A HISTORY OF POPULAR WOMEN'S MAGAZINES IN THE UNITED STATES, 1792–1995

Recent Titles in
Contributions in Women's Studies

Before Equal Suffrage: Women in Partisan Politics from Colonial Times to 1920
Robert J. Dinkin

"Nobody Wants to Hear Our Truth": Homeless Women and Theories of the Welfare State
Meredith L. Ralston

Spanish Women in the Golden Age: Images and Realities
Magdalena S. Sánchez and Alain Saint-Saëns

Russian Women in Politics and Society
Wilma Rule and Norma Noonan, editors

New Perspectives on Margaret Laurence: Poetic Narrative, Multiculturalism, and
Feminism
Greta M. K. McCormick Coger, editor

Women Shapeshifters: Transforming the Contemporary Novel
Thelma J. Shinn

Petticoats and White Feathers: Gender Conformity, Race, the Progressive Peace
Movement, and the Debate Over War, 1895–1919
Erika A. Kuhlman

With Her in Ourland: Sequel to *Herland*
Charlotte Perkins Gilman
Edited by Mary Jo Deegan and Michael R. Hill

(Un)Doing the Missionary Position: Gender Asymmetry in Contemporary Asian
American Women's Writing
Phillipa Kafka

Historical Nightmares and Imaginative Violence in American Women's Writings
Amy S. Gottfried

Dissenting Women in Dickens's Novels: The Subversion of Domestic Ideology
Brenda Ayres

Deprivation and Power: The Emergence of Anorexia Nervosa in Nineteenth-Century
French Literature
Patricia A. McEachern

A HISTORY OF POPULAR WOMEN'S MAGAZINES IN THE UNITED STATES, 1792–1995

MARY ELLEN ZUCKERMAN

Contributions in Women's Studies, Number 165

Greenwood Press
Westport, Connecticut • London

In Memory of

David Allen Waller
and
Constance Waller

Library of Congress Cataloging-in-Publication Data

Zuckerman, Mary Ellen.
   A history of popular women's magazines in the United States,
1792–1995 / Mary Ellen Zuckerman.
      p.   cm.—(Contributions in women's studies, ISSN 0147–104X ;
no. 165)
   Includes bibliographical references and index.
   ISBN 0–313–30675–3 (alk. paper)
   1. Women's periodicals, American—History. I. Title.
II. Series.
  PN4879.Z83   1998
  051′.082—dc21   97–45646

British Library Cataloguing in Publication Data is available.

Copyright © 1998 by Mary Ellen Zuckerman

Library of Congress Catalog Card Number: 97–45646
ISBN: 0–313–30675–3
ISSN: 0147–104X

First published in 1998

Greenwood Press, 88 Post Road West, Westport, CT   06881
An imprint of Greenwood Publishing Group, Inc.

Printed in the United States of America

Contents

Acknowledgments

Over the time it took me to write this book many people and institutions aided me in a variety of ways. I thank them all for their support and guidance, without which I would not have been able to complete this work. Any errors in the book are my own.

This book began as a doctoral dissertation, ably directed by John Garraty at Columbia University. A National Endowment for the Humanities (NEH) Summer Seminar directed by Stan Engerman of the University of Rochester sharpened my thinking about the economics of the magazine business. Stan's comments on drafts of several parts of this book proved very useful. A New York University seminar on Biography directed by Ken Silverman enriched my ideas about the individuals involved with women's journals. An NEH Travel to Collections grant assisted me in the research. Grants from the Geneseo Foundation helped me to complete various aspects of my manuscript.

A year spent at the Freedom Forum Media Studies Center (formerly the Gannett Center for Media Studies) proved invaluable, both for the time and space provided, and the collegiality offered by the other fellows; it was a truly stimulating and productive environment. I especially thank Don Gillmor and the Center's director Ev Dennis for their comments and support. A Nuala Drescher scholarship offered through the SUNY system gave additional financial assistance during this year.

A Spencer Foundation Fellowship provided support which allowed me to finish writing this book, as well as to look more deeply into the life and work of editor Gertrude Battles Lane.

I am grateful to all the individuals, listed in the bibliography, who agreed to be interviewed. I also appreciate the help provided by Ellen Gartrell of the J. Walter Thompson archives; Gerald Young, formerly of Crowell-Collier Publishing Co.; and Virginia and Edward Lane. Librarians at the following institutions aided me patiently and skillfully in my research: The Library of Congress, New York Public Library, Rochester Public Library, SUNY-Geneseo, and the University of Rochester.

Numerous scholars talked with me and provided insights concerning aspects of this book. I thank Lynn Gordon, Susan Henry, Joan Shelley Rubin, and Jennifer Scanlon. I am especially appreciative of the efforts of Mary Carsky and Julia Walker, who read drafts of this book. John Tebbel offered encouragement and a wealth of knowledge throughout this process.

SUNY-Geneseo granted me several leaves to work on this project. Colleagues in the School of Business at Geneseo have always been supportive of my interest in women's magazines, which I appreciate.

A number of talented students assisted me with this book, including Gretchen Teal, Lisa Graulich, Ella Frankel, Sue Geraci, and Brendan Higgins.

Many people helped me in nonacademic ways during the years of writing this book and I thank them all. I would specifically like to thank the following individuals: Ann Berzak, Lois Camphausen, Joanne Gerr, Marge Hopkins, Ginny Keck, Carol Malach, Marjorie Baker Price, Susan Benjamin Rubenstein, and Ilene Wexler.

My sons David and Yoni provided me with a wonderful reason to take breaks from work on this book. They also helped me truly understand the value of much of the homemaking and parenting information in the women's journals.

My final and most important thanks go to my husband Miron, who has always believed in me and this book. He shared in the joys and difficulties of writing the book, and provided love and strength throughout.

Introduction

Women's magazines have long posed a mystery to me. I first became intrigued when I reviewed issues of *Good Housekeeping* and *Delineator* from the 1920s and 1930s for a project concerning investigative reporter Vera Connolly, who published her articles in mass circulation women's journals. Some items in these early twentieth-century titles seemed familiar (advice columns, fashion), but much about them appeared different from the publications my friends and I read. Some variations came from changes in styles and technology. But other alterations seemed more substantive. The earlier women's magazines were bigger. They carried lengthy articles on a broad range of social, political, and cultural topics. Famous writers, political figures, crusaders for social justice all appeared.

How did women's magazines change? Why? And with what effect on their readers? Seeking answers to these questions started me on a long journey, the results of which appear in this book. My primary purpose was to trace the development of popular women's journals and determine why they unfolded as they did. This led me to look at the creation and distribution of the publications, as well as the message they sent and how that message varied over time.

I soon realized that content alone did not spell success or failure for a publication; a broader framework was needed. I came to the view that business and industry forces formed essential shaping mechanisms for women's magazines. Individual editors, readers, advertisers, technology, and cultural and social forces also affected the creation of the journals, in diverse ways and with varying weight at different points in time. But from the rise of the mass circulation magazine industry in the post–Civil War years through the present, business pressures and industry competition have created the context against which these other elements have played out. Thus my approach has involved looking at the structure of the women's magazine industry over time and analyzing the major women's titles together, noting their impact on one another. I also evaluated the actions of key players such as publishers, editors, advertisers, writers, and readers within the context of the industry.[1] This book examines the shifting relations between these participants and tries to understand how these movements affected the product, the content that found its way into the hands of millions of American women.[2]

Despite publishing articles on political and social issues, women's journals generally reflected mainstream thinking. They did not typically try to radically reconfigure women's lives or society, although they did at times work to reform and improve both. The magazines were profit-oriented businesses that had to satisfy two groups of consumers: advertisers who bought space and readers who bought finished publications. The journals were part and parcel of the United States' consumer culture. The capitalist structure in which the magazines were and are embedded defined the boundaries within which they operated. The interesting question then is how and why they have varied over time within those confines.

Gender played a key role in the development of women's magazines. It was no accident that publications directed at women emerged with such strength and popularity at the same time that females were increasingly defined as the consumers in American society. As *Ladies' Home Journal* editor Edward Bok told an aspiring young publisher, the way to success did not lie in producing a magazine directed at young boys (as the publisher was doing) because advertisers were only interested in the female sex.[3] Publishers recognized women as a viable customer group, a view supported by advertisers. This influenced content in the magazines, which both reflected gender roles in American society and helped construct and reinforce them. The linking of periodicals targeted at women with the steering of females into the consumer role produced a complicated relationship, with ramifications for editors, advertisers, and readers, setting a pattern which has extended down through the present.

WOMEN'S MAGAZINES IN THE UNITED STATES

Journals directed at women in the United States emerged early in the life of the young republic. Women's magazines of the ante-bellum period differed from their descendants in distribution methods, financing, type of audience, and, to some degree, content. Yet titles such as *Godey's Lady's Book* and *Peterson's* confirmed the viability of the female reading segment, nurtured the reading habit in women, and provided outlets for female writers and editors. In these years, as later, women's journals stood at the forefront of the magazine industry in using creative promotional techniques and innovative print technologies.

After the Civil War more reliable distribution techniques, new printing methods, and the desire to reach national markets combined to create the mass circulation magazine industry. Leading in this effort were publications aimed at women. Titles familiar to readers today such as *Ladies' Home Journal, McCall's*, and *Good Housekeeping*, as well as less well-known names such as

Delineator, *Woman's Home Companion*, and *Pictorial Review* were founded by entrepreneurs in these years. Characterized by low price, high volume, and advertising support, these journals soon reached hundreds of thousands of female readers across the nation, becoming advertiser favorites at the same time.

Often billing themselves as trade papers, these journals carried numerous service departments designed to help middle-class women in their jobs as housewives, a change from the ante-bellum publications targeted primarily at the elite. Now columns appeared advising readers about cleaning, cooking, making clothes, buying goods, supervising servants, child care, and the home needs of husbands. By the early twentieth century, these magazines also published abundant fiction. Nonfiction pieces on political, cultural, and social topics appeared, often written by well-known figures such as Theodore Roosevelt and Ida Tarbell. Campaigns were waged against adulterated food and drugs, contaminated drinking water, dirty stores, and venereal disease. In the early twenties women's journals ran vigorous voter education programs. However, by the late twenties competition had caused a decrease in such articles. The economic crunch of the Depression accelerated this trend. Competition for advertising and readers bred editorial caution. The remaining material focused on women as homemakers and sex objects, both stressing women's role as consumer. The beginnings of Betty Friedan's "feminine mystique" can be seen here. While women's journals have continued to discuss social, political, and cultural issues of importance to females, they do so in less detail and with less emphasis than in the early twentieth century.

During both World Wars women's magazines played a significant role, preaching conservation and describing activities women could undertake to help the war efforts. During World War II women's journals aided in the campaign to encourage American women to work outside the home. However, the 1950s saw a renewed emphasis on domestic activities, although the magazines also continued to show women in the public sphere. In this decade women's journals faced a crisis, as the steady success of television drew away both audiences and advertisers. In response, women's titles eventually emphasized a comparative strength, publication of concrete information that could be saved and returned to. Fiction, which had changed the least of all women's magazine content categories throughout their history, began to decline under pressure from television and inexpensive paperbacks. To win back advertisers, women's titles developed segmentation strategies, breaking their purchasers up into definable groups with appeal to advertisers, a tactic the entire magazine industry eventually employed. This set the terms for a different world, the one we see today, with publications targeted to special interest groups, ones attractive to advertisers who remain as important as ever.

In addition to competition from television, women's magazine content of the seventies, eighties and nineties has been affected by the women's liberation movement. Existing titles sought strategies to deal with women's changing attitudes and behaviors, and new journals appeared to address the emergent, diverse interests of American women. As the job of being female in America has transformed, so necessarily have the publications that provide advice and guidance to women. Some females continue the traditional women's role albeit with modifications; others are tackling new tasks. Thus women's titles now offer a great deal of information, often in highly condensed form, on practical matters such as decorating, quicker ways to clean house and cook, juggling children and career, how to get back into the job market, and fashions for home and work.

Throughout, editors, advertisers, and readers all influenced magazine content. Characteristics of editors changed over time. In the nineteenth century, for example, it was acceptable, at times preferable, for females to edit women's journals; it was like having another woman come into the household. By the early twentieth century, with mass circulation women's journals big business, men predominated as editors-in-chief. This male dominance held until the 1970s and 1980s. In today's women's magazine world, females reign, with no major women's title edited by a male. Women's journals have attracted a variety of editors and writers, offering good money and the chance to reach millions of readers. For female journalists the opportunities present at women's publications were for many years the best available. Many women had conflicting feelings about writing for these magazines; some, such as Dorothy Thompson, wrote differently for these publications than for other outlets.

Advertising accompanied the major mass circulation women's titles from their beginnings. Indeed, several major publications, including *Delineator*, *McCall's*, and *Pictorial Review*, were started specifically as promotional vehicles to advertise their founders' patterns. With the transformation of the U.S. economy into a national market, reaching consumers across the country became imperative for large volume manufacturers. Mass media provided the means to do so, and women's journals effectively reached the desirable female consumers. Ad revenues allowed women's periodicals to reach millions at a price below their cost, fueling the journals' growth. Ad dollars attracted quality writers and artists into women's magazine pages. Initially advertisers looked to publishers and editors for guidance. By the 1920s advertisers had realized their power relative to the women's magazines. Strong editors continued to resist advertising pressure, but it was always there, affecting content in various ways and influencing the path taken by the journals up through the present.

Readers also influenced women's magazine content. Letters and other material sent in to the journals, opinions expressed in market research studies, and actual purchasing behavior all sent unmistakable messages to editors, swaying content decisions. Of course, reader's preferences resulted in part from availability of particular titles, which in turn could be a function of distribution muscle, postal rates, technology, and marketing and promotion. But this study points up the significant role of readers in the development of popular women's magazines.

Has the women's magazine formula changed? Women's journals today still address their readers as women, slanting material through a female perspective; the attention to issues of concern and importance to women as women remains. Fiction, once so popular, has all but vanished. The investigative articles, the crusades, the in-depth analyses of political and social issues are shadows of their former selves, victims of competitive pressures and weak constituencies. What remains are journals emphasizing their information value, often expanded now to help women with their careers and with handling job and family. The magazines provide entertainment. They interpret things female, whether that be sex, fashion, or health issues. They exude intimacy and a kind of sisterhood. With magazines still funded by advertisers, the sell message persists. As has been true throughout their history, this adds up to publications both helpful and limiting to the women they target.

IMPLICATIONS

Studying women's journals illuminates issues beyond the publications' own histories. Women's magazine content reveals the possibilities and limits of popular media journalism. Women's journals operate on a continuum: at times they lead, at times reflect, at times lag in their presentation of women's lives. Always, they remain embedded in the consumer culture that gave birth to them.[4]

The history of women's magazines reveals clearly the active role of the audience. Readers responded to these publications, writing in with praise and criticism, sorrow and joy. Women did not passively take in the content presented to them. Editors considered what their audience wanted and the number of readers requesting certain kinds of material. And the magazines did not provide smooth, homogeneous messages. Throughout their history women's journals published conflicting and various material, from which readers could pick and choose.[5]

Women's magazines also tell us a great deal about the construction of gender in U.S. society. Within these journals certain aspects of women's lives were emphasized, other dimensions downplayed or ignored. Topics discussed, images displayed, activities presented all affected women's perceptions of themselves, their possibilities, and the world.

Finally, the history of women's journals sheds light on the conflation of gender and consumption. These magazines aided in defining consumers of most goods as female and reinforced the message that to be female was to be a consumer. This tale played out in the pages of the women's periodicals, affecting all participants.

METHODOLOGY

My focus in this book is on popular, mass-circulation women's journals. I was interested in the development and content of the highest circulating journals, the ones that reached the largest number of readers. These were directed primarily at middle-class (broadly defined), white females, although other women (and men) read these publications. I discuss the rise of some working-class journals, magazines directed at African American women, suffrage publications, as well as the elite fashion journals, but these titles are reviewed primarily in the context of their effect on the mass circulation women's journals. Throughout the book these large circulation publications are the ones I refer to unless otherwise specified.[6]

The section on women's journals from the 1950s through the present may seem small proportionately. Many patterns for women's magazines were established around the turn of the century and elaborated in the twenties and thirties, so I wanted to explore these years in great detail. Also, other scholars have recently given attention to women's publications in the post–World War II years, describing women's journals and analyzing their role in American women's lives.[7] Thus these last forty years, while clearly important, needed less detail.

I relied on both primary and secondary sources. I read innumerable issues of women's journals across the decades. I systematically reviewed issues of *Woman's Home Companion* for alternate years from the 1890s through the 1940s. I read other top circulating women's journals. I performed a comparative content analysis of the leading women's titles existing in 1912. I reviewed issues of contemporary women's magazines. I also analyzed women's journals' coverage during particular events, such as the two World Wars and the fight for female suffrage. While focusing on all major content categories of the magazines (fiction, nonfiction, departments, and advertising), I did not systemically review changes in art and design, although some aspects of these changes are discussed. I supplemented my reading of women's publications with results found by other scholars, refining and revising my findings within the context of their work.

I also drew on a variety of other sources. These included autobiographies, biographies, and manuscript collections of writers, editors, and publishers of women's magazines, as well as of individuals and companies involved in the advertising industry. I conducted a series of interviews with individuals working for women's periodicals today. Trade journals and general interest publications provided information. All of these helped me flesh out the picture of how these journals operated and evolved. Please see the bibliography at the back of this book for an explanation of the abbreviations used in my Notes sections at the end of each chapter.

Women's journals and their content resulted from the interplay of industry competition, editorial vision, reader preferences, advertising pressures, publishing company fortunes, social mores, national and international events, availability of writers, and technology. These journals influenced women, bringing them information, recommendations, and ideals. The effects were both positive and negative.

These journals became a part of American culture. Edith Wharton had Ned Winsett write for one, Tennessee Williams' Amanda Wingfield sold them. When Erica Jong's Isadora Wing sought cultural roots for her woes, she looked in part to the day's popular women's journals.[8] These writers, separated by time and temperament, all drew on the pervasive imagery of women's periodicals. Women's magazines are an inescapable piece of our society, of our consciousness, of our lives, one we need to know and understand.

NOTES

1. My conceptualization of women's magazines from the industry perspective was influenced by Porter, *Competitive Strategy*. This business framework differs in its emphasis from the focus on gender taken by Damon-Moore in *Magazines for the Millions*; and by Scanlon in *Inarticulate Longings*, both excellent studies.

2. As Richard Ohmann has said, material in mass circulation magazines is "an expression" of the marketplace relations between manufacturers, editors, ad agents, publishers, and reader/consumers; see Ohmann, "Discourse of Mass Culture," in Ohmann, *Politics of Letters*, p. 152.

3. Story told in Hungerford, *Publishers*, p. 21.

4. See Zuckerman, "Educated Citizen," pp. 97, 98.

5. To use the terminology of Antonio Gramsci, the mass circulation women's magazines participated in the cultural hegemony that reinforced the status quo, with respect to gender, race, class, and sexual orientation in the United States. However, while many readers legitimated the ideas put forward in these journals, it was not a closed but rather an open process, one characterized by some fluidity and the possibility for contradictions; see Lears, "Cultural Hegemony," pp. 567–93.

My understanding of the role of readers has been deepened by the work of Carl Kaestle and Janice Radway; see Kaestle, *Literacy*; and Radway, *Reading the Romance*.

6. General reviews of British women's magazines exist, such as White, *Women's Magazines*; Ferguson, *Forever Feminine*; and Winship, *Women's Magazines*. Frank Luther Mott's classic, five volume history of magazines provides good individual portraits but fails to look at women's titles in relationship to one another; see Mott, *History*, I; II; III; IV; V. For materials relating to the history of women's magazines, see Zuckerman, *Sources*.

7. See for example McCracken, *Decoding*; Meyerowitz, "Feminine Mystique"; and Zuckerman, *Sources*, pp. 73–104.

8. Wharton, *The Age of Innocence*; Williams, *The Glass Menagerie*; and Jong, *Fear of Flying*, p. 253.

A HISTORY OF POPULAR WOMEN'S MAGAZINES IN THE UNITED STATES, 1792–1995

PART I

WOMEN'S MAGAZINES, 1865–1918

The roots of the mass circulation women's magazines lie in the last quarter of the nineteenth century. However, journals created specifically for women existed in the United States almost a century earlier. No later than fifty years after the appearance of the first general interest magazine in the colonies, a publication designed especially for women started. Although short-lived, *The Lady's Magazine and Repository of Entertaining Knowledge* (begun in 1792) proved the first in a long line of periodicals catering to and playing a significant role in the lives of American women.

The women's magazines that appeared in the decades following that 1792 pioneer (over one hundred by the outbreak of the Civil War) bear some resemblance to the mass circulation publications that form the focus of this study. Targeted at females, addressing gender specific topics, providing an outlet for female writers and editors, these early women journals created a female sphere emulated by later women's titles. The best known of these, *Godey's Lady's Book*, is often seen as a model for later women's publications. These early publications targeted an elite class of readers, carried little or no advertising, were relatively expensive, and generally contained literary, etiquette, and fashion material.

After the Civil War a new chapter began. Innovations in print technology allowed publishers to produce hundreds of copies of magazines in a short time. The railroad system, improved roads, and a better and more favorably priced postal service permitted more efficient and reliable distribution. Entrepreneurial publishers aggressively sought advertising, which allowed them to cut journal prices for readers. Women's magazines led the industry in these areas, as well as in attracting writers and promoting their publications.

Women's journals enjoyed great popularity. This encouraged advertisers to place copy in the pages of these publications. During these years of growth, the staffs experimented, trying out numerous promotional techniques, varying editorial content and format. Publishers used various ploys to court advertisers, offering better placement within the magazine, cleaner copy design, research into ad effectiveness and product markets, and editorial support of ads. By the end of the era, much of the experimentation had ended; relations between the publications and their advertisers and readers had settled into fixed patterns. Practices established then became norms for the women's magazine industry throughout the rest of the century.

The shifts in production, financing, and distribution brought larger audiences to the women's journals, which now focused on middle-class women rather than the elite "ladies" targeted in the ante-bellum years. Increases in literacy also expanded the potential audience. As readership enlarged and women's role in the home and economy changed, so too did the nature of the women's magazines. Increasingly, women's job as consumer received attention, most particularly through the newly important ads and the ever growing service departments. Both provided advice and guidance to middle-class women in their jobs as housekeepers and purchasing agents for the home. The entertainment function of the journals persisted, as did advice about women's role, and articles on cultural affairs and other nonfiction topics that had appeared in the ante-bellum periodicals.

1

Birth of the Big Six

Over fifty girls are employed to keep the subscription books during each day
and a dozen others come to work at six p.m. and remain three hours every
night.
—Ladies' Home Journal, 1887[1]

The death of *Godey's Lady's Book* publisher Louis Godey in 1878 and that of
its editor Sarah Josepha Hale the following year symbolized the end of an era
for women's journals. This queen of the antebellum women's magazines had
fallen on hard times, unable to keep up with the changing interests of readers.
A spate of new women's magazines appeared in the 1870s, 1880s and 1890s.
Changes in market demand, print technology, transportation systems, and financing worked to place magazines in the hands of ever greater numbers of readers.
As Americans gained more leisure time and became more literate, they turned
to magazines for education and relaxation. The time when a circulation of
150,000 (*Godey's* peak, obtained in the 1860s) could be considered an astound-
ing success was past.

By the end of the nineteenth century, several journals had emerged as leaders, titles that would go on to top circulation charts in the first half of the
twentieth century. Known as "The Big Six," these magazines led in circulation,
attracted large advertising dollars, and were treasured in the homes of thousands
of loyal readers, causing journalist Charles Hansen Towne to term them "old
homes in a city of perpetual change," referring both to the time of their founding and the intimate role they played in readers' lives.[2] These journals, familiar
to so many women, were *Delineator, McCall's, Ladies' Home Journal, Woman's
Home Companion, Good Housekeeping,* and *Pictorial Review.*

The Gilded Age entrepreneurs engaged in these ventures spent little time on
thoughts of pioneering an industry. They focused on the more immediate goal

of making money. Yet individuals such as Cyrus Curtis and Jones Wilder, by creating and nourishing journals such as *Ladies' Home Journal* and *Delineator*, ended up leading the magazine industry. These publishers capitalized on technological changes and improvements in transportation, enabling them to reach large audiences. They kept prices down by attracting national advertising. They responded to the preferences of readers. The methods these individuals employed changed the shape of the magazine business as a whole, and began setting the pattern sustained by women's publications throughout the twentieth century.

In these decades the presence of a clever publisher and a distinct market demand for the existence of a publication proved the key components for survival. Once established, editorial talent, appeal to advertisers, and the willingness of a financially healthy owner to invest in the magazine moved to the fore as competitive factors. But initially the publisher played a pivotal role. Most founders of the winning magazines had prior business experience, either specifically in publishing or in running a company.

Readers of these new journals generally came from the whole spectrum of middle-class females, a shift from ante-bellum audiences. Like their predecessors these readers sought entertainment and amusement. But they also looked for concrete information that could assist them in their job of overseeing the household. Such home management advice formed the foundation of one group of successful journals. *Ladies' Home Journal*, *Woman's Home Companion*, and *Good Housekeeping* started as women's advice page supplements to newspapers or as publications directed at the home in general, filled with homemaking tips and service departments.

From another direction, a different type of publication arose, created to promote the fashions of pattern manufacturers. Initially making little pretense of being other than advertising vehicles, by the beginning of the twentieth century several of these fashion publications, including *Delineator*, *McCall's*, and *Pictorial Review*, had expanded to focus on women's concerns more broadly defined.

Both types of journals targeted the same group of educated, middle-class white women. Both developed editorial content, price, and distribution channels with these customers in mind. Eventually, each kind of publication influenced the other, with the pattern sheets enlarging to include household advice, stories, and essays, and the home journals forced to add fashion news and patterns.

In the magazines' early years, editors of necessity published a wide variety of material, some sent in by readers, some written by the owners, some penned by professional writers. This mix inevitably led to the inclusion of diverse viewpoints, some contradictory.

Nothing exposes so clearly the business nature of mass circulation women's magazines as their origins. These beginnings also highlight the extent to which the vision of woman as consumer propelled these publications. The depth of this view varied from journal to journal, but its seed, implanted in all the titles from their inception, took root and flourished on the diet of national advertising all the publications came to rely upon. The gendering of magazine audiences had been present since the late eighteenth century; such gendering of consumption had not. The new journals rested on females' role as consumers and advertisers' desire to reach these consumers.

A review of these publications' early years reveals their commonalities and differences, as well as their departures from the practices of ante-bellum journals. In the first decades of the mass circulation women's magazine business, the titles appeared diverse, various, and eclectic. Over time, however, they increasingly came to resemble one another.

THE *LADIES' HOME JOURNAL*

The *Ladies' Home Journal* and its first publisher and editors, Cyrus Curtis, Louisa Knapp Curtis and Edward Bok, led in creating the new women's magazine. As publisher, Cyrus Curtis played a crucial role in the *Journal*'s early years. His background, manner of starting the *Journal*, and subsequent promotion of the magazine all capitalized on changes occurring in the publishing industry, the advertising business, and among the American public. Before other publishers Curtis realized that large circulations could be maintained at a low cost to subscribers by the use of national advertisers. He tested this theory first with the *Ladies' Home Journal*, later with the *Saturday Evening Post*. He employed sound financial management, publicized the *Journal* extensively, and solicited advertisements for his own magazine, building the *Journal* into a top circulator. Talented editors Louisa Knapp Curtis and Edward Bok ensured that Curtis' product matched his promotion.

Curtis came to the *Journal* with an extensive background in advertising and publishing.[3] Born in 1850 in Portland, Maine, Cyrus H. K. Curtis had created and distributed a weekly paper while still a young teen. After high school Curtis left Portland for Boston, where he clerked in a dry goods store, using his spare time to solicit for an ad agency. Curtis founded a fiction magazine, then worked as advertising manager for the *Philadelphia Press*. When he and a partner started *The Tribune and Farmer*, a four-page agricultural weekly, Curtis saw clearly the benefits gained from large-scale advertising, as farm journals were among the first publications to carry extensive advertising.

In 1875 Curtis married Louisa Knapp.[4] Mrs.Curtis showed her value as a partner in a realm beyond the domestic. *The Tribune and Farmer* carried a column directed at farmer's wives, titled "Women and Home." Like many women's pages of the day, this department published material clipped from press exchanges; although uneven in quality, these second-hand items provided a fast, cheap way of filling space. When Mrs. Curtis commented disparagingly about the column, Curtis offered its editorship to his wife. She accepted and rapidly improved selection of the material, even writing some articles and household tips herself. Mrs. Curtis concerned herself with what her readers (housewives like herself) wanted and gave them articles designed to help them in their work in the home and as consumers.

Mrs. Curtis' women's department became increasingly popular, as letters sent in by readers attested. Observing that an actively interested audience existed for this home-oriented material, and realizing the desirability of these readers to advertisers, publisher Curtis decided to expand the column to a full page. Curtis then went further, transforming the women's section into a monthly supplement to the *Tribune and Farmer*, at a cost to readers of fifty cents a year.

The first issue of this supplement, the *Ladies' Home Journal*, "conducted by Mrs. Louisa Knapp," appeared in December 1883. The name came into being inadvertently. Curtis told the printer that the new sheet was "sort of a ladies' journal," and the engraver, drawing a little house in the middle of the title to indicate the contents, added the word "home," thus producing one of the best known titles in U.S. magazine history.[5] Eight pages of small folio sheets printed on cheap paper, with a woodcut picture on the front comprised the first issues. Contents included fiction, household hints and recipes, fashion notes, and articles on gardening, needlework, and handcrafts.[6] From its first issue the *Ladies' Home Journal* included advertising.

Success came to the new publication and it boasted a circulation of 25,000 by the end of its first year (the *Tribune and Farmer* had taken five years to reach a circulation of 48,000). Sensing greater good fortune to come, Curtis decided to devote all his energy to the new title. He sold out his share of *Tribune and Farmer*. In October 1884, the Curtis Publishing Co. became owner of *Ladies' Home Journal*.

Throughout, Curtis remained a consummate businessman. He saw the *Journal* as a media product filling a void in the marketplace. *Godey's* still existed but had not prospered in the post–Civil War era. Another ante-bellum success, *Peterson's*, continued to appear, but failed to aim accurately at the middle-class audience of housewives who formed the largest portion of readers. Other women's magazines emerged, as entrepreneurs discovered this fertile market. Yet Cyrus Curtis exploited this market most fully, through innovative promotion and management techniques.

On the business side, Curtis focused on three areas: raising the circulation of the magazine, increasing advertising *about* the magazine, and soliciting advertising for inclusion *in* the magazine. One of his main stratagems to increase circulation involved clubbing, an especially effective technique for a new publication. At the ordinary rate, the *Journal* cost fifty cents per year. Curtis offered a group price of $1.00 a year for a "club" of four women: each member paid only twenty-five cents for the subscription at a time when *Godey's* cost $3.00 a year, *Harper's Bazaar* $4.00, and *Peterson's* $1.50. *Delineator* and the *Queen of Fashion* (*McCall's*) were still primarily pattern publications. His main competition, then as later, came from *Woman's Home Companion* and *Good Housekeeping*, both near to the *Journal* in price and content. The *Companion* matched Curtis' rate, also selling for fifty cents annually during the 1880s. Although

Good Housekeeping cost more, it competed with Curtis' publication in its focus on the household; however, its $2.50 a year price made it significantly more expensive than the *Journal*. Curtis' pricing tactic worked and within six months (mid-1884), circulation rose to 50,000, 90 percent of it at the club rate.[7]

To publicize his magazine Curtis turned to the advertising agency of N. W. Ayer & Sons.[8] Curtis believed strongly in the efficacy of advertising; he saw it "not as an expense but as an investment: it creates an asset in the business in name and goodwill, and as such cannot be charged as an expense."[9] His initial outlay of $400 for promotional advertising proved effective; circulation jumped to 100,000 by the end of 1884. The next expenditure for advertising, larger than the first, yielded another doubling of circulation in six months: subscriptions reached 200,000.

Curtis actively solicited for advertising to appear in his journal, asking for $200 a page the first year.[10] He succeeded and by 1888, the *Ladies' Home Journal* contained three times as much advertising as any other women's publication.[11] This enviable state actually gave Curtis financial problems in his early years when circulation rose more rapidly than he could increase ad rates. The *Journal* proved popular with advertisers in part because it reached so many potential consumers, but also because former adman Curtis understood the advertiser's point of view. Curtis revealed this empathy in a speech to advertisers:

Do you know why we publish the *Ladies' Home Journal?* The editor thinks it is for the benefit of the American woman. That is an illusion, but a very proper one for him to have. But I will tell you; the real reason, the publisher's reason, is to give you people who manufacture things that American women want and buy a chance to tell them about your products.[12]

Curtis recognized women's new role as purchasing agents for the home, as well as advertisers' need to reach these female consumers.

In editorial matters Curtis appreciated the need to print high quality material to retain readers initially attracted by promotions and club subscriptions. He also understood the advertising value of a well-known writer's name. Acquiring the work of celebrated authors could be difficult. Other publications had already contracted for the work of many popular story tellers. Also, some writers believed that appearing in an inexpensive household publication such as the *Journal* would hurt their reputation. Curtis attacked these problems with spirit, traveling to the homes of desired writers, talking with them personally, overcoming their objections. He persuaded "Marion Harland" (Mary Virginia Terhune), well-known author of domestic tales, to give him a story. The piece cost $90, horrifying Mrs. Curtis, who knew the precarious financial state of the magazine. Curtis remained unalarmed, next visiting an egg-beater manufacturer who admired Mrs. Harland. Curtis convinced the merchant to place $90 worth of advertising in the *Journal*. Curtis captured Louisa May Alcott by promising $100 to her favorite charity for an article. By such ploys he signed up writers whom he then advertised in his "List of Famous Contributors."[13] Household departments and fashion pages still occupied the majority of the magazine, however.

By the spring of 1886, circulation reached 270,000. With improvements in the magazine's quality Curtis decided that he no longer needed to offer discounts. He discontinued the clubbing rates. This signified a major shift, since almost all his readers had subscribed at the discounted rate. However, subscriptions continued to pour in at the fifty-cents rate, with readers attracted both by the list of famous authors Curtis kept in the public's eye and by the newly enlarged magazine. Curtis also spent $20,000 on a newspaper advertising campaign and began using premium offers to attract subscribers, publishing a 20-page catalog describing the gifts available.[14] Circulation rose to 400,000, then 440,000, by 1889. The advertising rate commanded by the *Journal* increased to $2.00 an agate line.

During these six years Louisa Knapp Curtis edited the *Ladies' Home Journal*, aided by two female assistants.[15] Louisa Knapp Curtis' ability as a talented editor played a key role in the initial success of the *Journal*. She unerringly selected articles, household advice, fashions, and stories with appeal. She paid attention to her readers and encouraged their responses, saying "Try to write to us goodnaturedly, but if you cannot, then write to us anyway."[16] Upon interviewing her a reporter for the trade magazine *The Journalist* described Mrs. Curtis as

an editor who has proven her natural ability to win the loyal love and constancy of her readers, holding the half a million subscribers which might be *obtained*, perhaps by a liberal outlay of money in advertising, but could never be *retained* but for Mrs. Knapp's wonderful instinct as to the effect of an article and appreciation of the unspoken demand of the reading public.[17]

The reporter, a female, went on to reassure that "Mrs. Knapp is first a true woman, and next an editor." The article stressed Louisa Knapp Curtis' homemaking skills and devotion as a wife and mother. But Louisa Knapp Curtis' competence and accomplishment as an editor were demonstrated by both this coverage in a professional trade journal and her salary: $10,000 a year, more than any other female journalist for similar work. When the reporter questioned husband and publisher Cyrus Curtis on that point, he replied that "the services of an editor who can hold nearly a half million subscribers is worth fully the amount which is paid her."[18]

However, maternal responsibilities to her daughter weighed heavily on Mrs. Curtis, and by 1889 she wanted to step down from her editorial post. She did so secure in the knowledge that by then the *Journal* had firmly established a place in both its readers' hearts and the marketplace.

In fact, the *Journal* had prospered so greatly that Cyrus Curtis decided once again to upgrade its quality. As of July 1, 1889, he doubled the *Journal*'s size to thirty-two pages, added a cover, and raised the price to $1.00 a year. To retain circulation Curtis advertised extensively in religious weeklies, general interest magazines, and some other women's journals.[19] Ad agent N. W. Ayer believed in Curtis' business ability, so gave him credit for the ads the agency placed. Ayer also guaranteed the credit Curtis received from his papermakers, worth $100,000.

The financial gamble paid off, and when all the fifty-cents subscriptions ran out in 1890, Curtis had a circulation of 488,000, all at $1.00 per year.[20] Curtis never doubted the wisdom of this pricing shift, calculated to acquire a slightly higher class readership; his business and advertising skill, coupled with the necessary financial credit, allowed him to pull off this transformation. He initially had used a penetration pricing policy typical when introducing a product; he shifted to a more profitable and selective pricing strategy when he knew consumers had tried his product and developed loyalty to it.

With the business side of the magazine expanding under his skilled hands, Curtis needed someone to replace Mrs. Curtis. His choice was a man who, like Curtis himself, had worked in advertising and publishing. Edward Bok had little experience editing for a female audience. Yet in teaming up with Cyrus Curtis in 1889, Bok took up where Mrs. Curtis left off, building the *Ladies' Home Journal* into the largest circulating magazine in the United States.

WOMAN'S HOME COMPANION

The *Ladies' Home Journal* faced competition, most directly from the *Woman's Home Companion*. The forerunner of this title appeared in 1874, when Frederick and S. L. Thorpe of Cleveland, Ohio, began publishing a monthly called *The Home*. Only eight folio pages in length, *The Home* served primarily as a mail order paper, supported by numerous ads. It also carried some fiction, supplemented with housekeeping information.[21] This combination proved attractive to readers and the journal prospered. It lived through several incarnations and the hands of a second owner before Mast, Crowell & Kirkpatrick, of Springfield, Ohio, its publishers for the next fifteen years, took over in 1883. Circulation of the *Home Companion*, its name at the time, totaled 18,000. In describing its existence up until that point, the new owners termed it "a waif on the troubled sea of Western journalism," a situation they planned to remedy.[22]

Mast, Crowell & Kirkpatrick had the publishing and financial expertise to help the *Home Companion*. Phineas Price Mast was a successful manufacturer of agricultural machinery. His nephew, Thomas Kirkpatrick, had persuaded Mast to publish a farm magazine advertising Mast's agricultural goods. Former newspaperman John S. Crowell served as general manager and Kirkpatrick became editor of the journal, called *Farm and Fireside*.[23] It first appeared in 1877, and by 1879 Mast had organized the separate publishing firm of Mast, Crowell & Kirkpatrick.

Farm and Fireside succeeded and the firm moved to larger quarters in 1879.[24] The partners' interest in the *Home Companion* stemmed from the popularity of *Farm and Fireside*'s women's page; like Cyrus Curtis, Kirkpatrick and Crowell predicted that a magazine devoted wholly to the interests of women and the home would flourish.[25]

Acknowledging their commitment to the women's market, the firm changed the journal's name in 1886 to *Ladies' Home Companion*. Gradually the quality of this semimonthly journal improved. It carried better fiction than before, illustrated by woodcuts. The magazine also included housekeeping departments and articles on beauty, manners, health, and fashion. News about women's clubs and information about home study and university extension work appeared.[26] As had the original *Home Companion*, its descendant carried a large amount of mail-order advertising. The publication cost fifty cents annually.

By 1888 circulation had passed 40,000. It doubled the next year, and by 1890 more than 100,000 subscribers took the *Ladies' Home Companion* (compared to almost 500,000 buying *Ladies' Home Journal*). The *Companion*'s circulation rise continued through the nineties, hitting 220,000 by 1898. As the magazine expanded and prospered, Mast built new headquarters equipped with the most modern presses. The constant support and stability of the publishers helped make the *Ladies' Home Companion* a success.[27]

In October 1893 *Ladies' Home Companion* raised its price from fifty cents to $1.00 annually, matching its chief rival, the *Ladies' Home Journal*. The earlier disparity in content quality between these two competitors (with the *Journal* always a clear winner) slowly began to diminish. The *Companion*'s paper and print quality began to improve. In 1891 the pages had been enlarged. The first formal front cover appeared on the magazine on December 15, 1891, its Christmas issue.[28] With increases in readership and revenues, the *Companion* expanded its content, augmenting the departments and beginning to print serials. Fashions and dressmaking received more space than previously and patterns became available as premiums; competition from the pattern catalogs had forced the *Companion* to include dress patterns.[29] Non–mail-order advertising increased, a function both of manufacturers' growing interest in advertising and of the *Companion*'s swelling circulation.

In March, 1896, *Ladies' Home Companion* switched from semi-monthly to monthly publication. The following year, the owners changed the title to *Woman's Home Companion*, in part to differentiate the magazine from the *Ladies' Home Journal*.[30]

As circulation expanded so did the publishing facilities. In 1891 fifty feet had been added to the Springfield plant. A further addition in 1903 brought the printing capacity up to 450,000 sixty-four-page copies.[31]

By 1898, when Mast's name disappeared from the cover page, *Woman's Home Companion* was well established. The publishers built an effective editorial formula consisting of home service departments, fiction, and nonfiction articles reporting on society, travel, and leisure.[32] Support for these editorial pages came from the ever growing number of advertisements making the magazine prosperous.

Arthur Vance took over the editorial seat in 1900, set to pilot the successfully launched title into the twentieth century. The publishers continued to invest money in the magazine; as one staffer wrote in 1904, "Everyone says the magazine is improving. Its great fun to work on it and to feel that there's plenty of money behind it."[33] The thriving journal caught the eye of another experienced business person, New York City printer Joseph P. Knapp. Knapp bought a majority interest in the Crowell Publishing Co. in 1906 for $750,000 from John Crowell. Knapp's technological expertise as well as financial resources allowed the magazine to maintain its prosperous course.[34]

GOOD HOUSEKEEPING

Good Housekeeping began as a journal devoted to the home, a focus it retained even more strongly than its competitors. Started in 1885 and published from Holyoke, Massachusetts, *Good Housekeeping* carried the subtitle, "A Family Journal Conducted in the Interest of the Higher Life of the Household."[35] Publisher and editor Clark W. Bryan was an experienced newspaper editor, printer, and publisher. He already put out a number of publications, including the trade journal *Paper World*, when he started *Good Housekeeping*.[36]

Good Housekeeping appeared semimonthly, contained thirty-two pages, and initially cost the subscriber $2.50 annually, an amount higher than that charged by competing women's journals. The contents, reflecting the interests of Bryan and the availability of material, ranged widely from fiction and poetry to puzzles and columns for readers' questions. Household tips, articles on cooking, home decoration, dressmaking, and fashion filled much of the publication.[37] Bryan encouraged readers to write in with questions, suggestions, poetry, stories, and household advice. The magazine printed assurances to readers that their contributions would be given careful attention: "The winnowing of the wheat from the chaff will be done with tender care and kind consideration."[38]

In part, this policy of including readers' offerings showed good business judgement, enticing subscribers with the promise that they too could participate in the creation of this magazine. However, it also reflected the scarcity of material; readers' submissions in fact helped fill out the journal. Contributors had a real sense that the magazine was *theirs*, an enterprise they took part in, an arena where they were respected as experts on the topics (home and housekeeping) they knew best. Since *Good Housekeeping* paid its readers for their writing, it also provided a way to earn money.[39] All the women's magazines eventually fostered such active participation on the part of readers. Such contributions formed crucial links between readers and the magazine world, and worked to heighten the importance and influence of the journals in the lives of their turn-of-the-century readers.

Material submitted by its readers formed only a part of *Good House-keeping*'s content. Nonreader contributors included writers Marion Harland and Catherine Owen (writing a column called "Keeping House Well on $10.00 a Week") and cooking expert Maria Parloa.[40]

By 1891 *Good Housekeeping* had shifted to monthly issuance, the subscription price had dropped to $2.00 per year, and the average length ran to fifty pages, smaller in size than previously. The content continued to span a fairly broad range of interests, including fiction, poetry, illustrations, songs, and nonfiction articles. Small amounts of advertising appeared, primarily for mail order products. Circulation at this time stood at a modest 25,000, but by 1895 had jumped to 55,000.[41]

Owner Bryan became ill and eventually committed suicide in 1898. Although his other publications died, *Good Housekeeping* lived on. John Pettigrew purchased the magazine, delivering it into the hands of his printer, a common practice. Within two years the printer, George Chamberlain, sold it to E. H. Phelps, head of Phelps Publishing Co., a concern with offices in New York City and Springfield, Massachusetts, which already put out four agricultural journals.

Backed by this experienced publishing firm, *Good Housekeeping* survived, in large part because loyal customers continued to purchase the magazine (now edited by James Eaton Tower), valuing the useful household information it printed. William Randolph Hearst, beginning to put together a media empire, saw *Good Housekeeping* as an attractive property and his company purchased it in 1911 for $300,000 in bonds.[42] The promotional, distribution, and editorial clout of the Hearst organization would enable *Good Housekeeping* to capitalize on the strengths it had already developed.

DELINEATOR

Delineator had the earliest start of the Big Six women's magazines. Founded in 1873 *Delineator* began as an advertising catalog directed at women, created to showcase the patterns of Ebenezer Butterick. *Delineator*'s early years serve as a prototype for the evolution of several women's magazines begun to advertise patterns.

Tailor Ebenezer Butterick had developed the idea of making men's shirt patterns out of stiff paper. Butterick placed his patterns on the market in 1863. They proved popular and Butterick soon began creating patterns for children's and women's clothes.[43] The increased availability of Elias Howe's sewing machine, invented in the 1840s, contributed to the patterns' rapid acceptance. The combination of the sewing machine and Butterick's tissue-paper patterns (sized and notched for better fitting by 1867) simplified the whole process of home dressmaking, bringing fashion and style to women outside the wealthy classes. While not cheap, Butterick's patterns were affordable to most middle-class women in the United States. And as pattern production increased, prices declined.[44]

Initially, Butterick sold the patterns entirely by mail. But by 1869 the distribution channels had enlarged; department stores carried the Butterick patterns and the Butterick Co. itself opened branch offices. Butterick shifted his operations from Fitchburg, Massachusetts, to New York City, opening a sales office in 1864. As the organization grew Butterick hired two men to help him: Jones Warren Wilder, who became the distribution agent and marketing genius of the firm, and Mrs. Butterick's brother, Albert W. Pollard, office secretary.[45] In 1867 these three men became partners in the reorganized firm of E. Butterick & Co. Under Wilder's influence the company confined its attention to the profitable women's and children's fashions.

To promote and advertise its wares, Butterick Co. needed a catalog. It first put out a publication featuring gentlemen's fashions. Then, in 1867, the company created *The Ladies' Quarterly Report of Broadway Fashions*. The following year Butterick Co. started another fashion journal, *The Metropolitan Monthly*. Two-thirds of the magazine carried fashions, with the remaining articles devoted to fashion, women's role, and relations between the sexes.[46] These catalogs so effectively advertised the patterns across the country that by 1871 Butterick Co. had sold 6 million patterns. By the 1870s Butterick Co. worked out of 100 branch offices and had 1,000 agencies selling patterns across the United States and Canada. By 1876 the company had opened offices in London, Paris, and Vienna.[47]

Recognizing the efficacy of promoting through periodicals, in 1872 Butterick Co. planned a new fashion monthly, based on a merger of *The Metropolitan Monthly* and *The Ladies' Quarterly Report*. The combination resulted in *The Delineator, A Monthly Magazine Illustrating European and American Fashions*, which appeared in January 1873. Named after a tailor's pattern used to cut clothes in different sizes, the *Delineator* consisted of forty-eight pages devoted to fashions, at an annual cost of $1.00 (fifteen cents for a single issue). The cover, identical for every issue, featured a decorative archway, the title of the magazine, and the name of E. Butterick & Co. printed prominently. Inside, styles appeared according to age of the wearer and the type of clothing, illustrated by woodcuts. Few advertisements other than for Butterick's own patterns and products filled the pages.[48]

Delineator grew in popularity. Women wanted both fashion news and the patterns enabling them to dress in the latest modes. Since the tissue paper patterns were a relatively new product, the journal contained explicit guidelines for users; "Instructions for Selecting Patterns" remained a feature of the magazine for many years.[49]

By 1876 circulation had reached 30,000, with new subscriptions coming in at the rate of five hundred per day.[50] By 1880 annual subscriptions had climbed to 85,000, a circulation increase of one and a half times within a four year period.[51] To entice readers to the new publication and to promote its other business, Butterick gave away patterns as subscription premiums. This strategy increased brand and name awareness for both products.

Editorial duties at *Delineator* had been taken over by Robert S. O'Loughlin, Jones Wilder's son-in-law.[52] Throughout the late nineteenth century, however, *Delineator* adhered to the policy followed by many journals of omitting the names of editors in the magazine itself. Thus editorial changes remained unknown to the readers.

The 1880s brought changes in *Delineator*. In 1885 H. F. Montgomery became the new editor, with Charles Dwyer working as an associate editor. The parent company also changed; in 1881 the firm reorganized under the name Butterick Publishing Company, LTD, reflecting the significant publishing interests of the pattern organization. At this point Ebenezer Butterick, now a very wealthy man, separated himself from most of the work of the firm.

Butterick Co. continued to publish several other fashion magazines in the 1880s and 90s, all promoting the fashion business.[53] These other publications undoubtedly helped the survival of *Delineator*, as they provided more expertise in magazine operations, more financial steadiness, and greater name recognition for Butterick publications. *Delineator* proved the strongest of the group and the title that survived the longest.

Butterick Co. also purchased two other pattern companies and their fashion magazines to forestall competition. The Standard Fashion Co. founded *Designer* in 1887 to promote its fashions; in 1900 Butterick Co. bought the company and added *Designer* to its stable of publications. And in 1902 Butterick Co. purchased the New Idea Pattern Co. and its *Woman's Magazine*. Both new publications emphasized service departments and were priced slightly under *Delineator*. When selling advertising space the company bundled together *Delineator*, *Designer*, and New Idea *Woman's Magazine* as the Butterick Trio.

Charles Dwyer took over as editor of *Delineator* in 1885, a position he held until 1905. Under Dwyer the magazine expanded; by 1894 each issue of *Delineator* averaged between 150 and 200 pages. It continued to publish patterns, fashion, and sketches of clothes. But it no longer remained simply a fashion magazine, now carrying articles on travel, flower arranging, and beauty as well as columns on household affairs.[54] By 1894 average monthly circulation reached 500,000.[55] Throughout this period *Delineator* maintained its price of fifteen cents an issue, $1.00 for a yearly subscription. By 1902 *Delineator* appeared in five languages, and the journal claimed to have "the largest paid circulation of any Fashion magazine in the world."[56]

Butterick initially had targeted *Delineator* to upper-middle-class readers. In the 1880s *Delineator* had boasted that, along with *Godey's Lady's Book* and *Harper's Bazar*, it was read by the elite. And in 1895 its advertising agency still wrote, "Is it any wonder that its circulation reaches a large proportion of the wealthiest and most appreciative feminine buyers of the country?"[57] Some of Butterick's other journals targeted women lower down in the middle-class, as evidenced in the patterns shown. For example, some publications carried no designs for formal evening clothes. *Delineator*, on the other hand, featured styles for elegant evening dress in its early years. But by the turn of the century these distinctions among the Butterick publications had lessened, and *Delineator* was clearly aimed at the entire middle-class market.[58]

The Butterick Co. used *Delineator* to advertise other goods it produced. These included sewing tools such as embroidery scissors, button-hole cutters, and dressmaker shears, and beauty aids like manicure scissors and cuticle and corn knives. Butterick also advertised its other publications in *Delineator*.[59] Predictably, in a magazine created to promote its publishers' own products, advertising for other company's goods started out sparsely. In the first years ads other than for Butterick Co. wares appeared only on the inside back cover of the *Delineator*. Products advertised related to fashion and dressmaking, with Milward's Helix Needles, Furs by F. Boss & Brothers, and Clark's Spool Cotton all showing up. By the eighties and nineties more ads had appeared, with many small notices crammed on to the last three pages of the magazine. Most ads featured clothing, with corsets predominating. C. G. Gunther & Sons Seal Skins consistently took the inside front cover. The back pages also carried the Butterick premium offers. The premium offers remained fixed in number, but the manufacturers' ads grew in quantity.[60]

This increase in ads was due in part to the efforts of newly hired ad manager John Adams Thayer who came to Butterick in the 1890s. Extensive ad campaigns appeared in newspapers and magazines to promote the *Delineator*. Billboards shouted forth Thayer's slogan "Just Get 'The Delineator.'" The company spent $100,000 spreading this phrase, targeting advertisers and readers.[61]

Jones Wilder, who had become President of the company in 1881, died in 1894. Three trustees, O'Loughlin, Pollard and Salem Wilder (brother of Jones) took over management of the company. They expanded operations, invested in the magazines and ran the company profitably. In 1906 lawyer George Wilder, Jones' son, bought out the trustees and took over ownership of the company. George Wilder was firmly committed to the publishing side of the Butterick business. He bought additional publications, such as *Everybody's* and *Adventure*. He willingly spent to improve the magazines, including the company's flagship, *Delineator*, increasing the size, circulation, and advertising revenue of the journal enormously in the years after his takeover.[62]

MCCALL'S

Delineator was not the only broad interest women's magazine to evolve out of a pattern catalog. *McCall's* experienced a similar transformation. Started shortly after *Delineator*, *McCall's* also owed its existence to a tailor, James McCall. Its *raison d'etre* too was to advertise fashions. And, like *Delineator*, *McCall's* succeeded because of a strong publisher and his organization.

Born in Scotland, James McCall immigrated to the United States upon completion of his training as a tailor. He served as an agent for the "Royal Chart" system for designing patterns, then, with the assistance of his wife, set up his own pattern drafting business. Like Ebenezer Butterick a few years earlier, the McCalls quickly saw the need for a fashion catalog to advertise their patterns. Their first fashion sheet, *The Queen: Illustrating McCall's Bazar Glove-Fitting Patterns*, appeared in the fall of 1873, nine months after the inaugural issue of *Delineator.*[63]

The Queen initially contained four small folio pages, featuring woodcuts of the styles of McCall's patterns. Its pink pages caught the reader's eye. In space not given over to McCall's patterns, the editor ran notes about current fashions. Initially the paper appeared ten times a year, skipping the summer months.

Like Butterick, the pattern business of the McCall Co. prospered. Their patterns differed from others because they left unspecified the seam allowance for garments, allowing women to adapt the pattern to the peculiarities of their own figures.[64] Despite the advantages inherent in this superior product, the McCalls recognized the promotional value of their pattern catalog and they began adding supplements. By the late 1880s, for the subscription price of $1.00, a homemaker could receive a combined package of (1) ten monthly issues of *The Queen*; (2) two numbers of the *Bazar Dressmaker*, showing illustrations of the latest fashions from New York, Paris, London, Berlin, and Vienna; (3) spring and fall fashion catalogs; and (4) two colored fashion plates. Keeping desirable fashions in front of women's eyes, while simultaneously showing them how to make those very fashions by using McCall patterns matched the strategy employed by Butterick Co., capitalizing on the synergy existing between the pattern and fashion magazine businesses.

James McCall died in 1884, and his wife became president of the company. Mrs. George Bladsworth (better known by her pen name of "May Manton") filled the editorial spot, a position she held until 1891. Upon Mrs. Bladsworth's accession the magazine claimed circulation of 300,000.[65] Its pages had been reduced in size, but increased in number to eight. The journal still consisted primarily of fashions and patterns. Mrs. Bladsworth broadened this content to include more household information, homemaking tips, and ideas on handiwork. In 1891 the magazine acquired a new name, becoming *The Queen of Fashion*. The previous year the journal had been enlarged to twelve pages, and for the first time readers could buy this magazine separately, at the comparatively low price of thirty cents a year. Mrs. Bladsworth's husband George had taken over the presidency of the McCall Co. in 1890 but proved ineffective, and in 1892 Page & Ringot purchased the company. At this time audited circulation figures had fallen to 12,000. The lack of a strong, steady publisher slowed the success of the publication. This drop in circulation may also reflect inflation in the earlier figures, reported by the publisher but unverified. Decreases in the fashion magazine's circulation affected the pattern business of the company as well.

A change in leadership was clearly needed and in 1892 Mrs. Bladsworth yielded the editorial role to Miss Frances Benson, who held the position for four years. No notification of this switch appeared in the pages of the magazine.

In 1893 businessman James Henry Ottley took over the McCall Co. and the company's fortunes began improving. Ottley raised the magazine's subscription price to fifty cents annually and increased the number of pages to between sixteen and thirty per issue.[66] He accelerated the trend toward content expansion, although this change occurred more slowly than it had in *Delineator*. Fiction, one of the major components of women's magazines, appeared for the first time in 1894, the result of a contest offering a ten-dollar prize. Columns on a variety of topics including children's subjects, literary notes, health and beauty, and foreign travel began appearing.[67]

Ottley cut pattern prices to ten and fifteen cents and established agencies around the country to sell them. In a promotional effort, he published the letters of satisfied pattern customers in *The Queen of Fashion*.[68] By concentrating on both the pattern and the magazine business, Ottley brought the publication and the company back to financial health. Circulation picked up, hitting 75,000 by 1894.[69] The magazine contained several pages of small ads, placed at the back of the book, for items such as powder, soaps, and the ubiquitous patent medicines. McCall Co. offered premiums to subscribers and pictures of these gifts appeared in the back pages.[70]

With the September 1897 issue the publication took the name of its founder, becoming *McCall's Magazine—The Queen of Fashion*. The editor explained that this name change reflected the greater range of articles in the magazine, now no longer simply a fashion journal:

McCall's Magazine will contain nothing but the latest and most tasteful of Dame Fashion's creations, besides articles on current topics, beautifully illustrated by photographs; household hints that are really useful and practical; bright and entertaining fiction, and literature of interest to all members of the family.[71]

With its expanded material, recovered financial health, and renewed appeal to readers (and hence advertisers), this one-time pattern catalog was on its way to becoming an enduring general interest women's magazine. In 1913 the banking firm of White, Weld & Co. bought the title and formed the McCall Corp. They continued the effective management practices begun by Ottley, and invested in the corporation, ensuring its growth and success.

PICTORIAL REVIEW

Pictorial Review, a publication with origins similar to those of *McCall's* and *Delineator*, entered the magazine world some twenty years after these prototypes, in 1899. This magazine sprang up from the dress pattern business of German immigrant William Paul Ahnelt.[72] Ahnelt's firm, the American Fashion Company, published a number of fashion catalogs. *Pictorial Review* was the only one that would go on to great success as a mass circulation women's journal. Pictures of the American Fashion Co.'s patterns ran throughout *Pictorial*

Review and were tendered as premiums to those sending in five or more subscriptions. As later *Pictorial Review* editor Arthur Vance noted, "At its birth it
was rather a thin, little infant, more or less homely in appearance, but still
having within it the elements of a wonderful promise."[73] By entering the industry slightly later than its competitors, *Pictorial Review* benefitted from the
experience of the other magazines. From the first it contained more than merely
fashions. By its second year the journal included serials, reviews of plays and
books, as well as articles on fashion, health, beauty, home decoration, and
entertainment. A different cover appeared every month and could be framed as
a picture.[74]

Initially, *Pictorial Review—A Monthly Review of Trade Offerings in Fashions, Fads and Follies* cost ten cents an issue, $1.00 for a year's subscription.[75]
By the third issue the publisher tried to distance himself from the narrow image
of a pattern journal, despite the pervasive pictures of American Fashion Co.'s
styles. A new subtitle read more inclusively "An Illustrated Monthly Devoted
to Fashion, Society, the Stage, the Arts, and The Home." William McDowell's
name appeared on the cover for one issue but the magazine then lapsed into the
editorial anonymity customary at the time.[76] A typical issue ran about thirty-five
pages.[77] By the end of 1901 the publication announced an increase in pages due
to the "unprecedented success and enthusiasm that *Pictorial Review* has met
with in Advertising, Home and Fashion circles."[78] Generally, *Pictorial Review*
aimed at women of a higher social and economic bracket than the other Big
Six.[79] Slicker than the other women's journals, *Pictorial Review* took a more
sophisticated tone in its articles. In the early years the activities of social figures
such as Mrs. O.H.P. Belmont and Mrs. Hermann Oelrichs received attention,
as well as such events as the New York Horse Show. A regular column on the
Professional Women's League of New York appeared. A series focusing on
"Women of All Nations" began in 1900. Ads featured clothing more than any
other product.[80] When Arthur Vance took over as editor in 1908 the magazine
moved quickly out of its infancy stage and took shape as a general women's
publication for upper middle-class readers.[81]

OTHER ENTRANTS

Numerous other fashion magazines existed at this time. Some emerged from
pattern companies, such as *Demorest's Monthly*. This began as the quarterly
Mme. Demorest's Mirror of Fashions in 1860, seven years before Ebenezer Butterick brought out his first pattern catalog. Created to tout the patterns and
beauty products of Mme. Demorest and expanded to include advice columns,
temperance essays, music, and other material, the publication flourished,
particularly under the direction of the talented Jane Cunningham Croly ("Jennie
June"). However, Mme. Ellen Demorest and her husband turned the journal
over to their sons in the mid-1880s so they could concentrate on temperance
reform. They sold the pattern business as well. The Demorest sons proved

unable to guide the periodical through the rapid changes occurring in the magazine world, and by the turn of the century *Demorest's*, like *Godey's* and *Peterson's*, had folded.[82] Frank Leslie published a family of women's journals, including some fashion magazines, from the mid-fifties until the early 1880s, when he died. His wife Miriam Squier Leslie who took over the business concentrated on the company's general publications.[83]

Harper's Bazar (founded in 1867 and not to acquire its added "a" until 1929) and *Vogue* (founded 1892) focused on fashion, high society, and culture. *Harper's Bazar* was one of a stable of publications put out by the brothers running the Harper publishing concern. *Harper's Bazar* concentrated primarily on fashion, although in its early years also included articles on family and home topics. However, it gradually de-emphasized these, instead stressing fashion, style, and culture for the upper and upper-middle class, a mission it continued after being purchased by the Hearst Corp. in 1913. *Vogue* reported on the activities of New York City's high society from its start, as well as commenting on fashion and cultural matters. In the skillful hands of publisher Conde Nast, who took over in 1909, the publication more aggressively took on the role of fashion arbiter under the firm direction of editor Edna Woolman Chase. Once settling on their editorial strategy, both *Harper's Bazar* and *Vogue* achieved notable success in the specialized realm of high fashion. Such journals formed a special subset of the women's magazine market. They never moved, as pattern publications *Delineator*, *McCall's*, and *Pictorial Review* did, to extend their editorial coverage to gain larger audiences. Instead, they aimed at an elite segment of American women, working to "rigorously exclude all others," as *Vogue* publisher Conde Nast put it.[84] From a business perspective such a targeted strategy could be rewarding, but the influence of such journals on the lives of American women came nowhere near that of the mass circulators, except in the fashion arena.

Mail order magazines, marketing a large assortment of goods to readers through the postal system, gained huge circulations, especially in rural areas. The first mail-order magazines came out of Augusta, Maine, in the 1870s, published by E. C. Allen. They competed primarily on low price, typically stated as fifty cents a year; often, however, the publisher cared little about collecting payment. Readers were needed not for their money, but for their names, to swell the circulation list sold to potential advertisers. Many mass-market magazines underwrote their costs with advertising revenues, but the mail-order journals had little reason other than advertising for their existence. The expansion of content undertaken by the major women's journals moved them away from these purely mail-order publications. When the Post Office insisted in 1907 on seeing a list of paid subscribers for magazines wishing the second-class rate, many mail-order journals died; readers refused to pay much for these sheets. Two that managed to stay alive were *Women's World* (1901–40) and *Comfort* (1888–1940). *Comfort* survived by reducing its rate to fifteen cents a year and

Woman's World did so by pricing itself at twenty-five cents annually. Both competed to some degree with the major women's magazines for readers.[85]

Other specialized journals targeting women appeared; none achieved circulations to rival the large general interest women's publications. A number of women's rights magazines materialized. While these journals served to publicize the cause of female suffrage and helped foster community among its adherents, most had little money and were run by women's rights supporters with minimal journalism experience. Women's rights activists Susan B. Anthony and Elizabeth Cady Stanton founded the *Revolution* in 1868, with the backing of millionaire George Train. The editors called for female suffrage, equal pay for equal work, and an eight-hour day—radical ideas for the time. In 1879 competition emerged in the form of the *Woman's Journal*, a more conservative publication created by Lucy Stone, her husband Henry Blackwell, and the American Woman Suffrage Association. Experiencing severe financial difficulties once Train separated from the magazine, the *Revolution* disappeared by the early seventies. The *Woman's Journal* enjoyed greater support from both readers and financial backers and it continued into the twentieth century. In 1917 the National American Woman Suffrage Association purchased the title with money bequeathed by Miriam Squier Leslie and renamed it the *Woman Citizen*.[86]

At least five magazines targeting African-American women appeared, offering opportunities to black female journalists (who also wrote for women's journals targeted to white females) as well as information and entertainment created specifically for this audience. The A.M.E church sponsored *Our Women and Children*. Founded in 1888 in Louisville, Kentucky, it carried articles on education, the home, and social issues such as female suffrage and temperance. Two other family-oriented magazines for black women appeared in 1900 and 1907. Boston offered *The Woman's Era*, an outgrowth of the city's Women's Era Club, with women's rights activist and club president Josephine St. Pierre Ruffin at its helm. A minister's wife, Julia Ringwood Coston, started a fashion journal for African-American women in the 1890s. *Ringwood's Afro-American Journal of Fashion* was so enticing that it attracted both black and white readers. Unfortunately advertisers failed to follow suit.[87]

Ethnic language publications, whether newspapers, newspaper columns, or magazines, continued to emerge.[88] Churches also sponsored journals for females. The appearance of all these specialized publications testified to the existence of important segments of female readers, defined differently than simply as women, homemakers, and consumers. However, unless subsidized by churches, clubs, or individual donors, most ultimately failed due to poor distribution and inadequate support from readers or advertisers. Increasingly, in this time of the new mass circulation magazine industry, ability to attract advertisers proved crucial to success.

Many historians cite 1893 as a watershed year for the magazine industry, the beginning of a time of low-price, high-volume publications underwritten by advertising revenues. During that year of financial panic, S. S. McClure started *McClure's*, priced at fifteen cents, John Brisben Walker of *Cosmopolitan* cut his price to twelve and one-half cents, and Frank Munsey responded by dropping *Munsey's* to ten cents. These price decreases caused corresponding increases in circulation; for example, Munsey's went from 40,000 to 200,000 in a year, reaching 500,000 by 1895.[89]

Yet in focusing on these 1893 events, historians have shortchanged women's publications. Women's journals prefigured this magazine revolution, in price and in use of advertising. Their success was reflected in their circulations, large even before the nineties. In 1891 *Ladies' Home Journal* boasted a circulation of 600,000, *Delineator* one of 393,000, and *Woman's Home Companion* one over 125,000. *Munsey's*, a title cited as evidence of the "magazine revolution," only boasted 35,000 readers in 1891; *McClure's* did not yet exist. Even *Harper's*, one of the most successful of the older, established journals, only had a circulation of 175,000 in 1891. Clearly, women's magazines had grown large earlier than other mass market journals.[90]

NOTES

1. "Ladies' Home Journal," *Journalist*, p. 10. Portions of this chapter appeared in Waller (Zuckerman), "Business Side of Media Development."

2. Towne, *Adventures*, p. 190. On ante-bellum women's magazines see Tebbel and Zuckerman, *Magazine in America*, pp. 27–38.

3. Bok, *Maine*; Wood, *Story of Advertising*; Fuller, *Cyrus H. K. Curtis*; and "Man Who Founded the Journal," pp. 11, 12, 103.

4. Knapp had worked prior to her marriage as a private secretary to Dr. Samuel Gridley Howe; see Bok, *Maine*, p. 74; "The Journalist's Birthday," and "Women as Editors," *Journalist*, pp. 1, 2.

5. Bok, *Maine*, p. 94; and Mott, *History*, IV: 537.

6. Wood, *Magazines*, p. 211.

7. Bok, *Maine*, p. 107.

8. Hower, *History*.

9. Bok, *Maine*, p. 107.

10. Mott, *History*, IV: 530.

11. Weibel, *Mirror, Mirror*, p. 147.

12. Quoted in Steinberg, *Reformer*, p. 19.

13. Mott, *History*, IV: 537, 538.

14. Ibid., 539; "Ladies' Home Journal," *Journalist*, p. 10; and *LHJ* Scrapbook, p. 23, CCP, File Drawer 1.

15. "Women as Editors," pp. 1, 2.

16. Quoted in *Short History of the LHJ*, p. 16, CCP, File Drawer 4.

17. "Women as Editors," p. 1.

18. Quoted in ibid., p. 2.

19. Presbrey, *History*, p. 481.

20. N. W. Ayer & Son, *American Newspaper Annual*, 1890.

21. Mott, *History*, IV: 764.

22. Mast, Crowell & Kirkpatrick booklet of 1898, quoted in *Printer's Ink* notice (November 16, 1898), p. 43.

23. Mott, *History*, IV: 764.

24. Young, *Crowell-Collier*.

25. Peterson, *Magazines*, p. 133.

26. Kerr, "First 75 Years," p. 37.

27. Young, *Crowell-Collier*.

28. Mott, *History*, IV: 766.

29. Waller-Zuckerman, "Women's Journals," pp. 99–108.

30. *WHC* (January 1897): 15.

31. Quoted in Crowell, *Crowell Company*, p. 3.

32. *WHC* for 1897; and Kerr, "First 75 Years," p. 38.

33. GBL to Ella Lane, March 30, 1904, GBLVLP.

34. Stote, "Crowell," p. 9.

35. Mott, *History*, V: 126.

36. Ibid., 129.

37. Fisher, "Housekeeping Emerges," p. 81.

38. Ibid.

39. Mott, *History*, V: 130; and WHA to MVR, February 16, 1907, MVRP.

40. Mott, *History*, V: 131; and Fisher, "Housekeeping Emerges."

41. Presbrey, *History*, p. 485; and Mott, *History*, V: 131.

42. Winkler, *Hearst*, p. 173.

43. Daggett, "Delineator," p. 365.

44. Woodward, *Lady Persuaders*, p. 43; Kidwell, *Cutting*, p. 83; and Daggett, "Delineator," p. 366.

45. Mott, *History*, III: 481.

46. "Origins and Progress," pp. 59–61.

47. Daggett, "Delineator," pp. 365, 366.

48. Weiland, ed., *Needlework Nostalgia*; Mott, *History*, III: 482; and issues of *Delineator* for 1875.

49. *Delineator*, yearlong issues for 1875, 1884, 1891.

50. Daggett, *"Delineator,"* p. 419.

51. Mott, *History*, III: 483.

52. Daggett, *"Delineator,"* p. 419.

53. Mott, *History*, III: 482.

54. See e.g., *Delineator* of July, 1891; and Mott, *History*, III: 483.

55. N. W. Ayer & Son, *American Newspaper Annual*, 1894.

56. J. Walter Thompson Co., *Advertising*, 1899–1900, p. 76, JWTP.

57. Lord and Thomas, *America's Magazines*; and *Story of a Pantry Shelf*.

58. Bryk, ed., *American Dress*; J. Walter Thompson, *Advertising*, 1899–1900, JWTP; and issues of *Delineator*, 1875, 1884, 1885, 1891, 1898.

59. See e.g., *Delineator* (February 1884); and *Delineator*, yearlong issues for 1875.

60. See *Delineator*, yearlong issues for 1875, 1884, 1891.

61. Thayer, *Astir*; and Waller-Zuckerman, "Women's Journals," p. 104.

62. Ridgway, "Magazine Makers," p. 56.

63. Mott, *History*, IV: 580; and Tebbel, *American Magazine*, p. 161.

64. Mott, *History*, IV: 580.

65. Ibid., 581.

66. *Queen of Fashion*, yearlong issues for 1894.

67. *Queen of Fashion*, 1894; and Mott, *History*, IV: 58.

68. *Queen of Fashion*, yearlong issues for 1894.

69. N. W. Ayer & Son, *American Newspaper Annual*, 1894.

70. *Queen of Fashion*, yearlong issues for 1894.

71. *McCall's* (September 1897): 8.

72. Hinds, *Magazine Magic*, pp. 54, 55.

73. *PR* (November 1924): 1; and "Premiums! Premiums!" p. 25.

74. *PR* (August 1900): 2.

75. *PR* (September 15, 1899).

76. *PR* (December 1899).

77. *PR* (September 1899–February 1900).

78. *PR* (September 1901): 30.

79. Stevens, "Contents."

80. See e.g., "Boudoir Gossip," p. 16. Advertisers included Koted Silk Underwear Co., *PR* (December 1900): n.p.; various and tailors, *PR* (February 1900): 16; and the "Bon Ton" Corset, *PR* (May 1899): p. 33.

81. Austin, "Woman Looks," pp. 64, 66, 69.

82. Ross, *Crusaders*; and Kidwell, *Cutting*, pp. 81–83.

83. Mott, *History*, II: 437–41, 462.

84. Nast quoted in Seebohm, *Vogue*, p. 80.

85. Mott, *History*, IV: 20, 365–67; and Kennedy, "Postal Rates," pp. 93–112.

86. Steiner, "Finding Community," pp. 1–15; Masel-Walters, "Burning Cloud," pp. 103–10; Masel-Walters, "Hustle," pp. 167–83; and Masel-Walters, "Revolution," pp. 242–51.

87. Bullock, *Afro-American*, pp. 167–71, 209; Snorgrass, "Black Women," pp. 150–58; *Journalist* (January 26, 1889): 2–20; Dunnigan, "Negro Women in Journalism," pp. 178–79, 193, 197; and Coleman, "Woman's Era," pp. 36, 37.

88. E.g., "American Jewess," pp. 57–63.

89. Peterson, *Magazines*, pp. 13, 14; and Wood, *Magazines*, p. 60.

90. *Ayer's Directory, 1891*; Peterson, *Magazines*, p. 60; and Ohmann, "Mass Culture," p. 90.

2

Leaders in the Field

The WOMAN'S HOME COMPANION has seen more than thirty years of this growth—it has seen the field it once occupied alone become overcrowded with magazines modeled closely upon it, in form, in character and in name.

—*Woman's Home Companion*, 1904[1]

Surviving precarious financial situations, economic downturns, rapid technological changes in the print industry, and inexperienced advertisers, six titles, *Ladies' Home Journal*, *Woman's Home Companion*, *Good Housekeeping*, *Delineator*, *McCall's* and *Pictorial Review*, emerged as winners in the women's magazine race. From their origins as advertising pattern sheets and barely expanded women's pages, these journals stood poised on the edge of becoming the mainstays and delight of millions of homes, as well as the favored mediums of twentieth-century advertisers.

By the turn of the century these women's journals had moved into a growth period and were leading the magazine industry overall in the techniques of mass circulation. The successful women's magazine publishers had mastered the problems posed by mass manufacturing and distribution. They had laid out an effective strategy of low price, advertiser underwriting and targeting of female customers.

Now, for women's publications as for some other industries in this period, product differentiation, promotion, and cultivation of customers offered the best way to gain a competitive edge. While financial and entrepreneurial acumen had been crucial in the seventies, eighties, and nineties, marketing ability and editorial skill moved to the fore as critical factors after the turn of the century.[2]

Careful attention to the major components of a marketing strategy—the product itself, pricing, promotion, and distribution—allowed the Big Six women's magazines to consolidate and capitalize on their achievements. The prosperous publications attracted talented individuals who crafted the journals' messages. The market of potential readers continued to expand. And it was in these years, from the 1890s through World War I, that patterns for these media vehicles formed that remained for the rest of the century.

THE MAGAZINE INDUSTRY

Rapid growth characterized the magazine world in which the women's journals operated. In 1865 only 700 magazines existed; by 1890 the number had risen to over 4,400.[3] By 1904 monthlies alone amounted to 2,835, with sales amounting to $75 million.[4] Between 1890 and 1905 circulation of these monthly periodicals rose from 18 million to 64 million per issue. By the end of the teens, mass circulation magazines had become an institution in the lives of most Americans.

Several factors made possible the continued success of mass market publications in the early twentieth century. An increasingly educated American populace possessed more leisure time in which to read. Urbanization made those readers easier to reach. Ongoing industrialization of the American economy generated manufacturers who sought an advertising medium through which to reach a national audience. More sophisticated and professionalized advertising agents encouraged national advertising. These advertising revenues increasingly underwrote a substantial part of magazine production costs, bringing a consequent drop in prices. Strong, creative editors who cared about the content of their publications ensured ongoing success.

Magazine circulations had reached unprecedented heights by the early twentieth century, with publications attempting to break the one million mark. The low price of periodicals (ten and even five cents) allowed their purchase by an increasing number of Americans, as the ever-growing circulations showed. These buyers fell primarily into a broadly defined middle-class. Members of the working class, both male and female, as well as some special groups, such as immigrants and blacks, typically could not afford even such relatively inexpensive items as the new mass magazines; when such individuals saw the journals, it was often through "passed along" copies.

Advertising held a key position in the publishing structure. Advertising revenue kept prices down, allowing circulation to stay up, which in turn attracted even more advertising. Editors popularized the contents of their magazines, broadening and improving the editorial pages, making their entire product more diverse. Such expansion reflected an awareness of the interests of the magazines' middle-class audience, as well as the predilections of the editors. The newly available advertising dollars helped attract talented contributors.

Women's journals such as the *Ladies' Home Journal* and its publisher and editor, Cyrus Curtis and Edward Bok, led this media expansion. By 1900 *Ladies' Home Journal* was nearing one million in circulation, a readership larger than that claimed by any other magazine. In 1913 profit on the *Journal* amounted to half a million dollars. But the *Journal* did not stand alone in this success; the other members of the Big Six had established themselves by the early twentieth century. A listing of the top eleven advertising media published at the turn of the century included the names of *Ladies' Home Journal*, *McCall's*, *Woman's Home Companion*, and *Delineator*.[5] In the first two decades of the twentieth century, publishers of women's journals innovated in the areas of production, distribution, promotion, financing, and editorial content. Favored with expanding audiences and growing ad revenues, women's magazine publishers dominated the magazine field. A look at the key components of these publications' marketing mix helps explain their success.

PRODUCT

In these growth decades women's magazines increased their size, improved their print quality, and diversified their contents.

Improvements in technology and organization in the print industry had been necessary preconditions for the appearance of mass circulation magazines. Technological developments included use of the rotary press, stereotype plates, and photoengraving. Printing shops began using mass-production techniques such as assembly lines, conveyor systems, and timed production scheduling. Development of the rotary press resulted in production at ten times the rate previously achieved by the older flatbed press. Printing innovations reduced the cost of publishing and allowed larger runs of issues to be printed in a shorter amount of time. Since many printing expenses were fixed, this structure favored the publisher with the highest volume circulation over which to spread the fixed costs.[6]

The new presses also made reproduction of art work simpler and cheaper. Previously, reproductions had been engraved by hand, an expensive process. Photoengraving lowered the cost. By the end of the century a multicolor rotary press had been perfected by R. H. Hoe. Curtis Co. installed the first one in 1908. The perennially popular pictures could now be printed and sold at a price within reach of large numbers of consumers. Companies publishing women's magazines played pioneering roles in this technological revolution.

Curtis Co. built a new printing plant in 1895 in response to high subscription requests for the *Ladies' Home Journal*.[7] In 1901 a trade journal noted that Curtis Co. owned a printing plant housing custom-made machines including forty-nine presses and twenty-one binding and cutting machines with a daily capacity of 25,000 copies.[8] The *Ladies' Home Journal* used color printing before any other magazine and innovated with two-, three-, and four-color printing.[9] Curtis Co. began building another, larger building on Independence Square in Philadelphia in 1909, and completed it in 1911. Cyrus Curtis insisted on keeping his plant and offices in Philadelphia to hold down expenses. In the twenties Curtis Co. followed the lead of other magazines, moving some editorial and the advertising offices to New York City, but leaving behind the printing and distribution facilities.

The Crowell Co., publisher of the *Woman's Home Companion* and *Farm and Fireside*, had also enlarged by the end of the century, making room for more editorial personnel as well as new printing and binding machinery. Expanding on the original office on West High Street in Springfield, Ohio, the company made periodic additions from 1880 through 1903. Crowell Co. also bought one of the first "high-speed" rotary presses.[10]

The success of *Woman's Home Companion* propelled the company's expansions. A 1903 promotional pamphlet attributed the need for new machinery using the latest technology to the increase in the *Companion's* circulation from 75,000 (1880s) to the current 450,000.[11] Additions to the Crowell pressroom in 1903 were "especially constructed for the particular needs of this publication [the *Companion*] in order to produce the finest results in printing."[12] By 1900 the magazines, which previously had been folded by hand, were pressed into shape by a machine capable of folding twenty-five thousand copies a day. By 1912 the Crowell Co. had again been forced to increase its space and add printing presses, some for color production.[13]

Crowell Co. used a sophisticated filing system and the Mergenthaler linotype machine to keep track of its increasing number of subscribers. Inserts based on this information, called the subscription "Flier," appeared in the journal. Rationalization of the manufacturing process occurred, a necessary move as volume increased. Nineteen separate departments handled the work by 1910.[14]

Butterick Co., now printing the Butterick Trio (*Delineator*, *Designer*, *New Woman*) as well as other fashion publications and the popular Butterick patterns, operated a modern printing press in New York City. By 1907 almost 2,000 people worked in the large fifteen-story building located at Spring and MacDougal Streets. The basement contained an enormous printing plant, used to produce both the magazines and the patterns; the company claimed that only the Government Printing Office in Washington, D.C. was larger.[15]

These acquisitions by major women's magazine publishers demonstrate the crucial role played by efficient and cost effective print technology in the development of mass market publications. Publishers had to continuously modernize their machinery in order to keep up with the volume of work generated by constant growth, much of it stemming from their women's titles.

PRICE

Early mass market magazine publishers initially sold their products at a low rate to gain subscribers and capture a substantial part of the market; advertising dollars closed the revenue gap. The ten or fifteen cents per copy charged by the women's journals in the 1870s, 1880s, and 1890s marked a crucial change from the twenty-five to thirty-five cents being charged by quality periodicals aimed at an elite readership. Once within the lower price range, magazine purchasers proved somewhat price insensitive.[16] Readers developed loyalty to a magazine and continued to buy it.

Price differences in the 1870s and 1880s, reflecting the journals' varied origins and missions, were evened out by the turn of the century, when all but one charged $1.00 for twelve issues (*McCall's* charged fifty cents). Confident of the established nature of their product, publishers of women's magazines raised their prices gradually in the early 1900s. However, publications exercised caution in announcing increases. For example, when the *Woman's Home Companion* raised its price on the anniversary of its 700th issue, the editor presented a laudatory history of the title before mentioning the price hike.[17]

Mass market women's journals generally did not compete on the basis of price in these years, all staying within close range of one another (see Table 1). Readers responded better to promotional techniques, attractive content, and editorial appeals. Prices never rose in proportion to the cost of producing the magazines; advertisers bore that expense.

Table 1
Big Six Women's Magazines, 1912[18]

Title	Prices		Circulation
	Cover	Annual	
LHJ	$.15	$1.50	1,538,360
McCall's	.05	.50	1,084,902
Delineator	.15	1.50	930,600
WHC	.15	1.50	758,155
PR	.15	1.00	616,156
GH	.15	1.50	300,000

PROMOTION METHODS

Women's journals employed a variety of promotional methods including personal selling, advertising, and sales promotion. Reader-agents, predominantly female, sold subscriptions. They were paid with a combination of cash and gifts including books, teaspoons, and pictures. Some agents sold titles for several publishing companies. Magazines ran clubs for their agents to encourage them, instill a sense of independence, and promote competition. The *Journal* had its "Girl's Club," the *Companion* "The Pin Money Club," *Delineator* the "Clover Club for Girls," and *Pictorial Review* its "Daughters of the Golden Treasure."[19] The *Companion* offered free yearlong copies to readers who gave subscriptions as gifts to two friends.[20] Curtis Co. used "boy sales," youthful agents who received special directions for selling *Ladies' Home Journal* to women. A 1912

Curtis Co. manual for such boy agents devoted a whole section to selling the *Journal*. The booklet not only encouraged door-to-door sales, but also directed agents to approach women out shopping.[21] The *Companion* used a "Pony Man," who organized sales teams of young boys in rural neighborhoods.

All the magazines ran announcements advertising for reader agents and subscription solicitors, emphasizing the money and other prizes to be earned; fabulous sums were within every woman's reach. Typical copy promised "A Book for Every Girl" and ways to "Earn Your Education."[22] Individuals participating numbered in the thousands. In 1898 the Agency Department for *Woman's Home Companion* embraced "several thousand agents many of whom are schoolteachers."[23] This included both professional and amateur agents. *Ladies' Home Journal* reported employing about 30,000 in 1901; by 1903 Crowell claimed to have that same number affiliated with the *Companion*'s Department of Agents.[24]

In the 1890s publishers still relied on techniques from earlier years such as subscription clubs, discounts, premiums, and reader-agents to increase circulation. After the turn of the century, however, more sophisticated methods evolved, designed to keep old readers and attract new ones. Subscription clubs and premiums were dropped or de-emphasized, as publishers endeavored to assure themselves, their advertisers, and the U.S. Post Office that readers were willing to pay full price. Increasingly, publishers used professional subscription agents. Sales teams planned strategy, mapped out sections of towns for solicitations, and gave householders a polished sales pitch. Aiding the sales force was the subscription department at headquarters, which maintained huge files on readers. Renewal notices from the subscription manager appeared in the front pages of the book, those from McCall Co. printed in a bold pink to catch subscribers' attention.[25]

Advertisements appeared in other periodicals, in newspapers, and on newsstands. Led by Cyrus Curtis, all the women's magazines advertised extensively to attract readers. Publishers selling more than one title used group advertising and tried to persuade readers of one publication to buy another put out by the same company, employing what later marketers termed a "brand loyalty" strategy. Publishers promoted each publication in the pages of their other magazines and offered special rates and prizes to their own subscribers. For example, a "Pretty Girl Calendar" would be sent to each *Companion* subscriber who sent in fifty cents for an annual subscription to another Crowell magazine, *Farm and Fireside*.[26] The inside cover of the *Companion* carried an advertisement for "The American Magazine, published by the Publishers of WHC."[27]

Magazine covers gained importance as newsstand sales increased after the turn of the century. Street cars provided strategic spots to post covers. Publishers also supplied newsstand dealers with promotional posters. *Companion* fiction editor Hayden Carruth suggested surveying these vendors to determine which covers sold best; such information could be used in selecting future "salable" covers.[28] Carruth also recommended that the originals of *Companion* cover pictures be entered in various exhibits. *Companion* cover originals appeared in the offices of a leading advertising agent.[29] *Companion* subscribers received reproductions of popular covers free of charge, but such gifts were linked to subscription renewals. The magazine warned readers that the offer was good only as long as the supply held out.[30]

Publishers maintained an "exchange list" of other publishers to be given complimentary copies of magazines. Journals also regularly sent out "clip sheets" to editors of newspapers and periodicals several weeks in advance of an issue's publication, showing the Table of Contents for upcoming numbers, describing the entire issue, and printing about ten pages of excerpts. Both parties usually benefitted from these tactics, which provided publicity for the magazines and copy for the editors. However, the arrangement could cause resentment. For example, after the turn of the century, with the *Ladies' Home Journal* well established, Cyrus Curtis decided to stop sending free copies to those on the "exchange list," provoking unfavorable comment.[31]

Finally, magazines did not neglect the most obvious way of advertising: they promoted themselves constantly in their own pages. Every issue featured descriptions of the exciting articles and stories to appear the next month. December and January numbers often carried full two-page spreads announcing the special offerings of the coming year, enticing readers to purchase the title in the future.

DISTRIBUTION

More reliable lines of distribution aided the purveyors of mass market publications. Women's magazine publishers distributed their goods through all available channels. They set up subscription bureaus, used the services of the American News Company (ANC) and eventually developed their own distribution capabilities.

Subscription customers presented few technical problems for publishers by World War I. With improved rail transport and more extensive postal service, publishers could be assured of reaching their subscribers reliably and promptly. The Postal Act of 1879 had allowed the application of low second-class mail rates to magazines, making mail distribution a cost-effective measure. The Rural Free Delivery Act (1891) provided publishers with access to rural markets. In fact, *Ladies' Home Journal* claimed to have influenced the size of RFD mailboxes, saying the boxes had been constructed so they could hold the 11-by-16-inch *Journal*. In the early twentieth century, however, publishers fought an ongoing battle to prevent postal rates from increasing, with mixed success.[32]

This period marked the consolidation of publishers' subscription services into rationalized, automated operations. The *Companion* stressed its efficiency and speed in this area, claiming in 1903 to have

the largest number of names and addresses actually set in type to be found anywhere in this country. Six to eight men are kept busy the year round keeping the list up to date and free from error.[33]

As the subscription process became more mechanical, publishers turned their attention to luring single-copy buyers. Railroad stations, hotels, office buildings, drugstores, department stores, and local grocery stores all provided attractive outlets for magazine sales. The transportation system had improved, so reaching these distribution points presented few problems. But publishers had to negotiate with outlet owners to ensure that their journals received prominent display positions. *McCall's* and *Delineator* enjoyed the advantage of having their own agencies already established in towns throughout the United States and Canada where customers could purchase patterns and publications produced by these companies.

Newsstands became more important for all magazines, including women's titles, after the turn of the century. In 1898 only about 8 percent of *Woman's Home Companion*'s sales came from newsstands.[34] Curtis Co. encouraged its local agents to supply newsstands, but Curtis itself preferred not to, as the amount per copy taken by the distributor, ANC, was so large that Curtis suffered a loss on each issue sold. Curtis did sell a small number of magazines to newsstands through wholesalers because the company recognized the promotional value in having its journals on display.[35]

The ANC proved problematic for many publishers in the late nineteenth century. Established in the 1860s, this wholesaler had a monopoly on the distribution of magazines, with thirty-two regional branches nationwide. While publishers valued the distribution service that ANC provided for them and their customers, they resented ANC's power. Since ANC typically took a commission percentage based on a magazine's cover price, the company preferred to handle higher priced titles. The independent Frank Munsey clashed with ANC when he reduced the price of *Munsey's* to ten cents and offered it to ANC for six and a half cents. ANC refused. Unhappy with the terms ANC then offered him, Munsey decided to circumvent the agency and distribute his magazine to newsdealers himself.

When Munsey succeeded in his distribution venture other publishers followed. Cyrus Curtis started sending the *Saturday Evening Post* directly to newsstands in the nineties, and by the early twentieth century did the same with all his magazines. To ensure profitability Curtis refused to accept returns of unsold copies. Beginning in 1910 Curtis entered into agreements with over 1,500 independent wholesalers, who signed contracts giving Curtis the right to approve all other periodicals sold by the retailer. Rival publications, such as *Woman's Home Companion*, were usually vetoed. The Federal Trade Commission disallowed the right of approval section of these contracts in 1917. However, Curtis Co. continued to use newsdealers heavily, still bypassing ANC. By 1922 newsdealers sold 64 percent of *Ladies' Home Journal* copies. This constituted a higher percent of circulation sold through newsdealers than any of the other Big Six, testimony to Curtis Co.'s strength.[36]

Hearst Co. began direct distribution of magazines (including *Good Housekeeping*) in 1913. Around this time Butterick Co. turned to the newly created

Publishers' News Company to distribute its trio of titles. In 1914 over 83 percent of *McCall*'s circulation went out through the mails, but in 1919 McCall Co. and Popular Science Monthly Co. formed the S-M News Company to distribute their publications. Eventually most publishers used a combination of their own distribution system and wholesaling companies. Crowell Co. remained the exception, continuing to rely on ANC.[37]

Some publishers placed their women's journals in department stores and sold their patterns through these same outlets. A reader could purchase *Delineator*, browse through it, spot an attractive fashion, and buy the appropriate Butterick pattern all in one stop. Butterick Co., McCall Co., Curtis Co., and the Pictorial Review Co. all used this sales technique. The publishers of *Woman's Home Companion* and *Good Housekeeping* steadfastly refused to sell their patterns through stores, preferring the cachet of keeping the patterns exclusive to their own readers. Drug stores also provided a popular point of distribution for women's publications.

Women's magazines also went overseas. *McCall's* cited readers in Mexico, Panama, Cuba, and Shanghai, among other countries. *Delineator* claimed distribution in at least twenty countries by 1916.[38]

By the beginning of the twentieth century, the mechanics of distribution no longer presented an impediment to large-volume sales of periodicals. Competition focused instead on the point of sale, and on the various methods for acquiring and retaining subscribers. Strategies in both these arenas were dictated by the characteristics of the customer market.

CUSTOMERS

The number of potential customers for women's journals expanded enormously between 1890 and World War I. Economic and demographic shifts, as well as conscious strategies on the part of magazine personnel, contributed to this broadened market. Industrialization and urbanization greatly changed women's roles, with much productive work moving out of the home and increasing numbers of households relocating to cities. Alterations in work and lifestyles caused women to seek reliable prescriptive manuals to guide them in living a proper feminine life. And publishers and editors also worked diligently to extend their circulations; publishers advertised extensively to reach potential customers and editors drew readers in through careful campaigns designed to foster close relations. With this enlarged customer base came the impetus to expand the range of material appearing in the magazines. Womens' journals widened their focus, targeting the home as well as the homemaker.

Simple demographics aided magazine sellers. Between 1890 and 1920, total U.S. population jumped from almost 63 million to 105.7 million. During the same period females in the population increased by about two thirds, going from 30.7 million to 51.8 million. The literacy rate continued to climb, reaching 94 percent for the total population in 1920.[39]

Not only were there more women with greater literacy in the population swelling the market; women who *did* read magazines frequently read more than one. In 1914 *Woman's Home Companion* conducted a mail survey among its subscribers, receiving 1,951 responses. Forty-nine percent said that they read five or more periodicals in addition to the *Companion*, and 85 percent claimed that they read at least three other magazines, listing a variety of titles. The top five were *Ladies' Home Journal, Pictorial Review, Ladies' World, Cosmopolitan* (at this time a fiction periodical), and *Saturday Evening Post. Delineator* and *Good Housekeeping* came in sixth and seventh respectively.[40] Thus females who purchased women's magazines were likely to buy more than one publication, and most often, they bought an additional *women's* title. While not unique to women's journals this duplicate readership did increase the overall demand for women's magazines. Few rival goods existed to interfere with this purchasing pattern: women's columns in newspapers offered the nearest competition and these necessarily provided less depth and intimacy.

Specific data on early readers are difficult to acquire, but some inferences can be made. White, heterosexual middle-class (including upper and lower middle-class) readers formed the bulk of the mass circulation women's magazine market. The budgets of most working class females did not allow them to purchase luxuries like periodicals.[41] African Americans and immigrants frequently could not afford the magazines, nor did editors target these groups. Editors geared stories and articles to the middle-class women and families they believed were buying their publications. Editors formed an impression about their readers in large part from letters written to the journals. Although these missives came from a self-selected sample, they comprised the response that editors saw and reacted to in making editorial decisions.[42]

The contents of the magazines and the editors' beliefs about their audience are significant; as Richard Ohmann notes, when no specific research on readers is available, "we are left with conjecture based on content, and (perhaps better) on what readership the editors were trying to reach, and what readership they thought they had succeeded in reaching."[43] Editors of major women's magazines such as Edward Bok, Arthur Vance, Frederick Collins, and Gertrude Battles Lane all believed they were editing for middle-class readers, even if individuals outside this group read the journals. *McCall's* boasted of itself that it "is a prosperous magazine, and is read by the prosperous women of the country; not all of them very rich, and not all of them very poor; but the great middle class, who are the real producers and buyers."[44]

Labor-saving devices had lightened the work burden for many middle-class housewives, giving them more time for reading than before. Women's journals entertained homemakers in their leisure moments, provided household information, and offered guidance about activities outside the home. Magazine departments focused on such issues as women's clubs (complete with schedules of recommended activities), scientific housekeeping, and educated motherhood. As woman's role shifted from producer to consumer, reading and learning about new products in the marketplace became part of the homemaker's job, and magazine experts helped the perplexed housewife in the new job of consumption. Typically, each publication carried information about one or more "causes" or crusades toward which readers could comfortably and easily direct their reform energies.

Women thus provided a ready and growing target market for magazine publishers.[45] Womens magazine editors also targeted other members of the family, swelling the potential audience even further. Articles, stories, and columns of interest to men and children appeared, with the overall effect of broadening content. Agents for *The Ladies' World* boasted in 1895 that "It is read by everyone in the family from the housewife herself to the bachelor brother," a claim many women's titles tried to make.[46] One source estimated that by 1898 approximately 750,000 families read magazines regularly.[47]

Women's journals achieved phenomenal growth; between 1895 and 1910 the *Ladies' Home Journal*'s circulation grew 75 percent, *Delineator*'s grew 39 percent, *Woman's Home Companion*'s grew 291 percent, *McCall's* grew 912 percent, and *Good Housekeeping*'s grew 331 percent. *Pictorial Review*, begun in 1899, reached 237,000 readers by 1910.[48] Such growth continued, and by 1916 five of the Big Six women's journals placed among the ten highest circulating magazines of all kinds.[49]

Initially publishers emphasized undifferentiated numbers or made unsubstantiated claims about the quality of their readership. However, in response to pressure from advertisers, publishers began performing research that revealed the reader-profile actually represented by the numbers. Publishers had already begun to categorize readers according to geographic regions, information easily obtained from their subscription records. For example, by 1908 *Woman's Home Companion* possessed a breakdown of its circulation by state and county. Analyzing this information, editor Frederick Collins noted that "Of this circulation probably over 80% is located in small cities, towns and country districts. A larger percentage than is usual in magazine circulation is to be found west of the MI River." Collins went on to note that "the quality of the WHC's constituency so far as education and financial stability is concerned has increased nearly 50%."[50]

Editors nurtured close relationships with their readers. Letters, suggestions, and advice from readers appeared in the magazines. Contributors usually received a small sum for their efforts. At the *Journal* in the 1890s, readers typically earned from $3.00 to $5.00 for poems and from $2.50 to $3.00 for household tips. Bok's staff offered encouragement to potential contributors and concrete directions on reworking material to those submitting pieces.[51]

Most journals carried a page where the editor addressed readers in a familiar fashion, drawing them into the magazine world. As *Designer* editor Charles Hanson Towne noted about his task of composing the monthly editorial page:

I went at it with fear in my heart, for I realized what a responsibility it was. But after I got it going, I enjoyed those talks with readers, and the correspondence proved the most interesting I had ever received. People would write in on every conceivable subject, and I felt almost as if I knew them all personally.[52]

One sentence from the *Companion* describes the feeling the journals tried to evoke:

So many people write to use about "our magazine," "our Companion," that we have come to look upon the three million or more people who edit, manage, manufacture, buy and read "our magazine" as one great family.[53]

Readers relied on and trusted the information printed in these journals, giving them and the individuals editing them an enormous amount of power, influence, and responsibility. Americans in general, both male and female, looked to the new mass magazines for advice and understanding about the industrialized and urbanized United States. At women's journals a strong tie developed between the female subscribers and the editors. Many readers did not work outside the home, strengthening the impact of the national media force. As the author of the narrative summary of the results of the *Woman's Home Companion*'s 1914 Reader-Survey reported,

The feelings carried away from a reading of the ballots in general is that they were written by a body of devoted and enthusiastic friends, to whom the Companion is a delight and an inspiration, *and for whom it is in many cases the only link with a broader culture than their surroundings afford*. (emphasis added)[54]

For many women this monthly journal truly provided a necessary connection to the world outside an isolated farm or city home.

Women's magazines encouraged dependence and customer loyalty in a variety of ways, carefully answering all inquiries, printing a representative sample of letters, recipes, and homemaking tips, running reader contests, and eventually, setting up reader bureaus, which assisted subscribers with problems. A *Woman's Home Companion* editorial blurb, oozing with intimacy, exemplified this approach: "There are three million editors of the WOMAN'S HOME COMPANION, and you are one of them. You have been invited to contribute to the magazine, to criticize, advise and complain." However, after talking of the "good-fellowship around the lamplight of Our Own Page," the journal also displayed its awareness of cold business facts: "ninety percent of all magazine readers are women."[55]

Edward Bok built up a large reader bureau at the *Ladies' Home Journal*. Readers could write to the *Journal* and receive professional, detailed advice on any problem from a staff of editors that eventually numbered thirty-five. Bok "encouraged and cajoled his readers to form the habit of looking upon his magazine as a great clearinghouse of information. Before long, the letters streamed in by the tens of thousands during a year."[56] *Ladies' Home Journal* received almost a quarter million letters from readers in the first six months of 1913. And as Curtis Co. boasted, "It answered them, each one—not briefly and publicly through its open columns, but fully, conscientiously, confidentially, through the mails."[57] To ensure staff compliance with responding to readers, Bok occasionally wrote his editors letters under a pseudonym.[58]

Woman's Home Companion established a similar reader service. Experts in each department answered reader correspondence; editors received a specified sum of money per letter answered. Readers believed editors answered out of concern and caring; in fact, the editors worked at piece rates, which by 1916 had reached fifty cents per letter, with department editors required to submit carbons of each response in order to be paid.[59] The *Companion* also had several special reader services including the Better Babies Bureau, the Good Citizenship Bureau, the Pin Money Club, and a column for working girls. In 1916 alone the *Companion* calculated that tens of thousands of patterns had been sent out, readers enrolled in clubs, and mail sent in.[60] Butterick Co. too developed a reader letter service in response to the thousands of inquiries and suggestions that poured in. *Good Housekeeping*'s Institute performed a similar function.[61]

This responsiveness to reader needs distinguished the women's journals from other magazines. At publications such as the *Century*, editors chose pieces appealing to their own tastes. S. S. McClure believed that editors must first please themselves. The increasingly popular *Saturday Evening Post* had nothing like the service bureaus of the women's journals. At women's magazines even editors like Bok who selected much of the *Journal*'s material according to his own views recognized the fundamental importance of understanding what readers wanted and providing it.

While rapid industrialization and urbanization made United States women more uncertain about their "proper role," and hence more dependent on these publications for guidance, the magazines continued to define themselves as business operations, not merely literary or advice journals. Women's publications led the industry in innovative business techniques, and some editors, such as Edward Bok and Gertrude Battles Lane, identified themselves as business-people.[62]

The magazines' twin missions as profit-making firms and advisors to women could sometimes operate at cross purposes. When editors concentrated clearly on their readers' needs for information and direction while publishers took care of the business aspects of publishing, the roles functioned harmoniously; when the two magazine purposes overlapped and clashed, the reader might lose out. However, viewing the journals as businesses also led editors into a closer relationship with their reader-customers, and influence flowed in both directions. Readers' letters carried weight with editors, who were still experimenting with form and content. As good business operations, women's publications responded to their customers' needs. Over the years this meant compressing their range to focus more specifically on topics defined as of interest to women.

THE WOMEN'S MAGAZINE BUSINESS

The expanding women's magazine industry offered attractive opportunities to talented individuals with entrepreneurial abilities, creativity, and self-confidence. The low barriers to entry that characterized the industry as well as the growing market of subscribers tempted many entrepreneurs. The removal of the most onerous obstacle, the start-up expense of high cost printing, allowed easy access into the field to enterprising publishers who could now print and distribute issues of a periodical with relatively little difficulty. Improvements in technology meant that the quality of production on a new magazine could rival that of an older, experienced journal. The growth and strength of the magazine field at the turn of the century gave individuals the opportunity to experiment, test new ideas, and take risks. Profitability in the industry allowed editors and publishers to operate with power and relative autonomy.

Staffs of existing journals everywhere increased, as additional writers, editors, illustrators, and ad managers were needed to produce the enlarged and expanded publications. By the early twentieth century, an estimated 40,000 professionals worked on magazines, and the industry supported nearly 200,000 employees overall.[63] A typical women's magazine staff had a managing editor and editors for art, fashion, food, home service, and children.[64] At the Crowell Co. the payroll amounted to almost $4,000 per week by 1910. The company was divided into sections, with greater specialization required to accommodate the growth of the business. Departments existed for "superintendents, accounting, advertising, editorial, circulation, main press, power, engraving, composing, electrotyping, job press, proofreading, pattern, shipping, folding, stencil, subscription, agents, installment."[65] At the *Ladies' Home Journal*, Edward Bok ruled over an editorial staff of thirty-five. Theodore Dreiser had thirty-two people under him when he edited the Butterick Trio from 1907 to 1910. The McCall Co. employed 700 people by 1913 when publisher James Ottley sold the company to the banking firm of White, Weld & Co.[66]

Despite these additions, staffs failed to keep pace with magazine growth and the personnel shortage offered advancement opportunities to enterprising individuals. Crowell Co. provides an example of such an environment. At *Woman's Home Companion* both Hayden Carruth and Gertrude Battles Lane performed a wide variety of editorial, marketing, and executive duties. When Lane joined Crowell in 1903, the *Companion* staff numbered only eight. Carruth came to the organization in 1905, when staff members still had numerous and diverse responsibilities. Carruth engaged in a multiplicity of jobs, including editing, writing, promotion, and distribution.[67] Lane moved from her position as editor of the household department to managing editor, to editor-in-chief, to vice-president of the Crowell Co. Such job diversity and advancement opportunity attracted ambitious, energetic individuals, who in turn contributed to the growth in scope and quality of the publications.

Moves to increase the professional staff formed one part of the overall rationalization process experienced by the Big Six in personnel, technology, manufacturing, distribution, and commissioning of material. Standardization and efficiency in policies became a point of competitive strength. The procedure for paying authors provides one example. Curtis Co. and the *Ladies' Home Journal* maintained a policy of prompt payment: the company mailed out a check on Tuesday for all material accepted to that point, an attractive policy to contributors.

As the magazines published greater amounts of material, work flows had to be more carefully organized. Issues were planned months in advance. Such organization helped promotional departments persuade advertisers to buy space, since topics for specific articles in future issues were known.

Of the Big Six all but the *Ladies' Home Journal* had shifted at least their editorial and advertising activities to New York City by the late 1910s. *Good Housekeeping* moved from Holyoke, Massachusetts, when Hearst and the International Magazine Co. purchased it in 1911. Butterick's printing and editorial offices had been in New York City since the 1870s. *Woman's Home Companion* moved its editorial, art, and eventually its advertising offices there after the turn of the century. Both *McCall's* and *Pictorial Review* had started and stayed in New York City. These early moves proved permanent, and offices remained in New York City where the publishing, art, and advertising worlds flourished.

Several major women's magazine owners became horizontally integrated, publishing more than one journal. Curtis Co., Crowell Co., Butterick Co., and Harper Brothers followed this strategy, with successful women's magazines providing a base for expansion. Several publishers brought out foreign editions of their titles, including *Vogue* and *Delineator*. Production, promotion, solicitation of advertising, and processing of articles all benefited from the economies of scale these publishers achieved. Publishers diversified by adding subscription agencies and shopping services to the pattern sales already offered. *Ladies' Home Journal* and *Woman's Home Companion* both sold reprints of their popular covers.[68] Curtis Co. integrated vertically, buying paper mills and even the trees producing the paper, a strategy it continued throughout the twentieth century. McCall Co. bought additional machinery and began printing other publishers' journals as well as its own.

These expansions in ownership by the women's magazine publishers did not go unnoticed. Upton Sinclair wrote bitterly about the Crowell Co. takeover of *American Magazine* in 1911 and the acquisition of *Everybody's* by the Butterick Co. He contended that monied interests controlled newspapers and magazines and commented in a particularly negative way about the contents of the women's magazines.[69]

By the outbreak of World War I, the women's magazine business had become highly concentrated, a characteristic that intensified as the century wore on. Five publishers put out 40 percent of the top ten circulators between 1910 and 1960: Curtis, McCall, Crowell, Butterick, and Pictorial Review Co.[70]

Women's magazines flourished in the Progressive era. Women's journals led the magazine industry as a whole. They lowered prices, used advertising revenues to subsidize production, and offered advertisers assistance with ad copy sooner than any other publications. Women's titles topped circulation lists. Publishers of women's magazines rationalized their production operations, buying the most advanced print machinery to do so. These pioneering strategies placed women's journals at the forefront of the mass magazine market. But it was the magazines' editors, working to differentiate their journals from one another, experimenting boldly, and fostering close relationships with their readers, who kept readers coming back, month after month.

NOTES

1. *WHC* (October 1907): 42. Parts of this chapter appeared as Waller-Zuckerman, "Old Homes."
2. See Chandler, Jr., "Beginnings of 'Big Business'," pp. 1–31.
3. Tebbel, *American Magazine*, p. 124; and Mott, *History*, IV: 5.
4. Casson, "Wonders," pp. 8, 9; and Presbrey, *History*, p. 488.
5. Cyrus Curtis, "Testimony in House Committee on Post-Office and Post Roads," *Rates of Postage on Second-Class Mail*, February 9, 10, 1914, p. 78; and Presbrey, *History*, p. 481.
6. Ohmann, "Mass Culture"; and Peterson, *Magazines*.
7. "Few Things We Have Done," p. 3; and WA to Shurman Sibthorp, February 16, 1903, WAL, December 1, 1902–August 8, 1904, CP, Box 4.
8. *Profitable Advertising* (December 1901).
9. Fuller, *Curtis*, pp. 20, 21.
10. Young, *Crowell-Collier*.
11. Crowell, *Crowell Co.*, n.p.
12. Ibid., n.p.
13. Casson, "Wonders," p. 9; and Young, *Crowell-Collier*.
14. Crowell, *Crowell Co.*, p. 8.
15. Swanberg, *Dreiser*, p. 119; *A History of the Butterick Company*, p. 1 (n.d.), BA; and *Butterick and the Story of Sewing* (New York: Butterick Co., 1975): n.p., BA.
16. Waller (Zuckerman), "Content Changes."
17. *WHC* (December 1908). See also Waller-Zuckerman, "Old Homes," pp. 734, 735.
18. Circulation from Ayer's *American Newspaper Annual*, 1912.
19. HC memo, November 8, 1907, HCP, Box 9; McDowell, "Children's Feature," pp. 43, 44; and Woodward, *Lady Persuaders*, pp. 103, 104.
20. *WHC* (December 1910): 12.
21. Curtis, *100 Copies Weekly*, pp. 50–59.
22. See e.g., *WHC* (January 1912): 83; *LHJ* (June 1912): 1; *McCall's* (January 1909): 347.
23. "When We Were Younger," *Good News* (January 1926):15 in HCP, Box 9.
24. "Few Things We Have Done," p. 3; Steinberg, *Reformer*, p. 10; and Crowell, *Crowell Co.*, p. 26.

25. "Circulation: 9,496,841," pp. 63–69ff; Crowell, *Crowell Co.*; Curtis, *Selling Efforts*; Wyman, *Circulation*, p. 11; and *McCall's*, issues for 1912, Table of Contents page.

26. *WHC* (January 1915): 44.

27. *WHC* (January 1915): inside cover; and WHC (December 1913): 71.

28. *WHC* (February 1907): 13; and HC to Mr. Messler, December 15, 1916, HCP.

29. HC Memo, July 1915; HC memo, May 18, 1909. An HC Memo, undated (u.d.) 1910, noted this hanging in the ad agency, but left the agent unnamed. All in HCP.

30. *WHC* (October 1907): 1; and *WHC* (December 1911): Announcement page.

31. See e.g., *The Journalist*, Vol. XXXII (November 1, 1902): 1.

32. "Few Things We Have Done," p. 3; "Why Magazines May Cost More," p. 4; Kennedy, "Postal Rates"; Committee on the Post-Office and Post-Roads, House of Representatives, February 13, 1900, *Hearings upon the Loud Bill* (H.R. 6071); and House Committee on Post-Office and Post-Roads, *Rates of Postage on Second-Class Mail*, February 9, 10, 1914.

33. Crowell, *Crowell Co.*, p. 5.

34. Mott, *History*, IV: 766.

35. Steinberg, *Reformer*, pp. 10, 11; and Sykes, "Periodicals," p. 830.

36. Bok, "Magazine with a Million," p. 16; Steinberg, *Reformer*, p. 11; and *Standard Rate and Data Service* (1922).

37. Quinlan, "Magazine Distribution," pp. 4, 5; and Wyman, *Circulation*, pp. 43–59.

38. *McCall's* (January 1909): 347; and *Butterick Transfer*, Back Cover.

39. *Historical Statistics of the U.S., Colonial Times to 1970*, Part 1.

40. *1914 WHC Reader-Survey*, p. 4, HCP, Box 10.

41. Kessler-Harris, *Out to Work*, pp. 120–22.

42. Waller-Zuckerman, "Vera Connolly," pp. 80–88.

43. Ohmann, "Mass Culture," p. 97.

44. *McCall's* advertisement in *Ayer's Directory* (1914): n.p. On Bok, see Transcript of Advertising Conference, 1915, p. 8, CP, Box 5; on Collins see FC to Edward Everett Hale, September 28, 1908, HCP; for Vance and Lane, see Crowell, *Crowell Co.*, pp. 11, 14.

45. Gale, "Younger Generation," p. 320; Mott, *History*, IV: 353; and Cohn, *Creating America*, pp. 65–76.

46. Lord & Thomas, *America's Magazines*, p. 26.

47. Crowell-Collier, unmarked promotional booklet, 1929, XX, CCP.

48. 1895 figures from Lord & Thomas, *America's Magazines*; 1910 figures from Ayer, *Ayer's Directory*.

49. Crowell-Collier, *National Markets, 1922*.

50. *WHC* Geographic Circulation Breakdown, 1908, HCP, Box 9; and FC to Edward Everett Hale, September 28, 1908, in HCP, Box 9.

51. See e.g., W. Alexander Letterbooks, November 16, 1891 to December 27, 1893, pp. 43, 45, CP, Box 4.

52. Towne, *Adventures*, p. 153.

53. *WHC* (March 1910): "Our Own Page."

54. *1914 WHC Reader-Survey*, pp. 6, 14, HCP, Box 10.

55. *WHC* (October 1907): 42.

56. Bok, *Americanization*, p. 174.

57. Curtis, *Selling Efforts*, p. 235.

58. Steinberg, *Reformer*, p. 56; and EB to CMF, January 13, 1914, Folder 1, Box 1. For answering reader letters Christine Frederick was paid fifteen dollars per hundred; see EB to CMF, March 18, 1912, Folder 1, Box 1; both in CMFP.

59. See Hayden Carruth Expense Notebook for 1916, 1917, 1918, HCP, Box 26.

60. *WHC* (April 1916): Table of Contents Page.

61. *History of Butterick Company*, p. 1; and Towne, *Adventures*, p. 124.

62. Steinberg, *Reformer*, p. 33; and Zuckerman, "Pathway."

63. Casson, "Wonders," p. 8.

64. Connolly, *Judy Grant*, p. 89.

65. Young, *Crowell-Collier*, p. 11.

66. Bok, *Americanization*; Swanberg, *Dreiser*; and "James Ottley," *National Encyclopedia of American Biography*, pp. 65, 66.

67. Carruth, "What's Going On" (February 28, 1918), HCP, Box 10.

68. HC Memo, April 9, 1907, HCP.

69. Sinclair, *Brass Check*, pp. 233, 237.

70. Analysis performed on data from Ayer, *Directory*.

3

Editing the Women's Magazines

Mr. Dreiser had recently taken charge of the *Delineator*; and as I had read his novel, "Sister Carrie," and had the highest regard for his literary ideals, I went down to see him. If the women's magazines, I thought on the way, were to put such men at the helm, they must surely be picking up.

—Charles Hanson Towne[1]

Editors emerged as powerful figures at magazines after the turn of the century. Editorial taste and vision played a major role in a journal's success. Previously the publisher had been the key figure. Now a skillful, committed publisher was a necessary but no longer sufficient condition for profitability and growth. With many production, distribution, and financial problems resolved, magazine content, that area overseen by the editor, became a prime sphere of competition. Readers' interests, advertiser expectations, and cultural norms all affected magazine content. But the editor orchestrated these influences and impressed his or her personality on a journal. The women's titles moving to the front all had skillful editors boasting wide-ranging interests, able to balance the demands of publishers, readers, and advertisers.

A group of new, young editors appeared on the magazine scene. These individuals became well-known figures, both in the publishing world and in the more secluded worlds of periodical readers.[2] Several of these talented editors went to the women's journals, attracted by the clear growth opportunities in that field. Even men who feared that working for a "women's" publication meant lessened status saw that women's magazines were becoming big businesses. And for female journalists the women's titles offered the best situations for advancement and reward. Edward Bok, Theodore Dreiser, Charles Dwyer, Gertrude Battles Lane, and Arthur Vance were just a few of the gifted editors who headed women's journals, stamping their personalities on them.

Because these individuals exerted so much power, understanding who they were and their attitudes about editing adds a crucial piece to analysis of the magazine world. Several generalizations can be made. The successful editors tended to be authoritative, forceful, possessed of a vision for their journals, yet attending to the interests and preferences of readers. Many had previous experience in advertising and/or other fields of publishing and understood the business realities involved with mass circulation magazine publishing. These editors expanded their staffs, hiring experts in various areas to take over specific departments. Overall, the editorial function became increasingly professionalized in these years.

The prosperity of the industry, operating with growing reader and advertiser markets, also provided editors with a relatively strong position, particularly vis-à-vis advertisers, stronger than would be the case in later years when competition for advertising became fiercer. Generally, editors of women's magazines in this period pushed the journals into broader paths. Some editors did so because of their own wide experience and interests. Others pursued broader coverage because they believed that female readers wished it. Still other editors expanded their magazines' content as they aimed at the general family and home audience; several took a broad editorial direction for all of these reasons. Such actions resulted in women's publications containing stories, articles, and departments spanning a wide range of interests, broader than in either the previous or following periods, offering readers conflicting ideas and role models—a full and diverse menu from which to choose. This strategy succeeded in attracting readers. Beginning in the teens, however, most of the major women's journals sharpened their focus in response to stated preferences from readers and wishes of advertisers. This resulted in strengthened service departments and in nonfiction articles filtered through the prism of "women's" interests, a pattern that took hold by the mid-teens.

EDITORIAL PHILOSOPHY

One of the most successful editors in these years was Arthur Turner Vance. Vance played a significant role in expanding the contents of women's magazines. He edited the *Woman's Home Companion* from 1900–1907, then moved to *Pictorial Review* in 1908 where he stayed until his death in 1930. Vance believed that females found a wide range of subjects appealing. His views guided hundreds of issues of women's magazines.

Vance started his career at a newspaper, the *Binghamton Leader*. He became editor of *Home Magazine* then moved to a position as associate editor of *New England Magazine*; he also authored *The Real David Harum*. Thus when he took the helm at the *Companion* Vance was an experienced writer and editor.[3] He conceived the magazine audience as including the entire family, not just the women of the household. The prosperity and growth of the magazine industry allowed Vance the latitude to experiment with the material he published. Later, when competition became keener, pressure from advertisers greater, and the industry as a whole more fixed in its methods and operation, such venturesome editing became more difficult.

Vance made changes when he arrived at the *Companion* in 1900, broadening the journal beyond its rural orientation. As he told his readers: "The key-note of our editorial policy is something to ENTERTAIN, INSTRUCT AND AMUSE in every issue."[4] He elaborated on his editorial philosophy in 1904:

It is a mistake . . . to suppose that only men stop in the streets to watch steel-constructed buildings go up. Women do. I mean that the woman of today is almost as much interested in the progress of the world in the fields of science and art and in human achievement as she is in purely household matters, This is why we strive to make the WHC a woman's magazine in the broadest sense of the term. It might be better classed as a family magazine.[5]

Articles in Vance's *Companion* spanned a broad spectrum of topics. The magazine participated in various exposés and campaigns, matching the muckraking tenor of the period. Cultural topics flourished. The *Companion* began to publish more fiction, Vance's area of special expertise, including satires with a wider scope than those printed previously. Overall the journal became less sentimental and domestic in nature. Leafing through Vance's *Companion* one has the sense of reading a general interest or "people's" magazine rather than a women's magazine. The departments geared toward the household remained a significant component of the publication, but diversity of content became its outstanding characteristic. Women and families responded well to Vance's innovations, and circulation mounted; apparently women *were* interested in areas outside the home, as long as the core homemaking material remained.

Vance hired editorial assistants to help him make these changes. Gertrude Battles Lane came in 1903 to direct the household departments. A woman with experience in the publishing world, Lane had worked as an editor at an encyclopedia publishing company and had contributed articles to two Boston newspapers before taking the job at the *Companion*.[6]

Hayden Carruth joined the *Companion* as fiction editor in 1905. Carruth's previous work included reporting experience with the *Chicago Tribune* and the *New York Tribune*, as well as newspaper work in the Territory of Dakota and in Minnesota. Carruth wrote the "Editor's Drawer" of *Harper's Magazine* from 1900 to 1902, and had various books and short stories to his credit before joining the *Companion*.[7] Margaret Sangster, a well-known writer and columnist, joined *Women's Home Companion* in 1905, where she edited, penned moral advice columns, and wrote poems and short stories. Her previous jobs included positions as editor of the children's page of *Hearth and Home*, associate editor of *The Christian Intelligencer*, editor of *Harper's Bazar*, and staffer at *Ladies' Home Journal*. She was also a prolific writer.[8] As experienced writers and editors, both Sangster and Carruth made valuable additions to the *Companion* staff.

When new management took over the Crowell Co., Vance left the *Companion*. He worked briefly at Butterick Co., then in 1908 took over the editorial seat at *Pictorial Review*. Again, he implemented an editorial policy calling for amplification. Previously thin and without clear direction, *Pictorial Review* blossomed rapidly and profitably under Vance's guidance. Vance himself immodestly judged that "the success of PR in such a short space of time is one of the outstanding achievements of the publishing world."[9] Vance attained his success by expanding the range of the journal, printing a great deal of popular fiction, and by addressing controversial issues, such as birth control and sex education, openly and directly. *Pictorial Review* took the lead among major women's journals in openly supporting female suffrage, even giving practical instructions for raising money for the cause. Throughout the teens Vance commissioned articles on the subject of feminist achievements in the United States and abroad. In the late teens he received assistance in writing about such topics from two female journalists, Mabel Potter Daggett and Ida Clyde Clarke; Clarke stayed on as assistant editor through the mid-twenties.[10]

Vance increased circulation, exhibiting mastery in both the business and editorial realms. As contemporary columnist Burton Rascoe commented, "Mr. Vance has had the courage to publish a great number of hitherto unheard of writers of merit, and to go counter to editorial superstitions without any appreciable falling off of circulation. On the contrary."[11] The rise in readership of both the *Woman's Home Companion* and *Pictorial Review* under Vance's editorship attests to the fact that addressing women's interests in a broad fashion and not underestimating their intelligence worked. Vance's policy helped both these journals join the Big Six group of highest circulating women's magazines.

Delineator began publishing articles of greater variety in the late 1890s under the direction of Charles Dwyer, who assumed the general editorship in 1887. Dwyer had graduated from London University and gave up a business career for one in journalism. Like Vance, Dwyer had worked as a reporter before joining a women's magazine organization.[12] Dwyer gradually added nonfiction articles, social commentary, and fiction to the fashion magazine. Strong household departments formed an especially noticeable addition. Dwyer summed up his editorial philosophy in 1904:

We stand for the home; though it may be necessary at times to strike the minor chord, it is the alert, helpful note that travels farthest and does most good in the world. The principle underlying the Delineator is helpfulness, and its policy is thoroughness.[13]

In 1906 Dwyer left the *Delineator*, after nineteen years as editor, to take over the *Ladies' World*, a mail-order magazine.

Another editor who demonstrated great skill, strength, and ability to expand the material in his magazine was Theodore Dreiser. Dreiser edited Butterick's

Delineator from 1907 through 1910. Building on the changes begun by Dwyer, Dreiser greatly increased the number of fiction and nonfiction articles published in the *Delineator*'s pages, and, like Vance, included features that would interest men and women, including a "Man's Page," written by and for males.[14] This formula proved as successful at the *Delineator* as it had at the *Companion* and *Pictorial Review*: editors willing to lead their journals in the direction of a "home" audience saw their readership increase. Circulation at the *Delineator* increased from 400,000 to 1.2 million during Dreiser's tenure; since his salary was linked to circulation, that rose commensurately.[15]

By hiring Theodore Dreiser *Delineator* again benefitted from the services of an experienced journalist, as publisher George Wilder, who had been anxious to hire Dreiser, well knew. Dreiser had already published *Sister Carrie* and he continued to write while editing the *Delineator*, working on *Jennie Gerhardt*. Before his move to Butterick, Dreiser had been editing dime novels at Street and Smith's and had also run *Broadway Magazine*.[16] His varied background coupled with his great talent and literary reputation allowed Dreiser to expand the *Delineator*'s horizons. He contacted and convinced a variety of individuals to write for the magazine, including authors Ludwig Lewisohn, Jack London, and Joseph Coates. He attracted writers on social issues such as David Graham Phillips and Gustavus Meyers. Political figures such as Woodrow Wilson and William Jennings Bryan contributed. Dreiser persuaded H. L. Mencken to collaborate on a series of baby care articles with Dr. Leonard Hirshberg, although since they appeared under Hirshberg's name, readers never knew that the articles were penned in part by the sharp-tongued critic of American culture.[17]

Dreiser edited forcefully, maintaining full control of the magazine. Charles Hanson Towne, who worked under him, observed,

He was a dominating personality, and I liked his directness, his undoubted executive ability. He worked incessantly. . . . Every department of the organization was under the control of Mr. Dreiser. Not a detail escaped his vigilant eye.[18]

Other Butterick workers shared Towne's admiration for Dreiser's editorial skill. "He was a damn good editor," said Arthur Sullivant Hoffman, who as *Delineator*'s managing editor worked closely with Dreiser. Katherine Leckie, another of Dreiser's staff, and a former newspaper woman, commented enthusiastically, "The greatest editor I ever worked under! . . . A very fine mind! . . . And he always gave the woman the same chance as the man. . . . One of the few who considered women as workers, and that sex did not enter into the situation."[19]

Dreiser possessed a keen understanding of how best to reach his audience. He wrote Mencken about revising an article on diphtheria:

The only trouble with this is that it, instead of talking at the mother, talks *about* diphtheria. . . . Thus, on page 8, it reads: 'Unluckily, there still lingers in the United States a superstitious dread of antitoxin.' Instead of saying this in this way, it ought to be about as follows: 'You probably know a great deal about doctoring your children and some one has told you that antitoxin is a deadly poison or a filthy drug. It is nothing of the sort; if you are a wise mother you will listen closely to the wonderful facts in connection with this discovery.'[20]

In addition to his skill in selecting and editing articles and illustrations, Dreiser demonstrated considerable administrative ability. He oversaw the *Delineator*, *Designer*, and *New Woman* magazines and had responsibility for the South American and German *Delineators*. He supervised the process of sifting through the 42,000 manuscripts arriving at the Butterick offices annually.[21]

Dreiser's editorial selections broadened the scope of the *Delineator*. One employee observed,

He made a strong virile magazine for women. . . . There was a man who came over from *The Woman's Home Companion*. He said, 'Make *Delineator* softer.' Dreiser said, 'Send a letter to all our readers, and ask them if they want a nambly-pambly magazine.'[22]

Dreiser achieved success as an editor while attempting to push the boundaries inherent in the mass market women's magazine field. He ran articles on spiritualism, servants' problems, and Emma Goldman. With publisher George Wilder's backing, Dreiser mounted an extensive Child Rescue campaign. His correspondence concerning articles shows his concern about presenting factual, useful information to readers. Yet Dreiser remained ever mindful of his audience, whose morals he knew only too well from the disapproving reception accorded *Sister Carrie* some years earlier. He acknowledged the constraints, writing, "We like sentiment, we like humor, we like realism, but it must be tinged with sufficient idealism to make all of a truly uplifting character." Dreiser himself was "personally opposed in this magazine to stories which have an element of horror in them, or which are disgusting in their realism and fidelity to life," and he ended enthusiastically, "We find really splendid material within these limitations."[23]

Dreiser pushed up to but not beyond the restrictions imposed by advertiser financing and the need to keep satisfied hundreds of thousands of readers with mainstream values. He occasionally took strong stands *against* advertisers and *for* including realistic detail in stories. He quarreled with the advertising department at *Delineator*, calling them "the Goddamned hyenas on the eighth floor."[24] He insisted a heroine be allowed to smoke a cigarette, as originally written by the author (at a time when "nice" women did not smoke). Yet at other times Dreiser advised writers to stick to conventional mores. The starkly realistic depiction of urban life appearing in Dreiser's novels did not touch the pages he edited. He knew his audience—middle-class American homemakers and their families, who possessed a strong sense of morality—and he took care not to offend them in the *Delineator*.

Editors not only shaped the content of the magazines, but increasingly, in a sharp departure from Gilded Age tradition, began revealing themselves to their readers. A trade journal of 1900 commenting on this trend observed that previously,

The editorial side of the magazine has been kept in obscurity. The average reader living away from the magazine-publishing centers may study the pages of his favorite periodical month after month, growing familiar with the names which appear on the Table of Contents, and yet remaining absolutely ignorant as to the personality of the man or the woman who, sifting out the vast amount of verse and prose and illustration, puts together the concrete thing which is sent to so many thousands of people in all parts of the country.[25]

The new editorial disclosures proved to be a good marketing ploy. Attaching a name, face, and opinions to the creator of a magazine personalized the buying and reading experience for subscribers, adding to the familial sensation women's editors consciously tried to build in their publications.

Ladies' Home Journal editor Edward Bok led in this movement toward editorial visibility.[26] He later described his strategy:

Edward Bok's biographical reading had taught him that the American public loved a personality. . . . He felt the time had come . . . for the editor of some magazine to project his personality through the printed page and to convince the public that he was not an oracle removed from the people, but a real human being who could talk and not merely write on paper.[27]

So that his readers might know him, Bok's name appeared regularly in the *Journal*. He signed his editorials and made his own views clear. For a small fee, readers could purchase a picture of the editor.[28]

Given this prominence and the personal nature of the relationship Bok cultivated with his readers, his attitude toward them takes on special significance. Although Bok broadened the contents of the *Journal* in an attempt to appeal to the family, the *Journal*'s major purchasers and primary audience remained women.[29] Yet when he took the *Journal* job, Bok was a twenty-six-year-old bachelor, having little knowledge of women and little wish to learn. The female he felt closest to was his mother. This detached attitude remained unchanged during Bok's years as editor. As Bok himself admitted,

It is a curious fact that Edward Bok's instinctive attitude toward women was that of avoidance. He did not dislike women, but it could not be said that he liked them. They had never interested him. Of women he knew little; of their needs less. Nor had he the slightest desire, even as an editor, to know them better, or to seek to understand them. Even at that age, he knew that, as a man, he could not, no matter what effort he might make, and he let it go at that.[30]

Bok justified this position on two grounds: first, he saw the editorial role as essentially that of an executive, directing, studying trends in society and picking out those topics best suited to the interests of his magazine: "What he saw in the position was not the need to know women; he could employ women for that purpose."[31] Second, Bok defined his magazine as being for "the home" rather than exclusively for women (as did Vance at the Woman's Home Companion), and he felt that he understood that entity quite well.

With his avowed ignorance about the female sex and his background in advertising, Bok fits squarely into the role of editor as businessman. He saw the magazine as a profit-making venture, with his job that of providing direction and keeping up circulation, which in turn attracted advertising, all the while maintaining editorial integrity.

Bok edited authoritatively, decisively; as managing editor William Alexander admitted, "we have some peculiar notions as to how things should be done."[32] In these years editors ordered some items, took in contributions from readers, and accepted and considered unsolicited manuscripts and article ideas from experts on topics such as household management, gardening, and dressmaking. Editors shaped their publications, but the range of contributors and the need for material meant that new and unexpected items made their way into the journals' pages. Yet Bok, along with other editors of this new generation, increasingly managed and took control over the magazine's direction.[33]

Bok's influence proved both positive and negative. Beneficial changes in the Journal occurred because Bok published articles he found interesting, ones he believed women and anyone in the home should want to read. Bok told George Bernard Shaw that the Journal comprised the world's "largest pulpit," and he made extensive use of it, calling for sex education, patronage of American designers, beautified cities, elimination of billboards, and simpler living.[34] Articles and editorials reflecting Bok's interests such as these made for a broadly based, general interest journal, rather than a narrowly focused, gender-bound "women's magazine"; this proved to be the successful formula for this period. This approach also had the salutary consequence of educating readers about a variety of issues. Occasionally Bok was forced to temper his views (on women's clubs) and give up reforms (the failed campaign to get women to stop buying clothing decorated with egret feathers) in response to reader reactions. And in the service areas, measurement of reader interest led to expansion or deletion of departments. But on broader issues it was Bok's vision that steered the Journal.

A negative effect resulted from Bok's failure to try to comprehend the needs and strivings of women as they endeavored to leave the home or extend beyond its boundaries. Bok believed that women belonged in the home. This view of woman's proper place permeated the contents of the magazine, shaping it powerfully. Bok stressed women's role as managers in the home. He attempted to elevate the status of housework. His Journal also emphasized women's job as consumers, aiding in the conflation of femininity and consumption that occurred around the turn of the century.[35]

Thus the most popular magazine for women of the late nineteenth and early twentieth century, the prototype for other women's journals of that period and for years afterward, was edited, in an autocratic fashion, by a man who admitted to having no understanding of his female readers, no desire to learn, and who believed women should remain in the domestic sphere. That women continued to buy the *Journal* testifies to Bok's genius for understanding what appealed to popular taste, as well as to the growing reader market. Yet his negative views on several issues of importance to women (suffrage, women's clubs) and his approach on others (female education) reveals a truly conservative view of women.[36] However, Bok's traditional view of women and domesticity mirrored the one prevalent in this period. From a business standpoint Bok's editing must be judged a resounding success. And as he admitted, he was not editing a magazine for the "intellectual" but rather the intelligent woman.[37]

Bok possessed in his own mind a clear image of his reader:

I have edited the magazine with one woman in view. I have never met her, but a year or two after I became editor Mr. Curtis and I made a tour of the smaller cities to study the needs of the American people. In one city I saw a woman who seemed to me, by her dress, manner, and in every way, to be typical of the best American womanhood. I saw her at church and at concert, with her husband and children. I passed her house and saw about it the same air of typical "hominess" and refinement I had noted in her. "That woman," I said to myself, "is the woman I shall have in view in editing the magazine."[38]

Other editors also visualized the women they wanted to attract. *Woman's Home Companion* editor Frederick Collins wrote to contributor Dr. Edward Everett Hale,

The average WHC reader is, I believe, about the same type of woman as the average member of a small town Congregational or Presbyterian church. . . . The letters which we receive from our readers are in the main intelligent expressions of opinion, well written and prosperous looking.[39]

Collins also revealed that, "I have always thought of the *Woman's Home Companion* reader as the woman who meets you at the door."[40] Collins, like Bok, saw his female readers rather specifically as home oriented, although both magazines contained a wide range of material, since they targeted the larger "family" audience. Other editors viewed their female readers more broadly. Editors Vance, Dwyer, Dreiser, and Lane all believed that women wanted to read about an extensive array of topics, and all worked to include such material in their journals. Erman Ridgway, when publisher/editor of *Delineator*, outlined in 1912 a similarly comprehensive view about women's capabilities and women's magazines.[41] Ridgway thought women's journals should cover diverse topics, but his view stemmed from the traditional belief that if women knew more, they would make better partners for men. Men and women were different but complementary in Ridgway's mind. While he thought that "there are many vital community questions they (women) can understand better than men," he also wrote that "the more they know about business and politics, the better men they will send into business and politics." Women themselves should not actively participate in these areas. Ridgway believed that social issues, politics, and business should appear in the *Delineator*, albeit for conservative reasons. Ridgway's philosophy would be echoed by women's magazine editors down through the century.

INDUSTRY PERSONNEL

Magazine personnel frequently shifted from publication to publication. The journalistic world operated like a small society, with each member and his or her work well known to all. As editor Charles Hanson Towne commented,

An editor who changes his locale, is much like the actor shifting from troupe to troupe; he is still of the theater, but playing under different management in another house; and he is apt to have the same people in his audience. He may even encounter other actors who have played with him before—all of which makes for a spirited camaraderie.[42]

Women's magazines participated in this game of musical chairs.

The career of ad man John Adams Thayer illustrates this cross-fertilization. Thayer began his working life as a printer. After a variety of publishing jobs, he left his position on the *Boston Journal* in answer to an ad placed by Cyrus Curtis requesting an advertising and print man. While working at Curtis Co., Thayer innovated in a number of areas including the appearance of ads printed in the *Ladies' Home Journal*, means of soliciting advertising, and refusal of certain types of advertising. When Thayer left Curtis Co. and joined the Butterick organization under George Warren Wilder he again implemented these policies, including the refusal of particular kinds of advertising.[43]

Charles Hanson Towne and Frederick Collins both moved in and out of the magazine world, varying their work there with other types of journalism. Arthur Vance and Charles Dwyer hopped from publication to publication. Sarah Splint worked at *Delineator* under Dreiser as the juvenile editor and at *McCall's* as a household editor. She served as editor of *Today's Housewife*, and later went to work under Gertrude Lane at *Woman's Home Companion*.[44] Such traversing, both within and without the women's magazine world, fostered the use of successful ideas and techniques. It promoted homogeneity on the one hand, as personnel used methods found effective at previous publications, but also brought variety and fresh points of view.

Now, as earlier and later, some successful editors found their niche and stayed with one magazine: Edward Bok, Gertrude Battles Lane, William Frederick Bigelow of *Good Housekeeping*, and eventually Arthur Vance, all renowned editors of women's journals, stayed with one publication for at least fifteen years, with their names and that of the journal they edited becoming synonymous.

The magazine environment, offering the chance to establish one's own way of doing business and to creatively exploit available opportunities, attracted entrepreneurially minded individuals.[45] Cyrus Curtis broke new ground in his use of advertising within and for his magazine. He allowed his editors (Bok on the *Journal* and Lorimer on the *Post*) freedom to exercise complete authority over the content of their magazines. Gertrude Lane, through quiet determination and strong belief in herself, became a leading magazine editor and a vice-president of a large publishing company, at a time when such careers for women were rare. Such individuals concocted an increasingly varied fare for their readers, both in fiction and nonfiction.

Edward Bok brought an additional element to his editorial role: familiarity with and deep interest in the techniques of advertising. From the time he left school at thirteen to earn money for his family, Bok had marketed his own literary publications, including a magazine and syndicated women's features. He also worked as the advertising manager at Scribner's where he solicited ads to be placed in two of the firm's publications. This practical experience enabled Bok to better understand the needs of advertising agents, advertisers, and his own publication's ad manager.

The actual creation of ads fascinated Bok, and he admitted that the "science of advertisement writing" held more interest for him than literary writing.[46] Bok's experience and strength in the advertising end of the business stood him in good stead in his editorial job at *Ladies' Home Journal*, where he advised advertisers; like his publisher, Cyrus Curtis, Bok understood the advertisers' point of view.

SEX OF EDITORS

In these years, as would be true through World War II and up to the 1970s, males were more likely to be top editors at women's journals than females.[47] Some exceptions existed, particularly at the fashion magazines. However, the prevalence of males as editors-in-chief reflected the realities of the publishing and business worlds, the position of women in U.S. society, and, to some extent, the preferences of readers.

The effect of the editor's sex on the contents of the magazines is difficult to sort out; while men edited the two magazines of broadest interest (*Ladies' Home Journal* and *Woman's Home Companion*) during some of this period, trends in the industry, origins of the magazine, pressure from advertisers, and responses from readers all played a role in shaping content. The problem of cause and effect also arises; if a journal was narrowly focused on women's concerns (such as the fashion magazines), the publisher might be more likely to hire a female for the editorial position. Also, the women who did succeed in making it to the top in this world typically led lives quite different from most of their female readers.

In 1920 Edward Bok commented on the idea of female editors for women's magazines:

There is a popular notion that the editor of a woman's magazine should be a woman. . . . In fact, we may well ponder whether the full editorial authority and direction of a modern magazine, either essentially feminine in its appeal or not, can safely be entrusted to a woman when one considers how largely executive the nature of such a position, and how thoroughly sensitive the modern editor must be to the hundred and one practical business matters which today enter into and form so large a part of the editorial duties.[48]

Here Bok ignored both rival editor Gertrude Battles Lane and his mother-in-law Mrs. Louisa Knapp Curtis, the woman who had successfully piloted the *Journal* for the first six years of its life.

To be successful as editors, females as well as males certainly had to possess a degree of business savvy. But despite Bok's pessimistic evaluation, women's magazines *did* provide editorial opportunities for women.[49] Female editors included Gertrude Battles Lane, Marie Meloney, and Honore Willsie Morrow (at *Delineator*). *Vogue* had had only women as editors from its inception: Josephine Redding, Marie Harrison, and Edna Woolman Chase. Other female editors of this period included Elizabeth Jordan of *Harper's Bazar*, Katherine Leckie of *Woman's Magazine*, and Juliet Wilbur Tompkins of *The Puritan*, Frank Munsey's short-lived women's journal.[50] However, no female moved into the position of publisher at a mass circulation women's journal.

Despite this failure to provide access to the publisher's role, women's magazines often offered women their *only* opportunities to work in journalism, and certainly often their *best* chance. The number of women working as journalists generally began increasing dramatically in the last decades of the nineteenth century. While in 1880 the U.S. Census counted 288 female editors and reporters, by the 1920s that number had increase to almost 12,000, constituting nearly 24 percent of the journalism profession.[51]

One reason for this growth lay in the increased job opportunities available due to expansion in the magazine field generally in these years, as both numbers of magazines and circulations exploded. Newspapers too were growing and the competition between publishers such as Joseph Pulitzer and William Randolph Hearst opened up possibilities for talented women who could help editors beat rival papers. Also, as advertisers clamored for female readers, editors turned to female journalists for help in creating material attractive to women.[52] Female journalists began establishing clubs to aid them in their career efforts. Such clubs provided support, advice, and professional contacts to members.[53] Women also benefitted from the fact that a journalist rarely needed a professional degree to obtain a job, constrasting with other fields such as medicine, law, and the academy which underwent a professionalization process from 1890 through

1918, with an accompanying exclusion of women.[54]

However, despite expanding professional opportunities, the network of feminine support and lack of institutional barriers, discrimination and prejudice still existed for female journalists, both in getting jobs and also, once the position was obtained, in pay and type of work assigned. Newspaper editors confined most women to reporting on society, fashion, etiquette, and the home. Some women performed "stunts" to get or stay hired, sensational feats popularized by the intrepid "Nellie Bly" (Elizabeth Cochran Seaman). Women who refused to engage in these and other activities designated as appropriate for females could encounter difficulties in being hired and kept by newspapers.[55]

The surest path to a job for a female with writing or editing aspirations lay at a women's magazine. Evidence for this lies in both the actual job experiences of many female journalists and in the advice to this effect given in career books and columns written for women.[56] At women's publications, despite being paid less than men, female writers and editors could excel by focusing on women's experience in an expansionary environment that held career possibilities.[57] For those who chose careers on the women's journals, these publications reaching millions of women, replete with advertising dollars, offered great chances for job advancement, influence over readers, and power in the journalism world.

NOTES

1. Towne, *Adventures*, p. 536.

2. Gale, "Younger Generation," p. 320; and Wilson, *Labor of Words*, pp. 40–62.

3. Gale, "Younger Generation," p. 319; "Arthur Vance," *NYT*, p. 25; *Who Was Who*, p. 1268.

4. *WHC* (February 1902): 4.

5. Vance quoted in Gale, "Younger Generation," p. 319.

6. Hoffmann, "Lane," pp. 363–65; "Gertrude Battles Lane," *NYT*, p. 23; Kerr, "Gertrude B. Lane"; and Zuckerman, "Pathway."

7. HCP, Boxes, 9, 10, 26; and "Our Own Folks," *WHC* (February 1914): 1.

8. "Margaret Sangster," *National Cyclopeadia*, p. 169; Clark, "Margaret Sangster"; and Towne *Adventures*, pp. 30, 31.

9. Vance, quoted in Drewry, "PR-Delineator," p. 56. See also Austin, "Woman Looks," p. 9.

10. Rosiere, "Suffrage Fair," p. 24; Daggett, "Appreciation of Pictorial Review's Stand," p. 7; and Daggett, *Women Wanted*.

11. Rascoe, *Bookman's Daybook*, p. 59.

12. Daggett, "Delineator," p. 365; and "Charles Dwyer," *Who Was Who*, p. 501.

13. Dwyer quoted in Gale, "Younger Generation," pp. 319, 320.

14. See TD to H. L. Mencken, March 21, 1910, in Riggio, *Dreiser*, 1: 46.

15. Swanberg, *Dreiser*, p. 118; Dudley, *Forgotten Frontiers*, p. 225; Ayer & Sons, *Ayer's Directory, 1910*; and May 27, 1909 Memo in TD Corr.

16. George Wilder to TD, n.d., DP; and Swanberg, *Dreiser*, p. 110.

17. Riggio, *Dreiser*, 1: 5, 14; W. J. Bryan to TD, May 1, 1909; Woodrow Wilson to TD, June 28, 1909; and Jack London to TD, July 1, 1909, all in TD Corr., Mss. II.

18. Towne, *Adventures*, pp. 122, 134, 135.

19. Sullivant, quoted in Swanberg, *Dreiser*, p. 127. Leckie, quoted in Dudley, *Forgotten Frontiers*, p. 224. See also Sarah Splint to TD, October 12, 1910; and Mabel Potter Daggett to TD, April 2, 1920, both in DP.

20. TD to H. L. Mencken, October 19, 1907, in Riggio, *Dreiser,* 1: 2.

21. Dudley, *Forgotten Frontiers*, p. 220.

22. William Lengel, quoted in Dudley, *Forgotten Frontiers*, p. 223.

23. Dreiser quoted in Jambor, "Theodore Dreiser," p. 34.

24. Quoted in Swanberg, *Dreiser*, p. 128.

25. "Notes on Some Magazine Editors," p. 357.

26. Ibid., p. 357; and Tassin, *Magazine*.

27. Bok, *Americanization*, pp. 162, 163.

28. Steinberg, *Reformer*, p. 52.

29. Damon-Moore, *Magazines for Millions*, p. 74.

30. Bok, *Americanization*, p. 168.

31. Ibid., p. 168.

32. WHA to MVR, February 18, 1907. See also EB to MVR, November 21, 1907; both in MVRP.

33. Both CMF and MVR sent their material on home management unsolicited to *LHJ*; see S. L. Lacien to CMF, January 29, 1912, Box 1, Folder 1, CMFP; and WHA to MVR, April 24, 1901, MVRP. On the aggressive stance taken by the new generation of editors, see Wilson, *Labor of Words*, p. 42; and Vorse, *Footnote*, pp. 46–48.

34. Bok quoted in Shi, *Simple Life*, p. 183.

35. Damon-Moore, *Magazines for Millions*, pp. 98–107.

36. Steinberg, *Reformer*, p. 86; and Weibel, *Mirror, Mirror*, p. 150.

37. Bok, *Americanization*, pp. 374, 375.

38. Curtis, *Selling Efforts*, pp. 233, 234. See also Frederick, *Mrs. Consumer*, pp. 19, 20.

39. FC to Edward Everett Hale, September 28, 1908, HCP, Box 10.

40. FC to HC, November, 16 1908, HCP.

41. *Delineator* (January 1912): p. 21.

42. Towne, *Adventures*, p. 123.

43. Thayer, *Astir*.

44. Swanberg, *Dreiser*, p. 126; and VNL to MEWZ, November 1, 1985.

45. Peterson, *Magazines*, p. 2; and Hughes, "Eight Tycoons."

46. Bok, *Americanization*, pp. 153, 154.

47. Waller (Zuckerman), *Popular Women's Magazines*.

48. Bok, *Americanization*, p. 160.

49. See "Journalist's Birthday," and "Women as Editors," pp. 9, 10.

50. Chase and Chase, *Vogue*; "Notes on Some Magazine Editors," p. 357; and "Katherine Leckie," *Who Was Who in America*, 1: 714.

51. See Zuckerman, "Pathway."

52. Dorr, *Woman of Fifty*, pp. 16, 17, 92, 93; Marzolf, *Up From the Footnote*, pp. 32, 33; and Schudson, *Discovering the News*, pp. 100, 101.

53. Blair, *Clubwoman*; Croly, *History*; and Kincaid, "New England Woman's Press Association," pp. 7–11.

54. Glazer and Slater, *Unequal Colleagues*.

55. Banks, *Autobiography*; and Dorr, *Woman of Fifty*, pp. 73–77.

56. Schuler et al., *Lady Editor*; Boughner, *Women in Journalism*, especially pp. 300–307; and Adams, *Women Professional Workers*, p. 292.

57. Glazer and Slater, *Unequal Colleagues*, p. 22; and Henry, "Changing Media History." For salary information see Transcript of talk given by Mrs. Roberts, December 21, 1915; and Interview with Helen Koues, both in BVIR, 1919, Reel 16.

4

Marriage of Convenience:
Advertising and Women's Magazines

It has become a recognized fact that the publications designed with a view to interest women are the ones that will carry the message of the advertiser to the actual consumer in a more effectual manner and quicker than almost any other means of publicity.

—About the Crowell Co., 1903[1]

A symbiotic relationship existed between mass market magazines and national advertising in the late nineteenth and early twentieth centuries. National advertising played a crucial role in the growth of the magazine industry, while mass market publications offered manufacturers of nationally distributed goods attractive promotional vehicles. No major circulation journal succeeded without advertising. Magazine publishers conceded the value of advertising to their enterprises, but were quick to point out their own role in advertising's phenomenal growth. As the *Companion* noted, "It is not an exaggeration to say that the magazines are to-day the most important factors in the advertising business."[2] National magazines offered national manufacturers the opportunity to publicize their goods to wide ranging markets and to build brand and trademark recognition.

Advertising in women's journals represented a special and especially significant case of this relationship. As the products being advertised shifted from the pervasive patent medicines of the 1870s and 1880s to goods targeted specifically at women (soaps, foods, clothing), manufacturers turned their attention to women's magazines, journals that efficiently reached this desired customer group. Advertisers willingly paid high rates for space in these publications' pages. In turn, women's journals came to rely heavily on the bountiful ad revenues that enabled them to commission articles, stories, and illustrations from well-known authors and artists, while keeping magazine prices low.

While revenues from advertisers allowed women's magazines to survive and expand, the women's journals also assisted the nascent advertising industry in several ways. Editors moved advertisements toward the fronts of their publications, out of the advertising ghetto existing in the back; next they began placing ads in close proximity to editorial material on the same subject. This trend accelerated through the course of the twentieth century; at this time, however, editors welcomed the ads but retained a fair amount of control over their content and placement. Women's magazine publishers led in the development of market research studies, probing the lives and preferences of readers and aiding advertisers in their investigations of ways to most effectively promote to women. By seeking out advertisers and describing readers in terms of their potential as consumers, women's journals also played a crucial part in developing what Edward Kirkland has called "the feminization of American purchasing," reinforcing women's role as consumer.[3]

Dependent on advertising dollars, yet powerful because of their access to desired female customers and their evolution as businesses, in these years women's journals occupied a strong position in the association developing between advertisers and magazine publishers. The journals retained authority and a fair amount of independence.

"GATEWAYS TO THE HOME CIRCLE"

The years from 1890 to 1917 saw an enormous rise in national advertising. Historian Daniel Pope estimates that total advertising dollars in the United States rose from $190 million in 1890 to $682 million in 1914.[4] A portion of that money went to national magazines. *Woman's Home Companion* reported in 1904 that advertisers spent over $30 million in magazines. By 1917 that figure had risen to over $45 million.[5] In 1892 Curtis Co. began charting the growth of advertising in its publications (initially *Ladies' Home Journal*, with *Saturday Evening Post* added in 1897, and *Country Gentleman* in 1912). In Curtis titles alone ad revenues climbed from about half a million dollars in 1892 to almost $23 million in 1917.[6] Women's journals shared in the abundant dollars being spent on national magazine advertising, consistently attracting almost a third of the dollars.[7]

Ladies' Home Journal led the growth in women's magazine ad revenues. In 1892, the year Curtis hired John Adams Thayer as advertising manager, ad revenues from the *Journal* totaled $250,000. When Thayer departed in 1896, they had doubled to $500,000. Soon after 1900 *Ladies' Home Journal* ad revenues topped $1 million.[8] In 1890 the *Journal*'s ad rates stood at $2.00 per page, rising to $3.00 a year later. Space on pages with editorial material or where such material preceded the ad commanded higher rates. By 1900 the *Journal*'s back cover had become the most expensive spot in any magazine: beginning in 1899 and continuing for several years, R & G Corset Co. paid $4,000 an issue for this position. By 1902 the price had jumped to $4,800.[9] In 1914, the *Journal* boasted the highest rates of any periodical, charging $6,000 for a full page.[10]

Other women's journals also imposed high rates in 1914, with *Delineator* charging $3,500 per page, *Woman's Home Companion* $3,240, *Pictorial Review* $2,800 and *McCall's* $2,160. A page in *Good Housekeeping* cost only $560, due to the smaller size of its pages, placement of all ads in the back, and lower circulation. *McCall's*, *Woman's Home Companion*, and *Pictorial Review* increased their ad rates over the first decade of the twentieth century, narrowing the gap with *Ladies' Home Journal* and *Delineator*. By 1914 women's journals charged higher page amounts overall than any other magazine except the *Saturday Evening Post*, attesting to their importance as advertising media and their large circulations.[11]

Women's magazines could charge high rates because they conveyed advertisers' messages effectively, offering advertisers, as the J. Walter Thompson ad agency put it, "Gateways to the Home Circle."[12] Showing awareness of the special role women's journals played in the new commercial culture, in 1898 the Thompson agency for the first time listed women's publications as a separate category.[13] A Lord & Thomas brochure of 1895 pointed out that

Publications that reach women and children—household, fashion and juvenile journals— are highly influential. She who "rocks the cradle" and "rules the world" is directly and indirectly head of the buying department of every home. The advertiser who makes a favorable impression with her may be sure of the patronage of the family.[14]

Publishers promoted their publications, spending large sums to reach potential advertisers, calling attention to the audience they could deliver, and stressing the value of magazine advertising. Ads run by the women's titles, complete with their circulation figures, appeared in contemporary trade journals such as *Profitable Advertising* and *Printer's Ink*.[15] Publishers also advertised in the pages of their rivals, the other women's magazines. Over time such promotional activity increased, with *Ayer's Directory* a favorite outlet for advertising of ad rates and circulation.

A 1903 Crowell Co. brochure pointed out specifically the wisdom of advertising in the *Woman's Home Companion*. The pamphlet emphasized the *Companion*'s large circulation, the quality of its contents, and the consumer potential of its subscribers. The brochure also offered advice to advertisers, giving information about advertising policy and rates, and noting Crowell Co.'s expertise in typesetting ads.[16]

In 1913 Curtis Co. published a pamphlet called "Selling Efforts," narrating the influence and accomplishments of Curtis publications. The booklet included a special section on advertising to women, ending with an economic argument proving how much money a manufacturer saved by advertising in the *Ladies' Home Journal* rather than using other promotional methods.[17] A 1914 Curtis Co. promotional brochure pointed out that "Woman is charged with the duty of spending 90 percent of the family income, and vexed with many problems incident thereto."[18] The *Journal* and its advertisers could assist women with these "many problems."

ADVERTISING INFLUENCE

Editors began placing ads strategically, positioning them next to articles focused on the same subject. Women's magazines led others in this practice, beginning as early as the late 1890s, when *Profitable Advertising* commented,

It is claimed for publications of the *Ladies' Home Journal, Woman's Home Companion*, and *Ladies' World* class, that their pages offer special inducements to advertisers from the fact that most of the advertising is not only alongside of reading matter, but when pages are properly made up, is contiguous to the department to which it is most nearly akin.[19]

The article listed the advantages to the advertiser of such a scheme: the reader's mind is occupied with the subject and thus more susceptible to the idea of buying; the reader can skip whole departments (and advertisements) that are uninteresting to her; and finally, placement next to an article "insures that it will be seen and read by those who would not wade through solid pages of advertisements that are bunched together in the regular magazine style."[20]

General interest periodicals copied this practice, a fact noted by contemporary social commentators including Finley Peter Dunne and Upton Sinclair. Sinclair observed that advertisers demanded

what they call 'full position', next to reading matter. . . . You start an article or a story, and they give you one or two clean pages to lull your suspicions, and then at the bottom you read, "Continued on page 93." You turn to page ninety-three and biff—you are hit between the eyes by a powerful gentleman wearing a collar, or swat—you are slapped on the cheek by a lady in a union-suit. You stagger down this narrow column, as one who runs the gauntlet of Indians with club; and then you read, "Continued on page 99." You turn to page ninety-nine, and somebody throws a handful of cigarettes in your face, or maybe a box of candy; or maybe its the clack of a revolver, or the honk of an automobile horn that greets you.[21]

This encroachment of commercial material on the sacred pages of literature may have been resented by some readers but from a business perspective it made eminently good sense. Edward Bok of the *Ladies' Home Journal* claimed to have initiated the custom of breaking up stories and articles in 1895, due to an overlong article that had run into the back pages.[22] Editors and advertisers soon became aware of the value of compelling readers to leaf through the whole magazine. It was a short step to juxtaposing ads and articles featuring the same subject matter.

Editorial support given to ads played an important role in fostering product awareness and acceptance of advertising among readers. Magazines backed advertising not only with special placement but also with guarantees, so that women came to trust the ads. Magazines solicited complaints from their subscribers about unsatisfactory products, accepting responsibility for and personalizing the advertising process.

Good Housekeeping provides the most obvious example of product guarantees offered by a publisher. In response to perceived reader needs, in 1901 *Good Housekeeping* established an Experiment Station. The station initially endeavored to test the usefulness of the housekeeping methods and products written about in the magazine. The staff performing the tests soon saw that before they could ensure a satisfactory outcome in cleaning, cooking, or other aspects of homemaking, they needed to check the reliability of the materials and equipment used. For example, the staff felt unable to advise on the best way to wash dishes if they had not offered some guidance on the best brand of soap.

In 1902 *Good Housekeeping* announced that it would only accept advertisements for products tested and approved by the Good Housekeeping Institute. While other women's journals guaranteed their advertising, in these years only *Good Housekeeping* systematically tested products advertised in its pages.[23]

In 1909 the Experiment Station expanded to become the Good Housekeeping Institute, directed by home economist Helen Louise Johnson. *Good Housekeeping* increased the Institute's services and visibility in 1912 when Dr. Harvey W. Wiley, former chief chemist for the U.S. Department of Agriculture, joined the staff. Wiley instituted the Seal of Approval for products tested and found acceptable. Manufacturers donated an item and the Institute tested it free of charge. If the product passed, the magazine reported this fact, providing a description, price, and the manufacturer's name as an informational service. January and August issues of *Good Housekeeping* carried listings of all goods reviewed. The manufacturer had the privilege of advertising in *Good Housekeeping* and could use ad copy showing the product stamped with the Seal of Approval in any publication.[24]

In addition to supplying subscribers with testing results and brand names, the *Good Housekeeping* Institute actively drew readers into the process of advising housewives on their role of consumer. In 1912 *Good Housekeeping* advertising manager Richard Waldo asked readers for the names of stores that explicitly conducted their businesses according to the *Good Housekeeping* ideals of Better Service, which included carrying branded, nationally advertised goods. Waldo promised to print an honor role of such shops in the magazine and to send ten dollars each to the writers of the best letters describing these businesses. His offer encouraged readers to join a community of consumers, guiding one another about places to shop, based on criteria set out by *Good Housekeeping*.[25]

Other women's journals also endorsed advertisements. In the 1890s *Woman's Home Companion* regularly ran a paragraph stating that it stood behind all products featured in the magazine; it continued this practice into the twentieth century.[26] *McCall's* published a product guarantee on its Table of Contents Page in every issue, stating that only ads from reliable firms were accepted and, "If subscribers find any of them to be otherwise, we will esteem it a favor if they will so advise us, giving full particulars."[27] *Pictorial Review* and *Delineator* offered readers similar guarantees.[28] Curtis Co. guaranteed *Ladies' Home Journal* ads in 1901, scrupulously reviewed the advertisements printed, and offered to reimburse readers for any losses they suffered from buying products advertised in the *Journal*'s pages.[29]

Woman's Home Companion educated its readers about what it considered advertising's merits. In 1912 the journal devoted a full editorial page to explicitly laying out its position: advertising helps women in their roles as the "purchasing agent(s) of the home," while "The publisher accepts only proper advertisements, because he knows that this is the only sane policy."[30] The magazine further protected the reader by serving as a safeguarding intermediary:

When the reader of the *Companion* buys anything advertised in the pages of the magazine, and is dissatisfied, the *Companion* returns the money to her. The *Companion* vouches for the honesty of its advertisers, and it vouches for the honesty of its readers. Both are on honor.[31]

Advertisers reciprocated the *Companion*'s support. Borden's Eagle Condensed Milk used one of the *Companion*'s "Better Baby" winners in its ads.[32] Beech-Nut ads displaying pictures of the company's manufacturing process carried a caption reading "to present to the readers of the *Women's Home Companion* a series of pictures of the Beech-Nut Plant."[33] Gossard Corsets tailored its ads to fit in the *Companion*'s Better Films campaign, headlining its ad, "Better Films—Beautiful Stars—Gossard Corsets."[34] Such touches by advertisers aided editors in their mission to make subscribers believe that through reading this particular publication they received privileged information. And the efforts of editors played a key role in the acceptance of branded goods and advertising by consumers.

Some women's magazines possessed enough power to set terms for advertisers. The *Journal*, strongest of the women's journals, banned patent medicine advertising in 1893, refused to give rate discounts to large advertisers, decreased its reliance on ad agents, and reduced the commission of those agents used. As early as 1894 it rejected ads designed to resemble editorial material. Cyrus Curtis established a clear separation between the editorial and advertising departments, and refused to allow advertisers to print any material from *Journal* editorials or other articles. He prohibited editors from accepting gifts or product samples. In 1910 Curtis Co. published the Curtis Code, a guideline for acceptable advertising; soon other magazines followed this company's lead. Editor Bok refused pressure from his own Advertising Department to keep lists of *Journal* advertisers' dealers because it would "harness the Editorial Department too closely to the advertising."[35]

Women's publications also participated in the campaigns being waged against false advertising. *Ladies' Home Journal* exposed duplicity in the patent medicine trade; *Delineator*, at the behest of ad manager John Adams Thayer, joined in the call for honest advertising; *Good Housekeeping* had its Testing Institute for articles advertised in its pages. Such publicized fights for credible advertising undoubtedly nurtured the trust readers held in the ads that did appear in the magazines.[36]

But while Curtis, Bok, and others asserted their independence of the advertisers, all recognized the importance of ad dollars to their ventures. Curtis and Bok were both former admen and like other editors and publishers, they accommodated advertisers in various ways. Ad salesmen from Curtis Co. apprised manufacturers of upcoming features that might tie in with their products. Readers criticized the bulk of the 11-by-16-inch *Journal*, but advertisers applauded the roomy pages.

Relations between the editorial and advertising departments on the journals did not always run smoothly. Edna Woolman Chase of *Vogue* remembered being pressured to support editorially products she deemed inferior. She fought back:

In one battle of my early career when our advertising manager was pressing me for editorial credits for merchandise I considered unworthy he flung out at me, "Remember, young lady, it's the advertising department that makes it possible to pay your salary." . . . I flung back at him, "And you remember that what I make is all you have to sell and if it's not right both you and I will soon be out of jobs."[37]

In these years, editors retained a fair amount of authority.

While magazines claimed to support their ads, contradictions and inconsistencies between ads and feature articles appeared. *Woman's Home Companion*, for example, carried an article on the dress needs of women, warning of the ill effects of using a corset. In the same issue, numerous corset ads appeared. The food editor's column discussing diet and nutrition was surrounded by ads for tempting, high-calorie foods.[38] Such mixed messages could only lead to confusion for readers.

Overall women's magazines fostered the growth of the advertising industry by supporting the ads appearing in their pages. The journals' fights against false advertising also aided the advertising business, as did the advice they gave to advertisers about ad copy. All worked to build consumers' faith in ads and to enhance the ads' influence. In these years, magazine staff, product manufacturers, consumers, and advertisers were defining a relationship based on editorial endorsement and reader belief.

READER RESEARCH

Two streams of research about female readers originated in this period, exerting a powerful influence on women's magazines and their audiences. Both arose out of the relationship between advertisers and women's journals. One area of investigation focused on the psychological dimensions of the individual reader/consumer, with an eye on how best to advertise to her. Ad agencies, spurred on by clients, encouraged by magazine publishers, and assisted by academics, delved into female psychology. With increasing sums spent on advertising, study of the best ways to persuade an ad reader to buy became crucially important.

While academicians and advertising practitioners explored the purchasing psychology of individual females, the publications themselves initiated the second area of research: studying magazine purchasers as a group, using quantitative research techniques for analysis of markets of readers/consumers. In theory, collection of this demographic information served the journals' staffs, as well as their advertisers. However, many editors already possessed a good understanding of their readers, both intuitively and from reading the numerous letters sent in. In practice, many market research reports developed by publishers fell quickly into the hands of advertisers and were written with that audience in mind. Explorations in both the psychology of female consumers and market research affected the development and content of women's magazines.

Psychology of Advertising

Studies in the specialized field of advertising to women emerged from contemporary interest in discovering the scientific principles underlying advertising and its effects. Throughout the late nineteenth and early twentieth centuries, advertising had been dominated by the "rational school," so called because it believed that advertisers should appeal to people's reasoning capacity. According to proponents of this theory, an advertisement should educate consumers, telling them where an item could be purchased and at what price. Ads might also relay to the reader the uses of a particular good. Consumers were believed capable of making their own decisions about whether to buy the product.[39]

At the turn of the century, psychologists entered the field of advertising, and with their appearance came two developments. First, psychologists focused less on decisions about an ad's use of space, layout, and design, and more on the reader's reaction to an advertisement, measured scientifically. Second, psychologists fed the nascent trend in the advertising community toward the use of suggestion and persuasion. This thrust toward the nonrational in advertising reflected the direction being taken by the field of psychology itself.[40] This new persuasive school held that an advertisement should not merely inform a consumer, but should actually create a desire. Gradually, more and more ads used this technique; by the twenties persuasive advertising techniques had gained predominance. The national character being taken on by the previously regional advertising accelerated this shift since persuasive selling techniques suited national advertising better than the simple recounting of information.[41]

Advocates of both advertising schools acknowledged the importance of the female market. One of the first to identify the special role of woman as the primary consumer was Nathaniel Fowler. Fowler drew on his extensive experience in advertising to assert that a direct pitch at women most effectively sold a good. "During my career as an advertising expert I have over and over again attempted to reach the men through the women, and by advertising in publications supposed to be read almost exclusively by women," he wrote in *Printer's Ink*. "It does not matter whether the answer to the advertisement appears to be in a man's handwriting or a woman's. I believe that in nine cases out of ten, no matter who writes the letter, that the woman is at the bottom of it."[42]

If, as Fowler noted, "Woman is the buyer of everything," then advertising copy must increasingly be directed to her.[43] With the increased focus on the nonrational thought processes of potential customers, and with the involvement of psychologists, the female consumer and her psyche became the center of much speculation and research. Men too were analyzed, but the experts considered women to be especially "persuadable," "suggestible," "sellable." Ads in the rationalist mode conveying welcomed factual information to housewives overwhelmed by the plethora of novel products slowly gave way to ads containing little that enlightened the reader; instead, these new ads created feelings of insecurity, joy, inferiority, and happiness in relation to purchasing a product. The new theories about how advertisements influenced readers affected the content and ultimately the visual presentation of ads in women's magazines as copywriters and illustrators began to work with "female psychology" in mind.

Many traditional notions and stereotypes about the female sex came into play. Advertisers felt that women preferred little complexity or technicality; they followed commands and directions more easily than men. Appeals needed to be directed to women's feelings, not their intellects. Illustrations worked especially well.[44] Ill-informed, emotional, and suggestible, females also paid more attention to advertisements: "The woman who will not read advertisements is not a woman," claimed Fowler.[45]

The work of academics supported the practitioners' observations. The first academic psychologist to make an impact on the business world was Walter Dill Scott.[46] Scott belonged to the nonrational school, believing in the powers of suggestion, association, and atmosphere, which he thought should underlie the design of ads. Ad writers needed to discover images that would appeal to the reader, pictures or words conjuring up pleasant feelings, which would then be associated with the product being promoted.[47]

Scott's work affected the advertising world because he communicated with ad men, presenting his findings at the Agate Club's annual banquet in Chicago in 1901. He published his articles in trade journals such as *Mahin's Magazine*, and later in several books. In part because of his businesslike approach, Scott's ideas received a great deal of attention.[48]

Scott's work held special implications for women and the women's magazines carrying ads targeted to females because he argued that suggestion could be used more effectively with women than with men. Concurring with others Scott noted, "It is quite generally believed that women read advertisements more than men."[49] Scott also categorized the ways individuals make decisions, drawing on the theories of philosopher William James about the will to action. With women

the decision is dependent upon a sudden spontaneity of an emotional nature and leaves but little for the advertiser to do. Women decide after this fashion more frequently than men. Here the advertiser can do most by appealing to the artistic and sentimental natures of the possible customers.[50]

Thus the manufacturer could best reach women through an emotional, suggestive appeal.

Development of Market Research

While practitioners and psychologists analyzed the components of effective advertisements directed to women, a related development began, also drawing on scientific and academic methods, to help advertisers better understand their market. This field, the embryonic area of market research, focused on the total market rather than the individual shopper. Several different organizations began research in this area including magazine publishers, ad agencies, independent contractors, and eventually manufacturers themselves. For the ad agencies, use of measurable results also meant the ability to advise manufacturers about how best to spend their dollars, a crucial function if the agencies hoped to gain repeat business from shrewd manufacturers insistent on proof that their money was being used wisely.

Despite efforts by other individuals and agencies, magazine publishers constituted the major force in establishing market research departments. Women's magazine publishers led the way in these efforts. In these years the work they performed was considered credible; later, their objectivity came into question. Publishing companies controlled and maintained access to crucial information about reader markets, product markets, and ad revenue. They created research units to assist advertisers. But the data collection and analysis remained in the hands of the publisher. These first endeavors by publishers consisted of studies of distribution and sales of goods, analyses of industries, and investigations into reader demographics and preferences.[51]

Curtis Co. took the lead in this area. In the 1890s editor Bok and publisher Curtis conducted some rudimentary market research to identify neighborhoods where *Journal* readers lived. Bok and Curtis hoped to use this information to attract higher quality advertisers.[52] Thomas Balmer, who worked for Curtis at the turn of the century as an ad salesman, performed some research on advertising effectiveness, which he then used to advise potential advertisers. On the editorial side, Curtis Co. kept systematic records of mail sent in by readers, noting the departments generating the letters and the subject matter of the letters themselves. These results guided some editorial decisions.[53]

In 1911 Curtis Co. established a separate Commercial Research Division under Charles Coolidge Parlin, who headed it for twenty-seven years, developing and applying innovative techniques to the study of markets.[54] The influence and preeminence of this department and the studies produced there forged another link in the relationship between advertising and the magazine world. Curtis, a farsighted, rational businessman who possessed a national perspective, recognized that industries needed economic, demographic, sales, and competitive advertising figures to promote products effectively. The Curtis Commercial Research Division provided this information. Of course, each report carefully noted that the Curtis Co. publications (including *Ladies' Home Journal*) very effectively reached the same markets as the manufacturers' goods.

The Research Department also collected figures on advertising dollars expended in magazines, an area where Curtis publications led. The first report appeared in 1914. This maiden effort proved to be the first in a continuing series of studies. All demonstrated the desirability of Curtis publications and Curtis space salesmen used this information when soliciting ads.[55] In 1914 48 percent of ad dollars spent in the top thirty-six publications went to Curtis magazines. Over the next six years the percentage rose slightly, hitting a high in 1917 when Curtis journals claimed over 50 percent, then declining a bit to 46 percent by 1920. Curtis Co. took a smaller share in the women's magazine category, reflecting the number of good women's journals providing competition: *Ladies' Home Journal* acquired 32 percent of all ad dollars going to women's titles in 1914, reached a high of 37 percent in 1918, and fell to 33 percent by 1920.[56]

Collection of this data points up Cyrus Curtis' belief in the usefulness of numbers and his understanding of the psyches of potential advertisers: nothing succeeds like success and the herd instinct among novice advertisers assured that when presented with these triumphant numbers, a manufacturer or ad agent would be convinced that the Curtis magazines were *the* place to advertise.

Other women's magazine publishers soon followed Curtis's lead.[57] Crowell Co. had been collecting data and employing research techniques in the early 1900s. By 1908 *Woman's Home Companion* staff could draw on a geographic breakdown and analysis of their readership. By the twenties Crowell Co. had established a formal research department.[58] In 1914 the *Companion* conducted one of the first large consumer preference surveys concerning editorial material. Formally titled *The Reader Survey*, the editors called it a "correspondence convention" when describing it to readers.[59] In 1915 *Companion* fiction editor Hayden Carruth recommended undertaking an annual competitor analysis of the features and stories appearing in other women's journals, essentially a quantitative content analysis of their rivals' publications.[60]

The skillful way Curtis Co. and Crowell Co. used research findings spurred other publishers to set up similar departments. Butterick Co. was analyzing editorial and advertising content by the teens. McCall Co. and Hearst established research departments in the twenties and thirties. Publishers and ad agents alike realized that research on product markets and reader demographics and preferences would carry both the publishing and advertising industries forward.

As the field of market research developed, it bore important implications for female consumers of magazines. The market information unearthed eventually exerted a strong force on the content of the publications. As a clearer profile of the reader emerged, and as competition for advertising dollars became fiercer, editors increasingly tailored their material to the characteristics most desired by advertisers in female consumers: concern with physical attractiveness and home-making, and an interest in buying. As advertisers learned more about house-wives, in the aggregate as well as individually, they designed ads with particular females in mind. Advertisers then increasingly sought advertising media that directed their pages to this particular audience. In these first decades of the twentieth century, however, market research conducted by women's magazine publishers, while respected, shaped editorial matter with less strength and precision than it would later.

AD COPY AND CONTENT

Advertising in the Big Six

In the 1870s and 1880s ad copy received little attention, other than the general injunction to keep an ad simple and direct. Early ads were often very literally "announcements." Little theorizing was undertaken about what made advertising effective or appealing; instead, ad agents spent most of their time convincing manufacturers of advertising's value, while publishers simply tried to fill up empty space. Most ads assumed that potential purchasers had already decided to buy the product. With the exception of some patent medicine advertising, few examples of persuasive selling techniques existed in ad copy.

In the 1890s, as the result of work by publishers such as Curtis Co. and Crowell Co. and ad agencies like Lord and Thomas, advertisements began to look better. Illustrations and careful layouts characterized some of the better-known ads. Improvements in technology contributed to a higher quality appearance. The increased quantity of ads provided an incentive for creating more attractive copy, as each individual ad faced greater competition for readers' attention.

An analysis of five of the Big Six (*Good Housekeeping* excepted) in 1912 shows that by this time ads filled at least half of each magazine.[61] On average, *Woman's Home Companion* contained the highest number of ads per issue (59.5), and the largest number of ads in proportion to total pages in the magazine (70%). *Pictorial Review* placed the highest number of ads next to relevant editorial material (29%), making it difficult to distinguish between the ads and the editorial presentation of clothing and styles. All the former pattern journals published a high percentage of clothing advertisements; almost a third of the ads in *Delineator* and *Pictorial Review* featured clothing and material. All publications placed some ads in conjunction with editorial material.

By 1912 ads in these women's magazines employed a mixture of informational and persuasive approaches. The ads also mirrored tensions present in the editorial pages over woman's proper role. Grape-Nuts ads reflected women's changing role. One ad spoke to "The Business Girl" who "Needs a clear brain, strength and endurance."[62] John Muir & Co., Members of the New York Stock Exchange, advertised in the *Companion* to "Women who Have Saved and Women who are Saving."[63] At the same time the number of cosmetic and beauty ads gradually increased. "Mum" anti-perspirant had appeared by 1912 to assist women in being "odorless."[64]

Major advertisers (those featured on inner front, inner back, and outer back covers) included foods such as Heinz Baked Beans, Quaker Oats, Kelloggs Corn Flakes, Grape-Nuts, Cream of Wheat, Borden's Condensed Milk, Welch's Grape Juice, Coca-Cola, and Postum; soaps such as Fairbanks and Ivory; cleaning products like Old Dutch cleanser and Bon Ami; cloth and clothing manufacturers such as Munsingwear Underwear, Dymond Dyes, and R & G Corsets; and miscellaneous items like Roger Brothers Silver, Kodak, Colgate Toothpaste, Mennen's Talc, and Victor Victrola. Many advertisers placed copy in several women's titles. Food, soap, and clothing producers were among the largest advertisers generally at this time, and all appeared prominently in women's journals. All were products of interest to homemakers, and all could be placed next to related editorial material.

Advertising in the *Woman's Home Companion*, 1897–1914

Advertising in the *Woman's Home Companion* in these years illustrates trends visible in all the major women's journals. In the *Companion* developments in advertising, market research, psychology, and publishing blended together to produce the ads readers actually saw.[65] Several elements characterized these ads. Over time their quality improved significantly. Some items advertised regularly appealed to both men and women: travel announcements, seed offers, cameras, notices about the railways. However, many goods shown held particular interest for women: soap, food, clothing, household appliances. The ads targeted readers of a wide range of incomes; seemingly anyone who could afford the magazine was included in the undifferentiated target market of the novice advertisers.[66] The majority of ads employed scientific appeals. Many ads focused on health and conveyed factual information. However, toward the end of this period (by 1914), a greater number of ads used persuasion and a more emotional appeal.

In the 1890s the *Companion* printed few ads. Those appearing were small and bunched together at the back of the magazine. Curious readers could easily identify the ad section; the uninterested could just as easily avoid it. Many early ads promoted health cures and patent medicines such as Lydia E. Pinkham's

Vegetable Compound, sometimes advertised as a panacea for the blues, other times as a nerve remedy or a suitable replacement for a physician; clearly a "cure-all."

One of the few places in the front of the publication given over to advertisers was the front inside cover, a full-page spot that alternated between Ivory Soap and Sapolio Cleanser.[67] Ivory printed reproductions of paintings, often unrelated to its product. By sending in ten Ivory Soap wrappers, readers could obtain a copy of the painting.[68] Ads also appeared on the back outside cover. *Companion* regulars in the late nineties included Ferris Corset Waists, Baker's Teas and Spices, Walter Baker's and Co. Breakfast Cocoa, and Sapolio.[69] This advertising intruded little on editorial content, but by the late nineties ads began surrounding the Table of Contents, an area perused frequently by readers. Ads appeared there for soap (Pearline, the Modern Soap), health remedies (Scott's Emulsion, The Electropoise, Sulphume), food (Pillsbury's Vitos), and clothing (Shawknit Hosiery). A number of ads offered readers positions as "agents" for a variety of products, causing part of the page to resemble a help wanted section.[70]

After the turn of the century, the number of ads grew and more showed up in the front of the magazine. Copy and design improved. Soap ads appeared frequently, including Ivory Soap and Pear's; the latter often took the back outside cover. Fairbanks Soap Products also used space and Pearline Soap continued to advertise.[71] In June 1902 Eastman Kodak, featuring its camera and the Kodak girl, displaced Pear's on the back cover. Ads for pianos, organs, and Victor Talking Machines appeared regularly.[72] Other advertisers included Coca Cola, Gold Medal Flour, and AT&T Co.[73]

Notices about household appliances increased. One product featured frequently was the fireless cooker, a device often discussed in the *Companion*'s cooking sections. In January 1900 three out of four ads on the inner front cover promoted home fixtures and appliances: Perfection Basting Roaster, Standard Oil Co.'s Perfection Oil Heater and Rayo Lamp, and Standard Porcelain Enameled Baths and Lavatories (the fourth ad heralded the California Limited of the Santa Fe Railroad).[74]

Health themes persisted. An ad for Quaker Oats boasted that "The highest medical authority on foods, Sir James Crichton Browne, LLD-FRS of London, gives the best reasons for eating more Quaker Oats."[75] Postum also stressed health.

In 1906 Tiffany & Co. took a desirable spot on the right-hand column of the editor/subscriber page, keeping this position for several years.[76] Travel ads for rail companies showed up regularly.[77] Such ads appeared to be directed at couples and families, not simply women.

The amount of advertising kept increasing. In 1903 Crowell Co. claimed that over 3,000 advertisers had taken space in one year.[78] In July 1907 the publisher added eight pages to the magazine because advertising ran over the predicted number of columns.[79] By 1908 ads comprised two-thirds of the second half of the *Companion*. The number of large and visually arresting ads had multiplied. A few color ads appeared, including those for Niagara Silk Mills and Coca Cola. Cream of Wheat used a series of large pictures in 1910.[80] No longer could a reader peruse an article without being aware of the goods advertised. Ads began appearing regularly about a third of the way through the book. Articles and stories were broken up, finishing in the back of the magazine.

Despite explanations about advertising offered in the editorial pages, some readers remained confused about the origin and purpose of the ads. Hayden Carruth, in describing the letters he received as Postscript editor, wrote,

correspondents seem to read the ads, just as carefully as anything else. They write to The Postscript rebuking it for not commenting on the alleged fact that the flowers that ornament the Beechnut factory are not the right shade, or that a Resinol Soap lady hasn't the kind of nose that is being worn this year.[81]

Some ads mimicked editorial content in their design, purposely confusing readers. "Dr. Pierce's Favorite Prescription" attracted the reader's eye by stating, "health is womanliness: It is the foundation and the cap-sheaf of woman's attraction; a healthy woman is an attractive woman." It looked like an article; only halfway through would a startled reader realize that the "favorite Prescription" actually was a product being advertised.[82] Some ads in the *Companion*'s new Picture Section mirrored the size and tone of the editorial pictures; only upon close inspection would readers realize that the attractive photos were really ads for Coca Cola or Willys Overland Co.[83] Ads of this type increased over time and eventually were required to carry notices stating that they were ads.

By 1910 ads frequently received placement next to articles on related topics. This happened particularly with food and soap products. Cooking devices (ranges, cookstoves, aprons) as well as food were regularly displayed in ads on the cooking department pages, although the text, overseen by Fannie Farmer, did not use any brand or trade names. Material and clothing ads showed up on the pages of the fashion and pattern departments.

Just as the editors tried to keep subscribers involved with the magazine, so advertisers sought to include readers. In 1909 Colgate conducted a contest, asking readers to choose between two ads for its products.[84] Sixty thousand people wrote in, stating their preference. Ivory Soap offered readers prizes for describing the best use of their soap. Over 50,000 ideas from over 12,000 individuals were submitted.[85] The *Companion* highlighted this relationship:

The *Woman's Home Companion* through its intimate relations with the buyers in nearly 400,000 American homes, carried the advertisers' message like a letter—read, reread, and is passed along to family and friends. . . . The monthly visit of this periodical to nearly 400,000 representative American homes is the best and least expensive means by which patronage can be secured for any article of merit.[86]

Thus an ad constituted no mere commercial transaction; although trying to sell a good, the ad functioned as a visit from a good friend or a letter from a family member.

Through the tens and teens many *Companion* ads continued to emphasize health and factual information. Ads featured doctors or other experts, verifying the usefulness of the item, following the scientific and rational school of advertising. They commonly used statistics to persuade. Quaker Oats campaigned in this vein, heading its full page ad "Some Human Statistics regarding Oatmeal."[87] Crystal Domino sugar offered a booklet that told the story of sugar refining.[88] The truth in advertising movement affected ads. A 1910 Ivory Soap ad suggested that a remedy for a child's headache could be to soak his feet in hot water with some Ivory Soap. But the ad hastened to note, "It is the hot water that soothe's the child's nerves. Ivory soap makes the bath more efficacious. But Ivory Soap has no medicinal virtue. No soap has."[89]

Gradually, however, more psychological types of advertising took over. By the mid to late teens two trends had emerged in the *Companion*: advertising directed more specifically to women, and ads using persuasive, emotional techniques rather than scientific, rational arguments. Increasingly, the ads appealed to women, and in particular in their roles as housewives and mothers; the good housewife used Campbell's Soup, Crisco Shortening, Van Camp's Pork & Beans.[90] Canned goods would assist the housewife, not just to give convenience and leisure time, but to a higher standard in her work. Ads focused on women's insecurities and their desires to provide a good home. Royal Baking Powder noted that "Home Happiness and Good Food are so closely related that a proper start in the kitchen is of the greatest importance."[91] Appeals shifted from emphasizing health and time saving to themes that shopping and buying properly equals happiness and being good. More ads for cosmetics, creams and perfume appeared. Soap was no longer praised for cleansing, but for beautifying the user; Woodbury's Soap's famous slogan "A Skin You Love to Touch" burst on the scene.[92] Women were told that they needed to cultivate and enhance their beauty: "Beauty is An Asset, Cultivate It," warned Daggett and Ramsdell's Perfect Cold Cream, while Grace Mildred's Culture Course claimed "Beauty is a Duty. Make yourself as beautiful as Possible."[93]

Advertisements formed an integral part of the women's magazines. The evolution of ads appearing in the *Woman's Home Companion* illustrates this. Initially the ads were spotty and irregular. Gradually they began to improve, directing themselves at general home audiences, often containing useful information about their products. Eventually they narrowed their focus more directly to women and began to employ the persuasive style of advertising. All these trends affected and intersected with the magazine's editorial content.

NOTES

1. Crowell, *Crowell Company*, p. 16.
2. Casson, "Wonders," pp. 8, 9.

3. Kirkland, *Industry*, p. 273.

4. Pope, *Modern Advertising*, p. 26.

5. Casson, "Wonders," p. 8; and Peterson, *Magazines*, p. 26.

6. Curtis, *Leading Advertising Investments* (1928): 7.

7. Curtis, *Expenditures of Advertisers* (1920).

8. Mott, *History*, IV: 21; Presbrey, *History*, p. 481; and *Story of a Magazine*, pp. 3–15.

9. Steinberg, *Reformer*, p. 25; Presbrey, *History*, p. 403; and *The Journalist*, XXXII (November 1, 1902): 1.

10. *Advertising and Selling* (January 1914): 28.

11. Ibid. On the narrowing of the ad rate gap, see *J. Walter Thompson Advertising, 1904–1905*, p. 221; *J. Walter Thompson Advertising, 1906–1907*, p. 225; and *J. Walter Thompson Advertising, 1909–1910*, pp. 257–67, all in JWTP, Box 5.

12. *J. Walter Thompson Advertising* (1897): 50, in JWTP, Box 3.

13. *J. Walter Thompson Advertising* (1898), JWTP, Box 3.

14. Lord and Thomas, *America's Magazines*, pp. 10, 11.

15. See e.g., the June 1898 edition of *Profitable Advertising*, carrying ads for *The Housewife*, *The Household*, *Comfort*, and *Modern Priscilla* among others, on pp. 5, 7, 8; *WHC* ad in *Printer's Ink*, 25 (December 21, 1898): 18, 19; and "What Your Dollar Will Buy," p. 633.

16. Crowell, *Crowell Co.*, pp. 25, 28.

17. Curtis, *Selling Efforts*, pp. 241, 242.

18. Curtis, *Selling Efforts*, p. 229.

19. *Profitable Advertising* (June 15, 1898): 50.

20. Ibid.

21. Sinclair, *Brass Check*, p. 295; see also Dunne, "Mr. Dooley," pp. 539–42.

22. Bok, *Americanization*, p. 234; see also Steinberg, *Reformer*, p. 62.

23. Fisher, "Housekeeping," pp. 80–83 ff.

24. E.g., *GH* (January 1912): 67; and Wiley, *History*.

25. *GH* (January 1912): 36.

26. E.g., *WHC* (February 1897): Front Inside Cover.

27. *McCall's*, issues for 1912, bottom of Table of Contents page.

28. *PR* (September 1911): 1; and *Mrs. John Doe*, p. 91.

29. Curtis, *Selling Efforts*.

30. *WHC* (September 1912): 3.

31. Ibid.

32. *WHC* (January 1915): Borden ad.

33. *WHC* (February 1916): 67.

34. Naether, *Advertising*, p. 10.

35. Steinberg, *Reformer*, pp. 20–24; WA to Connellsville Construction Company, January 3, 1908, in WAL, January 24, 1907–October 29, 1908, CP; and Transcript of Advertising Conference, 1915, p. 13, CP, Box 5.

36. Weibel, *Mirror, Mirror*, pp. 152, 153.

37. Chase and Chase, *Vogue*, p. 107.

38. *WHC* (May 1912).

39. Curti, "Changing Concept," pp. 335–57; and Kuna, "Concept of Suggestion," pp. 347–53.

40. Curti, "Changing Concept."

41. Pope, *Advertising*, p. 8.

42. *Printer's Ink* (August 26, 1891).

43. Fowler, *Advertising*, p. 720.

44. Tipper et al., *Advertising*, p. 277.

45. Fowler, *Advertising*, p. 725.

46. See also Gale, "Psychology;" Coolsen, "Pioneers," p. 83; and Kuna, "Concept of Suggestion," pp. 347, 352.

47. Scott, *Psychology*.

48. Kuna, "Concept of Suggestion," p. 347; Coolsen, "Pioneers," pp. 83, 84; and Lynch, "Scott," p. 151.

49. Scott, *Psychology*, p. 138.

50. Ibid., p. 111.

51. For studies conducted by women's magazine publishers, see Zuckerman, *Sources*, pp. 147–60.

52. Steinberg, *Reformer*, p. 4; see also Bok, "Magazine with a Million," p. 16.

53. Wood, *Advertising*, p. 40; and Karl Harriman to CMF, May 5, 1914, Folder 1, CMFP, Box 1.

54. Alderson, "Parlin," pp. 1, 2; and Lockeley, "History," pp. 734, 735.

55. Lockeley, "History," pp. 733–36.

56. Curtis, *Advertising Expenditures*, 1920.

57. See Waller (Zuckerman), "Early Market Research," pp. 153–59.

58. Crowell, *National Markets*, 1922.

59. *WHC* 1914 Reader-Survey, HCP, Box 10.

60. HC to GBL, February 3, 1915, HCP.

61. Results derived by analyzing ads appearing in alternate issues of *McCall's*, *WHC*, *LHJ*, *Delineator*, and *PR* for 1912; *GH* was unavailable. For more see Waller (Zuckerman), *Popular Women's Magazines*, pp. 164–69.

62. *McCall's* (September 1912): 40.

63. *WHC* (January 1912): 33.

64. *McCall's* (September 1912): 49.

65. Qualitative analysis based on 1897–1917. For more on the methodology, see Waller (Zuckerman), *Popular Women's Magazines*, pp. 17, 18, 259–314. "Issues" in a cite means that the ad appeared regularly in alternate issues, starting with January, of the years listed.

66. For example one ad explicitly observed that Ivory, "knows no class distinction. The rich find it most satisfactory. The poor the most economical." *WHC* (January 1904): 3.

67. *WHC* (January through December, 1897 and 1898): inside front cover.

68. For example, see "Autumn Leaves," *WHC* (February 1898): inside front cover.

69. *WHC* (issues from 1897, 1898): back outside cover.

70. *WHC* (January 1898; December 1898; January 1899; and December 1899): Tables of Contents page.

71. *WHC* (December 1900); and issues of *WHC* for 1902 through 1908.

72. *WHC* (March 1902): outside back cover, for Kodak. *WHC*, 1906 issues, for Victor Talking Machine.

73. *WHC* (January 1910): 50, for AT&T.

74. *WHC* (January 1900): inner front cover.

75. *WHC* (January 1910): 37.

76. *WHC* (October 1906; November 1906; and December 1906): editorial page; and issues for 1907, 1908, editorial page.

77. *WHC*, issues for 1902; 1904; 1908.

78. Crowell, "Crowell Co.," p. 17.

79. HC to GBL, July 12, 1907, HCP.

80. *WHC* (April 1910).

81. Carruth in "What's Going On?" (June 1918; and July 1918), HCP.

82. *WHC* (February 1897): 10.

83. *WHC*, issues for 1916, 1917, Picture Section.

84. *WHC* (February 1910): 27.

85. *WHC* (February 1911): 2; and *WHC* (July 1911): 2.

86. Crowell, "Crowell Co.," pp. 19, 29.

87. *WHC* (January 1911): 51.

88. *WHC* (January 1912): 70.

89. *WHC* (April 1910): 2.

90. *WHC* (January 1915).

91. *WHC* (March 1915): 31.

92. *WHC* (March 1915): back cover.

93. *WHC* (February 1916): 75, 61.

5

What They Were Reading: Content in Women's Magazines, 1890–1918

Because of its position, its wide circulation and the interest with which it is read the best authors and artists are glad to place their best work at the command of The Ladies' Home Journal. It has put books among the best-sellers as it has introduced household articles to millions of homes.

—Curtis Co., 1914[1]

What was happening to the content of women's publications in these years when journalists flocked to the magazines' staffs, advertisers clamored to use their pages, and the industry expanded? Influenced by these developments, as well as the social, political, and cultural environment in which they flourished, the women's magazines moved through several content stages between 1890 and World War I.

In the nineties these former pattern journals and offshoots of farm publications began enlarging. To fill out their pages editors drew on any material available. The resulting publications appeared varied, eclectic, and unstandardized. Through the first decade of the twentieth century, women's magazines continued to extend their range, with editors at once planning each issue more carefully and taking risks with new and different material. To achieve higher circulation editors often directed their publications to the "family" and "home" rather than simply to women, broadening the contents to include stories and articles of interest to men and children, as well as the staples offered to housewives. Advertisers' dollars allowed editors to publish this broad range of material. Advertisers themselves were not yet sufficiently organized to exert undue pressure. Readers, competition, and the muckraking occurring in journalism generally also strongly affected content, producing rich, varied publications.

By the teens, however, most of the magazines had settled into an editorial focus targeting women's concerns. This reflected the preferences of many female readers, always the major audience for these journals. At the *Journal* Bok tried to attract men to his magazine, but realized that women and their particular interests must be the chief concern of his publication. *Delineator* expanded beyond its pattern business beginnings, crusading on social and political issues, but it came to frame its reforms within the context of domesticity and motherhood. *Good Housekeeping* standardized its format, particularly after its purchase by Hearst Co. in 1911, and by the teens was expanding and emphasizing its product Testing Institute, aimed at housewives. *McCall's*, failing to hit on a clear editorial vision, published a variety of material but retained an emphasis on fashions. *Pictorial Review* grew steadily after Vance became editor in 1908, but targeted women, even as it defined women's interests broadly. *Woman's Home Companion* moved from an unpolished women's publication filled with a mix of material to a family-oriented magazine publishing a wide range of topics. It shifted again, maintaining the content breadth, but filtered through the female viewpoint. Management's uncertainty and final decision were reflected in two of the magazine's subtitles; in 1900 the subheading read "A Popular Illustrated Family Magazine"; by 1912 this had switched to "The Woman Makes the Home," with the audience defined more specifically.[2]

This chapter looks at how each of the major content categories—service departments, fiction, and nonfiction—developed and changed. It ends by looking at the role women's publications played in World War I.

SERVICE DEPARTMENTS

Service departments offered readers guidance on topics from childrearing to career advice. Several editors and many readers felt that while fiction and articles offered entertainment and stimulation, service departments provided the magazines' crucial ingredient. In the 1914 *Woman's Home Companion* reader survey, "departments" ranked highest, garnering 38 percent of first votes, compared to 33 percent for fiction, and 28 percent for articles.[3] Departments ranged from marital advice, cooking, fashion, children, home furnishing, and home building to cultural interests and careers. The popularity of the service departments, chiefly focused on homemaking tasks, reflects the middle-class nature of the journals' audience; women buying them were homemakers, performing their own housework, often without friends and family to advise them.

Edward Bok never neglected the service departments. The *Ladies' Home Journal* not only provided excellent practical advice and information in its service department, but also maintained a huge bureau where readers could write with their problems. Readers interacted heavily with the departments. Christine Frederick, who served as Consulting Household editor at the *Journal*, remembered that "my *Ladies' Home Journal* mail often totaled nearly a thousand letters weekly."[4] By the mid-teens *Journal* service departments generating the most reader interest were food, children, and clothing, followed by interior decoration and gardening.[5]

Under Arthur Vance *Woman's Home Companion* asserted that "We have always maintained that the departments are the backbone of a family magazine."[6] Gertrude Lane continued and expanded this, stressing that

The WOMAN'S HOME COMPANION is above all things a magazine of service in the home. Its pages supply entertainment in its fiction, inspiration and information in its special articles, reliable suggestions in its departments and in its advertising columns. *But the most important feature of the magazine is the service work, which gives definite aid to the home-maker in reducing expenses and raising the standard of efficiency in her household.* (emphasis added)[7]

Some historians have criticized women's magazines' household departments for forcing higher standards of cleanliness and materialism on women, for creating new needs and additional work.[8] The information dispensed by women's journals undoubtedly had this effect, but in the early part of the century household columns also offered valuable guidance unavailable to many readers elsewhere in these pre-radio, pre-television years. The departments provided a real service, conveying the knowledge and opinions of experts. The increase in household standards and tangling of housework and feeling for family occurred over time. For example, Frederick at the *Ladies' Home Journal* advised readers to can goods "not because you love your family but because it is good business to do so."[9] By the late twenties and thirties this philosophy had been turned on its head, and women's publications counseled women to perform household tasks, often in a more labor intensive way (e.g., baking from scratch rather than a mix) because it proved their love for their family.[10]

Service departments focused on women's new job of consumption as well as the standard tasks of keeping house. *Pictorial Review*, for example, tried to help women become educated consumers by running a series on "Common Sense and Home Economics" that encouraged women to read labels, look for quality, and spend sensibly.[11] At the *Journal*, while many articles promoted consumption, Bok also advocated the "simple life," publishing ideas on how to live modestly, how to live on less, how to get value, and how to avoid waste. His cooking expert, Sarah Tyson Rorer, emphasized the creation of appetizing meals on limited incomes.[12] Women's magazines' coverage of the emerging consumption society and its special role for females paired with the journals' ever increasing dependence on advertising offers an example of the complexity of the publications' content in these years, when diverse influences could yield contradictory material.

Columns reflected not only changes in women's role as homemaker, but other changes in women's activities as well. For example, *Delineator* ran a financial advice column and *Designer* carried an Automobile Department.[13]

Departments devoted to children appeared. Editors hoped such features would give mothers a further reason to purchase the publications and would shape future readers. Some magazines presented a generic children's column, others divided it by sex. For example, *Delineator* in 1907 split its children's department into the Jenny Wren club and the Boys Knights of the Round Table, fostering early gender differences. The Jenny Wrens received instructions about buying patterns and sewing clothes for their dolls, while the boys' club encouraged members to think ahead to their future careers as writers, judges, maybe even president.[14] Daniel Carter Beard published a department directed at boys, first in *Woman's Home Companion* then in *Pictorial Review*, called "The Sons of Daniel Boone." It emphasized manliness and experience with nature for its young male readers, nurturing notions of gender difference and reflecting current adult beliefs about gender roles.[15] In the early teens cut-out pages became typical, featuring dolls, clothes, toy theater, and later toy movie cut-outs; these proved particularly popular in two of the journals also selling patterns, *Delineator* and *Pictorial Review*.[16] The *Companion* published the well-liked Kewpies series.

All the magazines included dress patterns in their pages, and the former pattern journals as well as *Ladies' Home Journal* regularly issued supplementary publications featuring additional fashions and patterns. The magazines with less expertise in patterns tried to claim specialization elsewhere, for example by hiring authorities on cooking. *Woman's Home Companion* boasted Fannie Farmer of the Boston Cooking School, an establishment where *Good Housekeeping*'s Maria Parloa also lectured.

All the publishers produced ancillary books and pamphlets, advising on topics such as needlework, canning and preserving, social life, beauty, good citizenship, and even "Employment and Professions for Women" (put out by Butterick). Such publications reprinted and extended the material appearing in the magazines, linked readers more firmly to the journals, and, since readers bore the cost of these items, provided advertising-free information to purchasers.[17]

Magazines often imitated and elaborated on the service ideas put forth by competitors. For example, Bok ran a column featuring affordable house plans drawn up by famous architects (an idea itself perhaps drawn from *Godey's Lady's Book*, which had run such a feature in the 1860s and 1870s). First *Delineator* then *Pictorial Review* copied this department, the latter adding the twist of providing estimates for materials, so readers could calculate costs themselves and possibly do without a contractor.[18] Both *Ladies' Home Journal* and *Woman's Home Companion* operated extensive services for infants and mothers, complete with detailed forms and individualized advice.[19] The *Journal* tried to mirror *Good Housekeeping*'s Testing Institute by having Christine Frederick establish her Applecroft Housekeeping Experiment Station.[20] Such practices furthered the industry along on the path of content standardization.

FICTION

Fiction played a major role in the women's publications, one that increased through the tens and teens. Stories drew consumers, who often read magazines for relaxation and entertainment. Keen competition existed for well-known authors, and the journals' promotional literature stressed the fictional offerings more and more.

The magazines spent a great deal of effort and money soliciting and obtaining fiction. With passage of the International Copyright law in 1891, works of U.S. writers cost no more than those of non-U.S. authors. Editors cultivated well-known, reliable authors, while constantly seeking out new talent. Hayden Carruth, fiction editor at *Woman's Home Companion* from 1905 until his death in 1932, spent much time traveling to visit established authors such as Elizabeth Stuart Phelps Ward, Margaret Deland, Alice Brown, and Kate Douglass Wiggin Riggs. He looked over their work to see if they had anything suitable for the *Companion*; if not, he tried to persuade them to write a future piece for the magazine.

The prices paid for stories offer some measure of the importance given to fiction, as well as the competitive forces operating. In 1906 Carruth offered Ward $1,000 for a story and was empowered to contract with Riggs for the same amount, the *Companion*'s limit. He discovered that *Harper*'s was paying Deland $1,500 a story. Later that year Carruth proposed the sum of $5,000 for a serial of six or seven parts to Ward. Lesser known authors received $250 or $300 for stories. These figures become more meaningful when compared with the prices paid for other features. In 1908 Edward Everett Hale received $125 for his *Companion* editorial page; a cover design by C. A. Gilbert cost the *Companion* $150. Two years later Anna Steese Richardson received $100 for each of her advice columns and $200 for an article.[21] Clearly, well-known fiction writers commanded top prices. Competition for some authors proved so keen that magazines contracted to take all their work for a specified period of time.[22]

Women's journals were willing and able to offer excellent prices to writers who could turn out stories with a sure appeal. Charles Hanson Towne, while working at *Delineator*, approached the popular writer Mary Stewart Cutting about commissioning a serial. Cutting agreed to write one, but at a price of $5,000 and with a firm contract before she had even written an outline. In Towne's previous experience on *Smart Set* (a literary monthly), the highest price he had paid was $2,000 for a 40,000 word novelette upon its completion.[23]

Editors sought to publish authors well known to the public but strove to avoid the unpleasant; fiction must be plausible, but not "distasteful." Carruth wrote resignedly about the "Episode," "I suppose this is a story that we can't use on account of its sadness, but it's pretty well written. The author says it has been declined by various editors who liked the story but couldn't stand for the pessimism."[24] Towne described a similar editorial policy in existence at *Delineator* under Dreiser.[25]

Carruth assisted writers, compiling an author's guide, describing the type and length of stories used by the *Companion*.[26] While helpful, such a guide also worked to standardize contributions.

Charles Hanson Towne described the experience of "ordering" a story when he worked at Butterick Co. Editors could do this with reliable authors because the requisite ingredients for a successful and satisfactory story were well known.[27] There could be no shocks, no surprises. As journals acquired staffs of writers and editors, standardized formulas for stories emerged. Publications gained in efficiency and reliability, but lost in novelty and freshness of submissions.

Magazines often used several stories or poems (carried in large quantity and popular with readers) written by the same author but published under separate names. Towne reported on this practice at *Delineator* and *Designer*, citing writer Justus Forman and poet Theodosia Garrison as individuals who published several pieces under different names in the same issue of the magazine.[28] Carruth used a variety of monikers for his *Companion* pieces; he also contributed unsigned pieces, and the Postscript column, which was edited under his true name. Unsigned or anonymous nonfiction articles also appeared, often by the same contributor. Bruce Barton wrote many articles this way, sometimes penning the anonymous replies. Onetime Crowell Co. employee Gerald W. Young noted that he had published under five different names.[29]

In addition to well-constructed plots and appropriately moral themes, other factors considered in selecting fiction included the value of the author's name for advertising and the illustration potential the story offered.[30] Cover illustrations formed an important component of the magazine product. Art directors chose covers carefully and rewarded artists generously.[31]

Once a magazine had signed a writer to do a serial, the author might be asked to produce a story, which could be printed prior to the serial, making his or her name more familiar to readers.[32] Publications also printed biographical profiles of writers, particularly females such as Kathleen Norris and Mary Roberts Rinehart, building a personal relationship between author and audience so the reader felt she knew the writer and hence might feel more loyalty to the writer's work (and the journal publishing it).

Advertising affected fiction indirectly because advertising dollars paid authors. For example, Edith Wharton, whose work appeared in *Pictorial Review*, was told by her literary agent that magazines could include more serious writers in their pages because of their growing advertising revenues.[33] Editors realized the need to exercise care in their fiction selections so as not to offend and in fact to attract the readers advertisers so urgently wanted.

Advertising conscious editors had to be vigilant in other ways as well. Commenting on a story written by Mary Heaton Vorse, in which she mentioned a fictitious cereal called "Ralston," Carruth noted "Another point: when we touch on breakfast foods *we are fooling with a subject where a big percentage of our advertising money comes from, and it never seems to me altogether safe*" (emphasis added).[34]

By the turn of the century women's magazine fiction featured a greater range of topics and style than previously. More stories appeared, and these of better quality.[35] The amount of fiction published increased both relatively and in real terms as the magazines grew in size. Publication of a number of high caliber pieces written by well-known authors testifies to the financial well-being and the editorial acumen of the women's journals. Authors such as Hamlin Garland, Sarah Orne Jewett, Bret Harte, and Jack London appeared.

Although most stories had a strongly moralistic vein and romance dominated the plots, even this category saw some expansion in range through the turn of the century, before the standardization of the teens took over. In the late 1870s and 1880s, heroines had embodied the romantic ideal: virtuous, attractive, moralistic, inactive, and unapproachable. Rarely did they work; if forced to earn a living, they usually taught. In the 1890s and 1910s, heroines underwent a transformation; still beautiful and moral, they now possessed independent spirits and were more practical and less fragile than their predecessors. Authors portrayed all these qualities as attractive to men. The Gibson Girl most fully represented this free and independent woman.[36] This more mature, adult heroine reflected American women more accurately than previous heroines. Her appearance in magazine stories also matched the movement toward increased diversity taken by the women's journals.

Numerous stories subjects appealed to general interests, not simply to narrowly defined "women's concerns." For example, a 1904 offering turned on an attempt to corner the zinc market. Another plot centered on stock speculation.[37] However, such topic breadth eventually narowed. And even with the appearance of some unorthodox stories and the transformation of the heroine, much fiction remained conventional and predictable. Most, particularly in the *Journal* under the conservative Bok, stressed women's roles as wives and homemakers and the need for self-sacrifice.[38]

NONFICTION ARTICLES

Spanning a wide range, nonfiction articles touched on politics, life overseas, social reform activities, female suffrage, child labor, and women's presence in the work force and in educational institutions. Articles described the lives of the rich and famous. Exposés uncovered corruption and injustice, with readers given specific directions about ways to right the wrongs detailed.

Crusades

By 1910 each of the major women's magazines had taken on a reform campaign. This reflected the Progressive spirit generally and the muckraking trend in journalism specifically.[39] These efforts also revealed the growing sentiment that women's proper sphere, the home, could be expanded to the larger community. Infused with this belief, many readers desired guidance in directing their energies toward social reform. Women's magazines responded.[40] Embracing a cause allowed women to feel part of larger movement, a whole family of readers all working in unison. Participation in a reform effort also made readers feel good about themselves and about purchasing the magazine, thus working to ensure their continuance as repeat customers.

Edward Bok of the *Ladies' Home Journal* led in publishing reform articles. He conceptualized the *Journal* as a magazine for the home, and this included fighting evils that threatened that abode, from infant mortality to poorly designed houses. Bok crusaded against Parisian fashions and venereal disease. He played a crucial role in the fight for pure food legislation, the first magazine editor to do so. He fought hard against the patent medicine advertisers, banning them from his publication and exposing their frauds against the public.[41]

Other journals began carrying crusading features, most notably *Woman's Home Companion* and *Delineator*; both joined Bok in the fight for the Pure Food and Drug Laws. Other *Companion* campaigns included fights for healthier babies, clean groceries, and packaged goods, and battles against obnoxious billboards, child labor, firecrackers, and city slums. In 1906–7 the *Companion* published a group of articles attacking child labor, starting a crusade the magazine maintained through the thirties. President Theodore Roosevelt spoke out on the issue in a signed statement appearing in the January 1907 *Companion*.[42]

Delineator ran a Child-Rescue Campaign from 1907 to 1909 while Dreiser was editor. This crusade matched homeless children with foster families, running stories of children destined for the orphanage if no home was offered; readers could write in to gain custody of a child. *Delineator* editor Honore Willsie started the "Save the Seventh Baby" campaign to lower the infant mortality rate in the United States. And the magazine later joined the movement pressing for pensions for needy mothers; this plan offered an alternative to placing children from indigent, single-parent families into orphanages or even into other, more financially stable homes, as the *Delineator* had earlier called for in its Child-Rescue effort.[43]

These pieces reflected Progressive era values, giving clear factual reporting, infused with morality. They invariably suggested actions for readers to take to right the wrongs reported. Investigative, reform-oriented articles became a standard women's magazine item, one expected by customers. With circulations growing and advertisers just familiarizing themselves with mass media, women's journals engaged in these fights relatively unimpeded by advertiser pressures, although they could be influenced by advertiser concerns. In later years, when advertisers possessed more power and had greater awareness of their strength, editors exhibited greater caution.

The reform efforts carefully targeted middle-class women; this meant campaigns focused primarily on home, children, schools, and health. Such issues fit neatly into the notion of woman as social housekeeper, a concept propounded by Jane Addams, whose work women's journals reported and commented on favorably.[44] While the intensity of muckraking journalism generally began fading by the mid-teens, women's magazine editors went against that trend and continued to publish strong investigative articles through the mid-twenties.

Women Outside the Home

When discussing females' roles in general, the women's magazines both led and reflected society. They presented some of the most progressive thought on these subjects, and at the same time mirrored Americans' conflicting and shifting views. Most clearly, they educated on this topic, presenting a continuous flow of information about women's expanded sphere of activities and commentary about the effects of these transformations. Readers of the mass circulation women's journals in these years could not remain unaware that women were moving into new areas.

A number of articles expressed anxiety about the future of the home. Much debate centered on the notion that women with educational or work experience would be reluctant to forgo this outside stimulation for marriage, housekeeping and motherhood.[45] Most discussions assumed women would give up their jobs after marriage if they could afford to. Creative problem solving for working women with children merited little space. Most articles directed to working women assumed the availability of servants.

Delineator explored the changing nature of women's work as it moved from home to factory.[46] *Delineator*'s journalist investigated the budgets of working girls, keeping in mind sociologists' claim that women spent their money frivolously; the author found this charge to be untrue. Photos taken by famed documentary photographer Lewis Hines illustrated this series. The piece closed with an analysis of the effects of cheap female labor on the economy.

Ladies' Home Journal ran an extensive series in the early nineties on careers for women such as dressmaking, stenography, teaching, interior decoration, art, telegraphy, acting, selling, and journalism.[47] *McCall's* published a series beginning in 1911, featuring stereotypically female professions such as dressmaking, stenography, and tea-room and millinery shop ownership, as well as less traditionally female jobs such as real estate agent and hotel owner. In the same issue as the article on dressmaking, the magazine published information about female pilots.[48]

Profiles of well-known personalities, a perennial favorite with readers, ranged from actresses, singers, and royalty to successful career women, all offering role models outside the private sphere. *Woman's Home Companion* ran a department called "About People," featuring males and females equally. Women presented included Harriet Quimby, "the first American woman to master the airplane," operatic star Felice Lyne, intercollegiate Bureau of Occupations administrator Frances Cummings, and clothing designer Madame Paquin.[49] *Good Housekeeping* published a more conventional series written by American actresses which focused on "the little-suspected home-hunger of the modern star."[50] *McCall's* addressed this same theme with "Should An Actress Marry?"

(yes, if she finds the right man).[51] *McCall's* also highlighted the careers of physicians Elizabeth Blackwell, Emily Blackwell, and two female doctors working overseas.[52]

General Interest Articles

In the early 1900s general articles of interest appeared, displaying the magazines' attempts to appeal broadly. At *Woman's Home Companion*, for example, Arthur Vance published pieces on topics such as "The Human Side of John D. Rockefeller" and "Wireless Energy, A Visit to the Home of Thomas A. Edison."[53] Vance printed two rather frightening essays on the "Wonders of Modern Warfare" at the time of the Russian Japanese War. The articles carried photos of weapons, boats, guns, trains, and explosives. One picture showed a smiling baby sitting near a gun.[54] Another piece featured the Panama Canal.[55] Such general interest articles gradually disappeared.

Women and Sex

Discussions of sex education proved the women's magazines' willingness to confront a forbidden topic. *Ladies' Home Journal* called for instruction about the sexual facts of life, then ran an explosive series on the need for public education about venereal disease. Hundreds of readers canceled their subscriptions, but Bok felt the subject an important one and ran the articles in spite of business considerations, albeit without ever explicitly using the term venereal disease.[56] *Good Housekeeping* printed several articles on sex education, noting that "Sex education of some kind must be given."[57] *Pictorial Review* daringly addressed the topic of birth control, opening a contest on the subject; the magazine claimed to receive thousands of letters. While *Pictorial Review*'s editorial page carried a boxed listing of birth control's pros and cons, the reader letters quoted all argued for birth control, primarily on the grounds of preserving mothers' strength and producing healthier children. *Pictorial Review* also offered a correspondence course in sex education.[58]

Women and Politics

Efforts to educate women about government yielded a steady flow of articles. Depictions of women in governmental positions provided role models as well as evidence that women could function effectively in the political sphere. The magazines described the mechanics of the different branches of the government.[59] *Woman's Home Companion* reported on women active in the 1912 Presidential campaign such as Jane Addams and novelist Gertrude Atherton.[60] *Pictorial Review* published a profile of Kate Barnard of Oklahoma, the first woman elected to state office.[61] *Good Housekeeping* reported on organized women's influence in getting national legislation passed, and reviewed the progress of women and women's issues in the 1912 election.[62] *Delineator* carried an article on Anna Rogstad, Norway's first female Parliament member.[63]

Delineator also ran a powerful series on women and the law written by William Hard, a former social settlement worker.[64] Hard's articles presented readers with information about various state laws dealing with divorce and child custody and the inequities women suffered under these laws. The series generated thousands of letters recounting difficulties experienced because of these laws, according to Hard. *Delineator* claimed to be instrumental in changing property laws affecting married women in several states.[65]

A long piece authored by presidential candidate Woodrow Wilson appeared in the *Companion*, specifically targeting women, and covering the kinds of political issues presumed to be appealing to them. In 1916 Republican presidential candidate Charles Evans Hughes conveyed his views on the tariff, preparedness, the federal budget, public administration, and U.S. policy toward Mexico, all as they related to women; the article included a large picture of Hughes and his wife.[66] These pieces contrast with earlier articles the *Companion* published in 1904 on presidential candidates Theodore Roosevelt and Alton Parker, which presumed a dual sex audience and were not slanted to female concerns.[67]

Female Suffrage

All the popular women's journals published articles on both sides of the female suffrage issue. Journals devoted explicitly to woman suffrage continued to exist. But even the *Woman's Journal*, the only feminist publication to boast more than 5,000 purchasers, could claim only a little over 10,000 subscribers in 1911, a year when *Ladies' Home Journal*'s circulation stood at well over a million.

Among the Big Six *Delineator*, *Woman's Home Companion*, *McCall's*, and *Good Housekeeping* all eventually supported female suffrage, albeit cautiously, basing their support primarily on the social housekeeping argument—women could clean up society. This matched the reasoning being used by the mainstream women's movement, an argument for expediency rather than for equal rights. *Pictorial Review*, which supported suffrage before the other four, did so based on equal rights for women argument.

The women's journals employed various strategies when discussing suffrage. One alternative was presenting several points of view, a tactic that paralleled the position of the General Federation of Women's Clubs, which debated the topic at its national conventions from 1904 on.[68] The *Companion* published an article exemplifying the multi-view approach, presenting the pros and cons of the issue, calling it "the-subject-you-can't-get-away-from."[69] *Delineator* also tried to take a nonpartisan approach, presenting a series of articles on suffrage in 1908, viewing it from a variety of angles.[70]

The editors of *McCall's* pressed heavily on the "social housekeeping" argument, noting that "With women, politics is either Municipal, State or National housekeeping, or it is—nothing."[71] The magazine published an article exploring the effect on the home of women entering the political arena, focusing on the theories of Ellen Key and Olive Schreiner. *McCall's* also ran an article by National American Woman's Suffrage Association President Shaw titled, "If I were President," in which she outlined her platform and designated individuals for various Cabinet positions, including Jane Addams as Secretary of State, businesswoman Hetty Green as Secretary of the Treasury, and Andrew Carnegie as Secretary of War.[72]

Good Housekeeping published a stirring series written by British militant suffragist Emmeline Pankhurst who effectively defended her disruptive tactics to the American audience. *Good Housekeeping*'s editors penned a sympathetic introduction, declaring "To all who have been fair-minded enough to read this story it has been a satisfactory explanation if not a justification, of the militant movement."[73] In a less radical vein, the magazine provided a survey of American suffrage movement leaders, framed reassuringly with an emphasis on their personal charms and housekeeping abilities.[74]

Over its life *Ladies' Home Journal* took several stands on votes for women. Louisa Knapp Curtis had advocated female suffrage, while Edward Bok shifted the magazine's stance, coming out against suffrage as early as 1892. He refused to believe that women of judgment and refined feelings wanted or needed the vote, even though surveys of his own readers showed they disapproved of these negative views.[75] Eventually, the *Journal* presented debate on both sides of the issue, including a prosuffrage essay by Jane Addams in 1910. But Bok still opposed giving women the vote, as he stated clearly in the *Journal*'s March 1912 issue.[76]

Pictorial Review under Arthur Vance unequivocally championed female suffrage, taking this position in 1913.[77] The magazine followed up with a comprehensive series describing women's actions in states where they had gained suffrage. By the next year the journal was urging its readers to work for the constitutional amendment to gain female suffrage.[78] *Pictorial Review* based its support for female suffrage on simple equality: "We believe when all is said and done, that if we recognize women to be human, it follows as a matter of simple justice that they have as much right to a voice in governmental affairs as the men."[79]

Delineator soon followed *Pictorial Review*'s lead. By the mid-teens, editor Honore Willsie pointed out facts on her editorial page such as the significantly lower infant mortality rate existing in countries where women voted, and a listing of foolish laws passed by men, for the edification of those fearful of laws women might legislate.[80]

For a number of years, *Woman's Home Companion* maintained an even-handed approach toward the topic, although as early as 1902 it printed an editorial on suffrage that pronounced "In the end it will doubtless succeed."[81] Readers enjoyed articles about women's suffrage, as the magazine's 1914 reader survey indicated.[82] Jane Addams argued working women's need for the ballot, and a three part series by Anna Richardson described the leaders and actions of the women's suffrage movement.[83] Presidential candidate Charles Evans Hughes expressed his personal support for female suffrage in a 1916 article.[84] Eventually, the *Companion* too gave editorial support to women's voting rights.

READERS AND CONTENT

Female suffrage offers just one example of a topic where reader responses affected magazine content. Readers' letters, suggestions, and written contributions all influenced and shaped the women's journals.

Despite increased use of experts and standardization of content, women's magazines still incorporated readers' tips and suggestions into their pages.[85] *McCall's* let readers know that "If there is anything in which you are particularly interested, write to us about it and we will be glad to publish the latest information on the subject," adding the cautionary "always provided, of course, that it is a suitable one for a wide-awake woman's magazine."[86] Gertrude Lane told J. Walter Thompson ad agents that Companion staff used information gathered in a reader survey to plan editorials, articles, stories, and fashions.[87] Butterick's *Woman's Magazine* boasted that it owed its very existence to reader requests to the pattern manufacturing New Idea Company.[88]

At the *Ladies' Home Journal*, correspondence to service columns was systematically tracked. With regard to departments editor Bok admitted that "in effect we edit the magazine out of the correspondence."[89] Bok routinely reviewed readers letters, staying home one day a week to do so in the early days of his career. He also offered prizes for responses to questions about what readers liked least and best in the magazine and why, and what feature they would like the *Journal* to run. Readers responded by the thousands.[90] However, although Curtis Co. publicly stated that "The readers of THE LADIES' HOME JOURNAL . . . determine what shall appear in it," and Bok appeared to agree, his actions at times contradicted this policy.[91] Bok preached against women's clubs and women's voting rights, even though his readers participated in the first and were interested in the second. Bok seemed most responsive in the service departments, arguably those areas where he held the least personal interest.

Just as readers undoubtedly affected magazine content, so the process worked in the reverse; women's journals certainly influenced their readers. This happened indirectly through the images put forth in the fiction. It happened more directly through information and guidance provided in the departments. The journals could also serve to stimulate women, show them untouched opportunities and new ways of thinking by calling on readers to act on social and political issues. Women responded, writing letters and working for passage of legislation in areas such as adulterated foods, widowed mothers' pensions, and marriage laws. But the many conservative messages inevitably affected women as well, as did the emerging vision of woman as consumer.

The magazines' content was at times contradictory. They carried articles on social and political issues, showing women active in all spheres, speaking out, capable. Yet editorially, in the fiction, and in the service departments, the magazines supported the traditional notion of women as self-sacrificing and belonging first in the home, raising children. Often the content categories dictated this split in attitudes. The fiction and editorial essays tended to be sentimental, moralistic, and conservative. Departments focused on homemaking. The nonfiction features carried factual reports about women in the United States and around the world pursuing work and independent interests.

McCall's offers a good example of this philosophical inconsistency. Despite articles on female doctors and one by NAWSA President Anna Howard Shaw, editorially the publication espoused a traditional view of women:

A wise, as well as a wealthy, woman recently had the inspiration to say that no woman is happy who does not work. Furthermore, that a woman is happiest when her creative ability expresses itself in marriage, the making of a home and the rearing of children.[92]

Other articles following this conservative vein included one bemoaning the disappearance of home life.[93] Yet at the same time, another essay called on women to work and to demand money for their labor:

Woman must work. This will make her well. She must demand for her work money as does man. She must hold herself to herself as an individual, an entity, and capable as such to be economically free. Then the world will acknowledge her as an individual.[94]

McCall's pages also reflected conflicting views about technology, housework, and the housewife's proper role. In one story a wife, liberated from staying at home to cook all day by the new "fireless cooker," began spending her days at clubs and teas. Her husband complained about his meals "being cooked in a box." The contrite wife (who admitted to disliking housework) realized she had been neglecting her duties and meekly returned to her full days at home.[95] Yet the magazine also published an informative article on electricity, touting appliances for their time and energy savings (an article sure to win the approval of advertisers).[96] *McCall's* printed a piece of fiction spoofing a husband who attempted to apply the techniques of scientific management to the home.[97] Yet an article on cooperative housekeeping by Charlotte Perkins Gilman appeared later that year, describing how "simple and elementary forms of co-operation (can save) some of each day's hours . . . for your chosen spending."[98] Clearly a tension existed between the use of innovative technological and management techniques to streamline housework, and a fear of what would happen if women no longer devoted themselves to this work full time. Presentation of contradictory outlooks reflected tensions in society at large and exposed readers to various viewpoints, allowing them to choose pieces that best fit their own beliefs.

Sometimes the conflicting ideas came about, as at the *Journal*, when the beliefs of the editor about a particular topic (such as the value of women's clubs) clashed with those of many readers.[99] The various viewpoints also reflected the magazines' incomplete movement toward standardization, a process occurring in these years, but which had not yet fully taken hold. Finally, the contradictory opinions reflected readers' own lives and thoughts; the diverse and at times conflicting articles may have mirrored women's own unsettled ideas.

The publications' impact reached beyond their purchasers. For example, *Ladies' Home Journal* pieces on venereal disease, appearing in 1908, were reprinted in pamphlet form and mailed to each female student at Kansas State Agricultural College.[100] Individuals frequently asked permission to use ideas or pictures presented in women's journals. Authors reprinted their own work.

WORLD WAR I

The war breaking out in Europe in 1914 had a profound effect on women's magazines. Women's contributions to the war effort forced Americans to reassess their ideas about woman's proper role, revisions provoked by and reflected in the women's magazines. War-related topics halted the narrowing of subject matter and in fact worked to broaden and deepen the material presented in the publications.

Wartime also revealed women's magazines' importance. The government drew on the staffs of these journals for assistance in its public information efforts. The magazines themselves carried significant information to millions of Americans about food and energy conservation as well as news of the war and its victims.

Even before U.S. entry in the war, but after the European conflict had broken out, women's journals began publishing articles on war relief efforts, economic opportunities for American industries, and the need for peace. Discussions of the pros and cons of American preparedness appeared. *Woman's Home Companion* reported on the strife and explained how women could help war-torn Europe. By 1916 each issue contained not only an editorial piece on the war, but also an article focused on the situation in Europe. *Delineator* and *Designer* strongly advocated preparedness, an issue also addressed in the *Journal* and the *Companion*.[101]

After the United States joined the war, the subject infused the women's journals, focusing on ways women could aid the war effort. Articles about clothing use and purchasing strategies appeared. Various volunteer opportunities were described. Columns provided practical information about the military touching on the concerns of wives and mothers.

Most commonly, however, the women's journals published information about food conservation and control. This work was especially important since in World War I, unlike World War II, compliance with conservation efforts remained voluntary. Women's journals carried pledge slips for women to sign, where they vowed to remain meatless and wheatless for a prescribed number of meals. This written commitment solidified signers' resolve and reassured women about their contribution to the war effort. The magazines wrote editorials in support of these programs, carried endorsements by Herbert Hoover (Head of the U.S. Food Administration), published recipes omitting the scarce items, and printed booklets containing food conservation ideas.[102]

While all women's magazines emphasized ways women could support the war effort, each sought to differentiate its approach to the emergency. *Delineator* filled its pages with articles passionately decrying the enemy. It created a "Woman's Preparedness Bureau" to assist readers in supporting the war. War victims in France and Belgium received a great deal of attention. *Designer* solicited candy from readers and their children for a Candy Ship that transported the sweets to Belgian children suffering from lack of sugar. *Delineator* editor Honore Willsie castigated the suffragists who marched on the White House during the war, calling such activities "mean and unpatriotic."[103]

Good Housekeeping used its Institute to provide information about food conservation and sent a correspondent overseas.[104] In fact most of the major women's publications hired journalists to report on conditions in England and the continent. These correspondents described not so much the war itself as the conflict's effect on the peoples involved, particularly those of England, France, and Belgium. *Good Housekeeping* sent Clara Savage, an assistant to editor William Frederick Bigelow.[105] Arthur Vance at *Pictorial Review* enlisted Mabel Potter Daggett to "go over there and find out just what this terrible cataclysm of civilisation means to the woman's cause."[106] Daggett penned a stirring account of women's contributions to war work in Britain, France, Germany, and Italy, pointing out the progress war brought where all the suffragists' efforts had failed.[107] Anna Steese Richardson served as a correspondent for *Woman's Home Companion*, as did Margaret Deland (on assignment in France for the YMCA). Butterick Co. editor Marie Meloney took a leave of absence and went overseas to do relief work with French children.[108]

Vogue sponsored a fashion fete in New York City in 1914, the first of its kind, with proceeds going to women and children in Europe. Conde Nast started British *Vogue* in 1916 in large part because of wartime conditions—French and Viennese fashion publications were no longer available, restrictions had been placed on paper in the United States, and a ban existed on all but necessary shipments between the United States and Britain.[109]

Ladies' Home Journal focused heavily on women's home front endeavors, in part because President Wilson had advised Bok to stress these activities rather than publishing reports about the war.[110] A regular "The Woman and the War" section appeared. In the February 1918 issue, for example, this segment carried a piece by the Head of the U.S. Fuel Administration on the need to save coal, a column by a U.S. Food Administration officer on the role played by grocery stores in the management of foodstuffs, and an article by Hoover on the recalcitrance of American men in the food conservation effort.[111]

The *Journal* published well-known names including Assistant Secretary of the Navy Franklin Roosevelt (telling mothers why their sons needed to enlist) and former President William Howard Taft, now chair of the Red Cross Central Committee. A piece by President Wilson appealed to readers to purchase Liberty Loans. Anna Howard Shaw, now Chair of the Woman's Committee of the U.S. Council of National Defense, conducted a regular department.[112] Editor Bok himself traveled to England and France as part of a group of editors and journalists and reported back to readers.[113]

The war crisis forced Bok to rethink women's role in society. The *Journal* showed women engaging in volunteer activities such as the Red Cross and in physical labor on farms. It also described the need for women to join the work force, even married women with children. Fictional heroines worked outside the home without sanctions. Bok himself recanted, noting that "it is time, whether peace is near or not, to begin to readjust ourselves to an amazing lot of notions and fetishes that we are going to be asked to throw into the scrapheap."[114] With such statements the magazine reflected the shifting views about women forced on society by the war.

When the hostilities ended women's magazine editors initially called for continuance of women's participation in the public sphere, whether through paid work or unpaid social improvement activities. *Good Housekeeping* suggested that women focus on poverty and hunger. *Ladies' Home Journal* called on women to unite as they had in the war crisis to deal with the problems of returning vets. And of course women's accomplishments during the war fueled the march toward the vote, something all the magazines recognized as inevitable by war's end.[115]

The rich coverage women's publications gave to a variety of war issues demonstrated their journalistic commitment to serious subjects, albeit with a feminine slant. This may have heightened readers' expectations, leading them to anticipate the continuation of such journalism in women's publications after the war. In turn this may have given editors the impetus and the freedom to maintain such variety.

NOTES

1. Curtis, *Selling Efforts*, p. 237.
2. See Waller (Zuckerman), *Popular Women's Magazines*, pp. 17, 18, 259–314.
3. 1914 *WHC* Reader-Survey, p. 5, HCP, Box 10.
4. Frederick, *Mrs. Consumer*, pp. 166, 167.
5. Transcript of Advertising Conference, p. 11, CP, Box 5.
6. *WHC* (December 1905): 56.
7. *WHC* (April 1914): 25.
8. See e.g., Cowan, *More Work*.
9. Frederick quoted in Scanlon, *Inarticulate Longings*, p. 53.
10. Schuler et al., *Lady Editor*, pp. 126, 127.

11. See Johnson, "Meaning of the Label," pp. 10, 54; and Johnson, "Consumer's Responsibility," pp. 18, 32.

12. Scanlon, *Inarticulate Longings*; Shi, *Simple Life*, pp. 181–89; and Weigley, *Rorer*.

13. Ryant, *Profit's Prophet*, pp. 22, 37; and *Mrs. John Doe*, p. 55.

14. McDowell, "Children's Feature," pp. 38, 39.

15. Mechling, "Collecting Self," p. 260.

16. Hill, "Toy Theater!" pp. 165–84.

17. Zuckerman, *Sources*, pp. 205–70.

18. *Delineator's Prize $3,000 Houses*; and "Solving the House-Plan Problem," p. 1.

19. Bok, *Americanization*, pp. 176–78.

20. Frederick, *Mrs. Consumer*, p. 167.

21. Expense record book, 1906 through end of the teens, HCP, Box 10.

22. HC to FC, April 10, 1908, HCP, Box 10. Towne, *Adventures*, p. 79.

23. Towne, *Adventures*, p. 79.

24. HC Memo, May 28, 1917, HCP, Box 10.

25. Towne, *Adventures*, p. 80.

26. Carruth, "What's Going On" (June 1918; July 1918), HCP; and *WHC* (February 1914): 1.

27. Towne, *Adventures*, p. 125.

28. Towne, *Adventures*, p. 57.

29. Carruth Scrapbook, HCP, Box 10; "Circulation: 9,496,841," p. 104; and GWY to MEWZ, January 19, 1985.

30. HC memo to GBL, June 16, 1908; HC to FC, June 10, 1910; and HC to FC, February 20, 1908, HCP. WA to Onotono Watanna, May 11, 900, WAL, October 13, 1899–June 15, 1900; and WA to C. M. Harger, May 22, 1901, WAL, May 1901–.

31. HC to GBL, February 2, 1915; and HC to GBL, August 8, 1916, HCP.

32. HC to FC, March 28, 1908, HCP, Box 10.

33. Lewis, *Wharton*, p. 484.

34. HC to GBL, April 29, 1908, HCP, Box 10.

35. See e.g., Waterloo, "Hair of the Dog"; Stoddard, "Tale of a Broken Oar"; and Bell, "Yessum." See also Wilson, "Rhetoric of Consumption," pp. 39–64.

36. See e.g., "By Advice of the Doctor," *WHC* (January 1902): 37, 38; Stineman, *Popular Women's Magazines*, pp. 33, 34; and Towne, *Adventures*, p. 62.

37. Waters, "Benefit of the Poor," p. 8; and Mayers, "Deal in Kanuka," pp. 7, 8.

38. Seaton, "Sex and the Nubile Girl," pp. 47, 48; see also Searles and Mickish, "Thoroughbred Girl," pp. 261–81.

39. Regier, *Muckrakers*; and Filler, *Crusaders*, p. 39.

40. See e.g., *McCall's* (September 1912): 50.

41. Steinberg, *Reformer*, and Bok, *Americanization*.

42. *WHC* (August 1906): 5; and *WHC* (January 1907): 4.

43. Hard, "Worldly Goods," pp. 217–18; "We Meant It and We Did It," p. 3; and Skocpol, *Protecting Soldiers*, pp. 434–39.

44. See e.g., *WHC* (October 1898; and November 1898), articles by Forrest Crissey on Hull House; and Addams, "Working Woman," p. 19.

45. See "Can a Man and a Woman Be Friends?" p. 16; Laurvik, "Modern American Girl," p. 13; Nearing and Nearing, "Four Great Things," p. 12; "Women Toilers," pp. 376, 377; and Logan, "American Home Life," pp. 12, 73.

46. "Women Toilers," pp. 376, 377.

47. Stineman, *Popular Womens Magazines*, p. 57.

48. *McCall's* (January 1911): 3; and Graham, "Women Who Fly," pp. 6, 7, 56.

49. *WHC* (January 1912): 24; and *WHC* (May 1912): 23.

50. *GH* (January 1912): 41.

51. Mannering, "Should An Actress Marry?" p. 12.

52. "Famous Women Doctors," pp. 28, 29.

53. Kaempffert, "Edison," pp. 3, 4.

54. Maxim, "Modern Warfare," pp. 13, 28–29, 54; and Maxim, "War," p. 7.

55. "Facts about Panama Canal," pp. 26–27.

56. Preston, "Girl's Preparation," p. 22; Wolberst, "Tragedy," p. 26; and Steinberg, *Reformer*, pp. 107–12.

57. Adler, "SEX Education," p. 22.

58. "Birth-control Contest," p. 31; "What Shall We Do About Birth-control?" pp. 24, 26, 76; and *PR* (December 1916): 31; and *PR* (December 1917): 49.

59. Sherman, "How Laws Are Made," p. 13; and Dufford, "Business Woman," pp. 17–18.

60. "Women of the Campaign," pp. 22, 23.

61. "Kate Barnard," p. 7.

62. Gibbs, "Woman's Capture," pp. 36–38; and Daggett, "New Chapter," pp. 148–55.

63. Knobis, "Only Woman Member," p. 7.

64. Hard, "Worldly Goods," pp. 217, 218.

65. "Program for Discussion," p. 437.

66. Wilson, "New Meaning," p. 3; and Hughes, "Women's Interests," pp. 7, 8.

67. *WHC* (October 1904): 30.

68. Cott, *Grounding*, pp. 32, 33.

69. Herrick, "Which Side," p. 16; and Cott, *Grounding*, pp. 32, 33.

70. Moyne, "Baroness Gripenberg," pp. 85–93; and Mott, *History*, III: 486.

71. Richardson, "Women as Municipal Housekeepers," pp. 8, 9.

72. Shaw, "President," pp. 8, 9.

73. Pankhurst, "Militant, III," p. 90; see also Pankhurst, "Militant, I," pp. 4–13; Pankhurst, "Militant, II," pp. 171–80; and "What the Editor Has to Say," *GH* (September 1917): 4.

74. Kinkaid, "Feminine Charms," pp. 146–57.

75. Damon-Moore, *Magazines*, p. 91; and "'Votes for Women'—As Seen by Edward W. Bok," Part 5, p. 3.

76. Steinberg, *Reformer*, pp. 68–73.

77. "Editorial Declaration," *PR* (March 1913): 3. Reportedly, reader response was overwhelmingly favorable; see "What Our Readers Think of Suffrage," *PR* (June 1913): 3; and "Comment and Compliment," *PR* (August 1913): 1.

78. "Three Things to Remember," p. 1.

79. "Editorial Declaration," p. 3.

80. Moyne, "Baroness Gripenberg," pp. 85–93; "Infant Mortality," p. 3; and "Majesty of the Law," p. 3.

81. *WHC* (March 1902). See "Look About You," *WHC* (January 1898): 13; "Why I Want the Ballot," p. 4; and Herrick, "Women Want the Vote?" p. 10.

82. *WHC* 1914 Reader Survey Results, HCP, Box 10.

83. Addams, "Working Woman," p. 19. Richardson, "Truth About Equal Suffrage," pp. 17–18; and Richardson, "Work of the Antis," p. 15.

84. Hughes, "Women's Interest," pp. 7, 8.

85. WHA to MVR on *LHJ* page; JET to MVR, March 16, 1915; and April 12, 1915, in MVRP.

86. "Editorial," *McCall's* (January 1911): 5.

87. Lane talk quoted in J. Walter Thompson News Bulletin, 84–B, March 25, 1922, p. 14, in JWTP, Box 1.

88. *Mrs. John Doe*, p. 56.

89. Bok quoted in Transcript of Advertising Conference, 1915, p. 6, CP, Box 5. See also Karl Harriman to CMF, May 5, 1914, CMFP, Box One, Folder One.

90. Scanlon, *Inarticulate Longings*, p. 21; and *A Short History of the LHJ*, pp. 17, 18, CP, File Drawer 4.

91. *National Advertising. THE Modern Selling-Force*, p. 36.

92. "Between You & the Editor," *McCall's* (July 1912).

93. Logan, "American Home Life."

94. "Earn Life or Lose It," p. 85.

95. Northend, "Romance," pp. 66, 67.

96. Talbott, "Electricity."

97. Converse, "Housekeeping."

98. Gilman, "Housekeeping." This hit a sensitive nerve with readers; see "Just Between Ourselves," *McCall's* (February 1913): 7.

99. Damon-Moore, *Magazines*, pp. 92–95.

100. WA to Mattie W. Thurston, July 14, 1908, WAL.

101. "I Didn't Raise My Boy," p. 23; and Steinberg, *Reformer*, pp. 114, 115; and Mott, *History*, III: 488.

102. See e.g., *100 Thrift Recipes*.

103. *Mrs. John Doe*, p. 54; *Designer* (December 1917): 16; "Women's Vote," p. 3; and "Dis-Service," p. 3.

104. "Editorial," *GH* (September 1917): 4.

105. CSL to Miss Kiefer, June 20, 1939, CSLP, Box A-157-3, File 71; and CSL to Marion, December 2, 1918, CSLP, Box 56.

106. Quoted in Daggett, *Women Wanted*, p. 14.

107. Daggett, "War Really Means to Women"; and Daggett, "War Jewelry."

108. *WHC* (February 1918): 1; Richardson, "Woman's War?" p. 2; and Ross, *Ladies*, p. 143.

109. Seebohm, *Vogue*, pp. 93–101, 123; and Chase, *Always in Vogue*, pp. 150, 151.

110. Mott, *History*, IV: 549. See also Steinberg, *Reformer*, pp. 113–42.

111. U.S. Food Administration's Head of Distribution, "Grocer," p. 32; Head of U.S. Fuel Administration, "Help to Save Coal?" p. 31; and Head of U.S. Food Administration, "'I Don't Care What Hoover Says,'" p. 33.

112. Mott, *History*, IV: 549.

113. Bok, "What I Have Seen," p. 1.

114. "Picture of Tomorrow," p. 13. See also Editor's note in Harmon, ed. "New Day for Women," p. 29; Harmon, "Must I Go to Work?" p. 22; and Newkirk, "Woman Past 40," p. 23.

115. Bigelow, "What the Editor Has to Say," *GH* (February 1919): 4; Blair, "Where Are Women Going?" pp. 37, 58; and "Ideas of Foreseeing Woman," p. 43.

PART II

WOMEN'S MAGAZINES, 1919–45

While women's magazines in the early twentieth century had been in a growth stage, publishing companies and their publications used the 1920s to consolidate their positions and expand. Circulations climbed steadily. The pages of the women's journals grew richer, visually and in text. This was a golden decade for advertising, which flourished by touting products designed to help Americans enjoy their seeming prosperity. Advertising's success spilled over to magazines and a significant portion went to women's journals, swelling their pages and pocketbooks.

At the same time, the women's magazine business experienced heightened concentration of readership and increased competition for advertisers as it moved into the mature stage of its industry life cycle. Publishers used persuasive promotional techniques to entice both readers and advertisers. Competition came from radio for advertisers, and from radio, automobiles, and movies for consumers' leisure time, increasing the pressure. The advertising industry and ad agents became more organized and more powerful, gaining increased influence over women's journals.

Economic depression put an end to the abundance of the twenties. The financial downturn following the stock market crash in October 1929 sharply affected practices of women's magazine publishers. Advertisers who had spent lavishly in the 1920s cut back their budgets in the 1930s. By the end of the 1930s two big names in women's magazines had disappeared—*Delineator* and *Pictorial Review*. Two names that would go on to become household words had emerged—*Woman's Day* and *Family Circle*. As in the previous decades, a complex interaction between economic forces, editorial visions, and readers' preferences yielded the varied and changing content appearing in women's titles during the twenties and thirties.

Attempts by the top journals to gain ever larger numbers of readers also influenced the content mix. In the prosperous twenties magazines could contain a smorgasbord of material, with something for everyone. By the thirties, with ad dollars cut back, editors were forced to keep those features with the broadest appeal, typically the fiction and the service departments. Hoping to draw advertisers, editors went after ever greater numbers of readers. This forced editors to operate on several assumptions: that all women resembled the white, middle-class readers they traditionally targeted; and that core subjects existed that were of interest to all women, such as housekeeping and beauty advice. This strategy contrasts with that used by editors of the "class" fashion periodicals *Vogue* and *Harper's Bazaar*, as well as that employed by editors in later years, when focusing on smaller reader segments became the tactic of choice.

World War II turned back the content trends of the thirties, as women's journals stressed information, telling women what they could do to help the war effort. The magazines joined the government campaign to attract females into the paid labor force. Attention to serious issues, seen through the female lens, characterized the wartime publications.

6

Women's Magazines
in the Interwar Years

The *Saturday Evening Post*, *Woman's Home Companion*, *Collier's*, *Delineator*, *Ladies' Home Journal*, *Pictorial Review*—are magnificent examples of adaptation to an industrial age of standardization. The amazing thing is not their limitations, but what is often accomplished in spite of them.

—Henry Seidel Canby, 1926[1]

The women's magazine industry continued to grow after World War I, with circulations, advertising revenues, and magazine size all expanding. The fight for readers and advertising dollars also increased. This intense level of competition affected all aspects of the business: prices stayed within an affordable range, promotional activities increased, and distribution methods extended. These components of the journals' marketing strategy as well as an analysis of the readers appear in the next chapter. This chapter focuses on the evolution of the publications themselves and on the characteristics of the market in which they were operating.

Magazine sales overall rose in the two decades between the wars, fueled by increases in education, income, and leisure. Sales were hurt by printer strikes in the early twenties, and circulations dipped during the worst years of the Depression. But by the early 1940s, 41 percent more magazines were being sold than in 1929, and the average family read about seventy issues of magazines per year, up from 1919 when families had read just under twelve issues yearly.[2]

Circulations of the top women's magazines kept rising throughout the twenties. Nevertheless, the race for additional readers never ceased, as advertisers wanted high numbers and publishers responded. Market penetration by magazines was coming perilously close to market saturation. The economic depression of the 1930s exacerbated the competitive forces in the women's magazine industry. Circulations stuck close to one another. In 1934, for example, circulations of the top six women's journals stood within 500,000 of one another.

Women's journals led in some areas and experienced certain magazine industry trends more intensely. Women's publications pioneered in innovative merchandising tie-ins and linkages with retailers. Advertising shrinkage during the Depression hit women's titles harder than magazines generally.[3] New periodicals sprang up in the industry generally (e.g., *Time*, *Life*, *News-Week*) and this held true in the women's field as well (e.g., *Woman's Day*, *Family Circle*). Radio affected all publications using advertising, although major women's journals were especially threatened, as radio soap operas drew some of women's titles' traditional advertisers.

Ever hungry for readers, some publishers started overseas editions, which frequently proved profitable. British versions of *Good Housekeeping* and *Harper's Bazaar* came out in 1922 and 1924 respectively. Conde Nast added to British *Vogue* (1916), publishing French *Vogue* and for several years in the twenties, Spanish and German editions. Even publishers unwilling to set up a separate business overseas sent copies of the American titles into foreign markets. For example, in 1933 Crowell Co. shipped over 28,000 copies of *Woman's Home Companion* to Canada and almost 5,000 issues to other countries. Curtis Co. sent tens of thousands of issues of *Ladies' Home Journal* overseas as well.[4]

The major mass circulation journals began to be published in groups, accelerating a trend begun before World War I. These combinations gave publishers greater power with advertisers, distributors, and authors and artists, as well as deeper pockets; it also left them more vulnerable to industry ups and downs. Curtis Co. had *Saturday Evening Post*, *Country Gentleman*, and *Jack and Jill* as well as *Ladies' Home Journal*. Crowell Co. put out *Collier's*, *American Magazine*, and *The Country Home* in addition to *Woman's Home Companion*. By the late thirties the McCall Group owned *Redbook* and *Popular Mechanics* as well as *McCall's*. Hearst Co. published *Good Housekeeping*, *Harper's Bazaar*, and, in the thirties, *Pictorial Review* and *Delineator*, among numerous other magazines.[5] Some publishers, such as Hearst Co., spanned the communications business, publishing newspapers and magazines, as well as holding movie interests.

Despite the claims made by each, contemporary industry observers considering factors such as reputation, financial strength, and circulation placed Curtis Co. first, Crowell Co. second, Hearst Co. third, and McCall Co. fourth.[6]

As parts of larger publishing entities, women's magazines were intimately affected by the overall health and strategies of the corporations owning them. This proved particularly true in the Depression years, when how well an individual title survived depended in large part on how well its parent company was run. Butterick Co., Hearst Co., and Conde Nast Co. had been overspending before the Depression hit, so found themselves unprepared to weather the financial storm very well. Even Curtis Co. proved to be in poor shape to ride out the severe economic downturn.

THE BIG SIX

The attributes present in the women's magazine industry as a whole affected each of the Big Six. Each of the titles also illustrates particular characteristics of women's periodical publishing in these years. *Ladies' Home Journal*, *McCall's*, and *Pictorial Review* all illuminate the advantages of having a good editor and the problems brought on by the absence of such an individual. The activities of *Good Housekeeping*'s prestigious Testing Institute reveal clearly the increased importance of such facilities. *Woman's Home Companion* demonstrates the success a magazine could attain through skillful promotion and merchandising activities. *Delineator* provides an example of a title published by a company with a related business (patterns), and how such a combination both helped and hurt.

Ladies' Home Journal

For *Ladies' Home Journal*, the unquestioned leader of the pre-war period, the twenties and thirties brought serious and at times successful challenges to its pre-eminence. The retirement of Edward Bok in 1919 threw the *Journal* into a slowdown from which it did not emerge until the editorial reign of Bruce and Beatrice Blackmar Gould. Bok had been forced to leave because he refused owner Cyrus Curtis' demand that he modernize the *Journal*, modifying the thirty-year pattern he had established. Curtis had for some time recognized something that the longtime editor had failed to see; change was necessary even with the most successful editorial formula. Bok tendered his resignation at a Curtis Co. Board of Directors meeting and Curtis quickly made a motion to accept.

Finding the right person to lead the *Journal* through the turbulent twenties, however, proved almost as impossible as getting Bok to change. Curtis' first offer went to popular writer Mary Roberts Rinehart, but she turned it down.[7] Instead, two temporary editors followed Bok in quick succession—Harry Orville Davis and John E. Pickett. They attempted to give the *Journal* a fresh image. *Saturday Evening Post* editor George Horace Lorimer was intimately involved in this process as well, since he was now overseeing all Curtis magazines. Editorials by Rinehart appeared as part of this refurbishing.

Then, in 1921, former newspaper man and *Country Gentleman* editor Barton Currie took over at the *Journal*, keeping the top position until 1928. Currie employed a strategy of consolidation, hewing to the outlines of past success. The *Journal* continued to publish popular fiction, strong service departments, and general interest articles. Currie understood that his female readers did not want to be patronized and edited his material accordingly.[8]

Currie relinquished the *Journal*'s helm to another newspaper man and former editor of *Country Gentleman*, Loring A. Schuler (who had served four years under Currie as managing editor of the *Journal*, from 1920–24). To keep up circulation Schuler enlisted writers such as Rinehart, John Galsworthy, Edna Ferber, and Booth Tarkington. Fashion and style departments were overhauled to give the publication a more modern tone.

Both Currie and Schuler failed to invest the *Journal* with the special edge it had maintained under Bok. The magazine sorely needed a new direction, one that would give readers the sense that reading the *Journal* let them in on the latest secrets in housekeeping, entertainment, and social trends. By the early thirties Curtis Co. President George Horace Lorimer was so dissatisfied with the *Journal*'s performance that he shifted the job of selecting stories and fiction for the title to *Saturday Evening Post* editors.[9] Circulation growth had slowed and by 1932 the *Journal* had slipped to the number three position, with *Woman's Home Companion* taking the circulation lead, and *McCall's* running close behind. A 1935 poll surveying readers' preferences among women's magazines showed the *Journal* in fourth place, just ahead of *Pictorial Review* and *Delineator*.[10]

Lackluster editing also cost the *Journal* its huge advantage in attracting advertising revenue. By the early 1930s advertisers had dubbed the *Journal* the "Old Ladies' Journal."[11] Like other women's publications the *Journal* lost ad revenues due to the Depression. But the *Journal* had more difficulty recovering, reaching a low in 1935 of $5,800,885 in ad revenues, which ranked it behind ad leader *Good Housekeeping* ($8,680,822) and chief rival *Woman's Home Companion* ($6,671,127).[12]

Onto this dismal scene burst Bruce and Beatrice Blackmar Gould, husband and wife authors. The Goulds took over in 1935 and immediately made changes at the unprofitable title, discarding over $500,000 worth of previously acquired manuscripts and illustrations in the process. Innovations included a new layout, more glamorous fashions, and campaigns against the high maternal death rate in the United States and for education about venereal diseases. The Goulds published results of polls taken among American women on a wide variety of topics, improved the fiction, hired new experts to modernize the service departments, and, perhaps most importantly, introduced a strong editorial presence. Dorothy Thompson's column began in 1937 (continuing into the 1950s) and Eleanor Roosevelt's biography, *This Is My Story*, ran serially that same year. The hugely popular *How America Lives* series, begun in 1940, profiling in depth a different family each month, generated strong reader interest as well as critical acclaim.[13]

By the end of the thirties, with the Goulds firmly in charge and circulation climbing, *Ladies' Home Journal* was once again playing the role of industry leader. Contemporaries saw the *Journal* returning to the glory of its days under Edward Bok. Readers responded with increased sales. The slogan created for the *Journal* in 1941 by N. W. Ayer ad agency signaled the Goulds' strong confidence in their readers and their magazine. Targeted at advertisers, the phrase reminded them to "Never Underestimate the Power of a Woman."

Woman's Home Companion

The fortunes of *Woman's Home Companion* rose steadily during these years due to the editorial skill of Gertrude Battles Lane and the business acumen of the Crowell Publishing Co. The company expanded with the 1919 purchase of *Collier's Weekly* from P. F. Collier & Son.[14] *Collier's Weekly* joined not only the *Companion* but also the *American* and *Farm and Fireside* (renamed *Country Home* in 1930, discontinued in 1939). The acquisition of *Collier's* gave the Crowell organization a publication in each of the major magazine categories (general weekly, general monthly, farm, and women's), a unique situation that proved advantageous when dealing with advertisers.[15]

Throughout the twenties *Woman's Home Companion* struggled to expand both its circulation and its advertising revenues. Despite steady increases in both, the title stayed in the number three or four position in readership until the end of the decade; then, advertising, pages in the magazine, and readership all increased significantly. By the April 1930 issue, the *Companion* had reached 204 pages, and by 1932 it achieved the number one spot in circulation, passing the *Ladies' Home Journal.*[16]

The *Companion* was hurt by advertising declines in the Depression, but quickly set on a profitable course through salary reductions and aggressive selling of advertising and circulation. All salaried employees at Crowell Co. took a 10 percent reduction in pay in 1932, except those earning less than $30 a week. Like Curtis Co., Crowell Co. also exercised economies on magazine production.[17]

Companion advertising lineage in 1933 fell to 61 percent of its 1930 performance, despite reductions in ad rates (although this was better than the industry as whole, which had declined to 52% of 1930 levels).[18] This in turn affected magazine size; in 1932 editor Lane noted that the fall issues were going to be "pitifully small."[19]

By the end of 1933, the *Companion* was again doing fairly well and in early 1934 editors received a salary increase.[20] Ad revenues improved by the mid-thirties, peaking in 1937. A management shake-up occurred at the company in 1934, when president Lee Maxwell had a disagreement with controlling owner Joseph Knapp. Maxwell left and former salesman Thomas Beck took over as president. Beck continued to push an aggressive selling effort (for advertising and circulation) on the part of all Crowell properties.[21]

The *Companion* held on to its position as number one in women's magazine circulation through 1940. Part of this circulation increase came from the consistently high quality editorial matter in the journal, particularly the fiction and service departments; part of the increase stemmed from the sophisticated and aggressive salesmanship of the Crowell organization's circulation department.

An observer described the successful techniques used by Crowell's circulation department by saying "It is simply merchandising in the full sense of the word— by overcoming the natural passivity of a buying public, by making purchase as convenient as possible, and by 'organized exposure.'"[22]

Good Housekeeping

Like the *Companion*, *Good Housekeeping* grew in the favor of both advertisers and readers, providng a successful mix of popular fiction, nonfiction reporting, and respected service articles.

The Good Housekeeping Institute provided a certain cachet for the magazine. By the end of the thirties, however, the Institute was no longer unique, although it maintained its leadership. Other journals had recognized the competitive importance of establishing such centers.[23] The *Journal* had its Workshop, *McCall's* its Consumer Center, *Woman's Home Companion* its Home Service Center, *Delineator* its Home Institute. All were costly to create, all served both readers (through testing products and procedures) and advertisers (who were frequently entertained in these centers, and whose products were approved there), all were promoted extensively.[24]

Good Housekeeping experienced problems in 1939 stemming from its Seal of Approval, long a point of competitive strength. The Federal Trade Commission (FTC) filed a complaint against *Good Housekeeping*, charging it with "misleading and deceptive acts and practices in the issuance of guarantees, seals of approval, and the publication in its advertising pages of grossly exaggerated and false claims."[25] Richard Berlin, general manager of Hearst Co. magazines, refused to sign a cease-and-desist stipulation, arguing that in no instance would the Commission be able to prove that *Good Housekeeping* had not fulfilled its guarantees. The case was fought for two years and included testimony from individuals working for rivals *Ladies' Home Journal* and *McCall's* who testified against their sister publication, arguing that Good Housekeeping's Seal of Approval constituted unfair competition.

The proceedings lasted twenty-one months and involved over 100 witnesses. As a reporter noted, "Only one incident afforded anything like a light moment in the long-drawn-out wrangling. Among GH-advertised (but not seal-approved) products introduced at the hearings was a Polish ham. Bursting open, it exuded such gamy odors that the court had to be cleared."[26]

In May 1941 the FTC issued a cease-and-desist order compelling *Good Housekeeping* to follow more clearly defined rules in its testing and to detail more specifically what was covered under its guarantees. The FTC also held that some of the publication's advertising contained deceptive claims. In October 1941, as a result of this ruling, *Good Housekeeping* announced a major policy shift; it would no longer test products that did not advertise in the title, as it had been doing; *Good Housekeeping* claimed that prior to this change, less than 30 percent of the products receiving the Seal of Approval had advertised in the magazine. The Seal's guarantee was changed, omitting the words "tested and approved." By 1946 the Seal only covered claims present in the advertising.[27]

Neither the FTC suit nor the cynicism of the advertising community about the Seal of Approval tarnished *Good Housekeeping*'s image with its audience. Readers continued to value and trust the information contained in the title, both editorial and advertising; in a 1938 survey sponsored by *Parent's Magazine*, respondents rated *Good Housekeeping* as the second most valuable periodical (behind *Reader's Digest*), and ranked it first in magazine advertising readers would be most influenced by.[28]

The Hearst organization overall, however, experienced severe financial problems in the thirties, and by 1937 Hearst Co. was almost bankrupt. Richard E. Berlin was instrumental in saving William Randolph Hearst's empire, negotiating with paper suppliers and banks for better terms. Hearst himself was forced to relinquish financial control of the company to an oversight committee, which sold or killed off unprofitable newspapers and magazines (including *Pictorial Review-Delineator*) and liquidated as many of Hearst's other assets (particularly his art and antique collections) as it could, to pay off the enormous debt the publishing lord had accumulated.[29]

Good Housekeeping itself remained steadily profitable and was spared the oversight committee's ax. The periodical's operating profit in 1938 stood at over two and a half a million dollars, in a year when magazine advertising generally dropped 22 percent due to a recession. *Good Housekeeping* outshone the other eight Hearst periodicals in this area, generating three times their total profit.[30]

Delineator

Much of *Delineator*'s fate in this period rested on Butterick Co.'s dual role as publisher and pattern maker. Clothing patterns had created the Butterick Co. and some saw patterns as the organization's mainstay. Other Butterick staffers viewed the company primarily as a publishing entity. These two groups fought, with first one party then the other gaining control.

In the late teens Butterick Co. was still publishing its three women's monthlies, *Delineator*, *Designer*, and *New Idea Woman's Magazine,* in which advertisers often purchased space at a package rate. Butterick owner George Wilder, while respecting the pattern enterprise on which the company had been founded, strongly desired to increase its publishing business.[31] He purchased the Ridgway Co., publishers of *Everybody's*, and set the company to publishing pulp magazines, including *Romance* and *Adventure*, which proved profitable.

In 1920 Butterick Co. bought *Good Hardware* and in 1922 launched *Progresive Grocer*; both trade journals achieved quick success. The decision to publish these titles grew out of Wilder's "Buy at Home Campaign," started in 1917, which encouraged consumers to purchase goods in local stores. As part of the campaign, Wilder announced that no mail-order advertising would be permitted in *Delineator*. Butterick Co. then began sending out a single page sheet called the "Delineator Buy at Home Bulletin" to all its pattern agents. This modest newsletter generated enormous positive response from store owners, Chambers of Commerce, and other associations across the nation. Butterick expanded its newsletter to four pages, and increased the mailing list to include merchants such as owners of hardware, grocery, and drug stores. Based on the wide success of this sheet, the company decided to enter the trade publication field.[32]

The "Buy at Home Campaign" illustrates how one segment of this company could negatively impact the other. In the twenties Butterick Co. was trying to place its patterns in chain stores and had specifically targeted Sears and Montgomery Ward. Those stores held Butterick in disfavor because of *Delineator*'s policy against accepting mail-order advertising, and the company's actual campaign opposing mail-order purchasing.[33]

In 1926 Butterick Co. underwent a momentous reorganization; for *Delineator* (and even more immediately for its sister, *Designer*) the change proved fatal. George Wilder, who had controlled the company since 1902, was aging and decided to step down. On April 21, 1926, he sent a memo to department heads throughout the company announcing that Stanley Latshaw and Joseph Moore had purchased most of the Wilder family stock.[34]

Stanley Latshaw, the successful advertising director of Butterick publications, had been with the company since 1914 and was responsible for the steady rise of advertising dollars flowing into *Delineator*. Prior to joining Butterick Latshaw had worked in advertising for the Curtis Publishing Co., and had been president of Curtis' pattern subsidiary, Home Pattern Co. Thus Latshaw had considerable experience in both the publishing and pattern businesses. He wanted to buy Wilder's stock himself, and the Oxford Paper Co. (Butterick's paper supplier) supported him. But Wilder felt that Latshaw should be joined by someone with more experience in publishing. Wilder introduced Latshaw to Joe Moore and insisted on a partnership between the two men before he agreed to relinquish his stock.[35]

In Joe Moore, Wilder believed he had found the perfect man to guard his legacy. Moore had worked at Hearst Co. for over ten years, serving as Hearst's assistant and treasurer and was credited, among other things, with building up *Good Housekeeping*. Moore soon revealed himself to be a passionate magazine man who believed that the pattern business was dying.[36] He had grand plans for making over *Delineator*. Latshaw remained in charge of advertising and took over the pattern business, while Moore governed the editorial and art departments.

This new ownership led to great transformations in personnel and in the periodicals. In that first year *Delineator* and *Designer* were merged, as were their patterns. This occurred despite *Designer*'s steadily increasing circulation— over half a million by 1926. The move saved the company the salaries of *Designer*'s eight staffers, all of whom were fired.[37] A new circulation director was brought in from Hearst Co., and another Hearst man, Henry Blackman Sell, was appointed General Manager for publications. Other new personnel came, usually at quite high salaries.

As fast as new staff were hired, old staff resigned, unhappy with the direction of the company. *Delineator*'s new mandate was to be modern, light, sophisticated, and upscale. This vision was reflected throughout the journal, from covers to articles to editorials to price, where an increase from twenty to twenty-five cents a copy signaled the targeting of a slightly more affluent readership. The Butterick offices were remodeled, including the Delineator Institute, which got a new Test Kitchen, laundry, testing lab, and dining room. Sell commissioned work from artists he had used at *Harper's Bazaar* as well as from newcomers. These craftsmen greatly enjoyed working on the revamped publication.

Unfortunately, readers had not been informed about the new direction, and they disliked the redesigned, newly combined magazine. Butterick Co. received hundreds of letters from outraged readers who refused to renew their subscriptions to a title that had changed so drastically, so quickly. Advertisers too distrusted the new approach, which essentially used a "class" strategy (suitable to *Harper's Bazaar*) on what had been a "mass" circulation publication. This unenthusiastic reception by both readers and advertisers led Latshaw to hire an advertising director, Myron Lechner, who could remedy the situation. Lechner advised going more slowly with the changes at *Delineator*, and recommended a price cut to ten cents to match the cost of all the other major women's titles except *Good Housekeeping*.[38] Lechner's strategy improved *Delineator*'s situation. The price was dropped back to ten cents. Both advertising and circulation began rising, although accompanied by large costs for circulation promotion. The pattern side of the business continued to be profitable despite competition (though less prosperous than before the management change), but *Delineator* sucked those profits into its promotional campaigns.[39]

Moore's influence waned as he experienced health problems, and Sell, his protégé and the architect of many of *Delineator*'s changes, left after two years.[40] Thus the publishing side of the business lost some of its chief support. Butterick Co.'s new managers decided to sell one of their big assets, the Butterick printing plant; Cuneo Press, Inc. bought it for nearly $1 million. Henceforth the company's publications would go to independent printers.[41] In a move symbolically as well as organizationally significant, in 1933 the Butterick Co. took over the Butterick Publishing Co. (a separate entity since 1902). These changes and expenditures left Butterick Co. in a poor position to weather the economic depression of the thirties, and indeed, the publications part of the business did not survive. All the magazines ran into trouble and soon only *Delineator* was left.

In January 1935 the Butterick Co. filed for reorganization under Section 77B of the Bankruptcy Act. Joe Moore resigned in May. Under the court approved reorganization plan, selection of new managers fell to the two chief creditors. They appointed Alfred Mayo (formerly of Crowell Co.) as president. *Delineator* continued to be published, providing work and an outlet for the services and goods of its creditors, but failing to make money; in fact the magazine continued to *lose* substantial amounts of money. Finally, Hearst Co., new owner of *Pictorial Review*, looking for a quick circulation boost, paid $1.00 for *Delineator* and agreed to take over its unfilled subscriptions.[42] *Delineator*'s name and some of its content was combined with *Pictorial Review*.

Some industry observers viewed *Delineator*'s demise as less the fault of either its parent company or its editor, and more the inevitable result of saturation in the women's magazine market.[43]

After selling off *Delineator* Butterick Co. continued to publish pattern publications. By focusing on the pattern business, Butterick Co. returned to prosperity.[44]

McCall's

New personnel and strategies set *McCall's* on the road to growth in these years. Owner White, Weld and Co. picked William Bishop Warner, a man with a merchandising background who had worked at department stores J. L. Hudson and Filene's in Boston, to give the company a firm hand and strong direction.[45] Hired in 1919, Warner moved quickly and effectively to build up the company in both the publishing and pattern businesses, achieving success where Butterick Co. had failed.

McCall Co.'s strength in the pattern business came in part from its early development and promotion of a printed pattern, an innovation directed by Warner. Women who used it developed a strong loyalty to the company. The patterns earned McCall Co. a good reputation, which the magazine built upon.[46]

Long considered little more than a cheap household journal, *McCall's* had slowly been improving its contents and Warner was willing to spend money to continue this process. *McCall's* had raised its price in 1917 to ten cents, putting it in the same price group with the other general women's publications. Simultaneously, the magazine stopped using premiums to gain subscriptions. This temporarily hurt circulation, which drooped in 1918. Advertising declined a bit as well, but both picked up by 1920.[47] Editors Myra G. Reed (1916–18) and Bessie Beatty (1918–21), a well-known foreign correspondent, failed to discover a winning formula for the journal. However, with the hiring in 1922 of Harry Payne Burton, another former foreign correspondent, *McCall's* found an editor who could consistently attract readers. Burton did this by filling the publication with big name fiction writers, including Kathleen Norris, Harold Bell Wright, Zane Grey, Booth Tarkington, and Mary Roberts Rinehart, among others. Burton mixed the stories with nonfiction articles, service features, and the ubiquitous McCall fashions and patterns, in color by the mid-twenties.[48] During the 1920s circulation practically doubled to more than 2.5 million, and advertising quadrupled to almost 8.5 million.[49]

Associate editor Otis Wiese took over Burton's seat in 1928. Called the "Boy Editor" because of his youth (23 years old) when given the top editorial position, Wiese continued Burton's strategy of including big name writers, and the patterns and fashions remained a fixture. To this mix Wiese added his own ideas, including an inventive redesign of the title into three parts in 1932. Fiction and News, Home Making, and Style and Beauty constituted the three sections, each complete with its own advertising, now moved up throughout the book. Another innovation was borrowed from sister McCall publication *Redbook* (bought with *Blue Book* by the McCall Co. in 1929): printing a complete novel in an issue. This feature proved extremely popular with readers.

In the 1920s *McCall's* envisioned its readers as ordinary, middle-class citizens, whom it referred to as living on "McCall Street." The company sponsored extensive reader research in the thirties and forties on its own and its competitors' audiences. Shrewd editing, attention to readers, and a healthy company allowed *McCall's* to survive the depression with its circulation only pausing, and its advertising significantly recovered by the end of the thirties.[50]

Pictorial Review

Pictorial Review gained circulation and stature in the 1920s under the wise editorial hand of Arthur Vance. Vance upgraded the fiction and added strong service and feature material to the fashion and pattern core of the magazine. The journal trumpeted its growing success to potential advertisers, claiming that "No publication in its class can duplicate the record of increases in circulation and advertising patronage during the last five years" (since Vance had taken over as editor).[51] By 1920 *Pictorial Review* had overtaken *McCall's* for the number two spot in circulation, which *McCall's*, at its lower price, had held throughout the teens, behind *Ladies' Home Journal*. By 1924 circulation was well over 2 million, giving *Pictorial Review* in that year the number one spot (achieved after a price drop from $2.50 to $1.50 annually, the same price charged by the *Journal* and *Woman's Home Companion*). *Pictorial Review* stayed in the number two spot for much of the twenties even after the *Journal* and *Companion* prices moved down to $1.00.

Fiction fueled this circulation increase. Under Vance the quality of fiction in *Pictorial Review* rose steadily.[52] He encouraged Edith Wharton in her ideas for a novel that became *The Age of Innocence*, paying her $18,000 in 1919 for the finished serial, which he published starting in July 1920. Vance continued to admire Wharton's work, publishing *The Glimpses of the Moon*, *The Mother's Recompense* (delivered early in response to a plea from Vance, for which she earned a $5,000 bonus), and *Twilight Sleep*.[53]

Vance challenged Theodore Dreiser to write a short story with neither a prostitute nor a kept woman in it, and when Dreiser did so, Vance published the well-written piece despite its lack of specific appeal to women; Vance published Joseph Conrad as well.[54] Vance was willing to pay well (sometimes more than other editors) for good fiction.[55]

Vance also had an eye for articles sure to captivate an audience; for example, in 1929 he ran a debate titled "Is America a Paradise for Women?" with journalist Dorothy Thompson emphatically answering in the negative and her then husband novelist Sinclair Lewis responding affirmatively.[56] Issues of significance to women had always been a concern of Vance's, who earlier had supported female suffrage and discussed birth control openly in the journal's pages; staffer Mabel Potter Daggett noted that "Among the feminists of New York he (Vance) had been known as the man with the vision."[57]

Pictorial Review had been founded to promote the patterns of the Pictorial Review Co., and the pattern business continued to play a key role in the company. The magazine always showed and promoted the company's fashions. The pattern arm of the company was, by the 1920s, strong and well-organized, doing an effective selling job and presenting potent competition to other pattern companies.[58] However, the company was not marred by the internal conflict that had characterized Butterick Co.

Percy Waxman succeeded Vance in 1930. Waxman followed Vance's winning formula in his editing for the next two years, with only partial success. *Pictorial Review* then changed hands and Theodore Von Ziekursch, whose experience lay with a tabloid newspaper and the pulp magazines, took over.[59] But the publication had lost the appeal it held under Vance. Sixth in circulation among the Big Six, *Pictorial Review* was taken over by the Hearst Co., which also purchased the Pictorial Review Pattern Co. Herbert Mayes was installed as editor, and in January 1935 the first issue of *Pictorial Review* under Hearst Co. direction appeared. Mayes attempted to revive the publication, redesigning the magazine, hiring *Best Short Stories* editor Edward J. O'Brien as a fiction consultant, and publishing book-length novels in one issue. Shirley Temple's autobiography appeared, as did a fictionalized version of the affair between King Edward VII and Wallis Simpson.[60] These features helped, but circulation never recovered and *Pictorial Review* stayed stubbornly in fifth place, with only *Delineator* behind it. Advertising lagged as well, not recovering as rapidly as that of its competitors.

Seeking a circulation boost, Hearst Co. acquired the ailing *Delineator*, which was merged with *Pictorial Review*. In May 1937 the first joint issue appeared, under the title *Pictorial Review-Delineator*, edited by Mayes. *Pictorial Review*'s format was retained, with the best-liked features of *Delineator* added to the mix.[61]

This merger increased the title's readers to over three million, vaulting it into first place for circulation. But circulation did not spell the whole story, and advertising failed to increase as much as needed. With the Hearst empire in disarray, all publications were eyed critically, with unprofitable ones sold or killed. In 1939 Hearst Co. announced that the March issue of *Pictorial Review-Delineator* would be the last.[62] The combined publication died, a victim of the economic depression and its tight advertising market, reader saturation, and the financial problems of the Hearst organization.

FASHION MAGAZINES

Fashion magazines flourished in this period, gaining in both advertising and circulation, although remaining smaller in readership than the general interest women's journals. Both the leading books, *Vogue* and *Harper's Bazaar*, continued to sell well, despite relatively high prices of between thirty-five and fifty cents. These rivals developed and expanded fashion journalism in these years, in part because of the keen competition between them. This journalism included astute reporting and writing on the fashions of the day, an international focus, and typographic excellence and innovation.

Vogue led in this latter area. Under art directors Heyworth Campbell and Dr. Mehemmed Fehmy Agha, *Vogue* was clean, modern, and pleasing to the eye. The work of skilled photographers such as Edward Steichen made *Vogue*'s pages artistic and handsome. *Vogue* showed readers the latest in fashion and beauty, wrote about the lifestyles of the rich and famous, and, after *Vanity Fair*, another Nast property, was merged with *Vogue* in 1935, published some good fiction. *Vogue*'s advertising revenues climbed in the twenties, and in 1926 were second only to those of the *Saturday Evening Post*. Ad revenues dipped during the Depression, but recovered in the mid-thirties. Circulation too rose in the twenties, dropped in the early thirties, but reached pre-depression levels by 1935.[63] Edna Woolman Chase, *Vogue* editor since 1914, continued to direct the publication on its successful course.

Conde Nast Publications, Inc. experienced huge success in the 1920s, when the company's earnings increased 213 percent between 1924 and 1928. *Vogue* contributed significantly to that growth.[64] Conde Nast's success was overshadowed, however, when, after suffering a huge financial loss in 1929, he was forced to relinquish control of his publications. Nast himself stayed on, running the company until his death in 1942.[65] During the Depression *Vogue* staff took a 10 percent pay cut and contributors reduced their rates. Nevertheless, the company showed first sharply declining profits, then, in 1932, a net loss. *Vogue* finally turned a profit again in 1934 and continued its recovery from that point on.[66]

Like sister Hearst Co. publication *Good Housekeeping*, *Harper's Bazar* had been expanded and promoted more aggressively when Hearst Co. acquired the title from its founder, Harper Brothers, in 1913. Advertising increased steadily in the teens, bespeaking the sales efforts of the publishing company.[67] The content of *Harper's Bazar* became more modern and sophisticated. Henry Sell, who had been editing the book pages of the Chicago *Daily News*, became editor in 1920 and gave the magazine the stylish look and tone he later tried to take to *Delineator*. Advertising continued to rise, providing Sell with the money to innovate. Sell introduced bleed pages (color all the way to the edge) and unposed photographs. He published Anita Loos' *Gentleman Prefer Blondes*, as well as works of other young writers. And like rival *Vogue*, *Harper's Bazar* showed the latest couture creations from Paris. The enriched content and skillful promotion caused the title to grow in circulation.

Charles Hanson Towne took over as editor of *Harper's Bazar* in 1926 for four years, continuing the focus on up-to-date fashions, fashionable people, and interesting fiction. The content was broader than that in *Vogue*. A second "a" was added to the title in 1929. Like its rival, *Harper's Bazaar* was ably designed, thanks to the work of French designer L'Aiglon Erte, who came to the magazine in 1915, and the Russian-born Alexey Brodovitch, hired by Hearst in 1934 as art director. *Harper's Bazaar* gained steadily in advertising throughout these years.[68]

In 1932 Hearst scored an enormous coup by stealing fashion editor Carmel Snow from rival *Vogue*. This move caused great bitterness and, more practically, hurt *Vogue* as Snow, an editor with a flair for fashion and an eye for innovative fashion photography, used the skill and contacts she had acquired at *Vogue* to improve *Harper's Bazaar*.

The emerging youth market also received attention from the fashion magazine world. Street & Smith, a publishing house best known for its dime and pulp novels, tapped the young women's market by bringing out *Mademoiselle, A Magazine for Smart Young Women* in 1935. "Mille," as its staff called it, featured affordable fashions, as well as food and fun. Editor Betsy Talbot Blackwell succeeded by creating departments targeted at college and career women, printing a broad spectrum of fiction and staying close to readers, who were encouraged to visit the publication's offices. Advertisers flocked to reach this group of consumers through *Mademoiselle*'s pages.[69]

In 1939 Conde Nast Co. started *Glamour of Hollywood*. Although covering the lives of stars, this was no ordinary fan magazine, joining the hordes of such titles that had sprung up in the teens and exploded after World War I.[70] *Glamour of Hollywood* also focused on the fashion and beauty needs of young women, offering them tips from film stars. Unlike Nast's other "class" publications, *Glamour* was aimed at the mass market. *Glamour* achieved quick success, as "fan" magazines were popular, but Nast found the Hollywood slant limiting. He redesigned *Glamour*, consciously copying the successful *Mademoiselle*. He retained some features on Hollywood, but hired a new editor, Elizabeth Penrose, former editor of British *Vogue*.[71] She gave readers fashion, beauty, and lifestyle advice, inexpensive yet stylish, targeted to young working women.

Publishing magnate Walter Annenberg observed the success of these fashion journals directed at young women, noting that during World War II some were forced to turn down advertising because of war-induced paper shortages. Recognizing opportunity Annenberg brought out his own fashion publication aimed at teens, with Helen Valentine, former promotion manager of *Mademoiselle*, as editor. *Seventeen* appeared in September 1944 and was an immediate hit; both advertisers and readers loved it.[72] Indeed, the magazine proved so popular that in January 1945 Annenberg was forced to kill another thriving journal to acquire the paper necessary for the newcomer. *Seventeen*, like *Glamour* and *Mademoi-*

selle, sold a significant portion of its copies on the newsstand, especially when it first started (94% *Seventeen*'s first year).

FURTHER MARKET SEGMENTATION

Despite increased and more concentrated circulations by the established women's magazine leaders, new entrants to the industry *did* appear during these decades, tapping newly identified market segments, starting the move toward specialization. New fashion periodicals targeting the youth market have been discussed earlier. Other titles destined to great success as women's service journals after World War II resulted from competition among grocery stores in the thirties. Some store publications, notably *Family Circle* and *Woman's Day*, moved beyond merely promoting products for their distributors to become wide-reaching women's journals, mirroring the path of some of the earlier pattern magazines.[73]

Family Circle started in 1932 as a free handout in food store chains. Harry Evans, a managing editor of *Life* magazine, conceived of this gimmick, produced it (with the help of Charles E. Merrill), and sold it to retailers such as Piggly Wiggly, Reeves, and Sanitary Grocery Co. (later Safeway).[74] The title remained free until 1946, when the publication switched from weekly to monthly and a five-cent charge was added. The number of grocery food chains carrying the magazine grew, giving it wider distribution. Shopping and homemaking tips, beauty and fashion, some coverage of movies and radio formed the nucleus of its content. Such material benefited retailers because it encouraged readers to buy products. The publication carried paid advertising from its first issues.[75]

Woman's Day appeared in 1937, a publication of the Great Atlantic and Pacific Tea Company(A&P). Started as a menu leaflet called *A&P Menus*, it became so popular the store decided to expand it into a magazine. It boasted a low price (2 cents by 1940, at a time when *Ladies' Home Journal*, *Woman's Home Companion*, and *McCall's* all cost 25 cents) and was sold in A&P grocery stores. The price rose throughout the forties, finally reaching the grand sum of seven cents a copy in 1951. By 1940 *Woman's Day* accepted outside advertising.[76] In 1943 Mabel Hill Souvaine took over as editor, a position she held for fifteen years. She led *Woman's Day* to great success, attracting almost 5 million readers.

Circulations of both these low-priced, home-service publications grew steadily. A third grocery-store-distributed magazine, *Everywoman's*, appeared in 1939. It expanded but remained smaller than the other two titles. Fierce competition and shifting circulation caused uncertainty, and in 1958, *Everywoman's* combined with *Family Circle*.[77]

Publications directed at women in smaller towns included the ever growing *Household*, *Women's World*, and *Needlecraft*; all were distributed primarily by mail. The late twenties proved a good time for these periodicals, which saw increases in circulation, advertising revenues, and ad lineage.[78]

Another new group of publications were the confession magazines, printing emotional first person tales of conflicts and problems. Bernarr Macfadden is credited with creating this genre, where highly personal, "true" stories, featuring liberal amounts of emotion and sex, were recounted for the reader. Macfadden, who had been publishing health titles, created the first confession journal in 1919. Called simply *True Story*, it immediately became popular and inspired numerous imitations, some published by Macfadden himself. Most purchasers were female, well over half from the working class.[79] Narrower in scope than the middle-class women's service journals, these confession magazines focused primarily on difficulties involving sex, marriage, and family. Rather than offering fantasy or escape, these stories strove to appear realistic. Action took place within a clear moral framework and all the tales were overtly prescriptive, imparting a lesson. In fact, by the 1950s, their publishers were calling these publications "Family Behavior Magazines." Some titles gradually added homemaking articles, but such information never comprised the journals' prime attraction. William Jordan Rapp, editor of *True Story* from 1926 to 1942, expanded that leader's focus to include social problems. But the most successful publications never lost sight of the personal emphasis readers loved so well.

Titles such as *True Story* and *True Confessions* did not compete directly with the Big Six, either for advertisers (who at first balked at placing their promotions in such publications) or for readers (working-class females). Many consumers of these journals had previously been infrequent magazine readers; many had limited education and purchasing power.[80] These latter traits branded them unattractive to most advertisers, and thus undesirable to most publishers. Eventually however, some advertisers became convinced of the wisdom of reaching these working-class consumers. By the 1950s Macfadden Publications was engaging in extensive research to persuade advertisers of the desirability of its readers, both in terms of spending power and in terms of willingness to be guided in purchasing decision.[81]

Confession journals filled a hole in the magazine market and lessened the chance that working-class women could be induced to buy the publications directed at middle-class women. Confession magazines also increased the market saturation the industry was beginning to experience in the twenties.[82]

Additional competition for working-class women came in the form of a new category of pulp magazine, the love pulp ("pulp" referring to the inexpensive, rough paper on which such titles were printed). While the pulp category generally targeted male readers with publications devoted to detective stories, adventures thrillers, and westerns, this new sub-group specifically aimed at women. Unlike the confession journals' "true" stories, love pulps were filled with romantic fiction. The first, Street & Smith's *Love Story Magazine*, appeared in 1921 under Amita Fairgrieve's editorship. Soon pulp publishers and magazine distributors clamoured for titles in this increasingly popular category, and new entries proliferated. These publications readily drew readers, if not advertisers. Pulps made their profit on high reader sales and low publishing costs and generally attracted little advertising. Free discussion of sex in the stories, permissible in the morally freer twenties, appealed to buyers, as did the romance.[83] *Love Story Magazine* stayed on top of the field, reaching a peak in the late twenties when, at fifteen cents, it sold almost 600,000 copies weekly, one of the highest circulations of any pulp magazine. Other top titles included *Love Fiction Monthly*, *Love Book*, and *All Story*, all edited by women. These publications offered purchasers predictable reading about romantic love. Right won over wrong, and good behavior was rewarded by glamorous romance. The audience tended to be working-class women, both housewives and those working outside the home, for whom these stories provided fantasy and escape.[84]

In the thirties circulations and prices of love pulps fell a bit due to the Depression, but new titles continued to appear. However, in the 1940s all the pulps (the loves included) declined in popularity, hurt by rising production costs and competition from first paperback books and eventually television, which offered similar kinds of entertainment.[85]

Fan magazines, capitalizing on the new intense interest in the Hollywood actors and actresses, revealed the lives and secrets of movie stars. Macfadden, Dell, and Fawcett put out the best-selling titles, all of which tended to die and be replaced fairly frequently. Working-class women formed their primary audience. Editorial and advertising worked closely together on these journals, often investing the mundane products promoted (soap, powder) with the glamour of the stars described.[86]

Some journals that had been published for years disappeared. *Modern Priscilla* expired in 1930, a victim of poor management, high price, and a poor quality subscription list.[87] *People's Home Journal*, targeted primarily at women in small towns, died in the late twenties, largely because of overcrowding in this field.[88] Neither *People's Popular Monthly* nor *Mother's Home Life*, both targeting more rural populations, survived the early thirties.

Magazines targeting black women continued to emerge. Some emanated from professional associations, such as the National Council of Negro Women's *Aframerica Woman's Journal* (1940–50) and the National Association of Colored Women's *National Notes* (1927–66). Others served more general interests, such as *The Negro Woman's World* (1934–36) and *The Woman's National Magazine* (1936–41).[89] None of the titles aimed at black women in this period achieved the mass distribution and circulation of the traditional women's publications targeted at white females. Journals edited for black women were hampered by the lack of a strong advertising base to provide the necessary financial support. Despite the nascent move toward specialization in the magazine world, most advertisers had yet to recognize the value of targeting a specialized group comprised of black female consumers.

Other specialized journals existed. The National Federation of Business and Professional Women's Association published *Independent Woman*. This organization also spawned state publications directed to business and professional women, including Nebraska's *The Goldenrod*, *The Iowa Business Woman*, and

The Business Woman of Missouri (all founded in the early 1920s).[90] Professional journals for women increased as women's numbers in the professions did, paralleling and reporting on women's professional activities.

Unlike the publications created to meet women's professional needs, the journals that had been promoting female suffrage found themselves floundering for a broader purpose after passage of the 19th Amendment, reflecting problems in the women's movement itself. All but two of the pro-suffrage publications died almost immediately. One survivor, the *Woman Citizen*, was converted in the twenties to a journal carrying news about social reform and the activities of women's clubs. The magazine had been the official publication of the National American Woman Suffrage Association (NAWSA), which used monies left to the organization by successful publisher Mrs. Frank Leslie to fund the journal. With the acquisition of suffrage, that organization transformed into the National League of Women Voters, and the *Woman Citizen* followed, serving briefly as the organization's official publication. The magazine became independent in 1921, although the NLWV continued to buy several pages in each issue to communicate about their programs. Throughout the twenties the *Woman Citizen* published articles about legislation of interest to women, firm in its belief that until women achieved power in organizations, businesses, and society at large, they still needed separate institutions of their own. Although supported by both subscribers and advertisers, the journal was plagued by financial difficulties. In 1928 the magazine went back to its original (pre-NAWSA) name of the *Woman's Journal*, hoping to attract a larger audience. The move failed and after a proud sixty-one and half year history, the title published its last issue in June 1931.[91] Another journal, *The Suffragist*, survived the passage of the 19th Amendment, becoming the official organ of the National Woman's Party (NWP). The party and the magazine dedicated themselves to passage of the Equal Rights Amendment. This amendment failed to gain widespread support, however, and was actively opposed by many female reformers who had worked for suffrage. The NWP itself was not large enough to support the magazine and *The Suffragist* died in 1922.[92]

These various publications offered readers alternatives to the mainstream women's journals directed primarily at white, heterosexual, middle-class women. None of the more highly specialized journals achieved the spectacular circulations of the general interest mass circulation women's titles, partially because of their more targeted content, partially because of the lack of a strong publishing organization and/or firm advertising support. Availability of magazines and the promotion efforts behind them had an impact on consumer choices.

In the early part of the century specialized magazines for men had existed, devoted to topics such as mechanics, hunting and fishing and sports. However, since unlike women, men were not defined generically by the work they did *as men*, no publications developed targeting simply "men's interests," as the major women's titles did for females; men's magazines were always more content specific. Even the *Saturday Evening Post* claimed to be targeting businessmen, rather than men as a generic category. General titles directed at men began appearing toward the end of this period. *Esquire*, a sophisticated journal of fashion, humor, and literature, with a sexual undertone, was successfully launched in 1933. *True* appeared in the thirties, and *Argosy*, a pulp for men since the 1890s, successfully transformed to a slick general men's journal in the 1940s. Adventure magazines appeared during World War II.

The slower, more diffused development of publications devoted to "men" also occurred because many advertisers did not find males as attractive a market as females. Men earned more income than women, but marketing studies had shown time and again that women made the majority of purchasing decisions. While certain product categories remained exempt from this rule (notably automobiles), generally in these years advertisers saw women as the primary consumers who had to be persuaded. Different gender roles spelled out for men and women and the specialization occurring in the magazine industry during these years meant that general publications directed at men never achieved the cultural pervasiveness as those targeted at women.

These years saw the perennial cries that women's journals were moribund. The desires of readers and advertisers for such publications was questioned. The women's magazines received their share of censure, as they had throughout their history. The *New Republic* published one critique of women's publications in each decade of the twenties, thirties, and forties. Disgruntled writers penned sarcastic pieces.[93] Such criticisms focused on the undue influence of advertisers, and the vacuity of the content. Calls came for new and different magazines to serve women of better taste and broader interests.[94]

However, despite these forebodings and condemnations, the economic depression, and radio, the women's magazine field continued to attract new entrants, to change in response to needs of readers and advertisers, and to flourish. New titles appeared, targeted at different groups of readers, creating the roots of reader segmentation, a strategy that grew to great importance.

NOTES

1. Canby, "Magazine Industry," p. 666.
2. JWTC News Bulletin, March 22, 1921: 72, p. 5, JWTP, Box 4; *Economic Facts*, p. 2; and Starch, *Advertising*, pp. 764, 766.
3. Ibid., p. 110.
4. *National Market* (1933): 176, 180; and Engman, "Gould Era."
5. Agnew and Dygert, *Advertising Media*, pp. 100, 101.
6. "Circulation: 9,496,841," p. 63.
7. Curtis wanted Rinehart so badly that he offered her an annual salary of $50,000 and promised to drop "Ladies'" from the magazine's title; see Cohn, *Improbable Fiction*, pp. 130, 131; and Rinehart, *My Story*, p. 286.
8. Mott, *History*, IV: 550, 551.
9. Gould and Gould, *American Story*, p. 151.
10. Ibid., p. 162.

11. Ibid., p. 161.

12. *National Advertising Records, 1935.*

13. Gould and Gould, *American Story*, pp. 169–75; and Drewry, "Ladies' Home Journal," p. 11.

14. Mott, *History*, IV: 467, 468.

15. "Circulation," p. 63.

16. Mott, *History*, IV: 770; and *Crowell Publishing Company Annual Report* (1934): 2.

17. On salary cuts, see GBL Diary, March 25, 1932, GBLVLP; on economizing, see GBL to BB, June 8, 1931; and GBL Diary, February 17, 1933, GBLVLP.

18. "Circulation," p. 110.

19. GBL to BB, June 22, 1932, BBP.

20. GBL to AC, February, 1934; and GBL to Ella Battles Lane, February 17, 1933, GBLVLP.

21. Anthony, *Where I Came In*, p. 326.

22. "Circulation," p. 110.

23. See DD to Max Whylie, January 20, 1943, DDP, File 19.

24. Ibid., p. 1; Tucker, *Recollections*; and Dignam, *Mrs. Jones.*

25. Quoted in Mott, *History*, V: 140.

26. "Tested and Not Approved," p. 51.

27. Mott, *History*, V: 140, 141; "Magazine Puts Seal of Approval," p. 192; and Mayes, *Maze*, pp. 269, 270.

28. *How Consumers Evaluate Magazines*, p. 28.

29. Mayes, *Maze*, pp. 249, 250; and Swanberg, *Hearst*, pp. 483–505.

30. Mott, *History*, V: 136; and "Hearst Magazine Earnings," p. 16.

31. Tucker, *Recollections*, pp. 6, 9.

32. Ibid., p. 25.

33. Ibid., p. 14.

34. Ibid., p. 29; and "Moore Heads Butterick," p. 7.

35. Tucker, *Recollections*, pp. 7, 30.

36. Ibid., p. 34.

37. *Story of a Pantry Shelf*, pp. 18, 19; "Butterick Magazines to Merge," p. 12; and Leckie, *Talent*, p. 80.

38. Tucker, *Recollections*, pp. 38, 39.

39. Ibid., p. 46.

40. Leckie, *Talent*, p. 86.

41. Tucker, *Recollections*, pp. 33, 46.

42. Ibid., pp. 48–51; and "Ladies' Line-up," p. 50.

43. "Ladies' Line-up," p. 50.

44. *History of Butterick Company.*

45. Tucker, *Recollections*, p. 18.

46. Ibid., p. 18.

47. Drewry, "McCall's," p. 304.

48. Mott, *History*, IV: 584, 585.

49. Hershey, *Pace and Pattern*, n.p.

50. Mott, *History*, IV: 585, 586; and Hershey, *Pace and Pattern.*

51. Ad in *N. W. Ayer*, 1914: p. 1857.

52. Copperfield, "Women's Magazines," p. 53; and Mayes, *Maze*, p. 258.

53. Lewis, *Wharton*, p. 459.

54. Dreiser, "Glory Be McGlathery," pp. 5–7; Rascoe, *Bookman's Daybook*, p. 97; and Austin, *Earth Horizon*, p. 343.

55. Lewis, *Wharton*, p. 447; Cohn, *Improbable Fiction*, p. 123; and Talmadge, *Corra Harris*, pp. 90, 98, 100.

56. Lewis and Thompson, "America a Paradise?" pp. 14, 15.

57. Daggett, *Women Wanted*, p. 14.

58. Tucker, *Recollections*, p. 18.

59. Copperfield, "Women's Magazines," p. 53.

60. Drewry, "Pictorial Review-Delineator," p. 383; and Mayes, *Maze*, pp. 257, 258.

61. Drewry, "Pictorial Review-Delineator," pp. 383, 384.

62. "Pictorial Review to Suspend," p. 18; and Swanberg, *Hearst*, p. 487.

63. Robinson, "Makers of Vogue," *Vogue*, p. 170. On *Vogue*'s 1926 revenues see Prior-Miller, "*Vogue*," p. 57.

64. Seebohm, *Vogue*, p. 282.

65. Ibid.; and "Conde Nast Dead," p. 39.

66. Seebohm, *Vogue*, pp. 308, 314, 318.

67. By 1917, *Harper's Bazaar* was second in women's magazine advertising linage; see *PI* (April 12, 1917): 172.

68. Pringle, "High Hat," p. 18; and Erte, *ERTE*, p. 116.

69. Levin, *Wheels of Fashion*, p. 84; and Schuler et al., *Lady Editor*, pp. 113–15.

70. Peterson, *Magazines*, pp. 304–6; and Gaines, "War," pp. 42–47.

71. Peterson, *Magazines*, pp. 334–39.

72. Cooney, *Annenbergs*, pp. 182–84; and "Bobby-Sox Forum," pp. 89–90.

73. Parts of the following appeared in Zuckerman, "Family Circle"; and Zuckerman, "Woman's Day."

74. Tabachnick, "Family Circle," pp. 122, 123; and Emmrich, "'Family Circle' Marks 50th," p. 10.

75. "Graduates of Life," p. 19.

76. *Magazine Circulation, 1937–1952*, p. 109.

77. Wood, *Magazines*, p. 266.

78. J. Esty, Transcript of Representatives' Meeting, October 25, 1930, pp. 6, 7. JWTP, Box 3.

79. Peterson, *Magazines*, pp. 294, 295; Macfadden and Gauvreau, *Dumbbells*; Cantor and Jones, "Creating Fiction," pp. 111–37; and Gerbner, "Social Role," p. 30.

80. Agnew, *Advertising*, p. 93.

81. Gerbner, "Social Role," pp. 29–40.

82. Stevens, "Inquiry"; and "Circulation," p. 106.

83. Uzzell, "Love Pulps," pp. 36–41.

84. Ibid., pp. 38–41; and Gerbner, "Social Role," p. 29.

85. Uzzell, "Love Pulps," p. 27; and Peterson, *Magazines*, p. 309.

86. Gaines, "War," pp. 42–47.

87. Hungerford, *Publishers Win*.

88. Transcript of Representatives' Meeting, October 25, 1930, p. 5. JWTP, Box 3.

89. Sims, *Progress*, pp. 213, 214.

90. "Reporters Who Get Results," p. 379.

91. "An Announcement," *Woman's Journal* (June 1931): 25; Lemons, *Woman Citizen*, p. 253; and Masel-Walters, "Burning Cloud," pp. 103–10.

92. Masel-Walters, "Hustle with the Rowdies," pp. 167–83.

93. Martin, "Women and 'Their' Magazines," pp. 91–93; Schlesinger, "They Say Women," pp. 125–27; Schlesinger, "Women's Magazines," pp. 345–47; and Copperfield, "Women's Magazines," pp. 22, 23, 53, 54.

94. Ford, "One Woman," pp. 37–43.

7

Targeting Readers

The Curtis publications through intensive and persistent efforts sought out in every city, hamlet and county in the United States those persons who would pay the full price for worthy merchandise and in turn made this market available to advertisers.

—Curtis Co., 1920[1]

To attract readers each of the women's magazines carefully crafted a mix of marketing elements calculated to appeal. Tactics centered on promotion, distribution, pricing, and, of course, the product itself. During these two decades technology and even editorial content could yield to promotion, merchandising, and research as the key points of competition. Research concerning readers intensified, as did advertiser interest in reader characteristics. Results of this research inevitably shaped editorial material.

PROMOTION AND DISTRIBUTION

Publishing companies employed a variety of promotional and distribution schemes in the intense fight to gain readers. A great deal of the competitive advantage held by certain titles came from distribution power and expertise.

Magazine organizations still used amateur salespeople, although they comprised a significantly decreased percentage of the sales effort. Reader-agents continued to earn money by selling subscriptions to friends and neighbors. Boy sales endured as well, used primarily by the Curtis Co., which had built a complex and sophisticated structure for these youthful salespeople.

In addition, however, aggressive teams of professional salesmen tramped neighborhoods in search of housewives who did not currently subscribe to their particular titles. Butterick Co. built up a strong field sales organization in the early twenties, promoting the Butterick Seven Reading Club; customers were offered a package deal of a three year-subscription to all seven Butterick publications at a deeply discounted price.[2] Butterick sent thousands of direct mail pieces to potential subscribers. It also maintained its Blue List department, where saleswomen called housewives, offering to sell them a subscription to *Delineator* at half price if the women would pick up the magazine at the nearest store selling Butterick patterns. Retailers with Butterick Pattern counters loved this plan, which forced customers to come into their establishments. Many turned over lists of their charge customers to Butterick telephone salespeople. Subscribers could place their *Delineator* subscription on their store charge.[3]

Crowell Co. too had a sales organization that by the 1930s was highly successful. In that decade Crowell's field sales teams sold more than twice as many subscriptions as those of any other publisher, as well as selling more of its magazines on the newsstand than any other company except Macfadden, and securing more subscriptions through direct reader request than any other company except Time, Inc. What particularly distinguished the Crowell Co. circulation department was its profitability. Unlike other publishers, Crowell Co. made money from the subscriptions it sold so forcefully. Crowell Co. sales teams worked out of offices called "Woman's Home Companion" Reading clubs, set up in cities of 50,000 or more; their women's journal was the company's lead product.[4]

Crowell Co. supplemented these efforts with other sales methods including independent agents, its Pin Money club (the reader-agent group run through the *Companion*), direct mail promotional pieces, a two-pay agency, and a catalogue agency. Crowell even used the expensive boy sales method to compete with Curtis Co.[5]

A large part of Crowell Co. publications' success in the 1930s, including the *Companion*'s jump to the number one spot in women's magazine circulation, came from the forceful and well-orchestrated circulation sales department. Crowell Co. president Thomas Beck, a former salesman, understood well the importance of strong efforts in that area. The company innovated by introducing the "paid-during-service" subscription (competitors called it "installment buying"). A customer purchased a two- or three-year subscription and paid monthly during the life of the subscription, rather than upfront. Crowell Co. and Hearst Co. were the only publishers able to handle these monthly billings, and it gave them an advantage with cash strapped readers.[6]

The magazine industry as whole needed to push their product to readers; more periodicals had to be sold than would naturally be demanded. Thus the need for aggressive sales strategies, such as those used by Crowell Co. Curtis Co. suffered during the Depression years in part because of the weakness of its selling organization, which it hastened to build up. Previously the Curtis subscription sales force had tended to wait for readers to write in for the popular Curtis magazines rather than seeking customers out.[7]

However, subscriptions gained through so much effort could prove costly. Intensive sales efforts were expensive, readers often paid a discounted price, and renewal rates from customers acquired through such methods could be low.

Perhaps most important, advertisers began expressing concern about subscriptions methods. Advertisers wanted measures of circulation quality and of how interested readers actually were in a journal. The Audit Bureau of Circulations, started in 1914 to verify circulations, began requiring publishers to report very specifically the different methods used to acquire subscriptions. Categories included percentage of mail and single copy sales (with subcategories for types of outlets), percentage sold with premiums, and percentage sold with advance payment versus payment by installment.[8] The deaths in the early 1930s of two journals directed at women, *Modern Priscilla* and *People's Home Journal*, were attributed by one analyst to subscription lists burdened with names acquired through "tricky" circulation schemes, which advertisers no longer welcomed.[9]

Publishers also sent crews to newsstands to ensure that their publications received favorable position and to set up promotional posters, reminding customers to buy.[10] Covers continued to be assessed in terms of potential for display posters.[11] The term "newsstand" covered a variety of outlets where single copies of journals might be purchased, including drugstores, department stores, rail and bus terminals, hotels, and book, confectionery, and stationery stores.[12]

By the 1930s all the major women's magazine publishers had broken away from the American News Company (ANC) except Crowell Co., which still distributed its publications through this organization, believing it received better newsstand placement because of ANC; most other women's journals used independent distributors.[13]

As time went on advertisers increasingly preferred high newsstand sales, believing that such purchases demonstrated the strongest interest in a title. As early as 1922 advertising agency J. Walter Thompson, speaking of the high percentage of circulation sold on newsstands by *Vogue* and *Harper's Bazaar*, concluded "that a higher percentage of its circulation may be of a more voluntary nature" than the circulation of other magazines.[14] *McCall's* was the first women's journal to sell more than a million copies on a newsstand in the late thirties, spurred by the presence of an entire novel in the magazine.[15]

The major women's journals differed in their reliance on subscription and newsstand sales, with *Ladies' Home Journal* highest in percentage newsstand sales throughout these years (over 50% in the twenties). In 1922 the overall rate for the major women's journals (plus *Designer*) stood at 37 percent sold on the newsstand and the remainder through subscriptions. This compared with a high of 52.4 percent sold on the newsstand by *Vogue* and *Harper's Bazaar*, and an average low of under 10 percent by journals such as *Needlecraft*, *Gentlewoman*, and *People's Home Journal*, which relied heavily on the mails to reach their smaller-town customers.[16]

By 1930 the numbers spanned from *Ladies' Home Journal*, with a high of 55 percent of its circulation sold on the newsstand, to *Delineator*, with 22 percent newsstand sales. In that same year, at the further extremes of journals directed to women lay the romance pulp *True Story*, with 96 percent of its sales at the newsstand, and, at the opposite end of the spectrum the former mail-order journal, *Household*, with almost 100 percent of its circulation (targeting rural households) derived through subscription.[17]

By 1937 the two highest newsstand sellers, *Ladies' Home Journal* and *Good Housekeeping*, had dropped considerably in the percentage of copies distributed that way; *McCall's* and *Woman's Home Companion* had fluctuated just a bit. After years of economic hardship, many readers had less discretionary money in their pockets to spend on an impulse purchase such as newsstand magazine buying. Customers may have looked for the lower price that could be had through subscription rates. However, two low-priced newcomers, *Family Circle* and *Woman's Day*, continued to be sold exclusively by single copy purchase in grocery stores chains through the early 1950s.[18]

Subscription customers became slightly more expensive to service. In 1917 Congress passed a Postal law revising the second-class mailing rates. This represented the culmination of an effort that had been ongoing since the end of the nineteenth century. The new rates, calling for postage hikes with increases in distance and volume of advertising, went into effect in July 1918. The law also mandated that publishers exclude from their lists of legitimate subscribers anyone paying less than 50 percent of the regularly advertised rate. Most publishers of women's journals sent individuals to Washington to lobby against the proposal. The measure passed, but publishers persisted in their fight to have the rates reduced.[19]

TECHNOLOGY

Technology played a less crucial role in magazine competition in these years than it had in the late nineteenth and early twentieth century, when it made a fundamental difference in the number and kind of publications available at a particular price. Innovations affecting periodicals often had more to do with advancing technology in other industries (movies, radio, and paperback books) that then posed competition. For magazines, this period saw refinements in print technology rather than great technological leaps.

Publications increasingly turned to photography. By the end of the twenties, color photography was available. At *Vogue*, editors spent $60,000 more on artwork than on photography in 1930; by 1933 that gap had been reduced to only $13,000, and by the end of the decade far more was spent on photography. Color steadily improved in quality. For example, in 1924 *Woman's Home Companion* had available for advertisers an innovative technique called the 4-color Ben Day process.[20] Overall, the use of color and the replacement of some illustrations with photography added variety and richness to the visual format.

While most magazines were not printed by their own companies, the major women's journals were part of huge publishing operations that in most cases *did* print their own publications as well as others, allowing them to stay on the cutting edge of print technology (as well as making them more vulnerable to economic swings in the publishing industry). McCall Co. built its own printing plant in Dayton, Ohio, in 1924. Butterick Co. maintained two huge printing plants until sold in the 1930s. Other publishers improved their printing plants. Crowell Co. introduced high speed gravure presses into its Springfield operation in 1934–35. In the late thirties Curtis Co. began using a faster machine for its four color printing, with a great improvement in results. In the 1920s Conde Nast bought a printing plant in Greenwich, Connecticut. He renovated it, making it one of the most advanced printing plants in the country.[21]

In this mature stage of the industry, the existing magazines became even more standardized and started looking more similar to one another. Size offers one example. *Ladies' Home Journal* increased its page size to the standard large-quarto in 1921 to better meet the needs of advertisers, and *Woman's Home Companion* reduced its pages to meet the same standard. In November 1924 *Pictorial Review* also altered its page size to match the other magazines in the women's field.[22] Only *Good Housekeeping* kept its smaller size.

PRICE

Loyalty to magazines meant that even during times of economic depression, other things were cut before a favorite journal, so circulations did not decline as much as might be expected. Strong feelings about favored titles also meant that readers did not necessarily respond to the lowest price or strongest financial incentive.[23]

However, price did have some effect. For example, *Ladies' Home Journal*, experiencing circulation declines when most of the other journals were steadily gaining readers, decreased its price from fifteen to ten cents a copy in October 1923 and saw a big jump in subscriptions.[24]

The top circulating women's journals engaged in some price experimentation and matching. *Ladies' Home Journal* kept its cost to readers on the lower end of the pricing scale throughout this entire period, in part because of the high advertising rates Curtis Co. was able to command. The *Journal* started this period in 1917 at $1.50 annually. By 1927 circulation leaders *Ladies' Home Journal*, *McCall's*, and *Woman's Home Companion* all had settled on an annual price of $1.00, an amount they stayed with until 1942 (when the *Journal* and the *Companion* both increased their prices to $1.50; *McCall's* soon followed). During these same years *Good Housekeeping* positioned itself at the upper end of the scale, arguing that it was really a trade journal and that the status and information provided by the Good Housekeeping Institute made it distinct and worth more money. It charged between $1.50 and $2.00 more than the three leaders. Readers were not scared off and *Good Housekeeping* maintained its circulation growth, although it stayed in fourth, fifth, or sixth place in overall numbers. *Pictorial Review* pitched its price lower than *Good Housekeeping*'s, but slightly higher than that of the other journals for much of this period; this premium did not appear to hurt its circulation. *Delineator*'s price fluctuated the most of the top women's journals. The price increased from $2.00 to $3.00 in 1927 when the management change occurred, but this price lasted only a few years. When readership fell (due to the radical changes in editorial content as much as increased cost) the price was dropped to $1.00 (by 1930).

Publications watched one another's pricing; all were careful not to stray out of a given range, defined at the top end by *Good Housekeeping* at $3.00 and the bottom by *Ladies' Home Journal*, *McCall's*, and *Woman's Home Companion*, at $1.00.

As in the tens and teens, price was seldom the most important purchasing consideration as long as it stayed within accepted limits. Price could denote prestige, as in the case of the Good Housekeeping. Since price to the consumer failed to cover the cost of producing and distributing magazines anyway (advertising picked up the rest of the tab), publishers were rarely forced into unwanted price increases.

PURCHASERS OF WOMEN'S MAGAZINES

Who were the readers of these women's journals, the ones to whom these promotion, price, and distribution strategies were directed? Some demographics give part of the story. The number of females purchasing women's magazines increased tremendously in the first decades of the twentieth century. Between 1910 and 1930, copies of women's journals sold grew from about 18 million to over 31 million.[25] The figure on women actually *reading* the publications was estimated to be much higher. A 1928 study sponsored by *Good Housekeeping* revealed that on average, women in "better homes" (defined as homes worth between $12,000 and $45,000) read just over three magazine titles regularly. By 1940 that number had risen to almost four and half issues a month, among females who read periodicals regularly.[26]

Women's magazine purchasing also became more concentrated over the course of these two decades. This resulted in a greater percentage of readers buying the top six women's journals than in the periods before and after this one. Numbers drawn from N. W. Ayer's directory, which recorded periodical circulations, show that in 1910 the top six women's journals took 44 percent of the total readers. In 1958 that figure stood at 43.6 percent. But in the thirties, a gradual increase in the percentage of readers purchasing the top six publications became apparent. In 1936 52 percent of all purchases went to the Big Six. By 1940 (with two of the Big Six gone) the leading six titles attracted almost 65 percent of all women's magazine readers.[27]

This created a problem for advertisers concerned about duplication of readership, namely, one woman appearing on two or three major women's journals' subscription lists. Advertisers considered duplicated names "wasted" readership in terms of their promotional efforts. To investigate the extent of this problem the American Association of Advertising Agencies (4 A's) hired researcher Daniel Starch to conduct studies on the subject. Starch discovered fairly low reader duplication among the top six women's journals (unlike the *Companion*'s survey earlier). For example, according to a 1927 Starch study, five of the major women's publications (excluding *Delineator*) had an average of 70 percent unduplicated readership; that is, on average, 70 percent of each title's readership did not purchase any of the other four titles.[28] A study in the 1930s confirmed this general pattern, showing that 65 percent of women purchasing a women's magazine at a newsstand bought only one such title in a given transaction, 23 percent bought two, and under 10 percent took three.[29]

While these low duplication figures were good news for advertisers, they fed publishers' fears of market saturation, a phenomenon commented on by media watchers; the women's magazine market was no longer in a growth stage. If most females bought only one major women's journal, then circulations could only expand as quickly as the population did, with additional increments from the 30 percent of the market that bought more than one title. If publishers wished to increase their circulations more quickly (and in these competitive years they did), they had to convince purchasers either to switch from one title to another, or to buy more than one magazine. To achieve this, the aggressive sales practices just described came into play.

Even with such tactics, gaining additional readers could be problematic. Since the turn of the century readers of women's titles had proved stubbornly loyal to "their" magazine. Direct advertising to readers proved consistently ineffective and expensive for the results gained; sophisticated (and costly) promotional pieces yielded disappointing results. Women knew which journal they wanted and tended to purchase it regularly. This behavior held true not just in subscription renewals, but also in newsstand buying. Women's magazines played the role of old friends to many female subscribers, and these readers returned loyally to their familiar companions, despite the blandishments of salespeople. Endorsement by an acquaintance, or a very low price could work to get a woman to *try* a new title. But overall, in this area female consumers made individual decisions and showed enormous allegiance.[30]

With competition for advertisers keen, publishers sought to establish the popularity of their media. In 1942 Curtis Co. hired an independent market research firm to carry out a study that would demonstrate that more women actually read the *Ladies' Home Journal* than the circulation numbers indicated. The company also wanted to prove that fewer people actually read Sunday supplements such as *This Week* and *American Weekly* than their circulation numbers showed. The former phenomenon was termed "fanning out" while the latter was called "shrinkage."[31] In 1941 a similar investigation had been conducted to demonstrate the "fanning out" of the four remaining major women's journals (*Ladies' Home Journal*, *Woman's Home Companion*, *McCall's*, and *Good Housekeeping*) in an attempt to convince advertisers of their superiority over radio and Sunday supplements. The study detailed the ways and places women received exposure to women's journals without actually buying copies.[32] These studies fit with those being conducted in the late 1930s by other major mass circulation publications such as *Life*, which had switched from measuring magazine purchasing to measuring magazine audience.

Despite the advertiser pressure on circulation, publishers did not compete for all readers. In fact, some readers were quite consciously excluded. Both Curtis Co. and Crowell Co. divided up sales territories based on wealth. Curtis Co. segmented cities into four sections (red, yellow, green, and blue) according to average property value. A salesman was told to "conduct circulation work in the better residential areas. . . . He was *forbidden* to do work in areas colored blue (for the most part with foreign-speaking or colored residents)" (emphasis added).[33]

Curtis ad salesmen argued that homes with more income were naturally more likely to purchase magazines, but admitted that this "natural flow" of periodicals toward the affluent homes was "supplemented by the direction of circulation effort toward such homes through the use of a control map."[34] The result was that in the mid-twenties the *Journal* claimed that it attracted more readers in all income groups over $1,000 than any other women's publication.

Crowell salesmen, like their Curtis counterparts, targeted the more prosperous homes, avoiding lower income readers. They too worked from colored maps, "with large areas blocked out in red that indicate regions in which 60 percent of the homes are not desirable and which are strictly *forbidden* to salesmen" (emphasis added).[35] In fact, the company refused to accept subscriptions from the lower income areas, thus allowing its publications to "provide(s) an entree for quality products into the most perceptive homes."[36]

This emphasis on readers' income, in response to desires of advertisers, influenced in turn publishers' ideas of who they wanted as their audience. This affected content and led eventually to a kind of literary disenfranchisement of a population segment. Thus, while publishers talked about mass and class magazines, many mass publications, influenced by advertisers, very explicitly did not include all the populace among their readership. Upon reviewing trade literature of the twenties and thirties, historian Roland Marchand found that advertiser estimates of those unattractive as consumers ranged from 30 percent to two-thirds of the population. Undesirable consumers included the same groups excluded from Curtis Co. magazines: blacks, the illiterate, and the poor.[37] The pressure on publishers to carve out of the American populace an audience with traits pleasing to advertisers intensified as the century wore on, ignored only by those journals not reliant on advertising dollars.

The delineation by publishers (pushed by advertisers) of welcome and unwelcome readers cemented the middle-class, white nature of the mass circulation women's journals, which continued down through much of the twentieth century. Such targeting inevitably affected the publications' content, which embraced particular images and subjects and rejected others. Certain groups were excluded (e.g., homosexuals) and others often presented with unfavorable or distorted images (the poor, immigrants, blacks) in the pages of these journals.

READER DEMOGRAPHICS

Research on readers revealed women's magazine purchasers to be on the whole relatively young, middle-income, married females distributed across the nation; race was usually not even reported in these studies, the assumption being that readers were white. Some differences in reader demographics existed between the Big Six titles. The audiences for women's journals in the class grouping (e.g., *Vogue* and *Harper's Bazaar*) and the confession and mail order category diverged significantly from the six leaders.

Female readers of all periodicals tended to be young, with readership peaking between ages twenty-six to thirty-five, according to one study. A slight decrease in magazine readership occurred between ages thirty-six and forty-five, with a big dropping off among women over forty-six.[38] These female reading patterns for general magazines held true for women's titles as well. A large percentage of all the major women's journals went to readers ages twenty-five to forty-five in these years, with lower amounts going to the over-forty-five age group.[39]

Facts such as these about readers, conveyed to editors, affected magazine content. The data was of interest to advertisers as well. *McCall's*, believing age an important variable in advertising placement decisions, began requesting this information from its readers in the thirties. In the late 1930s seasoned editor Gertrude Lane asked author Edna Ferber to delete a reference in Ferber's autobiography to Lane's approximate age when the two met in 1920; Lane feared it would hurt the *Companion* with advertisers if they knew her real age (approaching sixty at the time of this request), especially as the ad salesmen from *McCall's* and *Ladies' Home Journal* had been emphasizing the youth of their editors.[40]

With advertisers interested in readers' abilities to buy products, researchers at magazines, ad agencies, and trade organizations intensified efforts to collect specific data on purchasers' incomes and professions. Such investigations, revealing the buying power of a publication's readers, would become increasingly common and increasingly influential on editorial policy and advertiser decisions. The information also situated the traditional women's service journals in relation to other publications. For example, in 1927 women's magazines generally had 17 percent of their circulation going to families with annual incomes of $5,000 or more. This differed from general periodicals, which on average had 24 percent of their circulation finding its way into such homes. It diverged even more from the "class" magazines such as *Vogue*, which had between 42 and 51 percent of their circulation going to families with incomes of $5,000 or more.[41] As one commentator succinctly put it, to be called a "class" magazine "does not mean at all that they have a monopoly of readers with intelligence, culture, or manners. It means that advertisers and advertising agencies are convinced that the people who buy them have, on the average, more money."[42]

Of course, audiences for each of the major women's journals varied. One 1922 study, conducted by the J. Walter Thompson advertising agency, categorized subscription readers of women's magazines by occupation, creating three groups. The first was composed of jobs generally considered to be the highest paid.[43] In this categorization, readers of the top women's titles differed significantly, ranging from *Good Housekeeping*'s high of almost 72 percent in the first occupational group (in part reflecting its higher subscription price) to the *Companion*'s low of just under 34 percent.[44]

Ad agents kept these age and income numbers in mind when selecting media for their campaigns, as did editors when determining content. For example, McCall Co. found in its reader surveys in the late thirties and forties that younger women were generally more interested in fiction and style and beauty, and older women relatively more concerned with current events and social and economic topics. Poorer readers preferred fiction while wealthier readers were more likely to be attracted to contemporary events.[45] Editors thought both about meeting the needs of their current readers (such needs estimated in part by their ages and incomes) and about responding to advertisers, who preferred readers with a particular level of buying power.

Ladies' Home Journal editor Loring Schuler described his ideal readers as young in their thinking and "on their way up," defined by Schuler as having husbands who were doing well professionally.[46] As part of his program for attracting and holding such desirable readers, Schuler cut back on the *Journal*'s extensive reader service bureau, the pride of former editor Edward Bok. Schuler believed that higher class readers neither needed nor valued the service as much as lower-class purchasers. He called this reader service a "sideline" to the main business of creating a magazine. Schuler specifically referred to advertisers' interests when giving an additional reason for the reader service cutback, noting that "so many of the advertisers in the Journal are also offering service and we feel that if the advertisers are doing it, it is only fair that the editorial department should lead the way in encouraging people to write to the advertisers."[47] Schuler ignored the fact that guidance from the editorial staff might differ substantially from advice given by producers of goods.

Advertisers also demonstrated interest in other demographic variables concerning readers, including marital status, geographic location, and sex. *Delineator* had the highest percentage of married subscribers (91%), *Ladies' Home Journal* the lowest (73%).[48] *Good Housekeeping* proved particularly strong in big cities, *McCall's* was concentrated more distinctly in smaller towns, and the other titles spread out between.[49] Circulation became more evenly distributed geographically than previously as each of the Big Six became national in reputation.[50]

In the early part of the century, *Ladies' Home Journal* and *Woman's Home Companion* had aggressively promoted themselves as "family" magazines, which women *and* men could enjoy. The *Journal* in particular had stressed that it attracted male as well as female readers.[51] However, these efforts never worked effectively, with either purchasers or advertisers, and in the twenties and thirties the major women's periodicals kept their eyes firmly fixed on the demographics of their female readers, the customers most important to them and their advertisers.

Editors continued to possess a qualitative sense of their readership. *Journal* editors Bruce and Beatrice Gould wrote that they "felt a kinship with our readers," who were similar, they felt, to their own families. *Good Housekeeping*'s Herbert Mayes believed that the word "middle" embodied everything about his readership.[52] His intuition was confirmed by a 1930s' study conducted by ad man turned ad critic James Rorty. In his study of ten mass and class magazines (including women's titles), Rorty found that 51 percent of the titles went to middle-class readers, defined as individuals in the $2,000 to $5,000 income group.[53] As in the earlier part of the century, editors aimed their publications at middle-class readers, hoping to catch purchasers throughout this often ill-defined group.

INFLUENCE OF READERS

Readers continued to affect women's publications, but the nature of their influence shifted. The number of pieces written by readers decreased, in part because of the establishment by the major women's journals of testing institutes, which cut down on the need for homemaking "tips" from readers. As part of this trend toward standardization, the major women's journals also decreased reliance on freelance writers. By the mid-thirties, *McCall's* and *Pictorial Review* had their own staff writing all their nonfiction service, while *Good Housekeeping* commissioned only 5 percent and *Ladies' Home Journal* just 1 percent of such pieces.[54] Ad woman Helen Woodward attributed part of this standardization of content to professionalization of staffs, but also credited hidden persuasion by advertisers, who supplied increasing amounts of information to the journals' service departments in hopes of publicity for products.[55]

However, while fewer of their writings appeared in print, readers remained influential; their *opinions* still counted. The myriad reader surveys conducted by magazine publishers provided editors with useful information about readers' preferences with respect to features and stories, and this data inevitably affected content choices. When editors failed to consider readers, the results could be unhappy, as happened when *Delineator*'s new editors tried to make the title slick and sophisticated. *Delineator* learned its lesson and by the late twenties had put together a representative panel of women nationwide called "Consultant House-keepers," who provided input.[56] *Delineator* also supported a committee of a thousand women across the country who reported specifically on various beauty products. Advertisers as well as editors used such information. Such panels emphasized women's role as consumer.

Woman's Home Companion expanded and regularized this kind of reader input in 1935 with its Reader-Editor panel, one of the first formal consumer panels. For several years before setting up the official panel, *Companion* editor Gertrude Battles Lane and the Crowell Co. promotion department had mailed out numerous questionnaires to subscribers, attempting to discover the attitudes, behaviors, and life situations of *Companion* readers.[57] When the Crowell staff decided to form a permanent panel of respondents, they selected the first group through personal interviews where they stressed "the need of the magazine for closer contact with its readers, and the opportunity the individual would have to influence its make-up."[58] Staffers picked two hundred and fifty women this way and solicited the remaining 1,250 by letter from the *Companion* subscription list. The journal ensured continued interest by publishing a newsletter for partici-pants, filled with recipes, household tips, and letters. As friends, relatives, and other readers learned of the panel, the *Companion* received an increasing num-ber of requests to join.

Companion staffers used Reader-Editor information for editorial guidance and even as copy starting in 1936. Every month either a profile of a Reader-Editor or the results of a Reader-Editor survey appeared. Kitchen problems, travel plans, things to be thankful for, all received attention. Twelve Reader-Editors a year visited the Companion Home Service Center in New York City to discuss and test housekeeping ideas.[59] The *Companion* published articles covering the problems posed by Reader-Editors. Thus reader input yielded magazine content.

The staff used the Reader-Editor information in another way. The *Compan-ion* offered hundreds of service pamphlets to readers, covering topics from traveling with a family, to flower decoration, to care for expectant mothers, available free or at a nominal cost. Editors developing new brochures drew on the information garnered from the Reader-Editors.[60]

When the panel concept was introduced, the Companion told readers that this service had been developed for their benefit.[61] However, the panel had another purpose, one not as clearly obvious to panel participants or *Companion* readers; it helped meet the demands of the magazine's other customers, the advertisers. The *Companion* used the results from its Reader-Editor panels to convince advertisers that *Companion* readers comprised an audience worth reaching and to give advertisers information about the buying habits and prefer-ences of the publication's readers.

The panel worked in part because *Companion* editors had special access; women trusted the magazine. When public opinion researchers Paul Lazarsfeld and Marjorie Fiske evaluated the *Companion*'s pioneering panel, they noted the ready willingness of readers to participate as one of the advantages enjoyed by the periodical, a benefit many other users of such a technique would not have.[62] The panel endured and by 1947 had stabilized at 2,000 members.

Taking a different tact to getting close to readers, Bruce and Beatrice Black-mar Gould commissioned friend George Gallup to conduct opinion polls among their readers on a variety of subjects, including divorce, marriage, and birth control. Survey results appeared in the *Journal* starting in February 1938 and undoubtedly gave the editors a better understanding of their readers.[63] But the Goulds were not enamored of reader research. Although they wanted to know their readers' *opinions* on topics, they showed less interest in the numbers relayed to them by the research department about how particular articles and departments fared among their audience. Longtime *Good Housekeeping* editor Herbert Mayes agreed, asserting that editors should use their instincts. He believed that the only subject worth researching was magazine cover price. *Companion* editor Lane felt the same skepticism about editing by research numbers, noting succinctly that "To get a hundred percent readership . . . all you have to do is run a big cartoon on every page and give it a one line caption."[64]

The growing amounts of research being conducted at the major publishing companies meant that editors could not remain unaware of readers' views. And letters continued to pour into women's journals, both to staff generally and to authors of particular articles, offering ideas and asking questions.[65] Editors at several publications (notably *Woman's Home Companion* and *Delineator*) developed informational booklets on a variety of subjects to help answer reader queries. The Butterick organization claimed that with the specialists hired to respond to reader letters, "Our organization represents a composite encyclopedia, hospital, rectory, law office, university, and the house of a friend."[66] *Ladies' Home Journal* readers requested and paid for 800,000 booklets in 1933 on topics such as fashion, beauty, homemaking, and entertainment, and the *Journal* claimed that in an emergency, telegraph or special delivery would be used to ensure that information reached a reader in time. Through such services the magazines encouraged reader loyalty and served a truly valuable information function. In turn, reader responses to pamphlets put out by the *Journal*, *Companion*, and *Delineator* served as a measure of reader interest on topics, affected editorial decision-making, and helped to guide editorial policy.[67]

INFLUENCE ON READERS

Women read these publications in bits and pieces, in between other activities. Some read straight through, others leafed through the pages, stopping as something took their fancy. Still others quickly skimmed the whole journal before identifying those features that interested them most. Articles were read or skipped. In this relative freedom from structure (compared, for example, to that typically experienced in reading a novel) lay part of the magazines' appeal. But such unique reading experiences make difficult the task of describing any typical episode of reading and being affected by a women's publication at any point in time.

Women used these journals for entertainment, escape, and fantasy. They received information, guidance, and reassurance, gleaned money-saving tips and fashion news. Magazines gave women a connection to the outside world, allowing them to keep up with both social issues and the latest consumer products. Countless numbers of readers followed the advice on beauty, housekeeping, and childcare, which appeared in the teens, twenties, and thirties as well as the wisdom (ever changing) about attracting and keeping a man. The publications taught women the art of consumption, directly through the ads and indirectly through editorial material. Throughout, the magazines influenced women about what it meant to be female, even if simply heightening the impact of societal norms by mirroring them.

When articles called for specific actions, the effects of these journals can be assessed more directly. Bruce and Beatrice Blackmar Gould discovered the power of their publication the first years of their editorship when they saw the tremendous responses generated by their campaigns against high maternal death rates and venereal disease.[68] Women's magazine investigative journalist Vera Connolly noted the strength of organized women in her 1929 expose of the horrific conditions besetting the American Indians. Connolly's articles generated an outpouring of letters to Congress, then investigating the situation. *Good Housekeeping*'s 1921 campaign favoring passage of the Sheppard-Towner Act brought a similar flood of mail to Congress. *Woman's Home Companion*'s effort to educate women about politics and the vote in the early twenties resulted in thousands of women writing in for informational booklets about the mechanics of voting and party platforms.[69]

As effective as these campaigns were, in many instances editors and authors told female readers what to do rather than allowing them to take the initiative. Such methods may have encouraged dependence and a kind of intellectual passivity, although, at least early in the century, women, often unused to the public sphere, may have welcomed such direction.[70] Bruce Gould both complimented and belittled women when he wrote to *Journal* columnist Dorothy Thompson that

I find that women have no conception of their power and to get them to act is going to take years of exhorting. . . . I think you might well return to this idea of the real strength of women from time to time because it IS going to take some eloquent voice like yours to lead them on.[71]

Gould as well as other editors also wrote of the tension between giving readers exactly what they wanted and jumping a bit ahead of the audience. *Vogue* editor Edna Woolman Chase argued that pleasing the reader made for the best magazine, but even she talked patronizingly of including content that was "for the best interest of the reader."[72] Critic Elizabeth Schlesinger in 1934 wrote that in fact editors *should* do just that, give readers content that would broaden their perspectives and educate them, even if audiences did not necessarily want it.[73]

And editors were not above manipulating their audiences in small ways. Herbert Mayes admitted to adding a phony name to *Good Housekeeping*'s masthead, so it could be deleted to appease irate readers. *Companion* staff wrote missives published as reader letters.[74]

All of this emphasized the actual distance between the staff creating these journals and their readers, as did the growing use of experts. The magazine "family" editors had underscored in the early part of the century became a company run by professionals. Readers still held an important place in that family, but their activities and power in the household had shrunk.

NOTES

1. *Merchandising of Department Store Lines, Vol. BB: Retailing and Jobbing* (Philadelphia: Curtis Publishing Co., 1920), p. 95, CP, Box 5.

2. Tucker, *Recollections*, p. 26.

3. Ibid., p. 27; and *Midas Gold*.

4. "Circulation: 9,496,841," pp. 106, 108.

5. Young, "Who's Jim Thayer," p. 50, ff.

6. "Circulation," p. 108.

7. Wyman, *Circulation*, p. 23; and Cohn, *Creating America*, p. 238.

8. Wyman, *Circulation*, pp. 13, 80, 81.

9. Hungerford, *Publishers Win*, p. 30.

10. Tucker, *Recollections*, p. 26; and Wyman, *Circulation*, p. 55.

11. Seebohm, *Vogue*, pp. 184, 185; and LS, Transcript of talk at JWTC staff meeting, May 26, 1930, pp. 10, 11, JWTP, Box 8.

12. Wyman, *Circulation*, p. 33.

13. Ibid., p. 47.

14. "Analysis of the Subscription Circulation of Forty-four Magazines," p. 77, JWTP.

15. Mott, *History*, IV: 586.

16. "Analysis of the Subscription Circulation of Forty-four Magazines," pp. 33–86, JWTP.

17. Data from *Consumer Magazine and Farm Publication Rates* (1930).

18. *Magazine Circulation, 1937–1952.*

19. Kielbowicz, "Postal Subsidies," pp. 451–88; Kennedy, "Development of Postal Rates," pp. 93–112; and JWTC News Bulletin, June 11, 1917, p. 2, JWTP, Box 1.

20. See JWTC *Newsletter*, #33, June 26, 1924, p. 6, JWTP.

21. Engman, "Gould Era," p. 32; and Seebohm, *Vogue*, pp. 246–58.

22. Mott, *History*, IV: 550, 770; and JWTC *Newsletter*, #30, June 5, 1924, p. 6, JWTP.

23. Wyman, *Circulation*, p. 23; and Mabie, "'Popular' Stories," p. 3.

24. JWTC *Newsletter*, #18, March 18, 1924, p. 6, JWTP.

25. This includes all women's journals listed in Ayer's *Directory*, 1910 and 1930.

26. *Women in the Influential Homes*, p. 1; *Magazine Advertising Effectiveness*, J. Walter Thompson for *GH*, 1940, n.p., JWTP, Reel 221.

27. Ayer, *American Newspaper Annual* (1910, 1940, 1958). Concentration of readers appeared in the general magazine market as well; see Peterson, *Magazines*, p. 61.

28. JWTC meeting minutes, August 17, 1928, p. 6, JWTP.

29. Wyman, *Circulation*, p. 38.

30. Ibid., pp. 18, 19.

31. *Circulation Coverage vs. Housewife Reader Coverage of Ladies' Home Journal, American Weekly and This Week*, November 1942: in CP, Box 2.

32. *How Can Women's Magazines Cover so Many More Homes Than Their Circulation Figures Show?*, 1941, in CP, Box 2.

33. *Study of City Markets, 1928–1929*, p. 1.

34. Ibid., p. 1. See also Cohn, *Creating America*, pp. 238, 239.

35. "Circulation," p. 108.

36. *Crowell-Collier Circulations, 1939 Survey*, p. 10.

37. Marchand, *Advertising*, p. 64.

38. *Economic Facts*, p. 10.

39. JWTC, *Good Housekeeping Survey*, 1931, n.p., JWTP, Microfilm Reel 39.

40. *Tide* (December 1, 1936): 28; Gilbert, *Ferber*, pp. 305, 306; LS, transcript of talk at JWTC staff meeting, May 26, 1930, p. 23, JWTP, Box 8; and Frederick, *Mrs. Consumer*, p. 24.

41. Notes of Representatives Meeting, Tuesday, February 7, 1928, p. 3, JWTP, Box 1.

42. Pringle, "High Hat," p. 17.

43. "Analysis of the Subscription Circulation of Forty-four Magazines," pp. 10, 11, 16.

44. Ibid., p. 30.

45. *Qualitative Study of Magazines* (1946): 45, 47.

46. LS, Transcript of talk at JWTC staff meeting, May 26, 1930, pp. 23, 24, JWTP, Box 8.

47. Ibid., p. 4.

48. "Analysis of the Subscription Circulation of Forty-four Magazines," p. 31; and *Mrs. John Doe*, p. 44.

49. *The Ladies' Home Journal*, presentation by Mr. Parlin, n.d., CP, Box 3.

50. *Magazine Circulation* (Denney Company, 1919); and "The Market for Ladies' Home Journal," 1933, n.p., JWTP, Microfilm Reel 38.

51. Transcript of 1915 Advertising Conference, pp. 3, 4, 5, CP, Box 5.

52. Gould and Gould, *American Story*, p. 159; and Mayes, *Maze*, p. 75.

53. Rorty, *Master's Voice*, p. 124. See also Agnew, *Advertising*, p. 106.

54. Drewry, "Ladies' Home Journal," p. 11; and Peterson, *Magazines*, p. 122.

55. Woodward, *Lady Persuaders*, pp. 9, 10.

56. Dignam, *Mrs. Jones*, p. 38.

57. "Circulation," p. 106.

58. Lazarsfeld and Fiske, "The 'Panel,'" pp. 601, 602.

59. E.g., *WHC* (January 1936): 65; and *WHC* (July 1937): 78.

60. See *WHC* (May 1939): 10.

61. *WHC* (January 1936): 65, 66.

62. Lazarsfeld and Fiske, "The 'Panel,'" pp. 601, 602.

63. Gould and Gould, *American Story*, pp. 195–97; and Engman, *Gould Era*, pp. 83, 84.

64. Gould and Gould, *American Story*, pp. 166, 167, 319; Mayes, *Maze*, pp. 120–22. Lane quoted in Mayes, *Maze*, p. 121.

65. See e.g., account of letters flooding in to author Mary Roberts Rinehart upon publication of *My Story* in *GH*, in Cohn, *Improbable Fiction*, pp. 176–81.

66. *Mrs. John Doe*, p. 61.

67. See e.g., LS, Transcript of talk at JWTC, May 26, 1930, p. 5, JWTP, Box 8.

68. Gould and Gould, *American Story*, pp. 172, 173, 189–93.

69. Waller-Zuckerman, "Vera Connolly," pp. 80–88; "What the Editor Has to Say. Harding and Cox Both Favor Maternity Bill," p. 4; and Zuckerman, "Educated Citizen," pp. 86–105.

70. Woodward, *Lady Persuaders*, p. 121.

71. BG to DT, November 10, 1941, BG&BBGP.

72. Chase and Chase, *Vogue*, p. 169.

73. Schlesinger, "Women's Magazines," pp. 345–47.

74. Mayes, *Maze*, p. 128; and BB to GBL, February 24, 1925.

8

Creating the Women's Magazines

Magazines rise and fall entirely by the strength and ability of their editors. . . . There is something evangelistic in every successful editor. You have to want to do something for people. That is your primary drive. You never let the secondary drive, which is to make money through the magazine, supersede the primary one.

—Bruce Gould[1]

In the 1930s *Woman's Home Companion* began featuring new art work, which received favorable reviews from the magazine trade press. However, Joseph Knapp, chief stockholder of *Companion* owner Crowell-Collier Co., disliked the innovation. He sent a blistering letter to editor Gertrude Battles Lane and followed up with a personal visit. Lane listened to his complaint but when Knapp started shouting at her, she demanded that he leave her office, saying that her middle name was Battles and he had better take note of it.[2]

Lane won that dispute, as other successful editors often prevailed in struggles with their owners and publishers in the twenties and thirties. But the editorial role was changing as publishing companies grew larger, more rationalized, more concerned with stockholders and revenues from advertising dollars. A strong editor could still hold his or her own, but as organizations became bigger and more focused on profits, business pressures increased. An understanding of the implications of the business aspects of magazine making, always significant, was now crucial for editors, as was the ability to attract advertising. Editors walked a fine line. They needed a sensibility that allowed them to edit with integrity yet be realistic about advertisers' needs. It remained necessary for editors to stay in touch with their readers' interests, leading, but not straying too far ahead of, their audiences.

This chapter looks at the journalists editing and writing for women's publications in the interwar years: the experiences these individuals brought to their jobs, their editorial philosophies, and their attitudes toward women. The chapter closes with an examination of a particular group of women's magazine staffers, the experts on home management, to illustrate both the trend toward greater use of professionals and the complicated relationship existing between women's journals' staff and advertising.

EDITORIAL BACKGROUNDS

Women's titles attracted personnel with diverse professional experience, enriching the content of the journals. Newspaper reporting, writing, promotion, fashion, merchandising, and magazine work all appeared in the backgrounds of women's magazine staffers. No one path to the women's publications emerged.

Newspaper work provided preparation for a number of individuals. Such experience served those who switched to women's magazine work and the journals themselves well. Former newspaper reporters and editors usually brought to women's publications a broad perspective and skill with investigative techniques. Journalists generally found magazine work, with its monthly or semimonthly publication schedule, less taxing than newspaper work. For women attempting to combine a career with family, magazine work provided a sensible career option.[3] And women's journals continued to offer many females their best professional opportunities.

Marie Mattingly Meloney, the editor of *Designer* and *Delineator* and a former newspaper woman, used connections she had developed as a reporter and wrote on subjects she had previously covered. This yielded a wide spectrum of social and political topics. Meloney's work to encourage building of better homes, her crusade to buy radium for Madame Curie, and her focus on child welfare all grew out of her newspaper work. For example, when Meloney worked on the *New York Sun* she regularly covered the New York Children's Court. Such work led logically to her later inclusion of issues about children's welfare in the *Delineator*. Similarly, Meloney's earlier reporting on diplomatic news while a journalist in Washington, D.C. gave her an understanding of the importance of international issues, which she incorporated into the magazine's content.[4]

William Birnie, who took over at *Woman's Home Companion* in the 1940s, had also been a newspaperman, as was one of his top assistants, Roger Dakin. Under their leadership the *Companion* printed discussions on topics such as juvenile delinquency and racial and religious prejudice, which drew in part on their newspaper training.[5] Other *Companion* staffers with newspaper backgrounds included Anna Steese Richardson and Sophie Kerr.[6]

Bessie Beatty had served as a reporter, newspaper editor, and foreign correspondent before taking over at *McCall's* in 1918. The job provided a break from international journalism, but Beatty longed to return, and at the end of

1921 she left *McCall's* to travel to Russia as a correspondent.[7] Harry Payne Burton, who followed Beatty at *McCall's*, had also come from a reporting and editing background and had served as a foreign correspondent.[8]

Bruce and Beatrice Gould came to editing from newspaper backgrounds. They had graduated from the University of Iowa, where Beatrice Gould edited and Bruce Gould worked on *The Daily Iowan*. After brief stints on the *Des Moines Tribune*, both Goulds moved to New York, Bruce to report for the New York *Sun*, Beatrice to take a Masters in Journalism at Columbia University. They married shortly thereafter, in 1923. Beatrice began working at the New York *World*, where she started a woman's section, and Bruce moved to the New York *Evening Post*, serving as first aviation then literary editor. Bruce started writing books and plays, then magazine articles and short stories. He then served as an associate editor at *Saturday Evening Post*. Beatrice too began writing stories after her daughter Sesaly was born and she left her position at the *World*.[9] Such extensive reporting, editing, and writing activities honed the Goulds' journalistic abilities. Bruce Gould found this diverse background helpful in editing the *Journal*, deeming it a positive thing that neither he nor his wife had worked for a women's magazine before because it saved them from "cliche editing."[10]

Writers also served as women's journal editors. Honore Willsie Morrow, who edited *Delineator* before Meloney, was a writer, as was Meloney's eventual successor at *Delineator*, Oscar Graeve. Graeve had published numerous short stories and worked in magazine promotion departments. As an editor Graeve emphasized literature, culture, and entertainment, and published writers such as Edith Wharton, Ida Tarbell, and Edna St. Vincent Millay, though his promotional experience may have influenced his selections, including his belief that Cinderella makes "about the most durable theme, when it comes to selecting a background for present-day fiction."[11]

William Frederick Bigelow of *Good Housekeeping* gained his journalistic training on magazines, working on Hearst's *Cosmopolitan* for eight years where he rose to the job of editor before moving over to the helm of *Good Housekeeping* in 1913. Unlike some other women's journal editors, who lived in New York City (but like the Goulds), Bigelow resided in New Jersey; he maintained that living in a suburban community, sharing many interests with his readers, helped in his editing.[12] Concerns about the breakup of the family and the divorce rate led this Sunday School superintendent to commission and publish a number of articles exploring aspects of parenting and the family; eventually he edited a book on marriage.[13]

Women generally held few of the highest positions in the magazine world in these decades, and even at the women's journals the number of women in top jobs remained sparse. The visible exceptions included Gertrude Battles Lane, Marie Mattingly Meloney, and Beatrice Gould. Edna Woolman Chase (*Vogue*) and Carmel Snow (*Harper's Bazaar*) headed the fashion journals. Women edited all but one of the leading love pulps. However, men still owned and published all the major women's publications, a fact some critics pointed to when deploring the limited and commercial nature of the journals; such critics believed the magazines reflected men's views of what women wanted.[14]

Editors exerted great control over content, now ordering stories and articles rather than waiting to see what came in. Editing had always involved working closely with authors. But as readers' wants became better known, editors grew confident about and at the same time more wedded to their winning formulas. Editors actively sought and shaped material to fit their magazines; this was true for both fiction and nonfiction. Gertrude Lane was renowned for her work with novelists and short story writers such as Edna Ferber and Kathleen Norris. *McCall's* Constance Smith had a knack for helping fiction writers develop stories that would please the journal's readers. Barton Currie took an annual trip to England to visit writers, then moved on to Paris to see American authors living in that city. Later, the *Journal* had on staff Hugh Kahler and Laura Lou Brookman, who visited writers, literary agents, and publishing houses seeking out fiction. They read, edited, and cut manuscripts.[15]

Under Loring Schuler the editorial staff at *Ladies' Home Journal* typically outlined quite specifically for free-lance writers what they wanted in nonfiction articles. For fiction the editors generally gave less guidance, although Schuler cited examples where strong direction occurred in this realm as well. He mentioned "fiction for propaganda purposes—propaganda or some hobby that we may have as, for instance, a year or so ago we started Tarkington writing a series on business girls because we were very much interested in the woman in business."[16] Schuler admitted that the *Journal* was edited by a formula he calculated as "38% happiness, 37% entertainment and 25% general information." He and his staff abjured sex, sentiment, or high thought.[17]

Schuler's correspondence with popular writer Mary Roberts Rinehart about an editorial column she wrote for the *Journal* in 1931 and 1932 is instructive. While eager to have work by Rinehart in his magazine, Schuler encouraged her to "sugar-coat" her political opinions.[18] Rinehart wanted to include some serious topics and Schuler responded saying

Perhaps the subjects you have chosen so far have not been as big and internationally important as they might be, but the longer I stay in this business of editing the more I am impressed by the fact that what seem to you to be very unimportant details of life are tremendously important to the great mass of readers.[19]

Women's journals were not alone in exerting such control and dictating guidelines about content, structure (with serialization in mind), and length of fiction; these practices occurred in mass circulation magazines generally. For example, George Horace Lorimer and his editors at the *Saturday Evening Post* restricted material in terms of such things as politics and story tone with, for example, a happy mood preferable to a depressing one. Women's journal editors often imposed similar requirements, not solely because of the gender of their audience, but also because they were creating a popular, mass medium.[20]

WORKING ON A WOMEN'S MAGAZINE

Women's journal editors, staffers, and writers held various attitudes about woman's nature and her role in society, and harbored a multitude of feelings about working on publications devoted to females. Now as earlier discrepancies existed between their own lives and the lives of readers, a divergence that, in print, magazines were at pains to erase.

Some editors, such as Arthur Vance and William Frederick Bigelow, believed that male and female readers possessed similar interests, with the caveat that women also desired information on cooking, fashion, and homemaking. Many editors, including Gertrude Battles Lane and Bruce and Beatrice Gould, felt that while males and females liked to read about the same topics, a women's journal needed to give its articles a feminine slant. In general, editors addressed readers as women, with topics presented through the prism of traditionally female interests.

Gertrude Lane saw men and women as equally intelligent but fundamentally dissimilar in their reactions. Such beliefs dictated a special emphasis for a magazine directed to a female audience. In a judgement revelatory of mixed feelings about her own ambitions and achievements, Lane commented that "I do not believe a woman's success magazine would ever be a success, for women are interested in the success of others rather than their own personal success."[21] Aside from providing a partial explanation as to why the highly accomplished Lane herself kept such a low profile, this remark also suggests an editorial selection process filtering out self-help material geared toward worldly achievement and letting in articles calling for helpfulness toward others and actions leading to greater good for society. But Lane did not consistently advocate differential treatment for women. When Herbert Hoover's advisors recommended that he make a special address appealing to women in the 1932 election, Lane counseled against such a course, arguing that "women prefer to be considered a part of the whole electorate rather than a class by themselves."[22] Lane drew a distinction between women's preferences as magazine readers and as voters.

Bruce and Beatrice Blackmar Gould saw important distinctions between men and women. They believed that woman's most important job was in the home. After several years in the top position at the *Journal*, Beatrice Gould said,

I think that women these days are understanding their real job as women. They should retain their pre-eminence in their own field—in the home. In business, at best, they can hope for no more than second place. The importance of running a home with children has been minimized by too many women.[23]

Gould's belief that women could only aspire to second best in the business world inevitably shaped the material selected for the *Journal*. Her position on women's primacy in the home also revealed shrewd editorial judgement, as polls showed that most American women agreed with her.[24] And Gould claimed she was simply trying to get more value placed on the work women did in the home.

The Goulds modified their views about women a bit during the course of their editorial tenure, and the *Journal* gradually began discussing the subject of women, particularly wives and mothers, working outside the home. A January 1941 editorial (pre-dating American entry into war) stated forcefully, "The question becomes not one of **should wives work** but **under what conditions should they work**. Maternity leaves, adequate insurance, and community day nurseries can certainly nullify the possible bad effects of the employment of mothers" (*Journal*'s emphasis).[25] The Goulds continued to believe it was preferable for women to stay at home while children were young[26]; the Goulds' one child, Sesaly, was seven when Beatrice Gould took on the *Journal* job, and even then Beatrice came into the office only three days a week, working at home the other weekdays and on weekends. And while Beatrice Gould enlarged her ideas about women's role in the public sphere, as late as 1949 she still asserted that

I believe it is woman's job to be as truly womanly as possible. I mean to nourish her family, and to rest them, to guide them, and to encourage them. To be as pretty as possible, as loving as possible, as helpful as possible, so that if the whole rest of the world blacks out, each family has one center of warmth and comfort and cheer and tolerant good sense.[27]

Beatrice Gould stressed in public statements that one of her chief editorial roles was to provide her husband with the woman's point of view. The Gould's correspondence shows that Bruce Gould handled the business and administrative matters at the *Journal*, while Beatrice's contributions lay in the creative and editorial realms.[28]

In addition to providing a female point of view, women editors also had promotional value. In the 1920s Butterick Co. proudly reported to advertisers that several of its editors were also wives and mothers. One publication described *Designer* editor Gabrielle Griswold as "first of all, a wife and home-maker." Home Management editor Christine Frederick was depicted as "an interesting combination of professional woman and mother."[29] Marie Meloney was touted as "a wife, a mother and a writer."[30] Because they performed wifely and motherly duties such editors understood the needs of readers, Butterick argued, most importantly readers' consumption needs.

Some publishers ignored any special gender connection between female readers and their editors. Curtis Co. filled the top job at the *Journal* with former newspapermen and experienced Curtis Co. editors. Hearst Co. shuffled editors between properties—general, trade, and women's. A female, or someone particularly knowledgeable about women's interests, was not deemed necessary. This proved both beneficial and limiting for the female readers of these journals, as male editors selected material based on their understanding of readers generally and on their perceptions about female readers.

Did males edit differently than females, offering either a broader or narrower range of materials than women editors? Did female editors wed their publications more firmly to the woman's sphere? These questions prove difficult to answer in part because so few females edited the big women's magazines in these years. The fashion journals focused narrowly by their own definition, so their editors do not provide a good comparison. Other factors confounding our understanding of effect of sex on content include cultural climate, industry health, trends in journalism, and reader reactions, all of which affected editorial decision making. A fiercely competitive environment may have overridden sex differences. Corporate culture may have overshadowed these distinctions as well; women who rose to the top in these publishing organization may have borne more resemblance to their male counterparts than to their female readers. Large staffs also meant that a variety of male and female viewpoints were heard.

However, some observations can be made. Certainly both Marie Meloney of *Delineator* and Gertrude Lane of *Woman's Home Companion* offered readers a broad array of fiction, service departments, and articles on timely social and political issues. Both mounted crusades in their magazines aimed at empowering women. Yet Loring Schuler at the *Journal*, William Frederick Bigelow at *Good Housekeeping*, and the Goulds at the *Journal* did so as well. Some males insisted that they edited irrespective of sex. Bigelow maintained that he printed stories and articles that he himself would like to read; he believed that "men's and women's interests are largely identical."[31] Barton Currie believed that material should not be "feminized," that for the most part, articles should be of interest to both males and females.[32]

Bruce Gould, however, saw women as different than and inferior to men. He wrote that

I have always believed with Havelock Ellis that woman's charm is her greatest strength, as man's strength is his greatest charm. Persuasion, the quiet, amused revealing of another point of view, perhaps preferable, was woman's power. Absolute equality was our view—with the male slightly more equal than the female, but both equally enjoying the unequal arrangement.[33]

He valued stereotypical female virtues such as beauty and charm in women.[34] Bruce thought that Beatrice had been offered the coeditorship at the *Journal* in part because of her "very womanly nature."[35] However, it had been at his insistence that Beatrice Gould was included as coeditor.[36]

Some females editors, including Beatrice Gould and Marie Meloney, initially expressed ambivalence about working on women's titles. Others, such as Gertrude Lane and Edna Woolman Chase, found great professional success and happiness on these publications throughout their careers. Men may also have felt ambivalent about working on women's journals, but they could point with satisfaction to the magazines' commercial success with readers and advertisers. Bruce Gould chose to stay at *Ladies' Home Journal* rather than take on the editorship of the *Saturday Evening Post* if it meant giving up the *Journal*.[37] Women's titles were important properties in big publishing enterprises; heading one was a powerful job. This also partially explains the paucity of top female editors at these publications.

In the twenties, armed with funds from advertisers, women's journal editors enticed well-known writers to work for them. The writers came, albeit at times reluctantly; many of them too still held a prejudice about writing for a "women's title" and an audience of females, even as opportunities on these journals continued to be among the best in the magazine world, at least financially and in terms of reaching readers. Some authors believed that women differed from men in morality, lifestyle, and/or reading taste; others denied any differences. Enough editors and writers for women's journals felt that material had to be targeted distinctively to reinforce in the publications the idea that women differed from men.

For female fiction writers addressing issues seen as "domestic" or stereotypically "female," women's magazines offered an especially good market for stories. Over time female authors came to dominate in titles such as *Woman's Home Companion*, *Ladies' Home Journal*, and *Good Housekeeping*.[38]

Nonfiction writers also confronted the question of how to address a female audience. Investigative free-lance writer Vera Connolly believed that profound differences between the sexes existed and that the journals targeting women reflected this. When she arrived in New York City in the teens, Connolly worked at *Delineator* and *McCall's* as well as at the *New York Sun* and the *World Outlook*. These experiences convinced Connolly that her best chance for free-lancing lay with the women's magazines; she felt she could speak effectively to women's issues in a way that men could not.[39] Like social feminist Jane Addams, Connolly believed that women functioned as the "social housekeepers" of society; she wrote, "The home woman is needed as an influence in public affairs—which are just housekeeping on a larger scale."[40] This idea that women were morally superior to men, charged with the special role of cleaning up society and protecting the home, permeated Connolly's investigative articles, published primarily in *Good Housekeeping* and *Delineator*. In Connolly's pieces, whether describing abysmal conditions on Indians reservations, juvenile delinquency, or the dope menace in society, the message of separate spheres and activities remained constant.

Journalist Dorothy Thompson also used a special slant for a female audience. Thompson began contributing a regular column to the *Ladies' Home Journal* in 1937 at the request of Beatrice Gould, who felt Thompson's work would perfectly exemplify the new tone the Goulds hoped to institute at the *Journal*.[41] An authority on world affairs who contributed a phenomenally successful column to the *New York Herald Tribune* that was syndicated across the country,

Thompson revealed a different side in the *Journal*. Keeping her audience in mind, she focused primarily on the domestic sphere, idealizing it in the process. The joys of the household, gardening, progressive education, dieting, and the role of women as society's builders and protectors all served as column topics. Thompson defended her choices, arguing that for her *Journal* pieces, "One must . . . try to write about more enduring things than a current budget debate or international crisis."[42] Readers responded eagerly to Thompson's topics; as she observed,

I am a woman; month by month I have written about what interested me, and the mail has shown that (whether the correspondents agreed with me or not), they too, have been interested in the same matters. These essays have been more personal than anything else I have written, and the more personal, in general, the greater the response.[43]

In a fitting gesture the Goulds expressed their happiness with Thompson's work by remodeling the kitchen in her home at Twin Farms in Vermont.[44]

The traditional view of women Thompson espoused and the stereotypically feminine topics she discussed not only failed to broaden readers' world, but also sanctioned the notion of a separate sphere of female interests for all but the exceptional woman. The writing in the columns was lively, the topics various, the conventionally feminine presented in a positive light, but the message remained essentially conservative. Moreover, Thompson's independent, career-oriented life contradicted in many ways her *Journal* columns.

Writer Mary Roberts Rinehart also made distinctions between her own life and those of women's magazine readers, reinforcing traditional gender characteristics in the process. Rinehart had achieved great success as well as economic independence through her profession. But she also had a husband and family, and Rinehart insisted, in an interview published in *Good Housekeeping*, that most women would be unwilling to give up these relationships for a career. In a look at the twenties, which she termed "The Chaotic Decade," Rinehart wrote wistfully about the lost virtues of charm in a woman and strength in a man, characteristics missing in the independence and radicalism of that decade; she looked forward to a time when the "feminine" home woman around whom "the simpler virtues" were built would be valued, as well as the strong man who would protect her.[45]

The lives led by male editors clearly differed from those of their female audience, a distinction readers could easily see and ascribe to sex. Female magazine editors also maintained lifestyles that diverged from much of their audience, a contrast less immediately obvious and more complicated for readers. Top editor Marie Meloney followed a somewhat conventional pattern in that she stopped her successful career as a journalist when she married; she began working again outside the home only when she needed money. However, Beatrice Gould, wife and mother, worked while her husband was alive and earning good money. In fact, the husband-wife hiring of Bruce and Beatrice Gould forced Curtis Co. to drop its ban on married female employees.[46] Gould's situation gave her something in common with her readers (marriage, children), yet represented a contradiction in that she herself pursued a career outside the home while she encouraged her female audience to focus its energies primarily inside the home. Gertrude Lane was more dissimilar to her readers than the other two prominent female editors. Unlike most of her readers, Lane remained unmarried all her life, her only child an adopted French war orphan.

EXPERTS IN HOME MANAGEMENT

Money and the chance to reach millions of readers drew to women's journals not just well-known fiction writers but accomplished individuals from fields such as architecture, cooking, art, nutrition, and fashion. Such experts enriched magazine content and offered readers concrete, specific information in a variety of arenas.

One group of specialists increasingly employed by women's titles were home management experts, authorities who sought to put homemaking on a scientific, rational basis and to educate women across the country in the most modern techniques of household management. Some, although not all, of these home management authorities had received formal training in home economics, a profession that had been flourishing since the turn of the century.[47] Graduates of newly created university home economics programs found that magazines focusing on the home offered attractive job opportunities, providing a ready forum for carrying their messages. Home management experts working on women's journals included women such as Martha Van Rensselaer, Katherine Fisher, Christine Frederick, Lita Bane, Sarah Splint, Alice Blinn, and Mildred Maddocks Bentley.[48] A review of the work of several of these authorities illuminates some trends occurring on the women's journals. Home management experts provide a clear case of the general movement toward greater use of specialists. Their work illustrates the richness of information and variety of viewpoints (at times conflicting) present in the women's journals. Finally, the areas overseen by the home management authorities offered obvious territory for advertiser influence.

Martha Van Rensselaer, who served as Home Making editor of *Delineator* from 1920 to 1926, had been a pioneer in the home economics field. She established some of the first home economics classes in the United States at Cornell University. Much of the material Van Rensselaer published in *Delineator* came from activities and experiments on cooking and homemaking undertaken at the university. Through her pages in the *Delineator*, Van Rensselaer conveyed this knowledge to millions of women unable to attend home economics classes.[49]

Van Rensselaer found women's journals a logical choice for her home-oriented material. In her job as a school commissioner, she had visited many rural homes and realized the critical need to get homemaking information to women living in such situations. In 1900 Van Rensselaer started an extension program for farmers' wives at Cornell. For this program Van Rensselaer wrote bulletins covering topics often included in women's magazines such as child care, nutrition, sewing, decoration, and other aspects of housework.[50]

Armed with these bulletins, Van Rensselaer approached *Ladies' Home Journal* in 1901, asking if it would consider a copy of her "Reading Lesson: Supplement No. 1: For Farmer's Wives" as the basis for an article. The *Journal* expressed interest, and by 1907 Van Rensselaer was editing a column devoted to household economies. This department included both Van Rensselaer's expert advice and "tips" sent in by readers.[51]

Van Rensselaer's understanding of farm women's needs made her attractive to other women's journals, an indication that editors knew a significant portion of their readership was still rural in nature. By the teens Van Rensselaer had appeared in Butterick publications *Delineator* and *New Idea Woman's Magazine*, had been asked by *Pictorial Review* to take over their culinary and household department (she refused), had been featured in a *Good Housekeeping* article, and continued to contribute articles to *Ladies' Home Journal* and other women's publications.[52] A woman of stature in the home economics field who served as president of the American Home Economics Association (AHEA) from 1915 through 1916, Van Rensselaer was clearly viewed as an expert on domestic economy. Her wide contributions to women's magazines are a tribute to her ability to write well and get along with a variety of editors and her willingness to spread valuable knowledge about housekeeping for rural women. They also demonstrate the women's journals' recognition that many women needed and wanted such information.

When Van Rensselaer stepped into the top position at *Delineator*'s Home Making department she was already familiar with both the benefits (reaching a large circulation of women, receiving a comfortable salary) and the limitations (editorial oversight, space constraints, and awareness of advertisers' considerations) of working on a mass market women's publication.[53] In her articles Van Rensselaer emphasized thrift of time, energy, and money; community involvement; the need to run the home like a business; and the importance of homemakers caring for themselves as well as the household. She saw women's consumption role as significant but one that must be handled in a scientific, careful manner.[54]

Katherine Fisher, Director of the Good Housekeeping Institute beginning in the late twenties, also drew on practical and academic experience for her work. Fisher had taught domestic science, rising to the position of Dean of the School of Household Science of Macdonald College at McGill University in Canada. Paralleling Van Rensselaer's career, Fisher became involved in a kind of extension work, organizing an educational network aimed at rural Canadian women. Fisher then moved to Teachers College at Columbia University in New York City, where she instructed other home economics teachers. Finally she accepted the job at the Good Housekeeping Institute, overseeing all the product and service testing as well as supervising the Institute's editorial material appearing in the magazine. Fisher expanded the Institute's staff, which included home economists, chemists, and engineers. Well respected by home economists, Fisher maintained a high profile while at *Good Housekeeping*, attending conferences and traveling across the country. Her expertise and prestige in her chosen field enhanced the reputation of the Institute.[55]

Experts in household management such as Van Rensselaer and Fisher used women's journals to provide guidance to millions of women around the country, women responsible for maintaining homes and families. Much of the information provided by these authorities reduced the work done by women while increasing the efficiency and quality of the remaining chores. Undoubtedly they provided direction and reassurance, especially for novice housekeepers.

However, in focusing on the profession of household management and in setting high standards, the articles and advice offered by household editors such as Van Rensselaer and Fisher may have actually increased the burden of work on American housewives, raising their self-expectations. The material quality of life in the home may have improved, but higher standards meant additional work. And in addition to being advised to employ techniques for efficiency, women were eventually encouraged to view homemaking as an art, an expression of themselves and of their love for their families.[56] While articles did often emphasize saving housewives' time, the pieces did not focus on using that free time to leave the home and pursue a career; rather, the experts promised to take the drudgery and haphazardness out of homemaking, so that the home could be tranquil, modern, and smoothly run, leaving time for family and social activities. Experts' advice often carried an undertone branding those unwilling to use the new products and technological innovations as old-fashioned, backward-looking.[57]

Such notions pleased advertisers pushing new products designed to be used in the home. And given the overlap of subject matter, it was a short step for some home management advisors to becoming home manufacturer advisors. Christine Frederick provides a telling example of this cross-over from professional journalist and household management expert to advisor to manufacturers. Throughout much of her career, Frederick straddled the twin missions of educating consumers through women's magazines and other publications and assisting marketers.

Frederick, who had held the job of Contributing Household editor to *Ladies' Home Journal* in the teens, continued to write for women's publications, serving as Home Making editor at *Designer* in the early twenties. Like Van Rensselaer, Frederick had started her magazine career by sending in unsolicited material to the *Journal* (on efficiency in the home), and in her case too the editors responded with interest.

However, Frederick fit a pattern different from that of Van Rensselaer and Fisher. She had not trained professionally as a home economist; instead she had received a B.A. in English at Northwestern (where she also took a course with pioneering advertising psychologist Walter Dill Scott). Frederick schooled herself in the science of home management, setting up the Applecroft Experiment Station in her Long Island home to test new products and systems.

Frederick counseled women on scientific ways of managing their households, with the idea of making the work more efficient and less onerous. She disseminated her ideas through women's journals, two books, and a magazine published from her experiment station in the early teens called "The New Womanhood."[58] She argued that scientific management of the home would not only make housework easier and more pleasant, but also more dignified and professional. Frederick took a thoroughly businesslike attitude toward housework and urged others to do so, disagreeing with those experts who sentimentalized home tasks. Frederick received an enormous response from *Journal* readers anxious to both put their household work on a more professional basis and to free themselves from the drudgery of their job.

Frederick, along with many home economists such as Van Rensselaer, believed that modern housekeepers should learn to be educated consumers.[59] She cited advertising appearing in women's journals as a useful resource in this education process. Such ads, she argued, provided practical information concerning food, children, and housework, analogous to the data contained in ads in a trade publication such as *Iron Age*. Frederick pointed out that "I have often noted that the carping critics of advertising are not housewives, and do not possess, as we do, the manifold remembrances of the benefits and new ideas we derive from advertising."[60]

In addition to writing for consumers, Frederick also assisted manufacturers in making their products convenient, among other things advocating standardization in product design. Eventually Frederick moved from advising women on new products and scientific housekeeping, often in women's journals, to advising manufacturers on the best way to persuade consumers to buy their products. In the 1920s, while editing at *Designer*, she began writing numerous pamphlets for manufacturers, describing their products and persuading women to buy and use them.[61] In 1929 Frederick brought out her aptly titled book, *Selling Mrs. Consumer*, an advice manual to manufacturers on ways to make products and promotion more appealing to housewives.

Frederick's evolution from expert for housewives to expert for manufacturers traced a path taken by some service departments of the women's magazines. As production increasingly moved out of the home and many remaining jobs became mechanized, much work left for homemakers involved consumption. Here the women's journals found themselves with conflicting missions for their two groups of customers, readers and advertisers. As advisors to women managing the home, editors wanted to help housewives become intelligent, educated consumers.

At the same time these service departments and institutes, while driven in part by reader queries and problems, spent a great deal of time testing products offered by manufacturers. Under pressure from advertisers it was often easier to promote these products than to question more fundamentally the way house-work was divided and organized.

As the century wore on, with competition between magazines intensifying and advertisers becoming more sophisticated and powerful, articles questioning and unmasking aspects of the purchasing process decreased. The journals' function of training women in the crucial consumer aspect of homemaking shifted from a focus on intelligent, critical consumption to a focus on continuous consumption. The need for advertising influenced all magazine staffers, including the home economists.[62]

Manufacturers of home products recruited home economics experts to work for them and sought their support. Thus advice from home economists appeared in both the editorial and advertising sections of the women's journals. For a number of years the boundary between them remained blurred, both within the profession, where home economists both worked for manufacturers and also advised consumers, and, of course, for women's magazine readers.

Thus the energies of one group of women's magazine experts, the home management advisers, were eventually channeled to the purposes of the commercial and cultural status quo. And as the prosperous twenties gave way to the financially hard-pressed thirties, the necessity of pleasing advertisers increased.

NOTES

1. Gould quoted in Engman, *Gould Era*, p. 19.

2. Anthony, *Where I Came In*, p. 370; and MBB interview.

3. BVIR, *Journalist's Questionnaires*, Collected 1917, Reel 16.

4. Boughner, *Women*, pp. 251, 306; Wilder, "Delineator's Editor"; and history of Meloney's life in MMMP.

5. Mott, *History*, IV: 771; Edward Anthony, *Where I Came In*, pp. 341, 342; and Peterson, *Magazines*, p. 141.

6. *Who was Who in America*, II (1943–50): 50; and Boughner, *Women*, p. 279.

7. "Bessie Beatty," *Current Biography* (1944): 37; and Ross, *Ladies*, pp. 581–83.

8. Mott, *History*, IV: 584; and "Harry Payne Burton," *Who was Who Among English and European Authors (1978)*: 253.

9. Drewry, "Ladies' Home Journal," pp. 11–12; "Meet the Up-to-Date Editors," pp. 7, 8; and Gould and Gould, *American Story*, pp. 67–142.

10. BG to MEWZ, June 29, 1984.

11. Mabie, "Upon Graeve," p. 3; see also "Editorial," *Delineator* (November 1931): 5.

12. "William Frederick Bigelow," *Who was Who in America with World Notables*, Vol. IV, p. 85; and Mabie, "Editor of Good Housekeeping," p. 3.

13. Waller-Zuckerman, "Vera Connolly," pp. 87, 88; Bigelow, ed. *Good Housekeeping Book of Marriage*; and Copperfield, "Women's Magazines," p. 53.

14. Beard and Beard, *America*, pp. 741–43; Ulrich, "Why Women's Magazines?" p. 367; Copperfield, "Women's Magazines," pp. 22, 23; and Uzzell, "Love Pulps," p. 37.

15. Schuler, *Lady Editor*, p. 122; Zuckerman, "Pathway"; Gould and Gould, *American Story*, pp. 251, 252; "Workshop Housewarming," p. 189; Mabie, "Editor Needs Courage," p. 7; and LS, "How Many Miles to a Journal Page," p. 4, CP, File Drawer 3.

16. LS, Transcript of talk at JWTC staff meeting, May 26, 1930, p. 17, JWTP, Box 8.

17. Ibid., p. 20.

18. Cohn, *Improbable Fiction*, pp. 188, 189.

19. Ibid., pp. 194, 195.

20. West, III, *American Authors*, pp. 103–13; and Peterson, *Magazines*, pp. 118, 119.

21. Lane quoted in interview with *The Brooklyn Eagle*, 1929, copy in GBLVLP.

22. GBL to HHH, September 20, 1932, HHHP.

23. Gould quoted in "Meet the Up-to-date Editors," p. 8.

24. Chafe, *American Woman*, pp. 108, 177, 178.

25. "Editorial," *LHJ* (January 1941): 33.

26. "Should Mothers of Young Children Work?" cited in Engman, *Gould Era*, p. 81.

27. Gould quoted in "Workshop Housewarming," p. 214.

28. "Meet the Up-to-date Editors," p. 8; and BG&BBGP.

29. *Midas Gold*, pp. 84, 85.

30. *Story of a Pantry Shelf*, p. 15.

31. Drewry, "Good Housekeeping," p. 319; and Mabie, "Editor of Good Housekeeping," p. 3.

32. Currie quoted in Ulmann, *Portrait Gallery*, p. 48.

33. Gould and Gould, *American Story*, p. 201.

34. Ibid., p. 161.

35. Ibid., p. 155.

36. Ibid., p. 156.

37. Ibid., pp. 210–12.

38. Makosky, *Portrayal*, p. 19; and Dagavarian, "Content Analysis."

39. *Delineator* (September 1929): 4; and Waller (Zuckerman), "Vera Connolly," pp. 80–88.

40. 1928 article idea list in VCP.

41. Sanders, *Thompson*, p. 224; and Gould and Gould, *American Story*, p. 186.

42. Thompson, *Courage*, p. viii. This is a collection of Thompson's columns from the *Journal*.

43. Ibid., p. viii. See also DT to BG, January 21, 1954, BG&BBGP.

44. Saunders, *Thompson*, p. 352.

45. Rinehart, "Chaotic Decade," pp. 35, 172, 176ff; and Cohn, *Improbable Fiction*, pp. 106, 107, 194, 195.

46. Gould and Gould, *American Story*, p. 160.

47. Matthews, *Housewife*, pp. 145–71; Shapiro, *Perfection Salad*; and Strasser, *Never Done*.

48. Van Rensselaer worked for *LHJ* and *Delineator*, Fisher for *GH*, Frederick for *LHJ* and *Designer*, Bane for *LHJ*, Splint for *McCall's* and *WHC*, Blinn for *Delineator* and *LHJ*, and Bentley for *GH*, *LHJ*, and *Delineator*.

49. *Story of a Pantry Shelf*, p. 14; and MVRP.

50. "Martha Van Rensselaer," in *Notable American Women*, 3, pp. 513, 514; and "Martha Van Rensselaer," *Dictionary of American Biography* (2) XIX: 208, 209.

51. WA to MVR, April 24, 1901; and WA to MVR, February 12, 1907, in MVRP, Box 33.

52. Lilian Dynevor Rice to MVR, January 21, 1907; TD to MVR, November 16, 1908; TD to MVR, March 23, 1910; MVR to TD, 1910; Stella Reid Crothers to MVR, November 5, 1908; JET to MVR, November 5, 1908; JET to MVR, December 18, 1908; JET to MVR, September 27, 1909; Edith Burtis to MVR, August 9, 1910; and M. C. Bette to MVR, October 4, 1910. All in MVRP.

53. MMM to MVR, June 1, 1915; and MMM to MVR, September 27, 1915; in MVRP.

54. Van Rensselaer, "Big Business, This," pp. 26, 80.

55. Schuler et al., *Lady Editor*, pp. 124–26; and Frederick, *Mrs. Consumer*, p. 284.

56. Schuler et al., *Lady Editor*, pp. 118, 126; and Chafe, *American Woman*, pp. 106–7.

57. See e.g., Bane, "New Values," pp. 37, 124; and LS, Transcript of talk to JWTC Staff, May 26, 1930, pp. 9, 10, JWTP, Box 8.

58. CMFP, Folder One.

59. Strasser, *Never Done*, p. 249; and Waller-Zuckerman and Carsky, "Contributions of Women," pp. 313–18.

60. Frederick, *Mrs. Consumer*, p. 336.

61. Zuckerman, "Mrs. Christine Frederick."

62. See e.g., K. Harriman to CMF, September 22, 1915, CMFP.

9

Attracting Advertising

> Perhaps the prominence and dominance of *Woman's Home Companion* can be most clearly defined by emphasizing the obvious fact that it long functioned as a huge trade paper. A super-stupendous-Gargantuan salesmanship operation, delivering the goods, or the latest news concerning them, direct from producer to consumer.
>
> —Amos Stote, "Crowell," 1945[1]

The 1920s saw steady increases in ad dollars expended in magazines generally. Experiences in World War I set the stage for this boom. During the war ad agents had effectively demonstrated the power of advertising by promoting Liberty Bonds, encouraging food conservation, calling for Army recruits, and boosting public morale. This work raised the status of the whole profession as well as demonstrating the persuasive powers of advertising. The passage of the excess profits tax in 1917, which allowed advertising expenditures to be deducted as business expenses, also spurred on companies' use of advertising. Once started, such spending proved heady, and advertising expenditures showed no decline with the 1922 repeal of the tax.[2]

Advertising volume increased enormously in the twenties. Approximately $682 million was spent on advertising of all kinds in 1914, $1,409 million in 1919, and $2,987 million by 1929.[3] Magazines consistently took in about 15 percent of dollars spent on national advertising. The Magazine Advertising Bureau reported just over $28 million spent on periodical advertising in 1915, almost $94.5 million in 1919, and a jump to over $196 million in 1929.[4]

Advertising expenditures overall dropped precipitously in the 1930s as a result of the Depression, and magazine advertising suffered along with other categories as both ad volume and ad revenues declined. Publishers were forced to cut rates. But throughout the thirties magazines actually gained on newspapers in the percentage of national advertising carried. By 1939 firms advertising nationally placed more copy in periodicals than in newspapers. Magazines' overall share of ad dollars had risen to 19.8 percent by 1945, before declining to 12.8 percent in 1955. Advertising in women's journals typically followed the trends of general magazine advertising in these years.[5]

Advertising dollars remained highly concentrated in a small number of journals throughout the twenties, as they had been in the century's early years. Curtis Co. publications still enjoyed a large lead in overall ad dollars, a testimony to the lasting effect of the early, aggressive sales efforts made by Cyrus Curtis. For example, Curtis Co. reported that in 1920 its three journals took in 46 percent of all ad dollars placed in magazines, and noted that *Ladies' Home Journal* garnered 33 percent of all advertising going into women's journals.[6] Crowell Co. took second place in 1925, attracting 11 percent of all magazine advertising.[7] However, Curtis titles' dominance gradually declined, as its titles dropped from holding 49 percent of magazine advertising in 1925 to 31 percent in 1931, with a large chunk switching to Crowell Co. publications.

ADVERTISING IN WOMEN'S MAGAZINES

Advertising revenues in women's magazines soared in the 1920s, enabling editors to create ever larger and glossier issues. When Arthur Vance wanted Edith Wharton's work to appear in *Pictorial Review*, he could afford to pay her the large sums she demanded, something editors of more prestigious literary journals found difficult. While acutely aware that advertising dollars provided the lifeblood of the mass market journals, in these years of abundance most women's magazine editors focused chiefly on creating a good product purchasers would want to read and advertisers would want to use. When the Depression cut short the flow of advertising dollars, editors looked for ways to lure advertisers back. At times editorial integrity suffered.

Women's journals as a group consistently attracted about a third of all magazine advertising dollars throughout the twenties and thirties, reaching a high of 39 percent in 1932.[8] In some product categories women's journals attained far higher shares. For example, in 1927 women's titles attracted almost 72 percent of magazine advertising for soap and housekeeping supplies, over 70 percent for food and food beverages, over 48 percent for drug and toilet goods, and over 45 percent of all clothing and dry goods.[9]

Throughout the twenties ad dollars provided a growing portion of the revenue generated by the major women's journals. Magazines generally hit a high in 1930 when over 60 percent of their revenue came from advertising. The ratio for the most attractive advertising media could be much higher. Longtime advertiser favorite *Ladies' Home Journal* garnered over 80 percent of its total revenue from advertising in the prosperous 1920s, a figure that fell to the average for all Curtis Co. publications of 75 percent in the mid-thirties.[10]

Another measure of advertising's heightened importance comes from publications' editorial/advertising page ratios. *Ladies' Home Journal*'s ratio had reversed itself from about 60/40 (editorial/advertising) at the turn of the century to approximately 40/60 by the mid-1920s, a 50 percent increase in advertising volume.[11] In the early 1930s about half the pages in the major women's journals contained advertising, ranging from *Pictorial Review*'s low of 49 percent to *Good Housekeeping*'s high of 60 percent.[12]

Limits to the amount of advertising an editor could include existed. Bruce Gould at the *Journal* tried to keep his editorial/advertising ratio at 40/60. But he admitted that this ratio, which worked well with a 300-page journal, might founder with a magazine running only 100 pages. The acceptable amount of advertising stood higher at fashion titles, where editors believed that advertising constituted a crucial part of the product readers wanted. During the twenties and thirties, *Vogue* consistently contained the largest volume of advertising in a women's publication.[13]

Throughout the twenties *Ladies' Home Journal* led in advertising revenues. For its April 1922 issue, the *Journal* secured well over a million dollars worth of advertising, the highest amount captured by a single issue of *any* magazine up to that time.[14] In the early twenties the *Journal* attracted more than twice the advertising dollars of its nearest challengers.[15] And even though *Pictorial Review*'s circulation neared the *Journal*'s, the *Journal*'s quality image with advertisers enabled it to draw in significantly larger amounts of advertising.[16] However, when the Depression hit the *Journal* was poorly positioned to weather the crisis, suffering from a weak circulation sales team, uninspired editing, and reluctance to drop ad rates. By 1933 the *Journal*'s position as frontrunner had diminished, attracting only 21 percent of women's magazine ad revenues, down from 37 percent eleven years earlier.[17] The following year *Good Housekeeping* was out in front.

Of course, the Depression hurt all Big Six journals, as well as the magazine industry generally. Advertising as a whole dropped almost a billion dollars from 1929 to 1930, falling over another billion by 1933.[18] Just as the entrance of radio increased the competition for ad dollars, advertisers cut back, becoming more selective. Total advertising volume for the top six women's titles peaked in 1930, then fell off sharply.[19] Revenues from food advertising, a major ad category for women's journals, dropped 30.3 percent between 1928 and 1936.[20] Another important ad category, toilet goods, plummeted 40 percent in its spending on magazine advertising between its high of 1930 and its low in 1935.[21] By 1931, when it was clear that the economic depression was staying for a while, all the major women's journals were losing ad revenue. However, by 1934 four titles (all except *Ladies' Home Journal* and *Delineator*) saw their revenues start to climb back again.[22]

Previously much of the struggle for advertisers' dollars had centered on nonprice competition, with publishers vying with one another to offer services such as market research, audience surveys, and editorial support of advertised products; all these activities continued and accelerated during the Depression years, but economic conditions forced ad rate cuts as well. In earlier years large circulations had attracted advertisers, but in the Depression all most advertisers saw were the large advertising bills those mammoth circulations generated.

Many women's journals (including *Ladies' Home Journal* despite initial refusals) cut their ad rates, leading to lower ad revenues. Of the Big Six only *Good Housekeeping* did not cut its rates.[23] For some titles these rate reductions came as part of overall company policy. For example, Crowell Co. announced decreased ad rates for all four of its magazines effective July 1933, due to "country-wide" conditions.[24]

A sag in the economy in 1937 forced the *Journal* and *McCall's* to reduce their rates again. However, by 1938 recovery was apace for women's magazines, although advertising had not yet reached its earlier heights, and some titles, such as *Pictorial Review*, continued to struggle. Conversely, *Good Housekeeping* was experiencing great success; despite its fourth place in circulation in that year, the Hearst Co. title, which described itself as "The Buying Directory of the American Family," took in more advertising (pages and dollar amount) than any other women's journal.[25]

By 1940 the older women's journals still had not returned to their 1920s volume of advertising and they continued to compete intensively for the still limited ad dollars.[26] Their grip on advertisers' dollars spent in women's magazines had slowly diminished, with the percentage of advertising dollars garnered by the Big Six dropping from 78.4 percent in 1931 to 64.5 percent in 1938.[27]

The Depression hurt fashion magazine advertising, but the top journals rebounded. *Harper's Bazaar* climbed from almost $1.25 million of advertising in 1931 to almost $2.5 million in 1938. *Vogue* increased its ad revenues from just over $2.5 million in 1931 to well over $3.5 million in 1938, 7 percent of all ad revenues going to women's journals that year. Both titles dropped after a 1937 peak, but showed sharp advertising gains in 1943 and 1944.[28]

COMPETITION FOR ADVERTISING DOLLARS

Declines in advertising expenditures heightened the danger posed by radio. *Fortune* noted in 1937 that

Within the framework of their original pattern, the women's magazines have shown a fascinating adroitness in changing with the times—until recently. But they have as yet found no answer to the threat of radio, which, whether or not it lessens the attention paid to women's magazines, definitely has cut a deep gouge into women's magazine advertising.[29]

Magazine publishers had initially welcomed the new medium. In radio's early days *Harper's Bazaar* sponsored a fashion talk show on the airwaves, *Woman's Home Companion* featured stories about amateur radio operators, and

Curtis Co. conducted a market study of the radio industry.[30] Throughout the twenties ads for radios appeared regularly in *Good Housekeeping*, *Ladies' Home Journal*, and *McCall's*. However, the magazine industry watched anxiously as radio gained listeners, increasing from a presence in about sixty thousand homes in 1922 to 5 million in 1926.[31] But the real peril lay not in a defecting audience (readers stayed loyal and circulations continued to grow throughout the 1920s and 1930s), but rather in the potential abandonment by advertisers. As late as 1927 most broadcasting stations did not sell their air time. But by the late twenties the network affiliated stations had begun to do so, and radio's ability to attract ad dollars worried magazine personnel.[32] In the severest years of the Depression, radio's threat seemed especially strong, not just because spending-shy advertisers gave some of their scarce dollars to radio, but also because even as magazine advertising volume declined (cut in half from 1929 to 1933), radio's ad volume rose (increasing from almost nothing to $32 million in 1933). Radio's advertising revenues had not reached anywhere near those of magazines (over $97 million in 1933), but radio advertising's upward direction was troubling.[33]

Of course, even as they recognized radio as a rival for advertiser dollars, publishers also explored the promotional possibilities of the newcomer. *Woman's Home Companion* led efforts in this direction. It hired a nationwide team of women, each called "Jean Abby," to discuss products advertised in the *Companion* on the new medium. And the *Companion* used radio to publicize feats such as the opening of its model house in Scituate, Massachusetts, with Governor James Curley dramatically describing the house's features over the air.[34]

Radio hurt periodicals in terms of advertising lost, but the economic depression hurt much more. And newspapers lost more to radio in these years than did magazines.[35] However, women's journals had special fears, as the radio "soaps" targeted the same audiences (and hence potential advertisers) their pages did.[36]

The new confessional publications aimed at working class women, such as the wildly popular *True Story*, also posed threats to the traditional women's journals for advertising dollars. Initially shunned by advertisers, the circulation numbers these titles drew eventually overcame advertiser reluctance. By 1927 *True Story* carried over $3.5 million of advertising (more than the amount acquired by *Vogue*), and by 1931 it had attracted almost $4.5 million, as more and more advertisers recognized the title's readers as a big market with adequate spending power.[37] Fiction magazines such as *Cosmopolitan* and *Red Book* and the increasingly widespread movie titles such as *Motion Picture*, *Classic*, and *Photoplay* also provided competition for advertising dollars, particularly for products bought by young women such as cosmetics.[38] For example, in 1937 the trade journal *Printer's Ink* listed eight movie publications under its category "Women's Magazines." Together these titles took in 137,593 lines of advertising in one month, an amount slightly over the combined monthly total of leaders *Good Housekeeping* and *Woman's Home Companion*. Romance magazines and radio fan publications also contended with the traditional women's journals for the tightly held advertising dollars.[39]

As a group the major women's journals maintained lower ad rates than those of other monthly publications and those of weekly magazines. These rates resulted largely from the women's titles' big circulations. All other things being equal, the smaller the circulation, the higher the line rate, and the larger the circulation, the lower the line rate.[40] Page rates increased in the twenties, but since circulations of most major women's journals grew as well, the rate per thousand often stayed the same or declined. Frequently, advertisers received more for their money. Curtis Co. used this argument in the early 1930s when taking its initial stance of refusing to lower ad rates. Research director Charles Parlin stated that "the increase in rates since 1921 has been more than offset by the increase in circulation which those two publications [the *Journal* and *Saturday Evening Post*] have been delivering to the advertiser in excess of the guaranteed circulation."[41] But all that many advertisers saw was the large total cost.

Prestige fashion books such as *Harper's Bazaar* and *Vogue* set significantly higher rates per thousand than the mass circulation women's journals through the thirties and forties. In addition to the high-class audience they delivered, these publications also charged more because they offered superior quality in paper, design, and reproduction.[42] The younger women's fashion and lifestyle books, such as *Mademoiselle* and *Glamour*, set significantly lower rates than *Harper's Bazaar* and *Vogue*. *Mademoiselle*'s rate, higher than those of the Big Six, reflected the magazine's targeting of an affluent, albeit younger, readership. *Glamour* charged less, matching the rates of *Good Housekeeping*, *Ladies' Home Journal*, and the other major women's service titles. *Seventeen*, appearing on the scene in 1945, posted rates slightly lower than those of the big women's journals.[43]

Advertisers thus had a choice of rates, keyed to audience and circulation, but the marketplace forced titles with similar audiences to keep their rates close to one another.

EDITORS AND ADVERTISING

Women's magazines experienced special pressures because the editorial material frequently had a direct connection to products being advertised. As Bruce Gould admitted,

Problems of maintaining independence of the advertiser were more difficult on a woman's magazine than on the Post, which did not have pages of beauty aids or show pictures of ideal laundries (with trade-marked automatic dryers), did not use recipes (cake mixes, canned soups, coffee are advertisers).[44]

Service departments devoted to topics such as fashion, cooking, cleaning, and beauty felt the most obvious pressure to discuss advertisers' products favorably. Ad agent Helen Woodward reported that she had found the women's journals quite willing to print as service news the information she gave them about her clients' products. For example, Woodward enlisted the aid of fashion editors to help make gingham cloth a trendy material.[45] But not even fiction was sacrosanct. One 1930s critic of the women's journals noted that

No longer, for example, in many of these magazines, does our hero toss with over-wrought nerves due to a too generous shot of coffee. No more does the fictional house-wife complain of frigidity in her oil burning system. Nor have stenographers and office boys a monopoly on gum chewing; recently a well-known chewing gum firm communicated with the editor of one of our leading female publications, insisting that he wanted Nice People shown chewing gum as well.[46]

During the 1920s all the major women's magazine editors competed to match the advertising revenues generated by *Ladies' Home Journal*. Editors needed to do more than simply build circulation to catch up to the *Journal*. Strategies to attract advertising included building prestige (*Good Housekeeping*), developing a reputation as an up-and-coming publication (*Pictorial Review* and *McCall's*), creating an editorial environment supportive to advertising (the *Companion's* specialty), and regional advertising (pioneered by publisher Conde Nast at *Vogue*). Other moves involved redesigning the magazine, adding departments, and creating a flood of promotional materials directed at advertisers.

In 1925, for example, *Woman's Home Companion's* launched an eight-year campaign that featured a monthly editorial column extolling the virtues of advertising. The series claimed to be educating consumers, but had as its hidden agenda pleasing advertisers. Editor Gertrude Battles Lane believed that it would encourage advertisers to come into the *Companion's* pages.[47] The campaign illustrates the pressure felt by women's magazines to gain advertising. It also shows Lane's keen understanding of the crucial financial role played by advertising.[48]

The *Companion's* campaign for national advertising continued through the early thirties. It fit logically with the direction being taken by the Crowell Publishing Co. as a whole. Led by President Tom Beck, the company stressed that the *Companion's* pages could "pre-sell" goods for manufacturers, that is, expose consumers to branded goods in the service departments and features.[49] Over time the editorials received increasing support for their twin messages of educated consumption and the importance of nationally advertised brands. In the late 1920s the *Companion* started listing advertised products in a separate index. By the 1930s columns appeared devoted to new cosmetics and gadgets. By 1932 the journal had begun sponsoring its radio show, which told listeners where they could purchase products endorsed by the magazine.

While steady pressure came from advertisers, each editor drew his or her own boundary. *Woman's Home Companion* supported breast feeding of babies, angering advertisers of canned milk.[50] Early in their career at the *Journal*, the Goulds refused a quarter million dollars worth of advertising for a feminine hygiene product their experts found unacceptable. The pharmaceutical manufacturer retaliated by pulling out almost another quarter million dollars worth of ads for its other products from Curtis publications.[51] But, in general, with competition for advertising dollars steep, women's magazines cooperated with advertisers whenever possible. For example, when the J. Walter Thompson agency decided that its 1930 Cutex nail polish ads needed the backing of experts to give prestige and authority, staffers contacted beauty editors at the major women's journals, asking permission to use their names in the Cutex ads, as well as quotes from any articles the editors had published on manicuring. The agency secured agreement from beauty editors at all the Big Six magazines as well as at *Vogue* and *Harper's Bazaar*.[52]

PROMOTIONAL AND MERCHANDISING EFFORTS

Ladies' Home Journal prepared numerous promotional pamphlets targeting advertisers. A 1941 effort stressed the huge responses *Journal* articles generated, noting that in 1940 readers sent in over 1 million letters. This brochure also demonstrates the *Journal*'s aggressive merchandising efforts. It contained cards displaying products featured in *Journal* ads that retailers could set up in their stores. The folder also carried testimonials from large companies such as Kotex, Kleenex, Jergens, Knox Gelatin, and Gimbels department store, stating their satisfaction with *Journal* advertising, which they claimed yielded the lowest cost per inquiry.[53]

Curtis Co. was not alone in its retailer tie-up efforts. In the thirties McCall Co. began mailing out the McCall's Meal Planner to the newly popular self-service food stores across the country. The Meal Planner reprinted food and homemaking tips from *McCall's*, and allowed retailers to feature ten or more products carried by the store and shown in *McCall's*. The stores in turn used displays and promotions stating that the products were advertised in *McCall's*. Stores, products, and magazine all benefited. Readers gained information, but in the context of buying.[54]

Crowell Co. published several promotional booklets directed at advertisers. One particularly inventive creation, titled *Papa Gander*, featured rhymes and hand-colored pictures. It touted the services offered to readers in the *Companion* and described ways these features dove-tailed with advertisers' interests. The main message was the *Companion*'s superiority in preselling. One set of verses reassured advertisers about interior design editor Virginia Hamill, declaring that

The rugs she displays in a colorful setting—The fixtures that blend with the paper or pain—The silver and dishes on tables she's setting Might all be unadvertised goods—but they ain't. The linens are labeled—the blankets are branded—Why even the tile in the kitchen is yours.

The booklet ended with the cry: "The magazine whose force you've seen, Behind the versifying, Created Demand to beat the Band, And smooth road to buying."[55]

The *Companion* also promoted merchandise advertised in its pages through a national force of females. Under the names of Jean Abbey (for department stores) and Carolyn Price (for grocery stores), representatives hired by the magazine aired radio broadcasts discussing and decorated store windows with products featured in the *Companion*. Readers felt they had a local link to the publication (and its products) and advertisers received an enhanced promotion.[56]

Butterick Co. distributed a book in 1925 that highlighted the home service material in *Delineator* and *Designer*. The volume included a quantitative content analysis of the top women's journals, revealing the Butterick titles' high percentage of food and housekeeping articles, features that assisted advertisers. The company published another book that same year promoting its publications particularly to manufacturers of building, household, and decoration materials. This new piece argued that *Delineator* and *Designer* should be considered not simply "women's magazines" but "consumer trade magazines" in these areas.[57]

Good Housekeeping published promotional materials similar to those put out by Butterick Co. A 1930 effort directed at advertisers featured *Good Housekeeping*'s Studio of Furnishings and Decoration. The Studio displayed trade-marked items in its rooms and listed the manufacturers, making the products easy for readers to purchase.[58] The brochure noted that between two and three thousand readers wrote to the Studio monthly for details about items featured or for informational booklets, indicating powerful reader interest. Retailers also turned to the Studio, according to this pamphlet, requesting advance information about goods to be shown.

THE ADVERTISING GUARANTEE

Many women's titles continued to guarantee their advertising. *Good Housekeeping* did so most explicitly, with most goods and services appearing in its pages tested and approved through its Institute. Dr. Harvey Wiley, Director of *Good Housekeeping*'s Bureau of Foods, Sanitation and Health from 1912 through 1929, reviewed all ads for food, drugs, and toilet articles, sending product samples to a commercial laboratory for analysis before making his judgement.[59]

After Wiley retired *Good Housekeeping*'s standards appear to have declined. A study performed in 1935 showed that despite *Good Housekeeping*'s strong guarantee concerning the testing of goods advertised in its pages, exaggerated product claims slipped in, particularly for personal care items. For example, *Good Housekeeping* "permits Colgate to claim that the use of their tooth paste is 'a sure way to correct bad breath.' Bad breath may have an organic cause that no tooth paste can affect. Vita-ray is permitted to claim that it 'makes skin young again.'"[60]

Other titles guaranteeing ads in their pages included *Woman's Home Companion*, *Designer*, *Ladies' Home Journal*, *McCall's*, and *Delineator*. All carried ads that were at least deceptive if not outright dangerous, particularly for cosmetic and drug products. Only *Pictorial Review* did not carry any specific guarantee for items advertised in its pages.[61] These guarantees and seals influenced readers to believe the advertising they saw in their favorite publications.

Many attacks on advertising in the early thirties focused on cosmetics, drugs, and foods, all big advertisers in women's journals. Freckle cream and pain relief remedies in the *Delineator*, toothpaste and cathartics in *McCall's*, and vacuum cleaners in *Good Housekeeping* all received censure, as well as cosmetic products.[62] Criticism of ads in women's and general interest magazines formed part of the general efforts in the thirties to regulate deceptive advertising. This movement came to fruition with the passage in 1938 of the Wheeler-Lea amendment to the 1914 Federal Trade Commission (FTC) Act. Wheeler-Lea empowered the FTC to act against deceptive advertising and expanded its control over food, drug, and cosmetic advertising.[63] This enhanced power enabled the FTC to bring action against *Good Housekeeping*'s Guaranty and Seal of Approval the following year.

The campaign to strengthen governmental oversight of food and drugs had begun in 1933. Some women's magazine publishers fought these efforts in part because their advertisers opposed them.[64] *Woman's Home Companion*'s editor Gertrude Battles Lane refused First Lady Eleanor Roosevelt's request to write an article for the magazine in support of the proposed legislation. Indeed, Lane released a statement titled "The Press and the Tugwell bill," where she bluntly explained that she opposed the bill because it would prompt manufacturers in the food, drug, and cosmetic industries to cut back advertising expenditures.[65]

Hearst Co. fought the quality grade labeling provisions some consumer groups wanted included in the law because such regulations would have made *Good Housekeeping*'s Seal of Approval unnecessary. These provisions, also opposed by a majority of the food industry, failed to make it into the final legislation. Eventually the Federal Food, Drug, and Cosmetic Act of 1938 passed, much watered down from the original Tugwell bill, adding cosmetics to the products regulated by the Food and Drug Administration (FDA), tightening regulations against false product claims on labels, and forcing manufacturers to provide hard evidence of products' safety.

MARKET RESEARCH

Market research activities performed by women's magazine publishers escalated in the twenties and thirties. The Audit Bureau of Circulation continued to provide standardized information on circulation. In addition, publishers of women's titles designed studies to convince manufacturers of the importance and effectiveness of advertising generally. They attempted to point up the advantages of magazines as opposed to radio as an advertising medium. Each publisher also tried to prove that he had the highest quality readership.

Competitive circulation studies dominated the publishers' research of the twenties, with each magazine delineating the special characteristics of its own readership. By the thirties income, buying power, and neighborhoods formed categories of special interest. Large general interest publications like *Life* and *Saturday Evening Post* sponsored much research, but competition in the women's magazine market fueled many studies, often earlier than in the general interest field.[66]

Curtis Co. led in the use of in-home interviewing techniques in order to discover consumption behavior and preferences. As part of its program, in 1920 Curtis Co. canvassed an entire city (Sabetha, Kansas) and the adjacent 144 square miles. Interviewers noted all relevant features of the homes, marked down brands of goods in the house, and, of course, recorded the magazines present. To measure the use and consumption of grocery products, the company performed a national pantry inventory of 3,123 homes in 1931.[67]

Curtis also led in efforts to define neighborhoods by income and educational level. Curtis used a four-tier system, and assured advertisers that the editorial matter of Curtis magazines, as well as their selling efforts, targeted the top two tiers where individuals possessed the money to buy goods.

Crowell Co. conducted a wide variety of research, leading in efforts to collect data from readers. The *Companion*'s Reader-Editor panel, formed in 1936, provides an example of this. Composed of 1500 women chosen from the *Companion* subscription list, Reader-Editors faithfully filled out monthly questionnaires on a wide variety of topics. To avoid respondent fatigue or bias, readers could only remain panel members for three years.[68] The questionnaires yielded a high average response rate of 76 percent.

In addition to being used by *Companion* staffers to edit the magazine, Crowell packaged information culled from the Reader-Editors in ways useful to advertisers. Panel data formed the basis for numerous studies on particular products written with advertisers in mind.[69] As two observers of the panel noted,

The reports make no pretense at being market surveys, but the advertiser gets from them a very complete picture of how, for example, the 1,000 Reader-Editors spent the preceding Christmas holidays; what they served for dinner, what they received and gave as gifts, and the number of people they entertained.[70]

McCall Co. focused its work on combating competing women's journals. The company carried out a series of comparative circulation studies, complete with brightly colored maps, in the years 1929 through 1931. The presentation of results exemplifies the competitive pressure to show research results in an advantageous light. McCall Co.'s maps focused on the number of counties in which a publication held top circulation, highlighting *McCall's* lead in this statistic; in 1929, for example, *McCall's* ranked as the top circulator in 1,649 counties (correlating with the fact that it led in small towns, a widely dispersed population). In the accompanying statistics a title only reaped circulation figures from those counties where it led. This manner of presenting the numbers downplayed the fact that in total circulation, *McCall's* ranked fourth, behind *Ladies' Home Journal*, *Pictorial Review*, and *Woman's Home Companion*.

An active marketing department labored at *Good Housekeeping's* publisher Hearst Co. Here much of the researchers' work focused on readership studies. The primary emphasis lay in showing that readers valued *Good Housekeeping* over other publications. These studies clearly illustrate the credibility problem such publisher-sponsored research faced. A 1928 report of survey results published by *Good Housekeeping* had specifically attempted to meet the objections of advertisers who suspected bias in magazine sponsored research. The survey measured reader preferences, strength of preferences, and demographic characteristics. When discussing the survey's results, the publisher addressed head-on the credibility issue and explained that for this reason a number of different advertising agencies had conducted the research.[71] Each agency picked a geographic area to survey. Unfortunately, a reader of the 1928 report's results experiences the very suspicions *Good Housekeeping* hoped to allay; *Good Housekeeping* itself topped the list, both as a magazine mentioned as one read regularly and as the one magazine respondents would most like to have in the home.

PRODUCTS AND APPEALS

Ads appearing in women's journals influenced readers and formed a significant part of magazine content. Most obviously, ads conveyed factual information about products. More subtly, they helped shape women's vision of themselves.

The types of products advertised in magazines generally shifted from those seen earlier. In the twenties advertising for personal care products increased, advertising for apparel declined, and advertising for durable goods remained relatively steady.[72] Radios, automobiles, and electrical household appliances all made their appearances in ads. Women's journal advertising largely followed these general trends, although certain products, such as cosmetics and household items, tended to be more heavily advertised to women, based on perceived differences in consumption by sex; the targeted promotional strategies of advertisers in turn reinforced this gender stereotyping of consumers.

For several years after World War I women's magazines had featured a variety of car advertisements. In 1927 three of the major ad accounts carried by the *Ladies' Home Journal* came from car manufacturers Willys-Overland, Buick Motor Co., and Chrysler Sales Corp.[73] Automobile ads stressed features car makers thought would appeal to women such as ease, style, and model choice. Women in these ads examined or rode in the cars instead of simply serving as decorative objects.[74] The decline in car advertising in women's journals, coinciding with the economic depression, was not reversed until almost fifty years later.

Cigarette advertising appeared in women's publications very gradually. Women had begun smoking in greater numbers during World War I, often while engaged in war work. More women took up the practice in the twenties. Advertisers approached the potentially large female market with excitement tempered with caution, as women smoking in public still provoked controversy and debate.[75] But by the late twenties, some women's journals had dared to print cigarette or tobacco advertising. By the early 1930s all the major women's journals accepted cigarette advertising, later refused by *Good Housekeeping*.

Women's titles remained wary about alcohol advertising. *Ladies' Home Journal* explained itself on this issue by noting in a full page ad that

You, the readers, are the guests of the Ladies' Home Journal as soon as you step within our cover-walls. Advertisers too, are guests—welcome because of the great budget of news and helpful information they bring you every month! . . . There are some paying guests whom the *Journal* does NOT welcome! The *Journal* believes that every reader has the right to decide such questions for herself. **We will not try to influence you by taking liquor advertising.** The refusal undoubtedly has cost the Journal a great many dollars in recent years. (emphasis in the original)[76]

Crowell Co.'s weekly *Collier's* came out against Prohibition in the twenties, but Crowell Co. management directed the *Companion* to stay off the subject.[77]

Ladies' Home Journal had triumphantly and accurately declared the twenties to be the "Cosmetic Age." The personal care product category grew both in sales and advertising.[78] One conservative estimate put the amount spent on cosmetics and beauty products in 1930 at three quarters of a billion dollars. Christine Frederick calculated that in 1929 adult women in the United States bought, on average, over a pound of face powder and eight rouge compacts.[79]

Increasingly, cosmetic ads promised beauty and sexual attractiveness and featured models with such attributes. J. Walter Thompson's Helen Resor had first employed an explicit sexual appeal with her "The Skin You Love to Touch" campaign for Woodbury's facial soap in the teens and such strategies appeared increasingly in the twenties.[80] While sexual appeals appeared in ads targeted at men and women, female sexuality was the draw in both. This advertising both hastened and reflected changing attitudes about beauty products. Advertising did not create sex appeal, but it used this lure, taking advantage of the loosened moral code of the 1920s.

Cosmetic ads eventually came under severe attack in the 1930s, smirching the women's publications that published them in the process. Some criticism stressed the unrealistic hopes the ads created, promising women physical transformations. Christine Frederick censured the use of the "pretty girl" in ads, an image with a kind of chorus girl beauty, rather than the natural beauty of real women.[81]

Additional criticism centered on basic issues of product safety, a crucial point because readers had developed the habit of relying on women's journals to give them honest information. Such reader trust was at times ill-advised. For example, *Good Housekeeping*, which maintained perhaps the most stringent product standards, made news when it accepted its first ad for hair dye, allowing "Grayban" into its pages in the early 1930s. Yet testing revealed that Grayban contained a dangerous substance (bismuth salts) and completely failed in its claim to restore hair to its natural color. Other cosmetic products advertised in *Good Housekeeping* that proved either unsafe or misleading in their claims included the wave-set lotion La Gerardine and the astringent Ambrosia.[82] Ads for another dangerous hair dye, Mary T. Goldman's, appeared in the *Companion* despite the magazine's assurance that "The appearance of an advertisement in the *Woman's Home Companion* is a specific warranty of the product advertised and of the integrity of the house sponsoring the advertisement."[83]

ADVERTISING IMAGES

Physically, ads changed in size, placement, and color. In the teens a trend had begun for magazines to shift from "standard" to "flat" pages. This latter page type enabled advertising to mingle easily with editorial matter, and by 1920 most of the major women's journals had made the switch.[84] Ads used color with greater regularity than editorial material as advertisers forged ahead of magazine publishers in their desire and ability to pay for vibrant color and innovative graphics. Ads became larger and more colorful. By 1920 the *Journal* averaged almost forty pages an issue of colored ads.[85] The trend toward communicating with a full page ad continued; for example, an analysis of ads in *Vogue* for the years 1935 through 1944 found 44 percent of them full page. Some major advertisers even began taking out multiple ad pages in a single issue.[86]

The greater use of eye-catching color, coupled with larger ad space and the increasing movement of ads forward through the magazine left readers exposed more frequently and more intensely to selling messages. Color ads attracted readers' attention and memory, as did the bigger pictures that began to dominate ads, crowding out the copy.[87]

In the thirties ads shrank a bit in size, along with advertising budgets, but the color remained. Photographs became more common, propelled in part because they cost less than drawings. By 1932 the *Ladies' Home Journal* featured photographs in over 50 percent of its ads. Photographs also added an air of realism to the journals, although most ads still revealed what their creators believed readers aspired to, rather than an accurate reflection of the world.[88]

While advertisers experimented and innovated with research and technology to create better ads, content remained conservative. The basic message exhorted readers to buy. Female images in ads specifically aimed at women remained stereotypical throughout this period. Women were seen primarily as housewives or decorative objects, particularly in women's magazine advertising. The home provided the most frequent setting. Few ads presented women working outside the home, unlike earlier in the century when appeals to the "business girl" had showed up. Fewer servants appeared and women in ads increasingly performed their own domestic tasks with the aid of appliances, a reality for many women. Motherhood as a profession, a concept gaining approval in the culture at large, figured more and more in ads, even as the birth rate declined.[89]

Testimonials in ads, sprouting in the twenties, fit in with these traditional images, yet offered glimpses of women successful in the world outside the home. Helen Resor claimed credit for popularizing this tactic, which frequently used women. Ads featured actresses such as Joan Crawford, Janet Gaynor, and Clara Bow, socially prominent women such as *Vogue* publisher's wife Mrs. Conde Nast and Alice Roosevelt Longworth and feminist and society woman Mrs. O.H.P. Belmont as well as famous figures like aviatrix Amelia Earhart.[90] European royalty and medical experts appeared as well. While this technique continued on into the 1930s (photographer Margaret Bourke-White and actress Carole Lombard were among those featured), it attracted increasing attacks from the advertising industry and skepticism from the public.[91]

Advertising in general in the twenties made several kinds of shifts from earlier promotional appeals. Increasingly, ad copy emphasized the pleasures of consumption rather than the satisfaction of a utilitarian lifestyle. Historian Richard Pollay also documents a related change, a movement away from a product's attributes and toward the benefits to be gained by using the product, a shift Pollay found persisting through the 1930s.[92]

Not all product categories experienced these shifts. For example, an analysis of *Good Housekeeping* ads featuring new technologies and household equipment from 1918 through 1930 reveals that strategies used to sell new appliances differed from those employed for goods such as clothes, food, and beauty products. The former were much less amenable to emotional appeals. Ads featuring new and improved household equipment stressed better quality of life and reduced drudgery for homemakers, achieved through savings of time, energy, and money. Ads also promised higher standards of cleanliness, variety, and luxury in the home, *without* additional effort on the part of women, but *with* additional consumption, namely buying the advertised product. Product information, ease of product use, possible time and cost savings, and product demonstration proved to be the themes most commonly found in ads for products such as Gainaday Washer and Wringer, Simplex Ironer, Hoover Electric Suction Sweeper, and the 3 Minute Dishwasher.[93]

Despite differences in appeals by product type, all ads stressed women's role in the home, emphasizing the status and managerial responsibilities involved, as well as the significance of women's work as decision-making consumers. Ads also focused increasingly on the need to stay attractive in order to find and hold on to a man. The range of acceptable activities for women expanded, but primarily within the traditional female sphere of home.[94]

By the 1930s ads appealing to emotions had become even more numerous. Some appealed to negative feelings, such as shame, envy, and fears about social acceptability.[95] These negative appeal ads focused on everything from the right kind of toilet paper ("Watch Out for Harsh Toilet Tissue") and laundry soap (Fels-Naptha soap eliminated "tattle-tale gray") to facial soap; Camay soap asked "Why is one of these girls winning and the other losing this private BEAUTY CONTEST? You can't avoid these contests, you know, for everyone you meet judges your beauty, your charm, your *skin*."[96] In part these ads reflected the growing sophistication of advertisers and their research into consumer buying behavior. Eventually the Depression appeared. Ads directed at women showed a variety of ways they could protect their families by consuming the proper goods, warning mothers of the harm they could do their children if, through Depression-induced economies, they skimped on buying the right products.[97]

Agency and copywriter efforts to understand consumers met with mixed success. As one field worker who surveyed women about their feelings toward advertisements noted, "I found considerable bitterness on what women call lack of intelligence among advertisers in assuming that women were of ten-year-old mentality or, as one woman expressed it, 'nit-wits.'"[98] Women appreciated information in ads and disliked the fear appeals, which irritated them.[99] Indeed, a 1939 poll concerning attitudes toward advertising sponsored by *Ladies' Home Journal* reported that a bare majority (51%) of respondents believed claims in ads, while many registered complaints about advertising exaggeration.[100]

As advertising scholar Roland Marchand has said, advertising in the 1920s and 1930s reflected aspirations rather than realities.[101] Whether showing the hopes of many Americans or revealing the sentimental visions held by ad copywriters, female images in women's journals at this time reflected only a portion of women's activities and roles, and failed to accurately mirror American women's diversity in terms of race, age, and class.

NOTES

1. Stote, "Crowell," p. 10.
2. Olney, *Buy Now*, p. 183; Marchand, *American Dream*; and Pease, *Responsibilities*, pp. 13–17.
3. Pope, *Modern Advertising*, p. 26.
4. Peterson, *Magazines*, p. 26.
5. *Economic Facts*, p. 60; Borden, *Economic Effects*, pp. 56, 57; Compaine, ed., *Who Owns the Media?*, pp. 136–40; and Geller, *Advertising*, pp. 31, 38.
6. *Leading Advertisers* (1921).
7. Peterson, *Magazines*, p. 83; and Starch, *Advertising*, pp. 750, 751.
8. *Leading Advertisers* (1933); and *Leading Advertisers* (1936).
9. *National Advertising Records* (1927).
10. Borden, *Economic Effects*, pp. 927, 930; and Waller (Zuckerman), "Competition," Chart Two.
11. Olney, *Buy Now*, p. 140.
12. Agnew and Dygert, *Advertising Media*, p. 134.
13. BG&BBGOH; Pringle, "High Hat," p. 49; and Fogel, "Trends in Fashion Magazine," pp. 80–83.
14. *JWT News Bulletin*, May 1922, 15, JWTP, Box 15.
15. *Expenditures of Advertisers* (1923): 6.
16. Ibid., p. 6. In 1922, *Journal* circulation was 1,799,002, *PR*'s 1,765,430.

17. *Leading Advertisers, 1933*, p .4; and "The Market for Ladies' Home Journal," p. 3, JWTP, Microfilm Reel 38.

18. Wood, *Advertising*, p. 417.

19. "The Market for Ladies' Home Journal," p. 2.

20. "Circulation: 9,496,841," p. 110.

21. *Leading Advertisers, 1936*.

22. *National Advertising Records* (1931, 1932, 1933, 1935, 1936).

23. *National Advertising Records, 1932* (1933).

24. Announcement by Crowell Publishing Dept., April 8, 1933 in CCP, Box 1.

25. "Ladies' Line-up," p. 50; and "Buying Directory of American Family," p. 230.

26. *Printer's Ink* (April 26, 1940): 44.

27. *National Advertising Records* (1932, 1933, 1935, 1936, 1937, 1938, 1939).

28. *National Advertising Records* (1932, 1933, 1935, 1936, 1937, 1938, 1939); and Fogel, "Trends in Fashion Magazine," pp. 24, 25.

29. "Circulation," p. 110.

30. Barnouw, *Tower of Babel*, 1: 133; Douglas, *Inventing*, p. 297; and Curtis Co., *Merchandising of Radio*.

31. Volek, "Examining the Emergence"; and Spalding, "1928: Radio," pp. 70–79.

32. Leckie, *Talent*, p. 81; and Salisbury, "What Kinds of Advertisements?" p. 31.

33. *Economic Facts*, p. 60.

34. DD to Max Whylie, Memo, January 20, 1943, p. 2, DDP, File 19; and Anthony, *Where I Came In*, pp. 288–91, 324.

35. *Economic Facts*, p. 60.

36. Gould and Gould, *American Story*, p. 250.

37. Representatives Meeting, Tues., February 7, 1928, p. 3, JWTP, Box 1; *National Advertising Records* (1931); Marchand, *American Dream*, pp. 52–61; and Peterson, *Magazines*, pp. 296, 298.

38. Pond's Company Campaign, n.d., p. 7, JWTP, Microfilm Reel 52.

39. See *Printer's Ink* (April 8, 1937): 101.

40. Starch, *Advertising*, p. 772.

41. JWTC Minutes of staff meeting, October 20, 1931, pp. 7, 8, JWTP, Box 4.

42. Pringle, "High Hat," p. 21; and Agnew and Dygert, *Advertising Media*, p. 141.

43. *Magazine Circulation 1937–1952*, p. 126.

44. Gould and Gould, *American Story*, p. 170; see also Rorty, *Master's Voice*, pp. 106–14.

45. Woodward, *Lady Persuaders*, pp. 9, 133.

46. Copperfield, "Women's Magazines," p. 53; see also Bernays, *Biography*, p. 674.

47. GBL to BB, April 3, 1930, BBP.

48. For more see Zuckerman, "Educated Citizen," pp. 86–110.

49. "Circulation," p. 106.

50. Ibid., p. 106.

51. Gould and Gould, *American Story*, pp. 171, 179–82; and Engman, *Gould Era*, p. 34.

52. Minutes of Staff Meeting of JWTC, June 9, 1931, p. 6, JWTP.

53. *Things Happen When the Journal Comes Out* (Philadelphia: Curtis Co., 1941): n.p., CP, Box 2.

54. "*McCall's* Store Tieup," p. 28.

55. *Papa Gander*, n.p.

56. "Circulation," p. 106.

57. *Story of a Pantry Shelf*; and *Midas Gold*, pp. 78, 79.

58. *Studio Book*; and "Good Housekeeping Studio," p. 68.

59. Anderson, Jr., *Health of a Nation*, pp. 260, 261.

60. Reid, *Consumers*, p. 300.

61. See e.g., *Designer* (December 1917): 1; *Delineator* (December, 1920): 1; and Phillips, *Skin Deep*, pp. 179–202.

62. Kallet and Schlink, *Guinea Pigs*, pp. 178–89.

63. Waller-Zuckerman, "Federal Trade Commission," pp. 169–202.

64. Phillips, *Skin Deep*, p. 195.

65. Ibid., pp. 200, 201; and GBL to AC, November 23, 9133, GBLVL.

66. Mayer, *Madison Avenue*, pp. 171–91.

67. Curtis Co., *Digests*, 1946.

68. Robinson, "Use of the Panel," pp. 83–86.

69. See e.g., *Family Food and Grocery Purchasing*.

70. Lazarsfeld and Fiske, "The 'Panel'," pp. 605, 606.

71. *Women in Influential Homes*, n.p.

72. Pollay, "Subsiding Sizzle," pp. 24–37.

73. *Advertising in Ladies' Home Journal, 1927*; and *Automobile Markets*, n.p.

74. Waller (Zuckerman), "Changing Shape of Advertising"; Marchand, *American Dream*, p. 139; and Mulcahy, "Female Images," pp. 166, 167.

75. "Women and Cigarettes," pp. 25–27; and Williamson, "Inhibition versus a Market," pp. 34, 55, 56.

76. *Journal* ad quoted in Engman, *Gould Era*, 47a, no date.

77. Chenery, *So It Seemed*, pp. 180, 181; and GBL to BB, BBP.

78. Ryan, *Womanhood*, p. 297.

79. Allen, *Only Yesterday*, p. 88; and Frederick, *Mrs. Consumer*, pp. 188–97.

80. Scanlon, *Inarticulate Longings*, pp. 238–62; Mulcahy, "Female Images," p. 169, 171; and Fox, *Mirror Makers*, p. 87.

81. Frederick, *Mrs. Consumer*, p. 350.

82. Phillips, *Skin Deep*, pp. 179–202.

83. Quoted in ibid, pp. 189, 190.

84. Starch, *Advertising*, pp. 774, 775.

85. *Merchandising of Department Store Lines, Vol. BB* (Philadelphia: Curtis Co., 1920): p. 95, Box 5, CP; and *Leading Advertisers, 1928*: p. 6.

86. Fogel, "Advertising," pp. 37, 50; and Gundlach, *Facts*, p. 546.

87. Salisbury, "What Kinds of Advertisements," pp. 10, 11, 31; and Marchand, *American Dream*, p. 153.

88. Marchand, *American Dream*, pp. 149, 167.

89. Mulcahy, "Female Images," pp. 164–66, 172; and Marchand, *American Dream*, pp. 171–88.

90. Woodward, *Through Many Windows*, pp. 338, 339.

91. Marchand, *American Dream*, pp. 96–102; and Salisbury, "10,000 Women," pp. 756, 757.

92. Pollay, "Subsiding Sizzle," pp. 24–37.

93. Zuckerman, "Advertising." See also Gross and Sheth, "Time-Oriented Advertising," pp. 76–83; and Marchand, *American Dream*, pp. 171, 172.

94. Marchand, *American Dream*, pp. 175–79.

95. Pollay, "Subsiding Sizzle," pp. 24–37.

96. Mulcahy, "Female Images," pp. 175–77; and Waller (Zuckerman), "Popular Images."

97. Marchand, *American Dream*, pp. 288–301; and Mulcahy, "Female Images," pp. 179–80.

98. Quoted in Salisbury, "10,000 Women," p. 757. See also Marchand, *American Dream*, pp. 72–77.

99. Salisbury, "What Kind of Advertisements," pp. 10, 11; *How Consumers Evaluate Magazines*; and Adams, *Power to Advertising*, p. 124.

100. Pringle, "What Women Think About Advertising?" pp. 22, 60.

101. See also Pease, *Responsibilities*, pp. 38–40.

10

Magazine Content During
the Interwar Years

It may be difficult for outside people not to hold the chronicle responsible for the idiosyncrasies there expressed, and the mirror for certain absurdities, but it stands to reason that both are guiltless in the matter and reflect only what is to be heard and seen.

—Edna Woolman Chase, 1925[1]

A transformation occurred in the content of women's magazines during the interwar years. At the beginning of the 1920s, women's journals carried a great deal of serious, informational material on social and political issues, along with entertaining fiction and practical household departments. By the 1930s the departments had expanded, fiction had taken an ever greater role, and what nonfiction there was focused increasingly on light topics such as travel and leisure activities. The world shown to women had contracted.

Individual editors played a critical role in determining content, but magazines also needed funds to pay big-name fiction authors, support service department staff, and maintain a high quality publication. When a business prospered, then fiction, departments, and nonfiction could all coexist. But if a publication found itself squeezed financially by the company, the competitive environment, or the larger economy then nonfiction articles on social and political topics often became the first casualties. Readers liked fiction and departments; advertisers wanted departments focused on women's role as housewife, mother, wife, which helped sell products such as food, cosmetics, household appliances, furniture, and clothing. Nonfiction's constituency was less clear.

FICTION

Fiction fueled much of the magazine industry's growth in these years, and the successful women' journals capitalized on this, splashing fiction writers' names on magazine covers to lure purchasers.

Editor's comments, survey data, and the publications themselves all attest to readers' desire for fiction. Longtime editor William Frederick Bigelow observed,

I haven't the slightest hesitation in saying that it is next to impossible for any magazine to achieve a circulation of more than half a million without basing it upon good fiction, and that has been the policy which I have consistently followed during the last fifteen years.[2]

Despite *Good Housekeeping*'s pride in its illustrious Testing Institute, Bigelow used popular fiction to boost and keep circulation, regularly publishing writers such as Mary Roberts Rinehart, Kathleen Norris, Ring Lardner, Faith Baldwin, and Booth Tarkington.[3] *Woman's Home Companion* staffers elaborated on Bigelow's statement when they noted, "The editors work on the assumption that stories make friends for a magazine, whereas the departments and special articles keep them."[4] A *McCall's* survey in the late thirties confirmed that for female magazine readers, fiction provided a major attraction.[5]

McCall's published the most popular writers of the day, propelling the journal to circulation success. In 1937 *McCall's* began printing novels complete in one issue (the first women's journal to do so) to strong reader approval.[6] *Ladies' Home Journal* published fiction by Booth Tarkington, Zane Grey, and Corra Harris, John Galsworthy, Edna Ferber, and Willa Cather, among other popular writers.[7] *Woman's Home Companion* featured Sherwood Anderson, Sinclair Lewis, and Pearl S. Buck, as well as other authors.[8]

Editors proved willing to take risks with fiction, although such pieces were by no means the norm. Oscar Graeve at *Delineator* printed Edith Wharton's *The God's Arrive*, which had been rejected by the *Saturday Evening Post*, *Collier's*, and *Liberty* because of its depiction of unmarried lovers living together and an out-of-wedlock pregnancy. Graeve wanted to make *Delineator* the most liberal of the women's titles and he felt that Wharton's reputation as a writer was worth the possible reader outcry and $50,000 he paid for the serial.[9] Gertrude Battles Lane also published a story presenting an unwed mother, Edna Ferber's *The Girls*, appearing in 1921.[10] In 1926 *McCall's* carried Willa Cather's *My Mortal Enemy*.[11] *Designer* brought out serially Sinclair Lewis' *Arrowsmith*.[12] William Frederick Bigelow expanded notions of what would interest female readers by including adventure tales.[13]

The typical Big Six magazine carried four, five, or six stories, and one or two serials.[14] Given the large quantity, an editor could safely add to the mixture a spicy New Woman heroine, as long as the calming ingredients of more conventional females were present as well. However, fiction changed the least of all women's magazine features. While some nontraditional stories, some high quality narratives, and some tales defying conventional mores appeared, they proved the exception to the rule: stories focusing on love, romance, fantasy, and escape.[15]

Well-known fiction writers commanded large sums, even in the Depression years, although some fees were reduced. In the late twenties Edith Wharton received between $40,000 and $50,000 for novels published serially in *Delineator* and *Pictorial Review*. The *Companion* paid Kathleen Norris $85,000 for a serial.[16] More and more stories, particularly serials, were "ordered" from established and well-known writers.

With the onset of World War II magazine fiction declined in popularity, never to regain its draw with readers. Herbert Mayes at *Good Housekeeping* and William Birnie at *Woman's Home Companion* both recognized this and cut back their titles' offerings in that area.[17] The *Journal* alone continued to publish quantities of fiction by well-known authors such as Pearl S. Buck and Daphne Du Maurier.

SERVICE DEPARTMENTS

Most major women's publications established housekeeping "institutes" and "centers" in these years; such facilities became necessary weapons in the magazines' competitive struggle. Homemaking institutes enabled magazines to test manufacturers' products, give advice to both the manufacturer and readers about these goods, and experiment with new services for readers. They provided worthwhile advice to readers, but of equal importance, the institutes served as a draw for advertisers, who wanted the journals to emphasize the value of housework and the products needed to perform it.

Ladies' Home Journal opened its New York Workshop, complete with a model kitchen in New York City, in the 1930s, thus splitting this service function off from the *Journal*'s other editorial offices, which remained in Philadelphia. This positioning highlighted the service institute's interactions with New York City advertising agencies.[18] *Delineator* created a Home Service Institute with its management change in 1926, run by Mildred Maddocks Bentley. As a pattern publisher, Butterick Co. maintained an entirely separate unit given over to fashions. *Good Housekeeping*'s Institute, under the efficient direction of Katherine Fisher, continued to test products and create editorial copy. It added new departments in the thirties, including a beauty clinic, a needlework area, and a baby room, among others.[19]

Many of the factual pamphlets available to readers free or for a nominal sum emanated from these housekeeping institutes. *Ladies' Home Journal*, *Woman's Home Companion*, *Delineator*, and *McCall's* all produced books on topics such as family budgeting, time-saving cookery, manners, housekeeping, entertaining, and childcare, using information gained in their home centers. The actual operations of the institutes created good copy for the magazines as well, and contributed to the trend of increasing amounts of editorial material being written in-house.[20]

Competitive pressures forced all women's magazines to carry some clothing patterns. *McCall's* ran big fashion spreads featuring its patterns, available in hundreds of department stores by the early thirties; inevitably, the title's fashion departments stressed making clothes at home rather than buying ready-to-wear garments, advice also given by the other two pattern company women's journals, *Pictorial Review* and *Delineator*. Both McCall and Butterick Cos. developed new techniques to make home sewing easier and capable of producing better results. The pattern companies also put out a variety of other publications focusing on different segments of the fashion and home clothing market.

Recognizing that fashion formed an essential component of the women's magazine formula, the other women's magazines included them in their service mix and sought to find areas of competitive advantage outside the pattern field. The *Journal* established a Paris office in the twenties to report on fashions in a timely way.[21] *Woman's Home Companion* boasted that its Mrs. Little was the only one of the Big Six fashion editors to travel to Paris on an annual basis. The *Companion* also claimed to answer more personal letters than any fashion journal.[22]

Following the lead of *Vogue* and *Harper's Bazaar*, fashion editors at mass circulation women's journals worked ever more closely with retailers and manufacturers, creating merchandising schemes.[23] *Good Housekeeping*, *Ladies' Home Journal*, and *Woman's Home Companion* all developed various tie-ins with department stores, where fashions shown in the magazines' pages would be carried in stock at particular stores.[24] By the late thirties *Pictorial Review*, desperate for advertising, went the furthest of the Big Six by extensively listing names of manufacturers of the accessories shown on its patterns.

The major women's journals continued to experiment with shopping services. Some showed selected items readers could request through the magazine; others offered more extensive advising and purchasing services. These exemplify features that could be genuinely helpful to readers, particularly those in rural areas or small towns, but which allowed a tie-in with retail advertisers as well. As one commentator observed, "The most successful copy adroitly suggests needs and thus creates a desire for certain things."[25]

Women's journals carried service information on a wide variety of topics of interest to women running homes. Among these health issues received ongoing attention. *Good Housekeeping* regularly published factual articles on food, nutrition, and public health by Dr. Harvey Wiley through the twenties.[26] *McCall's* carried a diet and nutrition department in the 1920s, edited by Dr. E. V. McCollum of Johns Hopkins University. The *Journal* published an important story on the need to use pasteurized milk.[27]

Articles on education looked at public schools and school curricula; now that it was no longer novel, fewer pieces appeared about women in higher education.[28] Young children generated ongoing interest. Bureaus at *Ladies' Home Journal* and *Woman's Home Companion* continued to distribute information on prenatal and infant care, providing worksheets to record height and weight, and give nutritional and care guidance. The letters written to these ongoing columns familiarized staff at the women's magazines with the desperate need many women had for such advice, and the predominantly middle-class readership remained interested in the additional guidance offered on topics beyond basic childcare.

NONFICTION ARTICLES

Prior to World War I magazines had found it good business to carry crusades and material on social reforms; readers expected it and competing journals carried such articles. In the early twenties women's titles retained this Progressive reform impulse in their pages. The publications continued to give their readers substantive material with directives about how to effect change, laced with a strong dose of optimism. These articles typically focused on social improvement rather than individual betterment.

Such articles appeared particularly often in *Woman's Home Companion* and *Good Housekeeping*, both of whose editors had come to their magazines in the Progressive era. Nonfiction in the *Companion* through the mid-twenties retained the flavor of articles run in the years before the war, supplying facts and statistics, infused with a sense of right and wrong, providing steps for action. The *Companion* began reducing these articles in the late twenties and continued to do so in the thirties. Editor Lane knew that fiction drew readers in and that the departments held them; nonfiction social and political articles took space that could be used to further entice purchasers.

Ladies' Home Journal gradually cut back on investigatory pieces after the departure of Edward Bok. It expanded this area again once the Goulds took over. *Pictorial Review* had built its reputation on fiction, but editor Vance had also showed sympathy to women's issues. In the twenties Vance continued this stance, aided by his associate editor Ida Clyde Clark. Once Clark left the journal in the mid-twenties, Vance failed to place as much emphasis on social and political topics of concern to women.

Good Housekeeping provides the exception to this pattern of expansion and contraction. This publication, under William Frederick Bigelow, retained its crusading articles. Bigelow's commitment to such material and *Good Housekeeping*'s strong position vis-à-vis advertisers even in the Depression years, meant that thoughtful, lengthy nonfiction pieces continued to appear in the magazine. For example, in the thirties Bigelow published articles by investigative reporter Vera Connolly on the drug problem, the Traveler's Aid society, a school for poor mountain children, racketeering, Indian affairs, and the wretched conditions for female workers in sweatshops. Most were in-depth pieces, some running six and seven pages, which *Good Housekeeping* had the advertising to support; these can be compared to shorter pieces that Connolly wrote for *Delineator* in the same years.[29]

Women's fight for access to legal birth control received coverage, primarily in *Pictorial Review*. In the early thirties two articles appeared on the subject, focused, perhaps to avoid controversy, on figures involved in the birth control movement in England. The prominent British minister Reverend William Ralph Inge put the subject of population limitation into historical perspective, then stated that the means should be left up to individual couples. Two years later a profile of British sex education and birth control advocate Marie Stopes appeared.[30] *Delineator* carried an article about Margaret Sanger, chronicling her fight for birth control, describing her personal life, painting a very positive portrait of the crusader. Little of a specific nature concerning birth control appeared; rather, the piece noted that Sanger was fighting for bodily rights as the suffragists had been fighting for political rights.[31]

After the Goulds took over the *Journal*, it too addressed the topic of birth control, carrying more articles than the other women's journals.[32] The Goulds also ran a campaign against syphilis, reminiscent of Edward Bok's crusade against venereal disease early in the century. The Goulds enlisted the support of U.S. Surgeon General Thomas Parran for the pieces. They also waged a fight against poor treatment in maternity wards.[33]

In 1929 *Ladies' Home Journal*, recognizing the steady flow of women taking paid jobs (women constituted about 22% of the workforce at this time), started a department for "Women in Business," designed to give advice to those already working outside the home and those aspiring to it.[34] After a slow start the column received firm direction from public relations counselor Doris Fleischman. The department presented a broad array of job opportunities and role models, describing fields ranging from architecture and medicine to safety belt manufacturing and farming.[35] However, *Journal* editor Schuler sent readers an ambiguous message. In an editorial pronouncing that the Hoover administration would be hiring more women than ever before, and describing a variety of unusual jobs performed by women, Schuler ended by commenting approvingly, "The marvel of it is that so many of these modern women in business find time also to run charming homes and to dress better than women have ever before dressed in this world."[36]

Good Housekeeping too paid attention to the growing segment of women in business. For example, the magazine ran a financial advisory service for "business girls" in the late twenties (perhaps in response to the pervasive popularity of the stock market), which offered guidance on investing and provided information on specific stocks.[37]

Prosperity encouraged debate and diminished opposition to women in the workforce. Economic hardship changed this. In the thirties articles began lauding the home, scolding women for wanting to leave, proclaiming homemaking both the hardest and most rewarding work in the world. In the *Journal* one writer asserted that too many women were running to the workplace, thus undermining marriage and family. Home women should be proud of their job. For women who found homelife confining, the author gave directions for improving attitude and personality.[38] A *McCall's* editorial heralded housekeeping, "the most important business in the world . . . a task transcending all others in its universal appeal to human hearts and minds."[39]

This shift in attitude about women working outside the home in part reflected the culture and in part reflected the magazines' search for a purpose, an identity, for woman-defined publications in this new era. Politics and social housekeeping had gone out of fashion, jobs and careers appeared overwhelmingly diverse, as well as threatening to advertisers and many readers. Homemaking could still be a female universal. Also, these back-to-the-home articles reflected an economic reality in Depression America, where calls came for married women, women of independent means, and women generally to give up their jobs to men.

Women's publications had long been involved with the women's associations and they continued to work, directly and indirectly, with these organizations. Club pages and departments within the journals reported on club activities (national and local), offered advice about organizing and running women's associations, and provided topical programs for meetings.[40] At times the women's journals followed the agenda of the important women's associations, particularly the General Federation of Women's Clubs (GFWC) and the National League of Women Voters (NLWV). Editors commissioned articles and joined crusades on topics deemed significant by these groups.

The NLWV set as two of its main objectives in the first half of the twenties educating women for citizenship and encouraging them to vote and participate in the political system. Women's magazines emphasized these themes, while League branches established hundreds of citizenship schools. The League also supported the Sheppard-Towner Bill for infant and maternal health, as did the major women's journals. It advocated passage of the Child Labor Amendment, as did *Woman's Home Companion* and *Good Housekeeping*. The divisions within the League itself, as it struggled with decisions about its future direction, received coverage in women's publications as well.[41]

In the late teens and first half of the twenties, all the women's magazines covered the topic of women and politics. Some articles made predictions about the effect on government of the influx of female voters; others continued the pre-suffrage practice of featuring female politicians. Several titles, notably *Woman's Home Companion* and *Good Housekeeping*, mounted massive campaigns to educate the newly enfranchised voters about the mechanics of voting and the electoral process.

Pictorial Review, the first of the mass circulation women's publications to endorse female suffrage, kicked off the campaign to educate women voters even before passage of the 19th amendment. The magazine commissioned Colorado state senator Helen Ring Robinson to write a series on "Preparing Women for the Ballot." In a forthright manner Robinson addressed issues such as voter registration, laws restricting women of U.S. birth married to citizens of foreign countries, the need to work in groups to achieve political changes, and the importance of discussing the goals of democracy between elections.[42] Robinson challenged women to take the principles of cooperation and hard work they had used in the war effort and apply them to peacetime goals. She denounced arguments made by male politicians that women were too frail to seek public office, asserting instead that men actually feared that there would not be enough political offices to go around. Robinson ended fiercely, writing "A society that does not protect women from street sweeping should not lie awake nights planning how to protect them from bossing sweepers."[43] The pieces, thoughtful and provocative, went beyond merely educating women about the mechanics of politics and placed the election process in a larger social and political context.

In 1920, a year when all U.S. female citizens would vote in the Presidential election for the first time, the women's journals reflected on the power held by these new voters. *Pictorial Review* staffer Ida Clyde Clark spent a year canvassing women across the country from a variety of classes and political viewpoints about the problems they thought significant. She presented seven topics of top importance and advised the political parties to incorporate these issues into their platforms. These included (1) legislation for protection of infants and expectant mothers, (2) elimination of child labor, (3) expansion of public health services, (4) creation of a federal department of education, (5) better planning regarding food production and distribution and lowering of the cost of living, (6) more economy in the government, and (7) equal opportunity for women working outside the home, improved property rights laws for women, and uniform marriage and divorce laws.[44] Clark pointed out that few of these concerns were reflected in the current political party platforms. This list encompassed issues that women's magazines had been discussing and would continue to address through the early twenties.

Good Housekeeping addressed specific political issues, keeping up pressure to maintain financial support for the Sheppard-Towner Act and reporting on funding cuts.[45] Editor Bigelow's writings reveal a strong editorial voice, advocating bipartisan action by readers. His effort reflected the times (this was legislation that women's groups could unite behind) and the continuation of the Progressive spirit in women's magazine journalism. It also demonstrated realism, since the campaign to support Sheppard-Towner in part represented an attempt to improve the reputation of *Good Housekeeping* publisher William Randolph Hearst as a responsible journalist; Hearst's name had been tarnished because of his perceived pro-German stance during World War I.[46]

In 1920 *Woman's Home Companion* launched an educational campaign. The centerpiece of the effort was a column, initially designed to teach women about the mechanics of voting. "Good Citizenship, A Department for New Voters," appeared first in July 1920, subheaded "How, When, and Why to Use the Ballot." The department's placement at the beginning of the magazine on page two suggests the importance given it by the editor.

Run by *Companion* staffer Anna Steese Richardson, the Good Citizenship department defined itself as "the COMPANION'S first attempt to satisfy an insistent demand among readers for an opportunity to learn how to vote intelligently, by easy steps."[47] The department offered six informational pamphlets devoted to different aspects of voting and the political process to aid in such education. The column was to be interactive and Richardson solicited questions and comments from readers, reporting that as of January 1921, hundreds of letters had been received, and that one week alone had brought in requests for 8,000 informational pamphlets. By November 1921 the Good Citizenship Department had sent out over 38,000 Good Citizenship leaflets produced by the *Companion*; in October 1921 alone it had sent out almost 10,000 pamphlets provided by the National Republican and Democratic committees.[48] However, after the 1924 election the Good Citizenship campaign declined.

To some extent the women's journals' decreased coverage of political and social endeavors reflects the reduction of and fragmentation concerning such activity by organized women's groups. By the second half of the decade, these groups seemed less newsworthy, were perceived as less powerful, and offered less for the women's journals to report on. Women's publications' staffs may also have decided that readers were more interested in other kinds of features. Politically it had become apparent by the mid-to-late-twenties that women possessed limited power as a voting block. It proved difficult for the women's journals to hold readers by reporting on politics. With the New Deal, women regained some of their focus on issues of importance to them as females and as reformers.[49] But by then the women's magazines faced financial difficulties and were unwilling or unable to report on these concerns as they had in previous decades.

Some attention was paid to international affairs in the late twenties and thirties and *McCall's* proved especially strong in this area. Editor Otis Wiese sent Ida Tarbell to interview Mussolini in 1927 and to report on the situation in Germany in the early thirties. Mary Heaton Vorse reported on the Soviet Union.[50]

McCall's also attempted to bring women information through a department started in the twenties called "What's Going on in the World." This featured short columns written by notables, including Lord Asquith on European events, Helen Taft Manning (Dean of Bryn Mawr college) on current affairs of interest to women, and Colonel Edward M. House on world happenings. Reviews of plays, musical activities, and books also appeared. For example, in July 1926 Lawrence Stallings favorably reviewed Dreiser's *American Tragedy*.[51] By the late thirties, however, this feature had narrowed to focus entirely on "What Was Going On" in the movies; politics and cultural events had fallen in the face of the popular mass medium.[52]

In the late thirties *Ladies' Home Journal* managing editor Mary Bass Gibson started a series that made a powerful impact both within and without the women's magazine world. Titled "How America Lives" (HAL), this feature profiled a different family each month, describing its members, lifestyle, and beliefs. *Journal* staff also tried to solve some of the family's homemaking problems, broadly conceived.[53] Families received no monetary compensation, but their houses, wardrobes, larder, and so forth received make-overs courtesy of the *Journal*. The publication attempted to include a wide range of American families, and considered demographic factors such as income, geographic location, cost of living, occupations, and number of children when selecting the families.[54] Scheduled to run for a year, the feature proved so popular it continued into the 1960s.

HAL actually depicted a variety of American lifestyles, including, in the first year, black families, a family on government relief, and one involved with the Works Progress Administration, a southern sharecropper, as well as working class and middle-class families. Many realities of these families' lives were revealed; for example, incomes and budgets played an integral role in the articles. Economies practiced, comforts done without were all reported clearly. As editor Gibson later noted, "We were determined to tell this story without in any way glossing over the fact that poverty is a dreadful thing and that we have entirely too much poverty in this country. . . . The Journal handled it without gloves."[55] For some middle-class readers, these portraits provided a real chance to learn about the lives of those economically below them.

But while the portraits in one sense represented truly informational reporting, like much women's magazine fiction these profiles carried uniformly upbeat endings.The series also lacked any serious analysis of the circumstances in which the families found themselves, when such discussion would have been appropriate. Inquiry focused rather on solving practical, homemaking problems—how to decorate an oddly shaped living room, how to budget for the car that would be needed in two years, how to refurbish a wife's wardrobe on a limited income—most of interest to readers, but not provocative on a deeper level.

The economic depression of the thirties proved problematic for the women's journals, not just because of lost advertising dollars. Editors confronted the dilemma of how much and what to write about the economic and social consequences of the business slump. Predictably, editors did not publish many articles on how families might survive this time of financial hardship. Instead, they sounded themes of optimism and faith in the current system, touched on some specific problems, and stressed the need for all to pull together, work a little harder, and even spend a bit more.[56]

Ladies' Home Journal editor Loring Schuler declared in 1932 that it was "Up to the Women" of the country to turn the Depression around by spending more. Schuler asserted that "The JOURNAL reader who maintains at this time for herself and her family the highest standard of living that her income can afford, is the woman America needs to help end this depression. She has always courageously played her part."[57] In short, it was in her role as consumer that a woman could work to alleviate the Depression. Women had a duty to spend as much as they could. Schuler termed this "pocketbook patriotism." Supported by public relations expert Edward Bernays who helped orchestrate the effort, Schuler mounted a crusade stressing this theme.[58]

Schuler catalogued the Seven Points for Prosperity, activities that Schuler and a list of eminent economists suggested women follow as part of a plan to spend the economy back to health.[59] Editorials directed women to assess whether they really had little money, or only thought they did. One article encouraged women to dress well and be certain that their husbands did as well. Then followed a warning that women might lose their husbands and men their jobs if they practiced false economy and stopped spending money on clothes and their physical appearance.[60] These actions of course were doable only if the women in fact had money to spend, which many did not, as some readers indignantly wrote in to point out.[61]

Overall, the Depression appeared most often indirectly in the pages of the women's journals. When discussing the situation directly, the magazines most frequently proposed individual solutions and covered topics typically considered to fall within women's special sphere—children, the home, schools, and consumption.

NOTES

1. Chase quoted in Ulmann, *Portrait Gallery*, p. 20.
2. Bigelow quoted in Drewry, "Good Housekeeping," p. 320. See also *Cosmopolitan Market*, pp. 8, 9; JWTC *Newsletter*, Supplement to #17 (March 6, 1924): 1–3, JWTP; Leckie, *Talent*, p. 83; Seebohm, *Vogue*, p. 336; and Henderson, "Good Housekeeping," p. 9.
3. Mott, *History*, V: 133–36; and Drewry, "Good Housekeeping," pp. 319, 320.
4. Drewry, "Woman's Home Companion," p. 13.
5. *McCall's—Qualitative Study* (1946): 41, 43.
6. Mott, *History*, IV: 584, 585.
7. Drewry, "Ladies' Home Journal," p. 12.
8. Mott, *History*, IV: 769.
9. Lewis, *Wharton*, p. 502.
10. Ferber, *Peculiar Treasure*, pp. 264, 265.
11. Honey, *Breaking the Ties*, p. 5; and "Man in Woman's World," p. 68.
12. *Story of a Pantry Shelf*, p. 17.
13. Henderson, "Good Housekeeping," p. 9.
14. See e.g., the August 1926 issue of *McCall's*; Mott, *History*, V: 133; Mott, *History*, IV: 769; Waller (Zuckerman), *Popular Women's Magazines*, Chapter Five; and Waller (Zuckerman), "Delineator."
15. Chafe, *American Woman*, pp. 104–7.
16. "Companion Climb," p. 43.
17. Mott, *History*, IV: 771, V: 136; Mayes, *Maze*, pp. 84, 85; and Kerr, "First 75 Years," pp. 36–38, 118–24.
18. DD to Max Whylie, January 29, 1943, File 19, DDP.
19. Mott, *History*, V: 138.
20. Zuckerman, *Sources*, pp. 215–70.

21. LS, Transcript of talk, May 26, 1930, p. 22, JWTP, Box 8; and Mott, *History*, IV: 552.

22. "Fashion Comparison," 1932, pp. 6, 7, 8, CCP.

23. "Fashion Comparison," 1936, p. 9, CCP.

24. "Fashion Comparison," 1932, p. 4; and "Fashion Comparison," 1936, p. 5, both in CCP.

25. Boughner, *Women*, p. 230.

26. Wiley, *Autobiography*, p. 305; Anderson, *Health of a Nation*, pp. 259, 260; "History of Good Housekeeping Seal," p. 354; and Mott, *History*, V: 134.

27. De Kruif, "Before You Drink," pp. 8, 9, 162.

28. Gilles, *Materials on Education*; and Mather, *Education of Women*.

29. Waller Zuckerman, "Vera Connolly"; Copperfield, "Women's Magazines," p. 53; and Waller (Zuckerman), "Delineator."

30. Inge, "Question of Birth Control," pp. 12, 13, 51; and Allen, "Marie Stopes, Crusader," pp. 26, 27, 77.

31. Adams, "Crusader," p. 15ff.

32. Girard, *American Women's Magazines*, p. 390.

33. See "Never Underestimate the Power of a Woman," Speech by BBG to American Women's Association, September 22, 1948, copy in Box 13, Folder 30, BG&BBGP.

34. Engman, *Gould Era*, p. 8.

35. See LS, Transcript of Talk, p. 7, JWTP, Box 8.

36. Schuler, "Women in Government," p. 30.

37. Boyle, "Business Girl's Investments," p. 108; and Boyle, "Is this Stock High?" p. 112. See also Blair, "Books," pp. 104, 214–19.

38. Cook, "Kitchen-Sink Complex," pp. 12, 148.

39. "Housekeeping," *McCall's* (October 1928): 2.

40. Toombs, "Golden-Prairie Biennial," pp. 23, 172, 175, 176; A Companion Reader, "Woman's Club," p. 66; Shuler, "New Idea in Woman's Club," p. 16; and Winter, "General Federation," pp. 26, 202, 205.

41. Toombs, "Suffrage Jubilee," pp. 7, 8.

42. Robinson, "Ten Million Women," pp. 23, 78; Robinson, "Women's Work," pp. 2, 48; and Robinson, "Where Do We Go," p. 28.

43. Robinson, "Women's Work," p. 2.

44. Clark, "What Women Want," p. 26.

45. Wiley, "Maternity Bill," pp. 50, 133, 134; "Editorial," *GH* (February 1925): 4; Drewry, "Good Housekeeping," p. 320; and Lemons, *Woman Citizen*, p. 252.

46. Bernays, *Biography*, p. 248.

47. Richardson, "Good Citizenship, Department," p. 2. See also Upton, "Woman's View," p. 4; Lahman, "Begin at the Beginning," p. 24; Robertson, "Woman's Place," p. 15; and White, "Simplifying the Business," pp. 21, 22.

48. Richardson, "Good Citizenship Department," *WHC* (January 1921): 26; and Richardson, "Good Citizenship Department," *WHC* (February 1922): 22.

49. Ware, *Beyond Suffrage*.

50. Tarbell, "Greatest Story," pp. 23, 92–96; "McCall's Century," p. 10; and Garrison, *Vorse*, p. 361.

51. See "What's Going on in the World," *McCall's* (July 1926): 22–24.

52. "What's Going on This Month," *McCall's* (September 1937): 12, 13; "What's Going on This Month," *McCall's* (November 1937): 18, 19; and "What's Going on This Month," *McCall's* (January 1938): 4.

53. Mott, *History*, IV: 552; Stote, "Never Underestimate," p. 17; MBGOH, pp. 118–42.

54. Furnas, *How America Lives*, p. 7.

55. Gibson quoted in ibid, p. 14.

56. Rorty, *Masters' Voice*, pp. 106–8.

57. Schuler, "It's Up to the Women," p. 3.

58. Bernays, *Biography*, pp. 514, 516.

59. Schuler, "Pocketbook Patriotism," p. 3.

60. Crowther, "What YOU Can Do," p. 3.

61. Bernays, *Biography*, pp. 516, 518.

11

World War II

Every item of our apparatus and every operator thereof is now at our Government's command. Cheerfully we set aside our routine duties to undertake such emergency tasks as are assigned us.

—*Good Housekeeping*, February 1942[1]

When the United States entered World War II, women's magazines quickly sought ways to help their readers cope with the national emergency. The journals published information on government conservation guidelines, built morale, and brought news of the war as it related to women. They advised and guided women on homemaking related activities that war-time restrictions had changed, stressing women's role as guardians and managers of the home. When it became necessary to mobilize women to work in factories and other industries, the magazines promoted this initiative. They argued in editorials and articles and showed in fiction that participating in such work was patriotic. Articles still stressed femininity, motherhood, and responsibility for the home, but they acknowledged that females could manage jobs males had been doing.

Much of this advice on homemaking under conditions of scarcity and rationing came from government bureaus where officials again recognized the crucial role played by these mouthpieces to millions of citizens. However, women's magazine editors participated less directly in the government efforts than they had in World War I, in part because the government had expanded and bureaucratized and in part because additional outlets for governmental information existed, such as news magazines and radio.[2]

To coordinate communication about the country's needs, the government created the Office of War Information (OWI) in 1942.[3] A Magazine Bureau was formed in June 1942 as part of this establishment, headed by journalist Dorothy Ducas. The Bureau set out themes it wanted covered and provided magazines with pictures and story ideas. Women's journals' staffs and writers cooperated with the initiatives put forth by this bureau, most obviously the campaign to recruit women for war work.[4]

The traditional mission of the women's magazines, focusing primarily on women's roles as mothers, wives, and homemakers, shaped their dealings with government information, censorship, and propaganda. Even when showing women in the work force, the journals emphasized typically feminine roles. Women's titles interacted with the government less on issues of war news, more on home front concerns, just as in World War I they worked more with the U.S. Food administration than with the Committee on Public Information.

Women's magazines chiefly played a reflecting role during this war, covering governmental agendas and readers' interests (although not all readers' interests; black women remained almost invisible in both the governmental directives and in the publications responding to them).[5] Because this conflict created greater disruption in American lives and saw larger numbers of women take on jobs that previously had belonged to men, the Second World War also created greater tensions about women's roles than the first war had.

WARTIME REACTIONS

Even before direct United States' participation, women's journals had given some coverage to the conflict emerging in Europe. Ida Tarbell reported on Mussolini, Janet Flanner wrote about young women in Nazi Germany, and *Pictorial Review* carried a lengthy, derogatory article about Hitler.[6] *Woman's Home Companion* editorialized strongly against getting embroiled in the European strife.[7] In the summer of 1940, *McCall's* established a National Defense section in the magazine.[8]

Once the United States became involved in the war, the women's journals responded wholeheartedly. At *McCall's* editor Wiese scrapped the cover originally planned for the February 1942 issue then being made up (a frilly valentine) and instead featured a young woman who had joined *McCall's* consumer campaign, boasting a button emblazoned with "I've enlisted." Readers could enlist as well by signing a pledge and sending in the printed coupon; over one hundred fifty thousand did so within the first three weeks.[9] *McCall's* effort came as part of the government's "Consumer's Pledge for Total Defense" campaign, reminiscent of World War I promises to support wheatless meals and meatless days. This new pledge, emanating from the Office of Price Administration (OPA), emphasized women's role in the home; as *McCall's* noted, "You can start to serve the instant you have signed your name. Your post of duty will be where every wife, every mother, has always known she is needed most—at home."[10] By March 1942 *McCall's* had begun a section called "On the Home Front," featuring interviews with women, complete with pictures and solutions they had found to problems such as child care, balancing work and home, and managing with a husband gone overseas. The pieces, while realistic and detailed, remained upbeat. They stressed the essential femininity of women even as they coped with jobs and husbandless homes. When recruiting women to work outside the home became critical, this feature highlighted women engaged in such jobs.[11]

The war quickly saturated *McCall's*. Red, white, and blue appeared everywhere, as did ads for U.S. Savings Bonds and Stamps. The publication inaugurated a monthly "Washington Newsletter," carrying information on materials to be rationed, ideas for conservation, and tips for surviving in the war economy, all gleaned from the magazine's Washington bureau.[12] A short column by First Lady Eleanor Roosevelt, now Assistant Director of the Office of Civilian Defense, told *McCall's* readers what the Government expected from them, including advice such as "Remain calm," "Squelch rumors," and "Don't Be an Amateur G-Man."[13] Little appeared in *McCall's* on the actual events of the war itself. And the bulk of the magazine was still devoted to homemaking, fashion, and romantic fiction, items readers looked for when purchasing this journal.

Woman's Home Companion began its wartime effort in much the same manner as *McCall's*, emphasizing that "Preparedness Begins at Home." Even before U.S. entry into the conflict, the *Companion* had underscored the importance of women's work in wartime.[14] Later, the *Companion* shifted to spotlighting women's work in war-related jobs. In the first full year of war, 1942, war-related material took up about a third of the journal. The *Companion* sent former war correspondent Patricia Lochridge on a shopping trip around the country to see how much could be bought on the black market.[15] The "Companion Way" offered numerous healthful economic ideas for quick meals, war wedding etiquette, practical clothes.[16] Editorials addressed issues such as racial prejudice and criticism of government in wartime, while hard-hitting articles appeared on topics such as venereal disease and abortion.[17] The *Companion* boasted that it was the only women's journal to consistently keep a war correspondent in the European theater of war, and the first one to send a correspondent to the Pacific theater of operations.[18] The magazine also printed features such as a firsthand account of a female pilot's war experiences.[19]

The *Companion* published monthly opinion poll results, based on surveys of its Reader-Editors. The publication asked if women should quit their jobs after the war (three-quarters said yes), how women would vote in the 1944 election, what kind of war news women wanted, and what kind of solutions there should be for postwar peace.[20] The magazine also sponsored a long-running contest for the best letters from soldiers at the front, with the winning letters receiving prizes and publication.[21]

The war pervaded advice columns. Departments in both the *Companion* and *McCall's* counseled parents on ways to explain the war to children.[22] They discussed child care options for working mothers and highlighted the need for more child care establishments.[23] The beauty and style columns featured tips on how to stay well groomed and neat while working at wartime jobs such as airplane maintenance. The subtitle of a *McCall's* article said it all: "You'll like this girl.

She does a man's work in the ground crew, servicing airplanes, but she hasn't lost any of her feminine sweetness and charm."[24]

Good Housekeeping stressed practical homemaking information, geared to wartime conditions. Some of this came from governmental directives. For example, Harriet Elliott, Consumer Commissioner for the National Defense Advisory Commission, outlined for *Good Housekeeping* readers ten ways they could contribute to national defense. All but one focused on women's traditional jobs as homemaker, consumer, nurturer, and good citizen in the community. The exception advised women to hone skills in case they had to work in defense production efforts.[25] Features also appeared on etiquette for visiting service men at camp, gifts to send, and keeping servicemen's spirits high. Readers and authorities debated whether young couples should marry quickly in war time, especially when the man was enlisted.[26]

Ladies' Home Journal launched a campaign in 1943 called WINS (Women in the National Service), emphasizing women's role in watching over the family's health, keeping up morale, participating in volunteer activities, and working to conserve resources. Readers could purchase an informational manual as well as a conservation conscious uniform designed for volunteer activities. While blessed by the OWI and the Office of Civilian Defense, this campaign stressing the crucial role played by housewives was overshadowed later that year and the next by governmental efforts to draw women into the labor force.[27] *Journal* covers reflected this new direction with one in 1943 showing a woman in uniform and two others demonstrating women filling in for men on farm jobs.[28] The *Journal* also put together an exhibit of Women in War Work, featuring photographs of females engaged in a wide variety of war jobs.

The Goulds had called for American involvement in the European conflict in 1941, despite sister publication *Saturday Evening Post*'s stand against participation.[29] After the United States joined the war, General George Marshall and First Lady Eleanor Roosevelt wrote messages to American women for the *Journal*. Roosevelt advocated a year of compulsory national service for girls, a position Beatrice Gould supported.[30] A cartoon version of Walter Lippmann's insightful foreign policy analysis, *U.S. Foreign Policy: Shield of the Republic*, appeared.[31] *Journal* political and foreign affairs columnist Dorothy Thompson penned a forceful column urging readers to make sure that the war, with all its horrors, remained true to the goals of liberation rather than succumbing to imperialism or aimlessness.[32] British writer Dorothy Black sent letters almost monthly to the *Journal*, providing firsthand accounts of the situation in England.

The *Journal*'s regular How America Lives (HAL) series began reporting on the war's effect on families. Articles featured an electrician at a ship-yard who built battleships, a doctor who came back from retirement to take over his son's practice when the son joined the service, and a family living on an Army lieutenant's earnings. The OWI started broadcasting these profiles over the air in English-speaking countries, and reprints were sent to U.S. soldiers overseas. Later the series described families in countries affected by the war, for example,

"How England Lives." And when the conflict ended, HAL depicted veterans in a variety of situations, as well as portraying the plight of a war widow with two children.[33]

All the women's journals experienced paper shortages, logistical difficulties, and loss of personnel during the war. Limits on paper dictated a trade-off between magazine size (number of pages of editorial and advertising) and circulation (quantity of issues available for sale). Advertising and circulation were restricted, although ad revenues rose as publishers increased rates for the pages they could offer. Circulations grew as well, but not as greatly as they might have if allowed full throttle.[34] Most women's journals increased their prices.[35]

Advertising also reflected wartime changes. The War Advertising Council (WAC) had been organized in late 1941 as advertising agencies rushed to assist the government in promoting appropriate wartime behavior. Unlike the situation in World War I when advertising declined, advertising expenditures overall during this second conflict grew.[36] Many companies ran public service ads reinforcing behavior to support the war, to uplift morale, to remind readers of the war effort, and to reflect themes pushed by the OWI. Typically the company's name appeared only at the end of the ad. Kleenex Tissues discussed war job options for women, while Chrysler reminded readers that women worked on the company's tank guns.[37] Scott Tissues urged expectant mothers to think ahead since they would be allowed fewer hospital days and could count on less help once at home.[38] Camel cigarettes linked its product to war jobs, showing that women in the services needed steady nerves, implying that Camel cigarettes offered just that.[39]

POSTWAR ADVICE

Before the conflict's end, women's magazines discussed what life would be like in postwar America. Most frequently the journals talked of the plight of the returning vet, focusing on both the emotional and practical problems he faced. Columns offered solutions ranging from the individual (women should be supportive, understanding, nonintrusive) to the social (employers should give vets their prewar jobs if possible, otherwise the U.S. government should give them special loans). Experts advised women that their role was to assist the returning vets and help them adapt. As *McCall's* put it, women formed the "bridge" between the old world the vet left and the new one he would find on coming home.[40]

The picture painted in the women's magazines for a period after the war was filled with contradictory images. Correspondent Ray Josephs wrote admiringly (if a bit condescendingly) in the *Companion* about how American women had changed while he was overseas, becoming more serious, interested in politics, international affairs, and economics.[41] However, as early as 1944 Marynia Farnham and Ferdinand Lundberg mourned women's attempts to be like men, sexually, in the home, in school, in all arenas.[42]

Even during the war not all women's journal articles had assumed women would leave the paid workforce in peacetime. *Woman's Home Companion*, for example, published a piece about careers in science for women in 1943, specifically noting that training in such fields as engineering, chemistry, and physics would offer females lifelong career options.[43]

While not taking a leadership role in calling for women's right to remain in the workplace, women's magazines at least provided some facts. In its "Washington Newsletter" *McCall's* reported about an Equal Pay for Equal Work bill. The column pointed out that while job categories had opened up for women during the war, their pay, often for the same work, was 20 to 50 percent less than that of male workers.[44] *McCall's* also printed an article offering specific information about working women, countering myths and misconceptions. Author Elizabeth Hawes pointed out that even if there had been no war, about fifteen million women (three million more than in the prewar period) would be working, that the greatest increase in working women lay with married women, and that only about 15 percent of women reported working because of the war. Hawes emphasized that women working outside the home did not differ significantly from those staying at home to work. Further, "It's high time the U.S.A. came to a full realization that working women are a normal phenomenon in our country—and not a curiosity."[45]

Woman's Home Companion published a similar factual piece written by Senator Francis Myers, who cautioned against wholesale firing of women simply because of their sex. Like Hawes, Myers noted that most women worked because they needed the salary. He ended with the simple plea (italicized in the text) to "Employ men and women alike in accordance with their experience and ability, regardless of sex."[46]

Thus at least some women's journals recognized that not all women could afford to be laid off and tried to correct misimpressions about working women. The magazines' ambivalence on the issue and their inability to push further for women's rights in the workplace mirrored the doubts and consequent failure for action in society at large. Women's publications *could* have stepped out in front and taken a more commanding role on women's job rights and equal pay, but they chose instead to reflect and report on what was happening, publishing articles on both sides of the issue, rather than to fight for these rights.

Eventually, much of the postwar advice and emphasis turned to the personal rather than concerted political or collective action. It was easier to advise a woman on ways to help her man adjust to his individual postwar situation than to press for government sponsored child care centers. It was less complicated to guide women in reorganizing their own households than in laying out specific plans for world peace or equality in the workplace.

World Wars I and II produced different gains for women, different outcomes for the women's movement, and different reactions in the women's journals. Coverage in women's titles was broad during World War I and continued to be so through the mid-twenties. Conversely, in the wake of World War II, women's magazines made a few brave forays, then sank under the weight of postwar ideological, cultural, and business pressures to emphasize domesticity.

NOTES

1. "Good Housekeeping and WAR," p. 19.
2. See Ray, "Descriptive Comparison."
3. Winkler, *Politics*, especially pp. 1–4.
4. Honey, *Creating Rosie*, pp. 36–39.
5. Yang, "Selling Patriotism," p. 309.
6. Radziwill and Von Ziekursch, "Three Women," p. 7; and Flanner, "Generation," p. 16.
7. "We Must Keep Out," p. 2; Splint, "Faith," p. 10; and Splint, "Time to Build," p. 10.
8. Mott, *History*, IV: 586.
9. "Women's War," p. 58.
10. "How You Can Help," p. 45.
11. Jancke, "War Comes Home," pp. 6, 7, 108.
12. "Washington Newsletter," pp. 7, 8.
13. "Marching with Eleanor Roosevelt," p. 57.
14. New, "Women Wanted," p. 32; and Richardson, "National Defense," pp. 42, 43, 84.
15. Lochridge, "Black Market," p. 20.
16. See e.g., "Companion Way," pp. 51, 56, 57.
17. Roberts, "How to Behave," p. 2; Roberts, "I Am a Woman," p. 4; Palmer, "Your Baby," p. 4; and Lochridge, "VD," p. 34.
18. *Annual Report Crowell-Collier Publishing Co., 1945*, p. 2; Smith, "When It's Over," p. 4; Fleeson, "100,000 Men," pp. 4, 116; and Fleeson, "Feminine Touch," pp. 4, 132.
19. Fort, "Twilight's Last Gleaming," p. 19.
20. "Give Back their Jobs," pp. 6, 7; "How Will America's Women Vote?" p. 14; "Women Want More War News," p. 8; Martin, "Here's the American Woman," pp. 52, 53; and Maxwell, "After War?" p. 18.
21. See "Wanted—Letters," p. 17; "Winners! Five Lucky Ones," p. 60; and "Share Your Mail," pp. 35, 36.
22. Stoddard and Taylor, "Mom's Never Home," pp. 41, 79; "If Baby's Doctor Goes," pp. 62–65; and McKinnie, "Shall I Let My Child?" pp. 52, 53.
23. Taylor, "Women Wanted," pp. 74, 75; and Budd, "While Mothers Work," pp. 58, 59.
24. Fillmore, "Little Girl," pp. 104, 105, 112. See also Cades, "Hands," pp. 118, 119; and Rupp, *Mobilizing*.
25. Elliott, "Ten Ways," p. 42.
26. E.g., Ripperger, "Going with a Service Man?" p. 121; Ripperger, "Gone with the Draft," p. 70; Maxwell, "We Asked 1,000 Men," p. 10; and Anonymous, "Married My Soldier Anyway," pp. 33, 74.
27. Honey, *Creating Rosie*, p. 39.
28. Covers on *LHJ* (July 1943); (September 1943); and (October 1943).
29. Gould, "Freedom Shall Not Perish," pp. 22, 23.

30. BG&BBGOH, p. 405.

31. Ibid., pp. 488, 489.

32. Thompson, "This War."

33. Engman, "Gould Era"; and BG&BBGOH, p. 443.

34. "Some Interesting Facts about Journal Subscription Sales Since January 1, 1943," Memo from W. B. Detwiler, March 5, 1943, Folder 39, BG&BBGP.

35. *Curtis Co. Annual Report, 1942*, p. 6.

36. Fox, *Mirror Makers*, p. 170.

37. "But I've Never Worked Before!" p. 88; "Parts for Tank Guns," p. 71.

38. "Will Your Baby?" p. 73.

39. "Women in the War," p. 62.

40. Morriss, "From this Day," pp. 16, 17; Daniels, "Veterans' Chances?" p. 18; and Hartmann, "Prescriptions," pp. 223–39.

41. Josephs, "How You've Changed," pp. 4, 140.

42. Farnham and Lundberg, "Men Have Lost," pp. 23, 132, 133.

43. Antrim, "New Futures," pp. 72, 73.

44. "Washington Newsletter," p. 7.

45. Hawes, "Here Today," p. 22.

46. Myers, "Don't Take It Out," pp. 13, 76.

PART III

WOMEN'S MAGAZINES, 1946–95

At the end of 1956, the Crowell-Collier Publishing Company shocked the magazine world with the news that it was folding its two big publications, *Woman's Home Companion* and *Collier's*. The *Companion*, which had been number two or three in circulation among women's journals since the 1920s and had posted a profit of $2.5 million as recently as 1952, died after eighty-three years of regular appearances. *McCall's* and *Ladies' Home Journal* bought the defunct title's unexpired subscriptions.

While the reasons for the *Companion*'s demise seemingly lay within the broader scope of its parent publishing company, many industry observers speculated about the fate of the large circulation women's journals. Two mainstays of the 20th-century women's magazine industry, *Pictorial Review* and *Delineator*, had died before World War II. With this additional mortality the questions arose: Would women's journals as they had been known since the turn of the century soon be out of business? Would publications devoted to interests defined as female disappear?

In the decades following World War II a variety of social, economic, and business factors forced changes in the established journals and opened the way for a throng of new titles targeting women. The fifties and sixties brought turmoil and competition to the established women's magazines and saw the emergence of the "Seven Sisters." Television provided strong competition. The seventies saw the appearance of women's publications focused on the number of women who were entering the workforce and taking on careers. Journals appeared targeting special segments, including African American women and feminists. The eighties witnessed new entrants into the fashion category and publications emphasizing self. Advances in technology brought transformations from within the publishing field. These internal and external circumstances all affected the content of women's magazines.

The mass media recorded the difficulties besetting the big women's service journals, discussing their "dilemma," noting that they were "losing pep," talking of "sibling rivalry." Yet none of the problems proved fatal. In 1993 women's titles made up a fifth of the top hundred magazines (based on circulation), matching the percentage posted by women's journals in the top group thirty years earlier.

12

Big Six to Seven Sisters

Television will not take the place of the written word. In former days we worried about the effects of automobiles and motion pictures upon the reading public. These fears proved unjustified, and our surveys show that television . . . will have no major effect on the changing reading habits.
—Walter Fuller, CEO Curtis Co.[1]

After World War II both readership and advertising revenues of magazines shot up. The withdrawal of war-imposed restrictions allowed publications to expand. By 1955 the number of individual copies of magazines circulating exceeded the population, a considerable jump from earlier years.[2] *Ladies' Home Journal*, *McCall's*, and *Good Housekeeping* all saw steady growth. Even *Woman's Home Companion*, shut down in 1956, posted circulation gains until 1954.

Immediately after World War II, advertisers clamored to get into national journals. National advertising in magazines had risen steadily since 1938; magazine ad revenues outpaced those in radio and newspapers. In 1946 periodicals garnered $381 million of national advertising, while newspapers took in $228 million and radio $219 million.[3] By 1955 advertising revenues for magazines had almost doubled the sums of 1946 and had grown seven times greater than the dollars taken in during the Depression years.

Immediately after World War II, American consumption of periodicals, newspapers, radio, and movies had been fairly even. But by the mid-fifties it was clear that television could attract larger audiences than any of the older media, even with the cut-rate subscriptions increasingly offered by magazines. As consumers viewed more television, they cut back on their reading. Studies suggested that this occurred more with magazine than newspaper reading.[4] Readers who did purchase periodicals turned less and less frequently to them for entertainment and relaxation, looking to them instead for information.

Publications offering general interest fare—*Life, Look, Saturday Evening Post*— found that television eroded both their audiences and advertisers.[5] Circulation wars ensued, and in the late fifties and early sixties this combative trend hit the women's journals.

Readers continued to buy magazines, but circulation alone did not spell the whole story. Advised by Madison Avenue experts, advertisers began experimenting with television. While the black and white sets found in most homes in the fifties posed a disadvantage with promoters desiring color, television still drew off ad dollars. Advertising spending overall grew in the prosperous fifties, reaching about 10 billion dollars a year in 1957, twice the amount spent before the appearance of television. Advertising expenditures in magazines generally rose as well, jumping from $515 million in 1950 to $723 million in 1955. But magazines' *percentage* of overall advertising expenditures fell. Periodicals attracted 16 percent of national advertising in 1950; that had dropped to 13 percent in 1955 and plummeted to 8 percent by 1966. In 1954, five years after television began accepting advertising dollars, more ad money was placed in that medium than in magazines.[6]

Publishing costs such as subscription promotion and manufacturing had risen, shrinking profits; the average profit margin in the mid-fifties was just over 2 percent.[7] Paper prices shot up four or five cents a pound in the ten years after the war. Adding to the woes of magazine publishers, the Post Office increased the price of second-class mail delivery in 1962.[8] By the late fifties and early sixties a number of publications were generating few or no profits.

Faced with the heavy competition posed by television, the merchandising efforts that women's journals had always engaged in began to escalate. Market research efforts exploded, with each study showing its title at the top in some area. As one chronicler of these reports noted, "So full of numbers were the media studies that one adman said he expected at any moment to hear someone shout 'Bingo.'"[9] Magazines used techniques developed earlier in the century as well as new methods to attract advertisers and combat rivals. Merchandising tie-ins, product mentions, placement next to related editorial all continued. Publishers began offering split run editions allowing advertisers to test different ads. Geographically specialized editions offered advertisers the opportunity to reach segmented markets.[10] Use of color increased. A profusion of ingenious devices such as gatefolds, accordions, doors, and product samples became available for advertisers.

The fifties' trend toward suburban living led to greater emphasis on subscription readers, as fewer potential buyers strolled past newsstands, eyeing them for an appealing title. Newsstand sales for the top fifty-four magazines dropped from 47 percent of total circulation in 1946 to 35 percent of total circulation in 1954.[11] This hurt periodicals with advertisers, who considered newsstand buyers those with the strongest interest in a publication. Subscription customers were often costly to attain, frequently given discounts, and expensive to service. Advertisers remained leery of inflated circulations, often bought at great expense and producing purchasers not terribly interested in the magazine, including the ads. Yet subscription circulation rose from 48.6 percent in 1946 to 82.6 percent in 1960. In those same years discounted sales rose from 41.5 percent to 59.3 percent of all circulation.[12]

Advertising revenues and circulation continued to be highly concentrated in the women's magazine industry of the forties, fifties, and early sixties, in part because of failures in this intensely competitive environment.[13] While the *Companion*'s was the most spectacular, other shutdowns included the digest *The Woman* and Fawcett's women's service venture *Today's Woman*. *Better Living*, founded by McCall Corp. and distributed in stores, survived only five years, 1951 through 1956. Another death occurred in 1958 when Capper Publications folded the stalwart *Household* (circulation over 2.5 million) as part of its overall strategy to exit the magazine business. This home service title had been reaching women in small towns and rural areas since 1900.

Two Street & Smith publications for women started in the forties disappeared through mergers. The company had added *Charm* (1941) and *Living for Young Homemakers* (1947) to its already successful *Mademoiselle* as part of its efforts to move out of pulp and comic book publishing. However, when Conde Nast Publications purchased Street & Smith in 1959, *Charm* was immediately combined with Conde Nast's *Glamour*. Less than three years later *Living With Young Homemakers* merged with Nast's *House and Garden*.

By the 1960s a group of women's titles had taken the lead. They were called the Seven Sisters, both because of the female readers they served and because many of their new young staffers seemed to arrive from the all female Seven Sister colleges. The Sisters included matriarchs *Ladies' Home Journal*, *McCall's* and *Good Housekeeping*; relative newcomers *Family Circle* and *Woman's Day*; a revamped *Redbook*; and the shelter journal *Better Homes & Gardens* (some initially included the redesigned *Cosmopolitan* instead).

THE SEVEN SISTERS

Competition within the industry and with other media affected magazine content, as editors strove to increase advertiser and reader numbers. For example, *McCall's* shifted to brighter graphics and used the deep pockets of a new owner to purchase unusual and interesting but costly material such as Anthony Eden's account of the Suez Canal Crisis (pricetag: $300,000).[14] The *Journal* went after celebrity exclusives such as its 1961 feature on Jacqueline Kennedy, which led to a record sale of 8 million issues when the first segment appeared. But the basic formula changed little.

Ladies' Home Journal

Ladies' Home Journal emerged from the war years stronger than ever, an undisputed leader. By 1950 circulation had climbed to over 4.5 million. The previous year ad revenues exceeded $22 million.[15] High levels of advertising translated into a high advertising/editorial ratio. In 1946, for example, the *Journal*'s ratio of 55 percent advertising to 45 percent editorial topped the four leading women's journals and matched that of *Saturday Evening Post* almost exactly.[16]

Through the end of the forties and all of the fifties, Bruce and Beatrice Gould maintained the formula that had brought them success: strong fiction, solid service departments, and what they considered their distinctive contribution—features on politics, sociological conditions, community activities, and foreign affairs—all tuned to women's interests. The How America Lives (HAL) series continued, and the Goulds initiated another true life feature called *Profile of Youth*, outlining in dramatic form the dilemmas faced by young people.

In 1946 the Goulds established a Public Affairs Department under the direction of Margaret Hickey, a well-known lawyer, businesswoman, and advisor to the government who had just served as President of the National Federation of Business and Professional Women's Clubs. Under Hickey the Public Affairs Department focused on women's organizations and other groups working to improve communities. Hickey wanted to encourage citizen participation in the community and to show that such actions would not interfere with home life. The department and Hickey proved a hit. Each month an editorial by Hickey appeared, as well as an article covering some civic effort. The latter, a how-to piece, showed activities (such as the creation of a youth center, the work of a homemaker service, the operation of day-care centers) performed by volunteer groups. Directions on how other communities could emulate these deeds appeared. In 1953 the Public Affairs Department received the Benjamin Franklin award for public service journalism.[17]

A related effort, run under the auspices of the Public Affairs Department but more specifically aimed at involving women in politics, was Political Pilgrim's Progress (PPP), begun in October 1951. Articles showed women becoming active in the local political process and stressed the need to participate in politics as well as to vote. As was true of earlier editors working on political education articles, the Goulds received advice for these pieces from the National League of Women Voters.[18]

Despite its claim to depict the lives of real American families in these departments, some polishing took place. Mrs. Julia Ashenhurst, a housewife who received a *Journal* make-over in the fifties, complained that the magazine presented an ideal impossible for women to live up to—a woman on a pedestal who was an expert housewife, seamstress, decorator, cook, mother, informed companion, and attractive female. Constantly reading about such a paragon made women achieving less feel guilty. Ashenhurst described her own experience of being prepared to appear in the *Journal*: photographed in a dress unlike anything she would buy, differing from both her taste and her clothing budget; made-up by an expert (she herself never wore make-up); and given a hairdresser-styled hair-do that did not last more than a day. As this perceptive housewife wrote,

I cannot but question the wisdom and fairness of presenting me as the wife of a teacher and mother of four young children in clothes not my own with a face and hairdo not my own. Even my waist was not my own for I was hooked into a cinch corset which was nearly the end of me. How will my counterpart in apartments, farms, and developments all over the country feel as she sees this glamorous clothes horse and realizes that she cannot afford to dress like that and wonders why she cannot look like that?[19]

The increased use of photographs by the *Journal* intensified the impression that the publication reflected peoples' actual lives. The *Journal* began including more photo reporting stories, such as a series called "People are People," which showed families living around the world.

A condensation of Margaret Mead's *Male and Female* ran in the *Journal* as did an excerpt of the Kinsey report on sexual behavior in America.[20] The Goulds instituted a feature called "Tell Me, Doctor" to acquaint readers with medical news. Dr. Benjamin Spock was hired to write a column on raising children, and though his politics posed a problem for the magazine, his column was so well-liked the Goulds kept him on.[21] The Goulds also introduced the popular and longrunning "Can This Marriage Be Saved?," a feature that became identified with the *Journal*. Like the HAL series this too was purportedly based on real life accounts (drawn from clinical records), which added to its appeal.

The Goulds themselves traveled all over the world, reporting on social, cultural, and political topics. In 1952 they journeyed to India, visiting Nehru and Gandhi. They visited Japan and Korea, although did not cover the Korean War as extensively as they had World War II. In the 1950s they traveled to the Soviet Union and sent writer John Steinbeck and photographer Robert Capa to create a piece called "How Russia Lives."[22] The Goulds were cosmopolitan and internationally aware. Yet they always felt their mainstream, mid-western, middle-class backgrounds enabled them to interpret larger issues in ways meaningful to their readers.

In 1947 advertising taken in by the *Journal* totaled $25,627,000, more than the combined ad revenues at rivals *McCall's* and *Good Housekeeping*. Advertising continued a general upward trend in spite of some tough times in the early fifties. By 1957 the *Journal*'s competitors had made up some of the distance but each remained about $8 million short of the 29.5 million taken in by the *Journal* that year. However, the *Journal*'s reign at the top was soon to end.[23]

Two events contributed to this fall. The first, the defection of advertisers to television, hurt all the women's publications. The second, Herbert Mayes' move from the editorial seat at *Good Housekeeping* to *McCall's* in 1958, affected the *Journal* more specifically. Mayes launched both a redesign of *McCall's* and an all out circulation war with the *Journal*. Publicly the Goulds professed to be unworried by the assault, claiming ad agencies on Madison Avenue rather than actual female readers were the ones impressed by the refurbished *McCall's*. Privately they expressed concern.[24] Bruce Gould sought more money for advertising and circulation promotion, but Curtis Co., in financial straits, refused to spend the additional dollars. By 1960 *McCall's* had pulled even with the *Journal* in circulation. In the last quarter of that year, *McCall's* sold more copies than the *Journal*, albeit many at a discounted price.[25]

The *Journal* began losing money. It was cut to ten issues a year (it returned to twelve issues a year in 1964) and, for the first time, agreed to accept liquor advertising. In March 1962 Bruce and Beatrice Blackmar Gould resigned as editors of the *Journal* after twenty-seven years in the job.[26] Philadelphia managing editor Curtiss Anderson (previously at *Better Homes and Gardens*), a man the Goulds had groomed for the job, replaced them.

Anderson began the challenging job of shifting the *Journal*, for so long guided by the same editorial hands, into a new direction. In a cost cutting move, Anderson moved the *Journal*'s editorial staff to New York City.[27] A new publisher, John Veronis, was brought in. He aggressively pursued advertising, boosting ad lineage 20 percent in the first half of 1963. Under Veronis *Journal* editors felt more pressured to accommodate advertisers, as financial problems threatened the editorial boundaries the Goulds had staked out.[28]

Curtiss Anderson's tenure at the *Journal* was brief; he left after losing an editorial power struggle with Clay Blair, editor of the *Saturday Evening Post*, who had been made editorial director of all magazines. Blair fired a number of *Journal* staffers and others, including Dr. Spock, resigned. Blair appointed Hubbard Cobb, editor of Curtis Co.'s *American Home*, as new *Journal* editor. The unhappy Cobb soon returned to his old publication and *Saturday Evening Post* staffer Charles Davis Thomas took over the *Journal*. Newsstand sales of the *Journal* declined, in part because of the strong competition given by *McCall's* and in part because of the lack of editorial vision under Thomas, who drew extensively on *Post* staffers.[29]

In 1965 John Mack Carter came in, fresh from editing *McCall's*. Carter's sales experience and sound editorial instincts enabled him to successfully determine what would sell, both to readers and to advertisers. He emphasized name writers and a conventional formula. Carter's abilities were recognized and at the end of 1967 the company asked him to take on the dual responsibilities of editor and publisher.

Curtis Co., however, still faced financial troubles. In 1968, in an attempt to save the *Saturday Evening Post*, the company sold *Ladies' Home Journal*.[30] After eighty-five years its founding magazine no longer belonged to Curtis Co. However, the sale may have rescued the *Journal*. Downe Communications bought it and sister publication *American Home*. Downe formed a separate division to publish the two titles. Carter moved with the magazine and was named president of the new division, holding on to his job as *Journal* editor and publisher.

Carter's traditional formula clashed with the tenets of the emergent women's liberation movement, and in 1970 feminists targeted the *Journal* for a sit-in. An eleven-hour action resulted, after which Carter publicly promised change. He seemed genuinely affected by the confrontation, if not by the special eight-page supplement he allowed the feminists to create for which they were paid $15,000. Upon seeing it Carter was quoted as saying, "Formerly I had little patience with suggestions from non-professionals about the magazine. Now I have none at all."[31] However, a year after the incident Carter admitted, "Some of the complaints made about our magazines by the women's lib types were right. There has been a lot of silliness cranked out to sell products and life-styles to women, but it will never happen in this magazine again."[32]

Carter eventually moved up to the position of Chairman of the Board at Downe Communications, a spot he kept until 1973 when he resigned, bought *American Home*, and went briefly out on his own. Carter took over as editor-in-chief at *Good Housekeeping* in 1975.[33]

Upon Carter's departure executive editor Lenore Hershey took over at the *Journal*, a job she held until 1981. Hershey had been a senior editor at *McCall's* under Carter, but became frustrated when Herbert Mayes, then president of the McCall Corp., told her a woman would never be editor-in-chief of *McCall's*. At the *Journal* Hershey continued Carter's formula, but added material reflecting women's role as worker outside the home. For example, on the advice of financial columnist Sylvia Porter, Hershey published more information about personal finances. Hershey also instituted the *Ladies' Home Journal* Women of the Year Honors.[34]

In 1975 Charter Co. bought the *Journal*. It sold the title to Family Media, Inc. in 1982.[35] The year before, Myrna Blyth, previously executive editor at *Family Circle*, took over the *Journal*'s helm. Hershey began heading up a development company within Charter Co. Blyth, a polished editor, savvy about her readers and the magazine business, felt the *Journal* needed a lift, believing the title had not lived up to its reputation since the Goulds left in 1962.[36] Blyth strove to make the publication reflective of the diversity in women's lives and to raise its quality. She retained the service features the *Journal* had always carried, highlighted celebrities and human interest pieces, and stepped up journalism on contemporary issues.[37] Responding to the decreased time readers might have, Blyth compartmentalized the magazine, grouping beauty and fashion, and food, news, and decorating material separately. It took a while but eventually Blyth's formula gave the *Journal*, which had been wavering editorially, a new, strong identity.

Family Media, Inc., which increased the *Journal*'s ad volume and revenues, sold the title toward the end of 1985 to Meredith Co. Meredith already owned *Better Homes and Gardens* and acquiring another of the Seven Sisters seemed a good fit.[38]

In the nineties a relationship with CNN added relevant news briefs to the *Journal*, even as old mainstays such as "Can This Marriage be Saved?" were retained and others, such as "How America Lives," returned. Health and medical news were emphasized. The magazine went after advertisers typically found in fashion journals, such as Chanel, Estee Lauder, and Calvin Klein, and stressed the sophistication of its readership.[39] The successful Blyth eventually added the job of publishing director to her editorial role.

McCall's

Longtime *McCall's* editor Otis Wiese continued his success for a decade after World War II. He dropped *McCall's* three-section design format in 1950, keeping ads running throughout the magazine. He published and promoted the new memoirs of Eleanor Roosevelt, who had become disenchanted with the Goulds. He hired staffers from *Life* in an attempt to bring realism to the magazine. He established editorial offices on the West Coast.[40]

Wiese's biggest innovation, however, came with his "togetherness" campaign. Announced with great fanfare, this strategy to get men more involved in the household and women more involved in men's activities was designed to attract advertising, as well as to boost circulation. Editorially this direction meant more service material featuring men in home-related activities, more articles on sex and marriage, and more novels complete in one issue. "Togetherness" did not call for women moving into the workplace on an equal footing with men. For the magazine's ad space salesmen, the campaign meant more products that would be appropriate for the publication's pages. Unfortunately, the campaign failed to push *McCall's* past the circulation leading *Journal*.[41]

Ownership of the company was changing. Norton Simon, a West Coast financier and head of a group of investors, had begun purchasing shares of McCall Corp. in 1953. By 1956 this group had gained control of the company's board.[42] In 1958, when Simon passed over Wiese for the position of company president, Wiese and a number of loyal staffers resigned; as one weekly put it, "The house of togetherness had come apart at the seams."[43] Instead of caving in to Wiese's demands, Simon hired Herbert Mayes, the *Good Housekeeping* editor who had recently been dismissed by Hearst management in a dispute over editorial control.

The switch invigorated both Mayes and *McCall's*. Mayes brought a new look to the title that had been in Wiese's hands for almost thirty years. He redesigned *McCall's* pages, introduced bold graphics and many bleed pages (color all the way to the edge), created a new slogan ("first magazine for women") to replace the failed "togetherness" idea, brought in the concept of product testing he had overseen at *Good Housekeeping*, and thrust *McCall's* headlong into competition with circulation leader *Ladies' Home Journal*. Backed by Norton Simon's dollars and aided by some of his staffers from *Good Housekeeping*, Mayes succeeded mightily, passing the *Journal* in circulation in 1960, increasing circulation to eight million by the end of 1961. Advertising followed suit, exceeding the *Journal*'s revenues in 1960 by $2.6 million. Despite charges of excessive spending, *McCall's* earned a profit by the end of 1962.[44] By 1963 ad revenues neared $42 million. Advertisers loved the look of the visually exciting, up-to-date *McCall's*. It quickly became the most popular buy on Madison Avenue.

Mayes became president and CEO of McCall Co. in 1961, a position he held through July 1965. He continued as editor of *McCall's* briefly, then in 1962 turned the job over to executive editor John Mack Carter. Under Carter circulation rose, reaching over 8.4 million in 1965. Ad revenues remained sound, and in 1965 *McCall's* led its competition in this area; *McCall's* took in $51.4 million in ad dollars compared to $32.7 million for *Good Housekeeping* and $29.2 million for *Ladies' Home Journal*.[45] McCall Co. still owned its huge printing plant in Dayton, Ohio, the largest under one roof. It printed magazines for the McCall Co., but, unlike Curtis Co.'s printing plant, generated profits by also publishing for numerous other companies.[46]

When Carter departed *McCall's* in 1965 to take over at *Ladies' Home Journal*, editors followed in rapid succession for several years. Robert Stein, who had been editing sister publication *Redbook*, took over at *McCall's* in 1965, followed by running expert James Fixx in 1967. Norman Cousins, editor of *Saturday Review* (now owned by McCall Co.) and on the McCall Co. board, also exerted influence.[47] *McCall's* began to lose its identity with this quick turnover of male editors, and new McCall Co. president Edward Fitzgerald decided to try a woman; the only females editing major women's publications at this point were Geraldine Rhoads at *Woman's Day* and Helen Gurley Brown at *Cosmopolitan*. Fitzgerald first hired *Life* staffer and columnist Shana Alexander, who held the editorial spot briefly in 1970 and attempted to make the journal more responsive to changes in women's lives.[48] But Alexander's lack of experience as either an editor or a women's magazine staffer showed and she left the job in 1971.[49]

Patricia Carbine, executive editor of *Look*, followed Alexander. During Carbine's one-year tenure, journalist Gloria Steinem often appeared in *McCall's*. However, Carbine left in 1972 to work on the newly created *Ms*. After her departure Robert Stein returned and stayed in the editorial position at *McCall's* until 1986. Under Stein the publication took on a subtitle reflecting demographic shifts among its readers, calling itself "The Magazine for Suburban Women." Elizabeth Sloan, a protegée of John Mack Carter's, took over as editor in 1986.

Owners shifted as well as editors. In 1973 Norton Simon, Inc. sold *McCall's*. After being privately owned McCall's Publishing Co. was taken over in 1986 by a partnership of Time, Inc. and Lang Communications (sister publication *Working Mother* and Lang's original journal *Working Woman* were also in the group). The partnership proved unhappy, and in 1989 *McCall's* was sold to the New York Times Magazine Group, which already owned *Family Circle*, bringing another pairing of major women's titles. The new owner installed *Working Woman* veteran Anne Mollegen Smith as editor. She redesigned *McCall's*, which in 1990 claimed circulation of 5 million. Smith's mandate was to bring up the magazine's intellectual content while bringing down the average age of its readers, which stood at forty-three.[50]

In recent years *McCall's* has responded to changes in women's lives. Under Kate White, who took over the editorial seat in 1991, the journal has published more columns on health and legal issues, fewer and shorter pieces of fiction, and placed greater emphasis on celebrities, who now consistently grace the covers of all the traditional magazines. Diets, exercise, and beauty tips are all standard fare. This journal, which began as a pattern catalogue, stopped publishing patterns in its pages in the mid-eighties, more than a hundred years after its creation.

In June 1994 Gruner & Jahr, the publishing division of the German media company Bertelsmann, announced plans to buy the New York Times' Women's Magazine division, including *McCall's*. Gruner & Jahr International Publishing President Axel Ganz predicted a major repositioning for the publication. As part of that make-over, *McCall's* would be directed at a slightly younger readership.[51] In 1994 Kate White left to take the top spot at *Redbook*. Sally Koslow currently (1997) edits *McCall's*.

Good Housekeeping

Good Housekeeping came out of the war years in the capable hands of Herbert Mayes, editor-in-chief since 1942. *Good Housekeeping* remained fifth or sixth in circulation among the top women's journals. In the important ad revenue race, *Good Housekeeping* lagged the *Journal* in the forties and fifties, but remained profitable on its smaller circulation, reputedly clearing a profit of $2 million a year through the forties and much of the fifties.[52]

Mayes greatly enjoyed editing *Good Housekeeping*; he wrote of

my love affair . . . with *Good Housekeeping*. I felt married to it. . . . For me for two decades it was a multiclassroomed public school, with a roster of just under ten dozen resident teachers, and countless consultants, advisers, and contributors, and a syllabus that accommodated every subject under the sun, and I was principal of the school. We had millions on millions of pupils.[53]

Mayes identified his readers as middle Americans in every way and refused to be embarrassed by his journal targeted to them.

Mayes cut back on fiction in the forties, shifting to more factual material. He thought it difficult for stories to compete with real life characters such as Roosevelt, Churchill, Stalin, and Hitler, and real world situations, as reported in newspapers and on radio. Then, in the fifties, audiences could see events and find entertainment on television.[54]

However, in the fiction he did print Mayes tried to combine relatively high quality with mass audience appeal. He scored a hit when Daphne Du Maurier, who for years had published her work in the *Ladies' Home Journal*, wrote a horror story that Bruce and Beatrice Gould judged too scary for their readers. *Good Housekeeping* snapped it up: title, "The Birds." Mayes tried to get Shirley

Jackson's classic "The Lottery," but *The New Yorker* had already bought it. Other of Jackson's works, her lighter stories about household and childrearing, appeared in *Good Housekeeping*. Mayes initially liked Jackson's work so much the magazine put her on contract with a drawing account for her stories.[55]

Nonfiction at *Good Housekeeping* under Mayes included the perennial personality profiles, such as pieces on Perle Mesta, Harpo Marx, and Marilyn Monroe, and celebrity autobiographies, including ones by Maurice Chevalier and Kate Smith. Mayes routinely featured these items and the articles dealing with personal problems on the magazine's covers; this was the material often panned by women's journal critics. But other kinds of articles also appeared with regularity: informative discussions on infantile paralysis and cancer, a comprehensive guide to colleges, a description by Mrs. Khrushchev of women's role in the Soviet Union, and one by Golda Meir on life as the Foreign Minister of Israel. Admiral Rickover, Thomas Mann, and Cordell Hull all appeared in the journal. The profitable *Good Housekeeping* could afford to spend the time and money needed to develop and purchase such articles.[56]

Good Housekeeping maintained the focus that had built its reputation, that of providing advice and information on running the home. The Good Housekeeping Institute, headed by Willie Mae Rodgers upon the retirement of Katherine Fisher, continued to test products, advising readers and advertisers. Mayes expanded the Institute, adding kitchens, an engineering department, chemistry and textile laboratories, and a children's center, among other areas.[57] He created a section for the magazine (still running today) called "The Better Way," which contains short informational articles on such topics as health, finances, legal matters, education, and insurance.

While conceding that it would be stupid to alienate advertisers, Mayes claimed that at *Good Housekeeping* advertiser interests never stopped staff from doing an article. He cited *Good Housekeeping* investigations into airline practices and the diamond and insurance businesses as examples. Yet Mayes remained pragmatic, making it a point to stop by every large ad agency in the country annually for a visit. He kept his magazine's ad space salesmen informed about upcoming features that might be of interest to advertisers.[58]

When Mayes left *Good Housekeeping* in 1958, Wade Nichols, Jr., who had just quit as editor of *Redbook*, came and took over. Under Nichols *Good Housekeeping* retained its credibility with readers and its charm with advertisers. In October 1961 *Good Housekeeping*'s price was increased from thirty-five to fifty cents. In 1966, with the smallest circulation of the major women's service journals, *Good Housekeeping*'s pre-tax earnings of over $3.5 million far outpaced those of rivals *McCall's* and *Ladies' Home Journal*. *Good Housekeeping* refused to spend as much in the circulation race, disdaining readers who came reluctantly, through discounts.[59]

In 1975, with stints at *McCall's* and *Ladies' Home Journal* behind him, veteran John Mack Carter began editing *Good Housekeeping*. He stayed in the job through 1994.

Carter refined and adapted the formula he had succeeded with at his previous jobs and then stuck with it. Although by the eighties approximately half of his readers worked outside the home, Carter devoutly believed women bought *Good Housekeeping* to read about nonwork related topics: "We give them information on the home aspect of their lives. We are entirely service-oriented. We don't write about how to get raises."[60] The journal did support abortion rights and the Equal Rights Amendment.

Good Housekeeping continued to promote its Seal of Approval to readers, albeit now carefully circumscribed. Readers still trusted this symbol, and the publication assured advertisers that tests showed that use of the Seal increased sales.[61] The Good Housekeeping Institute still tested products and wrote reports rating particular items. The top rated brands in a product category would, of course, be interested in advertising in the *Good Housekeeping* issue where the report appeared.[62]

Carter's overall strategy worked, and in 1986 *Good Housekeeping* took in more ad revenue than any other monthly journal, women's or general.[63] In fall 1994 Carter left his position as editor of *Good Housekeeping*, a job he held for nineteen years, to take become president of a new magazine development group at Hearst Co.[64] Ellen Levine took over as editor, replacing the last male to head a major women's title and becoming the first female to serve as editor-in-chief of *Good Housekeeping*. Under Levine *Good Housekeeping* still publishes valuable homemaking information from its service departments, carries articles on celebrities, and discusses relationships. The publication also contains surprises, as for example a recent, offbeat short story by National Book Award winner Ellen Gilchrist. Readers have responded well to Levine's editorship.[65]

SUPERMARKET SUCCESSES

Supermarket titles continued to gain favor with readers. By the fifties pioneers *Woman's Day* and *Family Circle* had been joined by other titles. For example, in 1951 McCall Co. created *Better Living*. Printer John Cuneo and several food chains purchased *Everywoman's*. But the market proved unable to sustain so many publications. *Better Living* died in 1956. *Everywoman's* joined *Family Circle* in 1958, giving the merged *Everywoman's Family Circle* a circulation of 5 million and distribution in 12,500 grocery stores.[66] The winners in this category, *Woman's Day* and *Family Circle*, maintained the steady growth they had enjoyed since their inception despite the appearance of rivals. By the end of the fifties, *Woman's Day* and *Family Circle* were cutting into the advertising revenue pie of the traditional women's service journals, *Ladies' Home Journal*, *McCall's*, and *Good Housekeeping*.[67]

Both *Woman's Day* and *Family Circle* had expanded in the forties. Mabel Hill Souvaine came to edit *Woman's Day* in 1943, when it was still published by the A&P Co. and distributed through its stores. Souvaine increased circulation, drawing readers in with a mix of homemaking tips, childrearing advice, book reviews, money and time savers, all available at a low price (seven cents by 1951). Growth in editorial and advertising yielded issues totaling well over 200 pages by the 1950s.

Woman's Day had accepted advertising since 1940. In the early fifties the publication led supermarket magazines in advertising revenue, taking in almost $9.4 million in 1951. That same year 4,500 A&P stores distributed the title.[68] However, in the mid-fifties twenty-three retail grocers and two wholesalers brought a suit against three food companies advertising in *Woman's Day*, arguing that the money these companies spent advertising in the A&P publication constituted a benefit to the A&P chain, one not offered to these other food sellers. As the suit dragged on, advertisers became reluctant to use the title, and ad revenues sagged, dropping from over 9 million in 1955 to 5.5 million in 1957. *Woman's Day*'s owner began distributing the journal outside A&P stores in 1958, placing it in thousands of drugstores, newsstands, and other grocery stores. That same year the Fawcett Co., publisher of pulp magazines, purchased the publication.[69] Fawcett installed a new editor, Eileen Tighe. Tighe increased *Woman's Day*'s circulation to almost 6.5 million in 1963. Advertising neared $14 million.

In 1966 Geraldine Rhoads, an experienced women's magazine staffer, took over. Rhoads recognized the changes occurring in the lives of American women, particularly their readiness and need to enter the workforce as families spawned in the fifties grew up. She tried to reflect this new reality in her magazine. Rhoads also believed that "The reader is the most important person you'll ever know, and you must find ways to be indispensable to her—every single month," a necessity for this newsstand publication.[70] She defined *Woman's Day* as a trade journal for homemakers. By the late seventies Rhoads had added articles on health and money management. To give a spiritual element to this prosaic guide, the magazine published a biblical quotation on the top of the table of contents page, a practice it continues today.

Rhoads' approach appealed to readers and circulation climbed from 7.2 million in 1968 to just over eight million in 1978, fifth in circulation of magazines overall, and second only to *Family Circle* among women's titles.[71] *Woman's Day*'s reliance on single copy sales served it well through the seventies, as other magazines suffered from rising postal rates and the costs of subscription fulfillment. By 1979 the title appeared fifteen times a year. In 1980 it topped the women's group in ad revenues.[72]

In 1977 Fawcett sold its publishing business, including *Woman's Day*, to CBS Inc. In 1982 new publisher Peter Diamandis replaced longtime editor Rhoads with Ellen Levine. Levine's mandate was to update the journal in order to attract new readers while holding on to the old audience; as one staffer put it, "*Woman's Day* had become the type of magazine that no matter how old you were, it always seemed to be a publication for your mother"; Diamandis termed it "A little dowdy."[73] Levine ran articles on health, medical topics, and emotional issues, and gave the magazine "an infusion of reality."[74] She succeeded in increasing ad volume and revenues substantially, although circulation declined through the eighties, dropping 28 percent between 1978 and 1988, hurt by a general decline in single copy sales in the late seventies and early eighties.[75]

In 1987 Diamandis, along with other senior managers from CBS' magazine division and Prudential Insurance Co., purchased *Woman's Day* and the twenty other publications in the CBS group. The new business was called Diamandis Communications, Inc. However, the group had barely set up shop when Hachette S. A., a French conglomerate, bought the company as part of its plan to expand into the United States. *Woman's Day* was one of the chief attractions in this 1988 acquisition by Hachette, which had already successfully launched its fashion title *Elle*. Diamandis and his investors made a profit of just over $3 million on the sale.[76]

Hachette may have overpaid for the magazines. *Woman's Day* soon ran into trouble. In 1989 the aggressive entry of *First for Women*, owned by West German publishing company the Bauer Group, hurt *Woman's Day*. *First for Women* was distributed primarily on newsstands, as was Bauer title *Woman's World*, brought out in 1984.[77] *First for Women* heavily discounted its initial issues and competed intensely for display space. *Woman's Day* had resisted going after subscriptions (unlike rival *Family Circle*, which began doing so in the second half of the eighties), and so was hit especially hard by the newsstand newcomer. With 98 percent of its sales coming from newsstands, *Woman's Day* was forced to begin testing subscription sales.[78]

In 1989 Hachette had the opportunity to buy *McCall's* from the Working Woman/McCall's group, but offered an unacceptably low amount. *McCall's* went instead to the New York Times Magazine Group, joining *Family Circle*. *Woman's Day* remained the only Seven Sister without a sibling in her publishers' family, a disadvantage in the eyes of advertisers looking for combined audience reach and group discounts.

In May 1990 Diamandis Communications, Inc. (now owned by Hachette) put *Woman's Day* up for sale. However, the title was withdrawn because no buyers came near the $200 million reportedly being asked. This situation reflected both stagnant times in the magazine industry and lack of confidence in the strength of *Woman's Day*'s franchise.[79]

Yet staffers turned *Woman's Day* around. They put together a long term strategy for the editorial content, including a redesign under new editor Jane Chesnutt. They marketed the magazine aggressively to advertisers. By 1993 *Woman's Day* led all other women's journals in ad pages and had increased ad revenues by 7.6 percent. Subscriptions accounted for over a fourth of the publication's sales, although it remained the leading woman's title in single-copy sales.[80] Hachette Filipacchi Magazines continues to own *Woman's Day* (1995). The magazine remains a manual for the home, stuffed with coupons and providing valuable tips on everything from how to sharpen a knife to how to treat a burn to how to get rid of household chemicals.[81]

Competing supermarket publication *Family Circle* had been given away to shoppers in grocery store chains since its founding in 1932. This changed in 1946 when the publication began charging readers five cents a copy. At the same time it shifted from weekly to monthly publication. Three years later distribution increased considerably when the Kroger chain began carrying the magazine. *Family Circle* also began accepting paid outside advertising at this time. Shopping, homemaking, decorating, fashion, and childrearing tips formed the nucleus of its content, which expanded throughout the fifties. By 1951 8,500 stores distributed *Family Circle*, including Kroger, Safeway, and twelve other chains. The publication guaranteed 3.5 million in circulation in 1952, placing it second only to *Woman's Day* among the food-store magazines.[82]

Robert Endicott served as editor-in-chief for *Family Circle* from 1936 through 1954. Then Robert Jones took over, leaving a position at *Better Homes and Gardens* to do so. Both men edited the journal for time- and cost-conscious housewives. A healthy market existed for this information and by 1963 circulation reached about seven million.

In 1962 Cowles Magazines and Broadcasting, publisher of *Look*, bought *Family Circle*. Cowles was particularly interested in *Family Circle*'s distribution system and high single copy sales. Cowles eliminated the "Everywoman" in the title, taken on when the title merged with *Everywoman* in 1958. The content continued to consist of well-tested recipes, decorating ideas, fashion and beauty advice, laced with a few nonfiction features and a minute amount of fiction. Arthur Hettich took over as editor in 1965, a position he held for twenty years. Gay Bryant held the editorial spot briefly, then Hettich resumed the job until 1988. Under Hettich an emphasis on service features and do-ability became the magazine's watchwords, and these proved popular with readers. Gradually health and money management topics appeared. *Family Circle* increased frequency of publication, finally reaching seventeen times a year in 1979. Advertisers moved steadily into the magazine, making it a profitable property.[83] Editorial dropped from 51.2 percent of the journal in 1970 to 44.2 percent in 1980.[84]

When *Look* died in 1971, Cowles sold *Family Circle* and its other periodicals to the New York Times Co. For the next decade *Family Circle* jockeyed with rival *Woman's Day* for the top spot in women's magazine circulation, with each title boasting over eight million purchasers for most of that decade, both relying heavily on single copy sales.

By the eighties shelter journal *Better Homes & Gardens* had taken over the top spot in circulation. *Family Circle* held the second slot, but circulation numbers declined steadily. Newsstand sales of all magazines were hurt in the late seventies and early eighties. In the mid-eighties *Family Circle*, which had grown to greatness on single copy sales, began pushing subscriptions. *Family Circle* also started publishing more articles on children to attract readers in the 28- to 34-year-old group.[85] The journal's price remained a low ninety-nine cents. Each issue carried about 60 percent advertising, but advertising in *Family Circle* dropped 32 percent between 1978 and 1988.[86]

As circulation continued downward and competition for ad revenues heightened, *Family Circle* acquired a new publisher, Charles Townsend, in December 1986. He in turn hired a new editor, Jacqueline Leo, cofounder and editor of *Child* magazine. Taking over in 1988 Leo retained the basic *Family Circle* mix. However, to differentiate the title, particularly from competitor *Woman's Day*, Leo began running investigative articles on issues of interest to women. For example, *Family Circle* published an exposé of toxic waste in an Arkansas town, an in-depth piece that went on to win a National Magazine Award. Other articles discussed transportation of hazardous chemicals and child labor abuses among teenagers.[87] The magazine excerpted an important report about cluster diseases that originally appeared in the *New Yorker*, written by Paul Bodeur; *Family Circle* editors had Bodeur condense the 30,000 word story into 2,500 words for their readers. Carried in this large circulation journal the information received wide exposure. Leo explained her thrust toward cause journalism by asserting, "We are **the** magazine of family advocacy."[88]

Publisher Townsend worked to help strengthen sales by joining his distribution operation with Time Inc.'s, increasing by more than ten times the number of field representatives checking supermarket racks to ensure good placement for *Family Circle*.[89] However, circulation continued to decline, dropping 1.5 million between 1985 and 1989. Competition for single copy sales intensified. Bauer's newsstand publication *First for Women*, appearing in 1989, affected *Family Circle*, which in 1991 still sold over half its issues on the newsstand.

Despite competition from other newsstand publications and declining circulations, *Family Circle* still posted a $36.8 million net profit in 1991.[90] In 1993 *Family Circle* ranked thirteenth of all magazines in advertising revenues. By this time the publication had British, Japanese, and Australian editions. In March 1994 editor Leo ascended to the position of senior vice-president and editorial director of the New York Times' Women's Magazine Group, and staff veteran and deputy editor Susan Kelliher Ungaro became editor.

Gruner & Jahr USA Publishing's purchase of the Women's Magazine division of the New York Times Co. in June 1994 included *Family Circle*.[91] Gruner & Jahr reputedly paid $350 million for the group. Few changes were planned for *Family Circle*, at least in the near future. Gruner & Jahr International Publishing President Axel Ganz asserted that "Family Circle has a clear position in the market."[92]

Millions of readers purchase *Family Circle* and *Woman's Day*. While recognizing women's changing lifestyles these journals still focus editorially on the woman who either works as a full-time homemaker, or who identifies homemaking as her most important job.

OTHER CHOICES

Two journals joined the three survivors of the Big Six and the two supermarket winners in the Seven Sisters group. Shelter and home service publication

Better Homes and Gardens moved into direct competition with the traditional women's service magazines, at least in the eyes of advertisers. *Better Homes and Gardens*, founded in 1922 as *Fruit, Garden, and Home* by E. T. Meredith, targets the home with practical, how-to-do-it-yourself articles. It reaches a dual audience, with almost a quarter of its readership male, over twice the figure for any major women's service journal. Unlike the New York City titles with which it is compared, *Better Homes and Gardens* is edited in Des Moines, Iowa.[93]

Circulation of *Better Homes and Gardens* has grown steadily since its birth. Advertising declined during World War II when home construction slowed and related advertising was cut back. However, advertising zoomed in the immediate postwar years, and circulation took off in the family-oriented fifties, when people focused on improving their homes, inside and out. Circulation topped 4 million in 1954, exceeded 5 million in 1960, and reached over 6 million in 1962, outpacing, for example, *Good Housekeeping*, in each of these years. While readers might be attracted to *Better Homes and Gardens* for different reasons than the ones they have for purchasing titles such as *Ladies' Home Journal*, advertisers of appliances, home furnishings, and food see *Better Homes and Gardens* as a similarly effective way to reach consumers. Handsomely edited by Jean LemMon, the title carries many features that are similar to those in the other women's journals (food, decoration, health, family), but articles on fashion and beauty are missing.

Redbook has also been recast as a women's magazine. A general interest journal owned by the McCall Corp. since 1929, *Redbook* remained primarily a fiction publication through the 1930s. In the forties the title added more non-fiction. In 1949 McCall Corp. hired a new editor, Wade Nichols, Jr., to replace longtime head Edwin Balmer. Nichols switched *Redbook*'s focus to young married couples. Circulation climbed, hitting two million in 1950. The journal published articles on social and political topics, winning awards in the process.[94] Robert Stein took over at *Redbook* in 1958 and continued to increase advertising and circulation. In 1960 Sey Chassler joined the title as executive editor, then took over the top editorial slot when Stein moved on to sister publication *McCall's*.

In 1970 the magazine shifted from targeting young marrieds to zero in on the female half of the couple, in her role as mother. Chassler redesigned the publication in 1979 and offered advertisers a *Redbook Gold* edition targeted to affluent readers. During these years *Redbook* was considered the most intellectual of the Seven Sisters. Owner Norton Simon, Inc. sold *Redbook* to the Charter Co. in 1975. But after a poor performance in 1981 (mirrored by all the top women's journals except *Good Housekeeping*), Charter Co. sold *Redbook* to Hearst Corp. in 1982, where it joined *Good Housekeeping* and *Cosmopolitan*.[95]

Hearst Co. repositioned *Redbook*, telling advertisers that the publication reached "the Juggler," the 25- to 44-year-old woman trying to combine career, home, and family. Annette Capone was brought in from *Mademoiselle* to serve as editor. Fashion and beauty received more emphasis. Articles on nontraditional mothering occasionally appeared as well as pieces such as "Is There Sex After Motherhood?" The magazine's ability to attract advertising remained mixed in the early years under Hearst ownership.[96] One of *Redbook*'s distinctive features had been its strong fiction offerings, an area the other women's journals had all but abandoned. In 1982 fiction comprised over 30 percent of the editorial material in *Redbook*. Capone started to cut into this, eliminating the monthly novel excerpt (not original work, as Capone pointed out) and switching the traditional August fiction issue to focus on fashion. Capone argued that it was older readers who liked fiction and the magazine was trying to capture women in their thirties.[97]

Ellen Levine, editor of *Woman's Day*, took over *Redbook* in 1991. Levine attempted to move *Redbook* out of the Seven Sisters category, insisting that it be perceived instead as "an older sister" to titles such as *Cosmopolitan* and *Glamour*, a bridge between the traditional women's journals and the fashion publications. She dropped the cosy homemaking articles in favor of attention to subjects such as "Why I Date Your Husband," "If Sex Hurts . . .," and gays on campuses. Levine also stressed beauty and fashion, hoping to entice advertisers in those categories. The revamped *Redbook* was promoted to advertisers as "The Juicy Redbook."[98] The new strategy worked, attracting readers and advertisers, although competitors cried foul, pointing out that Levine claimed she was reaching 25- to 44-year-olds, when the median age of her readers was actually 40.3—the lowest of the Seven Sisters, but not quite the audience Levine presented to advertisers.[99] When Levine was tapped to take the top editorial spot at *Good Housekeeping* in the fall of 1994, Kate White left *McCall's* to become *Redbook*'s editor. White treads along the path carved out by Levine, focusing on beauty, clothes, relationships, and family.

NOTES

1. Fuller quoted in Goulden, *Curtis Caper*, p. 74.
2. Tebbel and Zuckerman, *Magazine*, p. 244; and *Magazine Circulation, 1937–1952*, p. 4.
3. *Sales Opportunities*, p. VII.
4. Bogart, "Magazines," pp. 153–66; and Baughman, *Republic*, pp. 9, 63–65, 74.
5. These three journals all ultimately folded, in 1972, 1971, and 1969 respectively.
6. Moskowitz, "Who Killed Collier's?" p. 4.
7. "Autopsy," p. 23; and Alpert, "What Killed Collier's?" p. 11.
8. Baughman, *Republic*, p. 127.
9. Seldin, *Golden Fleece*, p. 270.
10. Ibid., pp. 271–74.
11. Moskowitz, "Who Killed Collier's?" p. 4.
12. Seldin, *Golden Fleece*, p. 277; and *Magazine Circulation, 1937–1952*, p. 7.
13. Peterson, *Magazines*, pp. 84, 85.
14. Mayes, *Maze*, pp. 302, 303.

15. "Never Underestimate . . ." p. 64; and "The Ladies' Home Journal, 1946," March 3, 1947, in Folder 39, BG&BBGP.

16. "Total Editorial Linage & Percent of Advertising to Total, 1946," Box 6, Folder 39, BG&BBGP.

17. Mary Bass to BG and BBG, March 11, 1954, Box 6, Folder 39, BG&BBGP.

18. BG&BBGOH, pp. 530–35; and Engman, "Gould Era," pp. 71–73.

19. Mrs. Julia Ashenhurst to BG and BBG, September 17, 1956, Box 3, Folder 9, BG&BBGP.

20. MBGOH, p. 189.

21. Gould and Gould, *American Story*, p. 297.

22. MBGOH, p. 320.

23. Peterson, *Magazines*, p. 190; and BG to Katherine (Burt), January 7, 1957, Box 6, Folder 3, BG&BBGP.

24. "Maybe 'McCall's' Threatens," p. 154; BG to Edna Ferber, October 18, 1961, Box 7, Folder 36; and BG to Kent Mitchel, October 19, 1961, Box 6, Folder 38, both in BG&BBGP.

25. BG to Robert MacNeal, December 14, 1960, Box 6, Folder 38, BG&BBGP; Gould and Gould, *American Story*, pp. 321, 322; and G.B. McCombs to BG, October 26, 1964, Box 6, Folder 38, BG&BBGP.

26. BG to Robert MacNeal, February 1, 1962, Box 6, Folder 38, BG&BBGP; and "End of an Epoch," p. 112.

27. MH to Curtiss Anderson, April 16, 1962; MH to Ford Robinson, Chairman of the Pension Committee, November 21, 1962, Box VIII, Folder 14, MHP; and Goulden, *Curtis Caper*, pp. 206, 207.

28. Friedrich, *Decline*, p. 46; and Goulden, *Curtis Caper*, pp. 147, 148.

29. Friedrich, *Decline*, pp. 46–49; Culligan, *Curtis-Culligan*, p. 127; and Goulden, *Curtis Caper*, pp. 212, 213.

30. Ackerman, *Curtis*.

31. Carter quoted in "Liberating the Journal," p. 44.

32. Carter quoted in "Liberating the Magazines," p. 101.

33. "Ladies' Man," pp. 84, 85.

34. Hershey, *Between Covers*, pp. 44, 96, 97.

35. Sloane, "Charter," p. D4.

36. MB interview.

37. "Women's Magazines Lose Pep," pp. 72–73.

38. "Meredith Buys," p. 33.

39. Warner, "P&G," p. B5.

40. Peterson, *Magazines*, p. 204.

41. "Accent on 'Togetherness,'" p. 322; Mayer, *Madison Avenue*, p. 179; and Hershey, *Between Covers*, pp. 156, 157.

42. Peterson, *Magazines*, pp. 204, 205.

43. "Rival Women's Magazines," p. 88.

44. Peterson, *Magazines*, pp. 195, 206.

45. "Magazine Puts Seal on Success," p. 191.

46. "Battle Among Women," p. 54.

47. Hershey, *Between Covers*, pp. 42, 43.

48. Alexander, "Feminine Eye," p. 7.

49. "Lady at Top," p. 88.

50. Goldman, "Looks Like New Woman," p. M26.

51. Kelly, "Gruner & Jahr," p. 4.

52. Peterson, *Magazines*, pp. 216, 217.

53. Mayes, *Maze*, p. 296.

54. Ibid., pp. 84, 85.

55. Ibid., p. 79; and Oppenheimer, *Private Demons*, pp. 119, 144, 145, 185–87.

56. Mayes, *Maze*, pp. 90, 91.

57. Ibid., p. 282.

58. Ibid., pp. 102, 119, 225, 226.

59. "Magazine Puts Seal on Success," p. 191.

60. Carter quoted in "Women's Magazines Lose Pep," p. 73.

61. McCracken, *Decoding*, p. 182.

62. Ibid.; and Coleman, "Recipe for Success," p. 104.

63. Coleman, "Recipe for Success," p. 90.

64. Carmody, "John Mack Carter," p. D17.

65. Gilchrist, "Blue Satin," pp. 237–39; and "Brady's Bunch," p. 24.

66. Peterson, *Magazines*, pp. 106, 283.

67. Some of the material in this section appeared in Zuckerman, "Family Circle"; and Zuckerman, "Woman's Day."

68. "Food Store Magazines," pp. 108, 110.

69. Peterson, *Magazines*, pp. 288–90.

70. Rhoads, "How to Sell a Magazine," p. 61; and GR interview.

71. *100 Leading A.B.C. Magazines* (1968, 1978).

72. Lentini, "Balancing Act," p. S-64.

73. Senior editor Sally Koslow quoted in McFadden, "Women's Magazines," p. 16; and Diamandis quoted in Fannin, "Image Revision," p. 121.

74. Ellenthal, "Ellen Levine," p. 70.

75. McCracken, *Decoding*, p. 285; and Schmuckler, "Sob for the Sisters," p. 112.

76. Fabrikant, "Hard Times Hit," pp. A1, D17; and McCracken, *Decoding*, pp. 284, 285.

77. Teinowitz, "'First'," pp. 1, 66.

78. Fabrikant, "Hard Times Hit," p. D17; and Donaton, "'Woman's Day' cuts rate," p. 2.

79. Fried, "Hachette Fallout," pp. 41, 42.

80. Donaton, "'Woman's Day' Biggest," p. 54.

81. "How to Do It Better," pp. 23, 24.

82. Peterson, *Magazines*, p. 283; *Magazine Circulation, 1937–1952*, p. 108; and "Food-Store Magazines," pp. 108, 110.

83. Peterson, *Magazines*, pp. 283, 284.

84. McFadden, "Sibling Rivalry," p. 51.

85. Bryant, "Family Circle," p. 22.

86. Yoshihura, "Women's Magazine Dilemma," sec. IV: 1, 5; and Lentini, "Balancing Act," S-62, S-64O.

87. See Arbanel, "Toxic Nightmare," pp. 77–80; and Clark, "Poisoned Cargo," pp. 100–103.

88. Leo quoted in Masterton, "Profit Profile," p. 36.

89. Schmuckler, "Sob for the Sisters," p. 113.

90. Masterton, "Profit Profile," p. 36.

91. Fabrikant, "Gruner to Buy," pp. D1, D15.

92. Kelly, "Gruner & Jahr," p. 4.

93. Kraft, "Windows," p. 50.

94. Peterson, *Magazines*, pp. 208, 209.

95. McCracken, *Decoding*, p. 17; and Taft, *American Magazines*, pp. 105, 106.

96. Ellenthal, "Redbook Redux," pp. 142, 212; and McCracken, *Decoding*, p. 188.

97. McFadden, "Women's Magazines," p. 17.

98. Ward, "Sibling Rivalry," p. 38; and Reilly, "Once Considered Look-Alike," pp. B1, B7.

99. Hochwald, "Red-Letter Days," pp. 51–53.

13

New Contenders

The women's service magazines are 'dinosaurs,' doomed to be replaced by niche publications.

—*Magazine World*, 1991[1]

While competing media and changes in the magazine industry affected the way the Seven Sisters did business, the women's liberation movement and women's increased presence in the paid workforce presented challenges of another kind. The Seven Sisters responded cautiously, averse to tampering with formulas that had been successful for so long. Their tardy reaction opened the way for an assortment of new titles targeting the multitude of interests females were now perceived to have. New magazines such as *Ms.*, *Working Woman*, and *Essence*, and redesigns of old publications such as *Cosmopolitan* capitalized on carefully defined segments of the female reading public. Newsstand sales and advertising pages of older journals fell. While most new titles failed to make their way into the top hundred magazines ranked by circulation, these publications hurt the older books because their attractive positioning gave ad space buyers good reasons for using their pages. The new journals also influenced the content of the older journals, pushing them to broaden the topics covered and reflect more accurately the reality of readers' lives. A look at several of these titles illustrates their appeal, their messages, and their position in the market.

A successful redesign occurred at fiction publication *Cosmopolitan* in 1965. Helen Gurley Brown, who had just written the best-selling *Sex and the Single Girl*, approached Hearst Corp. with a prototype for a new magazine. The company jumped at her concept as a solution for the sagging *Cosmopolitan*. Brown rejuvenated the title with her vision of self-help and sexuality for the single woman.[2]

Brown's mix worked, perhaps appealing more to women's imaginations than to the way they actually ran their lives. The first revamped issue of

Cosmopolitan featured a cover with what would become the magazine's trademark pose: a three-quarter shot of a beautiful model, showing a great deal of bosom. Brown, who envisioned the Cosmo girl as "sexy, slender and bosomy," observed that "A beautiful bosom is a beautiful bosom. If you don't have one, you look on with awe and envy; if you do, you wonder, 'Are mine as good as hers.'"[3] Statements such as this enraged feminists. Betty Friedan's assessment of the new *Cosmopolitan* was harsh: "'an immature, teenager-level sexual fantasy' based on the 'ugly and horrible idea that woman is nothing but a sex object.'"[4] But Brown increased the circulation of *Cosmopolitan* by 2 million in her first fifteen years. And her focus on the self and discussions of sexuality were later taken up by other women's journals. By editing for independent working women in their twenties and early thirties, Brown attracted advertisers as well.

In 1990 *Cosmopolitan* celebrated the twenty-fifth anniversary of its remake by Brown. The commemorative issue sported Madonna on its cover, carried a nude picture of actor David Hasselhoff inside, and paid homage to age by identifying seven female celebrities who had improved over the quarter century. Replete with over 300 pages of ads worth $18.7 million, the issue testified to advertisers' continued confidence in the buying power of That Cosmopolitan Girl, and the ability of Brown, at 68 years old still the ultimate Cosmopolitan Girl, to keep delivering her audience of almost three million.

In recent years *Cosmopolitan* has conceded that women may actually move out of the single state; the magazine's advice has begun addressing the interests of married readers, those with children and those thinking of starting families. Half of the publication's audience is now married, with an average age of almost thirty-one; 75 percent work outside the home.[5] *Cosmopolitan* still advises readers about getting ahead in both work and love. For the most part it avoids political and social issues, failing to place even the women's topics (particularly workplace issues) it does cover in a larger context. One exception was a 1994 issue with a special section devoted to feminism, with supporters and critics alike writing articles on the subject.[6]

In early 1996, following the decline of *Cosmopolitan*'s newsstand sales for a decade, Hearst Co. announced a successor for Brown. The company selected an experienced journalist, Bonnie Fuller, to run *Cosmopolitan*. Fuller worked as deputy editor under Brown, then took over.[7]

Capitalizing on sexual liberation proved somewhat easier than capitalizing on economic and political liberation, as *Ms.* magazine discovered. While *Cosmopolitan* told women how to make the most of the system as it existed, *Ms.* questioned the system and called on women to make changes.

Ms. was the brainchild of Pat Carbine, Gloria Steinem, and other writers, editors, and women's rights activists.[8] It initially appeared as a forty-four page special insert in Clay Felker's *New York* magazine. This December 15, 1971, issue proved a hit on the newsstands and in spring 1972 the first free standing edition of *Ms.* was published. Its 300,000 copies sold out in a surprisingly short eight days. Warner Communications and *Washington Post* publisher Katherine Graham invested in the publication, giving it more financial stability.

Ms.' early issues featured some renowned female writers, adding to its marketability and credibility. Essays by Germaine Greer and Simone de Beauvoir, fiction by Doris Lessing, and writing by Lois Gould, Kate Millett, and Margaret Drabble all appeared. The magazine depicted women of various classes, races, ages, shapes, sizes, and abilities.[9] Practical columns discussed car mechanics, medical advice, and information on gaining credit and mortgages.

Ms.' circulation increased steadily in its first few years. Readers appreciated coverage of social and political issues of importance to women such as the Equal Rights Amendment, child care, women's health issues, financial and employment concerns, women's spirituality, aging, domestic violence, and lesbianism. The first issue generated over 20,000 letters, an amount ten times greater than the average women's journal issue, according to one women's magazine staffer. And letters continued to pour in.[10] By 1974, with the title two years old, circulation stood at more than 400,000 and by the late seventies topped 500,000.

Advertisers followed more slowly, unsure about the sales effectiveness of a nontraditional women's publication. *Ms.* issued guidelines for advertising acceptance, refusing to publish ads the staff considered sexist. For example, the Virginia Slims' "You've Come a Long Way, Baby" campaign generated an enormous amount of discussion between the *Ms.* staff and people at Virginia Slims' owner Phillip Morris, as they tried to work out an acceptable way to run the ad. Ultimately *Ms.* turned the ads down, at a cost of $80,000 in ad revenue. The refusal came because the ads were perceived as sexist, not because of the product. In fact, a major reader criticism of *Ms.* centered on its acceptance of cigarette advertising.[11]

Ms.' sales staff went after advertising accounts not traditionally placed in women's magazines, such as insurance, telecommunications, financial services, and cars. Publisher Carbine, ad sales director Valerie Salembier, and other *Ms.* staffers pioneered in making pitches to automobile executives in Detroit. Other women's journals followed, and eventually car ads returned to women's publications in number after being minimal for fifty years.[12] *Ms.'* staff wanted to obtain ad placement from these atypical categories because these advertisers would be less accustomed to receiving the editorial support more traditional female product groups, like food and fashion, expected. While *Ms.* salespeople had some successes, this strategy never worked completely. Ad pages began dropping in 1985, a signal that led *Ms.* to pursue more aggressively stereotypically female accounts. Advertisers remained unconvinced about the *Ms.* audience and leery of its editorial content; some advertisers willing to buy ad space specified types of articles they did not want their ad near.[13]

While *Ms.* scrutinized ads more closely than other women's journals and tried hard to attract ads from nontraditional categories, it had mixed success. One study shows traditional women's magazine advertisers such as personal appearance products (cosmetics, clothing, jewelry) increasing steadily from between 1973 and 1987. Products of questionable safety to women such as alcohol and cigarettes accounted for about 29 percent of ads in the fifteen years studied.[14]

Yet despite criticisms *Ms.* profoundly affected the women's magazine world, pushing back the boundaries of what could appear in popular women's journals. *Ms.* pioneered in questioning advertisers, forcing them to be more conscious of women as human beings participating fully in society when creating new ads. *Ms.* trained women and offered them opportunities in the business aspects of the magazine; many *Ms.* staffers went on to high positions on the business side of publishing.[15] And the editorial content presented a wider range of viewpoints, topics, and images than any other advertiser-supported women's journal.

Ms. switched to nonprofit status in 1979. While that lowered mailing costs, it also brought problems as it barred the publication from taking political positions. Any political issue had to be presented even-handedly. This inability to take strong political stands, competition from other new magazines, as well as the ethos of the times (with attention moving from the political and social focus of the seventies to success and money) all contributed to the declines in circulation and advertising *Ms.* experienced in the eighties. Some of *Ms.'* message had become part of the mainstream, at least in print if not practice. And in its own pages, *Ms.* turned to popular media topics such as money, careers, personal relations, and celebrities. Some argued that the journal had lost its edge.[16]

When Australian publishing giant John Fairfax, Ltd. proposed purchasing the magazine in 1987 (reputedly for between $10 and $15 million), the Ms. Foundation for Education and Communication (*Ms.'* owner) accepted. The offer looked promising. New editor Anne Summers had headed the Australian Office of the Status of Women. Sandra Yates, president of Fairfax Publications in the United States would be publisher.[17]

The results proved disappointing. The Australian company poured money into trade promotion, as expected, but emphasized the spending power of *Ms.* readers, diluting and narrowing the feminist message. The magazine itself was enlarged and redesigned, with celebrities placed on the covers. Editorial on fashion was added. *Ms.* began to resemble the more traditional women's journals.[18] Circulation grew to 550,000, boosted by strong subscription drives, but advertising failed to follow, partly because of editorial content, such as the title's strong support of abortion rights.

In June 1988 Yates and Summers formed a partnership called Matilda Publications and purchased *Ms.* and *Sassy*, a bold teen magazine, from Fairfax. However, the new company failed to show sufficient profits, in part because of troubles at *Sassy*. Investors forced a sale of both publications. In October 1989 Lang Communications, already owner of *Working Woman* and *Working Mother*, purchased the two titles. *Sassy* rebounded, but *Ms.* had suffered almost fatally from the eighties' decline and ownership changes.

Thus in 1989, a year before *Cosmopolitan* was celebrating its twenty-fifth year of commercial success, *Ms.* was starving for ads. Owner Dale Lang gave the magazine a hiatus. When *Ms.* returned it contained no advertising. Well-known feminist and writer Robin Morgan became editor, with Steinem serving as consulting editor. The company gambled that loyal, old readers as well as new ones craving a noncommercial, substantive feminist publication, would buy the reinvented title.

Despite gloomy forecasts by industry analysts, *Ms.* survived. A year after relaunch, the title boasted a circulation of 150,000 and was more than breaking even.[19] No longer constrained by the goals of advertisers, the new bimonthly publication has an international perspective and covers political, social, and cultural issues, led by former *Essence* editor Marcia Ann Gillespie, who took over from Robin Morgan in 1993. *Ms.* was sold in 1996 to a group of investors headed by Jay MacDonald.

Another segment of women, African-American females, received attention in a national magazine targeted at them. Reader research at the traditional women's journals had uncovered a market of black female readers.[20] Four black men saw opportunity in these demographics, and in 1970 Edward Lewis, Clarence Smith, Cecil Hollingsworth, and Jonathan Blount founded *Essence*. Edited for middle-class black women in all their variety, the magazine hit the right formula, and with persistence from its staff, succeeded. Several banks and Playboy Enterprises backed the business. *Good Housekeeping*'s John Mack Carter and several other experts provided advice. The publication was also bolstered by heightened awareness and pride brought by the black power movement.

Management quarrels early in the magazine's history and the ouster of founder Jonathan Blount in 1971 (when he protested *Playboy*'s investment in the title) created difficulties.[21] However, readers responded well to the journal and by the mid-1970s it boasted 450,000 in circulation. As publisher Edward Lewis put it, *Essence* tried to "make Black women feel good about themselves."[22] Originally targeted at middle-class, black females ages eighteen to thirty-four, the publication carried the traditional women's magazine focus on fashion and beauty but also broadened to include articles on social and political topics.

A key reason for the magazine's expansion and success lay in the 1972 appointment of Marcia Ann Gillespie as editor-in-chief. Gillespie enlarged the journal's mission to include service and lifestyle features tailored to the needs of black women. Initially she included aggressive coverage of political issues, but modulated that when it made the publication too strident. Instead she focused on issues of concern to black women: building a strong family and presenting positive images of black females. She wanted black women to be proud of their history and culture.[23]

In the seventies the magazine included stories by Alice Walker and Gayl Jones and interviews with Amiri Baraka and Fannie Lou Hamer, in addition to fashion and beauty pieces. Discussion of birth control, abortion, male-female relations, and white women appeared. Many articles mirrored those appearing in mainstream women's service, fashion, and self-help journals, but they reflected the black woman's point of view. And *Essence* mirrored the diversity of the black female community; as one analyst looking back on the journal's first decade noted,

The magazine was as schizophrenic as the times, and no matter what was printed, a vocal segment of our community was offended. It's a good thing Black women had no other magazine to turn to—otherwise ESSENCE might have been in a no-win situation.[24]

Advertisers reacted more cautiously than readers but enough expressed interest so that the magazine stayed afloat. Gillespie sought to convince advertisers of black women's strength as consumers and of their loyalty to a journal edited particularly for them. *Essence* also benefited from the earlier success of black general interest magazine *Ebony* (started in 1945), which had worked to educate advertisers about the African-American market. From the beginning *Essence* enforced a policy requiring ad copy to include black models and rejected ads that used only white models if no rationale existed for that choice. By 1976 the publication boasted over 500,000 readers and $3.7 million in ad revenues, up from just over half a million five years earlier.[25]

Essence has since expanded its audience, reaching readers ages eighteen to forty-nine, over a quarter of them male. About 20 percent of the readers are white.[26] The content focuses on traditional subjects of interest to women as well as important political, cultural, historical, and international topics, seen through a lens sensitive to the interests of blacks. While supported by advertising (which at times reinforces beauty ideals of the white world), *Essence* manages to go beyond merely serving as a commercial vehicle. The magazine stresses the importance of blacks using their political and economic power.[27]

Marcia Ann Gillespie resigned in 1980 and was followed briefly by Daryl Alexander. Susan L. Taylor took over as editor in 1981 and has continued successfully since then. In 1993 advertising revenues reached over $31.7 million and circulation hit 954,351.[28]

One of the first individuals to identify the need for a women's publication devoted to career and workplace issues and bring this idea to fruition was Beatrice Buckler, founding editor of *Working Woman*, begun in 1976. Buckler formulated the idea for this journal while working as an executive editor at *Family Circle* in the early seventies, where she was impressed by the statistics showing the number of women entering the workforce. She pitched the idea to management at the New York Times Magazine Group, which owned *Family Circle*. That company proved unwilling to back the venture, forcing Buckler on a search for capital. She had almost given up when she met business promoter J. Jay Frankel. Frankel gathered together a team of investors, and Buckler's magazine concept came to life.[29]

Working Woman initially tried to target women at all levels who worked outside the home. It attracted readers and advertisers and the publication looked like a sure winner.

However, problems developed between editor Buckler and owner Frankel. Frankel reputedly had links to the Mafia.[30] Buckler suspected Frankel of diverting funds from the magazine to his other enterprises, while Frankel charged Buckler with financial mismanagement. The controversy ended up in court, where Frankel was eventually awarded enhanced powers at *Working Woman*, although enjoined from removing Buckler as editor. Buckler felt that she had been reduced to a "mere figurehead," and she resigned from the publication in May 1977, a move followed by most of the staff.[31] Kate Rand Lloyd, who had previously worked at *Glamour* and *Vogue*, took over as editor-in-chief.

By the end of the year the enterprise had filed for Chapter 11 bankruptcy proceedings.[32] Dale Lang, who had just founded HAL publications, purchased *Working Woman* at the beginning of 1978. Lloyd was retained as editor-in-chief although Buckler thought she had a deal with Lang to come back in that position.[33]

Under Lang's ownership *Working Woman* steadily gained readers and advertisers. The magazine shifted its editorial strategy, focusing on higher-level, better paid professional women with careers rather than working women generally; newly promoted publisher Carol Taber called this audience "the cream of the crop."[34] The switch reflected the need to target specific audiences attractive to advertisers. As part of its sharpened focus, *Working Woman* cut back on discussions of women's conflicted feelings about working outside the home and emphasized ways to succeed in the workplace. Articles on leadership, management styles, and negotiation started outnumbering those on balancing home and work. Columns of consumer advice and legal information appeared, as well as profiles of successful career women. The publication also began an annual review of salary disparities between men and women in particular professions.[35]

Lang promoted *Working Woman* heavily, spending more than $5 million by 1982. Circulation jumped from 100,000 to 500,000 between 1978 and 1982 and ad pages climbed from 200 to 760 (with ad revenues rising from $500,000 to $6 million). Despite this success, *Working Woman* was still clearly a specialty title, with neither circulation nor ad revenues approaching those of the traditional women's service journals.[36] Circulation reached 905,000 in 1988, but slid to 867,000 by 1992. Anne Mollegen Smith came in as editor and in 1988 redesigned the magazine. Kate White edited the journal briefly in 1989 and 1990, replacing Smith, before moving over to *McCall's* in 1991.

Today *Working Woman* stays focused on workplace issues, career strategies, and investment advice for women. Under the editorial direction of Lynn Povich the articles offer solid information, are soundly researched, and use appropriate experts in the fields of management, human resources, financial planning, and so forth. Health and fashion have their spot, too, but are limited. The advertising reflects the subject matter of the magazine, with business products and financial services companies touching shoulders with the more traditional apparel and cosmetic advertisers.

OLD LOOKS, NEW LOOKS

An outpouring of additional women's titles has occurred over the past twenty years, reflecting new reader needs, new imperatives from advertisers, and the intensified trend toward specialization. Publishers, experienced and novice, spotted opportunity in the assortment of female interests and activities surfacing. The recession of the early nineties, with its cramping effect on advertising spending, somewhat dampened enthusiasm for new magazine starts, although titles continue to appear. Successes have ranged from Conde Nast's *Self*, capitalizing on the enhanced interest in health and self-improvement, to home decorating and lifestyle queen Martha Stewart's publications.

Many new journals focus on a particular segment of females. Such magazines attract circulations far lower than those of the traditional women's magazines, but advertisers generally view such specific targeting of consumer/readers very favorably. A few new titles have attempted to reach larger audiences, but, while succeeding in attracting over a million readers an issue, have not reached the volume of the established women's publications.

The fashion journal field was shaken up in the eighties by the appearance of French newcomer *Elle*. The longstanding rivalry between *Vogue* and *Harper's Bazaar* intensified with the appearance of this overseas competitor. Introduced into the United States in 1985 through a joint venture of Hachette S.A. and Murdoch Magazines, *Elle* hit the fashion world with a bang. Rich color, high quality paper, only partially retouched photos, mixing of designers' clothes on a page, and use of multiracial models all gave the magazine a modern, cosmopolitan, *young* look. Advertisers were thrilled to be given an alternative to the staid, ad filled pages of *Vogue* and *Harper's Bazaar*. Readers responded to the visual innovations and international flavor.

Elle influenced the entire women's magazine world, and fashion stand-bys *Vogue* and *Harper's Bazaar* were forced to react. Despite her long record of success (having built *Vogue*'s circulation from 400,000 in 1971 to over 1.2 million when she left), *Vogue* editor Grace Mirabella was replaced, a move she heard about on a five o'clock news program. British transplant Anna Wintour received the top slot at *Vogue*, despite mixed reviews on her redesign of *House and Garden*.[37] Wintour moved quickly to bring a younger, downtown flavor to *Vogue*, featuring Madonna on one cover and a model showing her navel above jeans and below a $10,000 jeweled tee shirt by Lacroix on another.

Two other entrants, *Lear's* and *Mirabella*, while not strictly fashion magazines, focused attention on older women, a growing reader segment. *Mirabella*, named after its creator Grace Mirabella, appeared in spring 1989, published by Rupert Murdoch's News Corp. *Mirabella* initally targeted women ages thirty to fifty; eventually, bowing to advertising realities, it stressed thirtysomething readers. While a fashion magazine, it carried more editorial (about 50%) than traditional fashion journals such as *Vogue*. Gay Bryant served as editor-in-chief.

Mirabella took advertising risks with its editorial. It ran an exposé of sunscreens, published a story about the hazards of second-hand smoke, and printed a piece discussing the dangers of wearing high heels. However, despite a talented staff and fresh ideas, *Mirabella* remained in fourth place in circulation and advertising in the fashion field. In 1995 Hachette Filipacchi purchased the title, reduced frequency to bimonthly and installed first Amy Gross as editor-in-chief, then, in 1997, Roberta Myer. In fall 1997 Hachette Filipacchi announced that the magazine would focus on upscale women in their mid-thirties.

Lear's burst on the magazine scene in 1988. *Lear's* pioneered in emphasizing the right of older women to have a publication edited for them. *Lear's* was sophisticated, addressing affluent older females in ways quite different from the traditional women's service journals, which continued to emphasize women's role in the home. Articles in one *Lear's* issue focused on investing, cars, fishing, and female entrepreneurs.[38] Feisty and direct, reflecting the spirit of founder Frances Lear, the publication went through several incarnations (as well as a portion of Lear's divorce settlement from wealthy television producer Norman Lear). The title was a throwback to earlier journals founded by individuals to express themselves or fill a need they found unmet, unusual in this time of corporate ownership. However, in 1994 Frances Lear folded the publication.[39] Although the journal had proved popular with readers, reaching over 500,000 in 1993, it never became profitable; one magazine expert estimated that *Lear's* lost between $20 and $30 million at least.[40]

Magazines for young women, focusing on fashion and lifestyle, continue to thrive, including leaders *Seventeen* and *YM*. Competition persisted in this attractive market and in 1997 Petersen Publishing merged the bold *Sassy* with *Teen*.

Glamour remained successful under the sure hand of Ruth Whitney, aiming at young women ages eighteen to thirty-four, a group slightly older than those sought by Conde Nast sister *Mademoiselle*. In 1991 Conde Nast launched a new title that declared its intent to take a tough look at the beauty and fashion industries. *Allure* flouted the received wisdom that fashion and beauty magazines had to give manufacturers of those products only favorable coverage. *Allure* triumphed, attracting both readers and advertisers with its mix of factual reporting and information.[41]

CONTENT

What was the effect of these new publications on women's magazine content? What pressures did editors feel from competition for both advertisers and readers? What did content in the women's journals look like?

Focus on Information

Women's journals today contain much less fiction than in their earlier years, though *Good Housekeeping* provides an exception, publishing fiction by well-known and popular writers. Female audiences can find entertainment and escape on television through soap operas, sitcoms, and talk shows; in paperback romance novels and mysteries; at the movies; and in celebrity magazines focusing on the lives of movie and rock stars, royalty, and other rich and famous personalities.

Instead of competing to entertain, women's journals have focused on a comparative strength rooted in their past: the ability to present detailed, useful information. The magazine format allows facts to be offered in an understandable form that can be saved and returned to as needed. Editors have cut the length of these pieces to accomodate consumers with attention spans shortened by television and the fast pace of modern life. Where articles used to extend for five, six pages or more, features of a page or two are common today.

Much information appears in digest form. *Ladies' Home Journal* teamed up with news channel CNN to bring readers a monthly CNN Newsline Report. *Good Housekeeping* still offers "The Better Way," a compilation of "ideas to clip and use." *McCall's* created the "McCallmanack."[42]

The magazines still preach ways to improve one's life, with articles on dieting, cosmetic surgery (pros and cons), fashion, beauty, love life, sex life, relationships with men, recipes, homes, decoration, and physical and mental health. But pieces also appear on serious issues of concern to women, many areas neglected by other media outlets. Equal pay for equal work, problems of abused and battered women, the difficulties faced by rape victims, what constitutes sexual harassment, and the glass ceiling confronting women in the workplace are just a few of the subjects reported on.[43]

Women's magazines continue to cover social and political topics through the time honored device of educating about an issue through an individual's story. Thus *McCall's* readers learned more about the bloody situation in Bosnia through the tale of a woman widowed there. The conflict in Rwanda came home to *Ladies' Home Journal* readers through the story of a woman's effort to rescue family members. An article on transracial adoption featured the battle over a real child. *Journal* editor Myrna Blyth described her own experience at the United Nations' Conference on Women in Beijing.[44]

Inspirational stories abound, tales of hardships overcome, illnesses battled, and good works accomplished. Often these stories are paired with informational boxes telling readers what they can do to help a particular cause, or how they too can set up such a charitable endeavor. For example, *Family Circle* runs a "Women Who Make A Difference" column. The profiles are optimistic and upbeat, showing both faith and problem solving abilities. Many activities recognized in such columns are achieved through individual initiative, often through unpaid labor.[45]

Popular Personalities

Almost all the women's journals include profiles of celebrities and well-known personalities. This is unsurprising in a periodical world where celebrity-driven *People* scored such a huge success. *Redbook* carries a section called "Celebrities," *Ladies' Home Journal* one titled "Personalities." In one month in 1994, *Ladies' Home Journal* featured talk show queen Oprah Winfrey on its cover, *McCall's* headlined talk show cohostess Kathie Lee Gifford, and *Good Housekeeping* displayed entertainment show hostess Mary Hart.[46] Stars from television and movies appear frequently; fewer celebrities are drawn from the realm of politics, arts, or business.

Influenced by movies and television talk shows, magazine articles have taken on a sensational edge. Child abuse, illness, and death are handled with great drama; some such pieces cite sources for additional information, but others contain fewer facts and more theatrics and bizarre circumstances.[47]

Women's journals today differ from those of earlier years in their overt and constant emphasis on sexual attractiveness. Explicit sexuality appears not just in the fashion and beauty pages; sex has moved squarely into advice columns, features, and health articles.

Audience

Editors still encourage the idea that their audiences comprise a community of women. *Family Circle*'s Jacqueline Leo likened her magazine to a Community Bulletin board and launched a Reader-to-Reader column; *McCall's* instituted a neighbor to neighbor page. The journals print tips, advice, and ideas from readers, as they did in the past. Readers receive a nominal amount for some write-ins; for others the pleasure of seeing their names in print has to serve as sufficient reward. *Woman's Day* began sponsoring reader lunches. The journals also publish letters to the editor, some critical. Printing such critiques makes readers feel that their negative feelings about articles or images can be part of the magazine. It also fosters the idea that the publications are open to criticism. All letters published must be viewed with some caution, however, as some may be written by magazine staff.[48]

Social Issues

Environmentalism has become popular, seen as an area logically of interest to women concerned with raising their families in a healthy world. Coverage has ranged from animal rights to fighting toxic polluters to tips on how to recycle.[49]

Violence has received attention, fitting in with the traditional view of woman as peacekeeper as well as mirroring a national concern. *Family Circle* listed the names and other details of all U.S. children killed by guns. *Harper's Bazaar* carried a piece on the way gun manufacturers target the female market. *Redbook* offered tips on stopping violence at the local level.[50]

Readers continue to turn to women's journals for health information. *Mirabella* even conducted a national symposium on women's healthcare in Washington, D.C., which First Lady Hillary Rodham Clinton attended. Nutrition, birth control, menopause, illnesses such as cancer, heart disease, lupus, all have been written about.[51] Stories on pregnancy and childbirth are mainstays. In recent years more articles have appeared on serious health concerns to women such as heart disease and cancer. Pieces often emphasize prevention.[52] Breast cancer surfaced in many publications. Articles advocated second opinions, provided information on treatment options, and gave lists of resources for support and education.[53]

The magazines have recognized and discussed mental and emotional illnesses. Stories acknowledge that alcoholism is an illness and portray the disease sympathetically. *Harper's Bazaar*'s annual special issue focusing on women over forty has often carried a piece on alcoholism. *Lear's* ran a regular column on addiction.[54]

Women's magazines have been accused of fostering eating disorders such as anorexia and bulimia. While conceding that eating disorders are an important female concern, women's journal personnel downplay the role of their publications in creating these problems. They point to forces such as other media (television, movies), other institutions (e.g., beauty pageants), and a range of factors such as individual personality, environment, and biology, which together contribute to eating disorders. They claim the women's titles only reflect the standards of the culture within which they are produced, and that readers themselves dislike it when publications use more normal weight models to show fashions; the clothes don't look right.[55] However, *Glamour* called for the creation of a National Eating Disorders coalition (analogous to the National Breast Cancer Coalition) to work for increased federal funding for research and programs, and other magazines have discussed the problem posed by eating disorders.[56] *Mode*, a title targeted at women who wear size 12 and higher, enjoyed a successful debut in 1997.

Mainstream women's journals eventually covered the feminist movement and wrote about some issues raised by feminists, such as equal pay and childcare. *Cosmopolitan* printed excerpts from feminist Kate Millett's explosive *Sexual Politics*. *Woman's Day* ran the results of a survey conducted by the National Organization of Women (NOW) about sexist television stations.[57] For the July 1976 bicentennial issue, *Redbook* editor Sey Chassler organized coverage of the Equal Rights Amendment (ERA); thirty-nine women's journals joined in this campaign and carried articles discussing the ERA.[58] Career information appears regularly in specialized magazines such as *Working Woman* and *Working Mother*. *Mademoiselle* has historically printed articles on jobs, as have *Glamour* and *Cosmopolitan*. These include useful tips on dealing with bosses, coworkers, subordinates, and the marriage-children-career balancing act.

Women's journals reflected U.S. society to the extent that women's issues received more extensive and more serious coverage in the 1970s than in the

1980s, when calls for changes in the status quo declined. Women's magazines never seriously questioned the economic and social system in which they operate. At the same time many advertisers co-opted the feminist message of equality, power, and independence, translating it into the right to purchase a wider range of products.

Advertisers' influence on content continues to be both direct and indirect. Competition for advertising remains stiff. Publishers promote their titles to advertisers heavily, offering research on readers as well as merchandising arrangements, continuing the patterns started earlier in the century. Value-added services include market research, couponing, contests, sponsorships, special sections and editions, and specialized marketing opportunities.

Many products advertised in women's journals are the ones traditionally seen in women's publications, while some new and some returning categories have surfaced, including spots for cars, insurance, travel, financial services, and office products. Grocery products remain the biggest ad category for the Seven Sisters. Cigarette advertising became an important revenue source for women's journals (except *Good Housekeeping*) after such ads were banned from television and radio (effective 1972). Acceptance of cigarette advertising inhibited the editorial coverage of cigarette related health problems for women.[59] Such ads have declined in recent years as the advertisers have sought other promotional outlets.

Females serve as the top editors at the major women's journals today. They are veteran journalism and media professionals, who, within the constraints of their organizations, stamp their own vision of what makes a successful women's magazine on their publications. However, in content decisions these editors are frequently bound, as were their predecessors, by the strictures of the market-place, by readers' tastes and advertisers' concerns. Editors rarely have a free hand to include the full range of subject matter they might like unless, like France Lear, they own the publication.

NOTES

1. Goldman, "New Woman," p. M26, recounting the opinion of magazine consultant Marty Walker.
2. Welles, "Iron Butterfly," pp. 65–73; and Brown, *Single Girl*.
3. Brown quoted ibid., p. 32.
4. Quoted in Friedman, "She Loves Being a Girl," p. 9.
5. Rothenberg, "Cosmo Girl," p. 32; SH interview; and e.g., Intrator, "Pregnant," pp. 154, 160.
6. Brown, "Feminism Now," p. 195.
7. Carmody, "Cosmopolitan Names Successor," p. D7.
8. "Feminist Forum," p. 104.
9. Wenner, "Ms.," pp. 267–69.
10. "Ms. A Personal Report," p. 6. For a sampling see Thom, *Letters*.
11. "Everything You Ever Wanted to Know About Advertising," p. 59; and

Steinem, "Sex, Lies, and Advertising," p. 22.

12. PC interview; VS interview; and "Everything You Ever Wanted to Know About Advertising," pp. 56–59, 90, 92.

13. VS interview; and Steinem, "Sex, Lies and Advertising," p. 26.

14. Ferguson, Kreshel, and Tinkham, "In Pages of Ms.," pp. 40–51.

15. Emmrich, "Daughters of Ms.," pp. M2, M3.

16. Milligan, "Sex Change?" pp. 17–21; and Diamond, "Steinem," pp. 50, 52.

17. Wayne, "Australia Concern," pp. D1, D22; and Schrambling, "A Sassy Approach," pp. 29, 44.

18. Guy, "Celebrities, Politics," p. 7B; and "Upstart to Mainstream," p. 72.

19. Roemer, "That Feminist Ms.tique," pp. 46–49.

20. Dougerty, "Negro Women," p. 71.

21. Fraser, "Essence Magazine Chief," p. 31; and Taft, *American Magazines*, pp. 244, 245.

22. Taft, *American Magazines*, p. 244.

23. McManus, "Essence," pp. 27–29.

24. Allen, "Essence," pp. 94, 95.

25. McManus, "Essence," p. 28.

26. Kennedy, "In Essence," p. D8.

27. See Lewis, "Celebration of Our Twentieth Anniversary," pp. 20, 25.

28. Britt, "Essence," p. G1; and "Top 300 magazines," p. 46.

29. BB interview.

30. Ibid.; and Raab, p. 22.

31. Farber, "Magazine Promoter."

32. "Chapter XI Filing," p. D8.

33. BB interview.

34. Taber quoted in Hirshfeld, "Working Woman," p. M-22.

35. E.g., Hellwig and Mann, "Salary Gap," p. 61. See also Taft, *American Magazines*, pp. 113, 114.

36. "Women's Success," p. 39.

37. Kleinfield, "Grace Mirabella," p. 13; and Maier, *Newhouse*, pp. 75–78.

38. *Lear's*, March 1994 issue.

39. Carmody, "Plug Pulled," p. D1

40. Kelly, "Innovative Lear's," p. 3; and Carmody, "Lear's Magazine."

41. Reilly, "Allure," p. B6.

42. Manly, "Makeover Contest," p. 31.

43. Donor, "Women's Magazines," pp. 38, 39.

44. Goodwin, "Brave Widow," pp. 80–84; Gallimore, "Save My Sisters," pp. 66–73; and Blyth, "Women Together," p. 10.

45. See e.g., *GH* Profiles; "Against All Odds," pp. 66–72; Groeber, "Blind, Deaf," pp. 42–48; and Wheatley, "Women Who Make Difference," pp. 15, 16.

46. February 1994 covers of *LHJ*, *GH*, and *McCall's*.

47. See e.g., Lowry, "Good Killing," pp. 100, 101, 154, 157; and Casey, "Beyond the Grave," pp. 104–8, 208.

48. PB interview.

49. Couturier, "Protecting," pp. 96–100; Arbanel, "Toxic Nightmare," pp. 77–80.

50. *FC*, March 1994, noted in "Scoops on Family," p. 3C; Horowitz, "Arms," pp. 166–69; and Antonio, "How You Can Stop Violence," pp. 77, 112–16.

51. Miller, *Descriptive Analysis*; and JL interview.

52. Ruggiero and Weston, "Popular Approach," pp. 47–62; Monson, "To Your Heart," pp. 41–47; and Lippert, "Women and Heart Disease," pp. 59–60.

53. Shannon, "Surviving," pp. 56, 57; Hales, "I'm Still Here," pp. 96–101, 192; Rock, "Breast Cancer," pp. 144–51, 220; Lang, "Find a Lump," pp. 104, 105, 155, 156; Arnot, "Can Talk Fight," p. 98; Woodman, "Life," pp. 98–105.

54. Kent, "Mental Health," pp. 519–52; Chalfant, "Alcoholic," pp. 19–26; and McCracken, *Decoding*, p. 167

55. Donahue, "Brown Lives," p. 2D; and NC interview.

56. Anderson, "Viewpoint?" pp. 139, 140. See also Callahan, "Cosmo's Update," pp. 230–33.

57. Hole and Levine, *Rebirth*, p. 264.

58. Butler and Paisley, "Magazine Coverage," pp. 183–86.

59. Ernster, "Mixed Messages," pp. 337, 339; Kessler, "Women's Magazines," pp. 316–22, 445; Whelan, "Alarm Clocks," p. A19; and Gritz, "Warning," pp. 4, 5.

Epilogue

Are women's magazines still the "old homes in a city of perpetual change" that Charles Hanson Towne wrote of in the 1920s? Will they continue to exist in the media city of the future? If so, what will they look like?

Women's journals will survive and flourish well into the twentieth century. They may shift their focus and redesign their pages. They may be supplemented with offerings on the Internet. But gender-oriented mass publications, supported by advertising, will endure. Advertisers still see these magazines as an efficient and effective way to reach female consumers. And women, despite changes in their lives, still value these journals, still want to plunge into a favorite title for entertainment, fantasy and concrete information on matters of importance to them, as they always have. Women may not like everything in these journals but at least these publications recognize and discuss the female experience.

Women's magazines play a different role in women's lives today than they have in the past. Other media compete vigorously for women's attention, at times diluting the impact of periodicals. Many females now work outside the home. But women still crave information on how to manage their lives, homes, families, and now careers. Publications focusing on fashion, beauty, health, and relationships also offer material women want. Magazines provide an efficient and convenient way to present ideas and facts, especially to working women who are traveling, commuting, fitting their information and entertainment needs into small pockets of time.

Today's women's titles address timely topics, carry reviews of books, movies, music, and art; dabble in politics and social issues; publish facts on health subjects. The celebrities profiled reflect the times. The material and messages, even if contradictory and read selectively, fall within a prescribed, relatively predictable range, dictated by the economic reasons for the magazines' existence. But the journals are fighting to identify, comprehend, and keep up with the interests of their readers.

Women's journals face greater competition than ever, for readers and for advertisers. Yet as magazine consultant Marty Walker has noted, "Family Circle and the other service books may be big dinosaurs, but they're also cash cows," still making money for their owners.[1]

A few trends for the future are apparent. New women's titles continue to appear. *Aspire*, *Latina*, and *Sports Traveler* are just a few recent entries. However, the field's keen competition, particularly for advertising, means that some die as well.

More magazines targeting older women will emerge as the population ages. Despite the difficulties of gaining support in the fifty-five plus category, financial realities will overcome cultural resistance to attending to older women's needs.

The emphasis on specialization will endure, as new publications target niches and old titles try to accommodate and reach defined reader segments. The mass circulation service journals have long been putting out ancillary publications aimed at particular groups of readers and they will continue these efforts, capitalizing on their brand names. The Internet may prove a useful tool in providing readers with additional specialized information, binding them more closely to a magazine. How well this forum will work for advertisers remains to be seen.

New technologies generally will lead to changes in the women's titles. Readers already reach the journals through fax and e-mail. Magazines generally are experimenting with on-line services. Here, women's publications are moving with other journals and will advance as rapidly as their publishers do.

Publishers will continue their efforts to shift more of their costs along to readers, as well as their attempts to shed marginal circulation and focus on core readers, that is, those highly interested in the publication and willing to pay for it.

Editorial content in the journals will continue to be shaped, as in the past, by the combined forces of readers, editors, advertisers, and the business and cultural environment in which the publications operate.

As for the three surviving Big Six titles—*Good Housekeeping*, *Ladies' Home Journal*, and *McCall's*—each looks optimistically toward the future. Each strives to keep up with reader and advertiser interests, as well as the competition. Inspiration and uplift, helpful tips and true-life stories rub shoulders. Advertising surrounds the articles and columns. Subject matter and content mix have shifted in two hundred years, but the focus on women as a special interest group has not.

NOTES

1. Masterton, "Profit Profile," p. 36.

Bibliography

MANUSCRIPT COLLECTIONS USED

William Alexander Letterbooks (WAL)
Bruce Barton (BBP)
Bureau of Vocational Information Records (BVIR)
Butterick Archives (BA)
Hayden Carruth (HCP)
Vera Connolly (VCP)
Crowell-Collier Publishing Co. (CCP)
Curtis Co. (CP)
Dorothy Dignam Papers (DDP)
Theodore Dreiser Papers (Lilly Library)
Theodore Dreiser Papers (University of Pennsylvania)
Christine Frederick (CMFP)
Bruce and Beatrice Gould (BG&BBGP)
Margaret Hickey Papers (MHP)
Herbert H. Hoover Papers (HHHP)
Gertrude Battles Lane (LC) (GBL Corr.)
Gertrude Battles Lane (Virginia Lane) (GBLVL)
Clara Savage Littledale (CSLP)
Marie Mattingly Meloney (MMM)
J.Walter Thompson Company (JWTC)
Martha Van Rensselaer (MVRP)

ORAL HISTORIES

Bruce and Beatrice Gould Oral History (BG&BBGOH), 1977 at CU Oral History Research Office.
Mary Bass Gibson (MBGOH), 1975 CU Oral History Research Office.

ORAL INTERVIEWS, CONDUCTED BY MEWZ

Mary Bliss (MBB) September 21, 1989
Myrna Blyth (MB) March 22, 1990
Beatrice Buckler (BB), April 17, 1990
Patricia Carbine (PC), February 13, 1990
John Mack Carter (JMC) May 1, 1990
Nancy Axelrod Comer (NC) March 14, 1990
Mary Bass Gibson (MBG) March 24, 1980
Seth Hoyt (SH) May 3, 1990
Jacqueline Leo (JL) April 13, 1990
Margaret Parton (MP) May 8, 1980
Geraldine Rhoads (GR) April 5, 1990
Valerie Salembier (VS) March 13, 1990

ISSUES OF THE MAGAZINES THEMSELVES

Abbreviations-Magazines

Advertising Age (AA)
Better Homes & Gardens (BH&G)
Business Week (BW)
Christian Science Monitor (CSM)
Family Circle (FC)
Good Housekeeping (GH)
Journalism History (JH)
Ladies' Home Journal (LHJ)
New York Times (NYT)
Pictorial Review (PR)
Printers Ink (PI)
Wall Street Journal (WSJ)
Woman's Home Companion (WHC)

Abbreviations-Individuals

William Alexander (WA)
Bruce Barton (BB)
Edward Bok (EB)
Hayden Carruth (HC)
Frederick Collins (FC)
Dorothy Dignam (DD)
Theodore Dreiser (TD)
Sally Easton (SE)
Gertrude Battles Lane (GBL)
Virginia N. Lane (VNL)
Clara Savage Littledale (CSL)
Marie Mattingly Meloney (MMM)
Loring Schuler (LS)
James Eaton Tower (JET)
Gerald W. Young (GWY)

BOOKS

100 Thrift Recipes. Philadelphia: Curtis Co., 1918.

100 Leading A.B.C. Magazines. New York: MAB of MPA, 1968.

Ackerman, Martin. *The Curtis Affair*. Los Angeles: Nash Publishing, 1970.

Adams, Elizabeth Kemper. *Women Professional Workers*. Chatauqua, NY: Chautauqua Press, 1921.

Adams, James R. *More Power to Advertising*. New York: Harper & Brothers, 1927.

Agnew, Hugh. *Advertising Media*. New York: D. Van Nostrand Co., 1932.

Agnew, Hugh and Warren Dygert. *Advertising Media*. New York: McGraw Hill, 1938.

Allen, Frederick Lewis. *Only Yesterday*. New York: Harper and Row, 1931.

Anderson, Oscar, Jr. *The Health of a Nation*. Chicago: University of Chicago Press, 1958.

Anthony, Edward. *This Is Where I Came In*. Garden City, NY: Doubleday and Co., 1980.

Austin, Mary. *A Woman of Genius*. Garden City, NY: Doubleday Page, 1912.

Automobile Markets—Influence of Women. Philadelphia: Curtis Co., 1920.

Ayer, N. W. & Son. *American Newspaper Annual*. Philadelphia: N. W. Ayer & Son, 1891–1960.

Banks, Elizabeth. *The Autobiography of a Newspaper Girl*. New York: Doubleday, Page & Co., 1902.

Banner, Lois. *Women in Modern America*. New York: Harcourt, Brace, Jovanovich, 1974.

Barnouw, Erik. *A Tower of Babel*. Vol 1. New York: Oxford University Press, 1966.

Baughman, James L. *The Republic Of Mass Culture*. Baltimore, MD: John's Hopkins University Press, 1992.

Beard, Charles and Mary. *America at Midpassage*. New York: MacMillan, 1939.

Bernays, Edward L. *Biography of an Idea*. New York: Simon and Schuster, 1965.

Bigelow, William, ed. *The Good Housekeeping Book of Marriage*. New York: Prentice-Hall, 1938.

Blair, Karen. *The Clubwoman as Feminist*. New York: Holmes & Meier Publishers, Inc., 1980.

Bok, Edward. *A Man from Maine*. New York: Charles Scribner's and Sons, 1923.

Bok, Edward. *The Americanization of Edward Bok*. New York: Charles Scribner's and Sons, 1920.

Borden, Neil. *The Economic Effects of Advertising*. Chicago: Richard D. Erwin Company, 1942.

Boughner, Genevieve. *Women in Journalism*. New York: D. Appleton and Co., 1926.

Brown, Helen Gurley. *Sex and the Single Girl*. New York: Bernard Geis, 1962.

Bryk, Nancy Villa, ed. *American Dress Pattern Catalogs, 1873–1909*. New York: Dover Publications, 1988.

Bullock, Penelope. *The Afro-American Periodical Press, 1839–1909*. Baton Rouge: Louisiana State University Press, 1981.

Butterick Transfer for Embroidery, Braidery, Etc. New York: Butterick Co., 1916.

Chafe, William. *The American Woman*. New York: Oxford University Press, 1972.

Chase, Edna Woolman and Ilka Chase. *Always in Vogue*. Garden City, NY: Doubleday and Company, 1954.

Chenery, William. *So It Seemed*. New York: Harcourt, Brace, 1952.

Cleveland and the Family Circle. Newark, NJ: Family Circle, 1943.

Cohn, Jan. *Creating America*. Pittsburgh, PA: University of Pittsburgh Press, 1989.

Cohn, Jan. *Improbable Fiction*. New York: Harper & Brothers, 1980.

Compaine, Ben. *Consumer Magazines at the Crossroads*. White Plains, NY: Knowledge Industry Publications, Inc., 1974.

Compaine, Ben, ed. *Who Owns the Media?* New York: Harmony Books, 1979.

Connolly, Vera. *Judy Grant*. New York: Dodd, Mead & Co., 1940.

Consumer Magazine and Farm Publication Rates. Skokie, IL: Standard Rate and Data Service, 1930.

Cooney, John. *The Annenbergs*. New York: Simon and Schuster, 1982.

The Cosmopolitan Market. New York: Hearst's Cosmopolitan, 1927.

Cott, Nancy. *The Grounding of Modern Feminism*. New Haven, CT: Yale University Press, 1987.

Cowan, Ruth Schwartz. *More Work for Mother*. New York: Basic Books, 1983.

Croly, Jane Cunningham. *The History of the Woman's Club Movement in America*. New York: Henry G. Allen Co., 1898.

Crowell Co. *About the Crowell Co.* Springfield, OH: Crowell Co., 1903.

Crowell-Collier Co. *The Story of Selling*. New York: Crowell Co., 1946.

Crowell-Collier Co. *National Markets and National Advertising, 1922*. New York: Crowell Co., 1922.

Crowell-Collier Circulations, 1939 Survey. New York: Crowell-Collier Co., 1939.

Culligan, Matthew. *The Curtis-Culligan Story*. New York: Crown Publishers, 1970.

Curtis Co. *Digests of Principal Research Department Studies*. Philadelphia: Curtis Co., 1946.

Curtis Co. *Expenditures of Advertisers in Leading National and Farm Publications*. Philadelphia: Curtis Co., 1920.

Curtis Co. *How to Sell 100 Copies a Week*. Philadelphia: Curtis Co., 1912.

Curtis Co. *Selling Efforts*. Philadelphia: Curtis Co., 1913, 1914.

Daggett, Mabel Potter. *Women Wanted*. New York: George H. Doran, 1918.

Damon-Moore, Helen. *Magazines for Millions*. Albany: SUNY Press, 1994.

The Delineator's Prize $3,000 Houses. New York: B. W. Dodge & Co., 1909.

Dignam, Dorothy. *Mrs. Jones Discovers the Most Interesting Home in the World*. New York: Butterick Publishing Co., 1931.

Donham, S. Agnes. *The Eastern Massachusetts Home Economics Association*. Eastern Massachusetts Home Economics Association, 1954.

Dorr, Rheta Childe. *A Woman of Fifty*. New York: Funk & Wagnalls Company, 1924.

Douglas, Susan. *Inventing American Broadcasting, 1899–1922*. Baltimore: John's Hopkins University Press, 1987.

Dudley, Dorothy. *Forgotten Frontiers*. New York: Harrison Smith and Robert Haas, 1932.

Economic Facts Pertaining to the Future of Magazines. New York: MAB at the Request of the NPA, 1944.

Family Food and Grocery Purchasing. New York: Crowell-Collier Publishing Company, 1941.

Ferber, Edna. *A Peculiar Treasure*. New York: Doubleday, 1939.

Filler, Louis. *Crusaders for American Liberalism*. Yellow Springs, OH: The Antioch Press, 1964.

Fowler, Nathaniel. *About Advertising and Publicity*. New York: Publicity Publishing Co., 1897.

Fox, Stephen. *The Mirror Makers*. New York: Vintage, 1984.

Frederick, Christine Frederick. *Selling Mrs. Consumer*. New York: The Business Bourse, 1929.

Friedan, Betty. *The Feminine Mystique*. New York: W. W. Norton, 1963.

Friedrich, Otto. *Decline and Fall*. New York: Harper and Row, 1969.

Fuller, Walter Dean. *The Life and Times of Cyrus H. K. Curtis, 1850–1933*. New York: Newcomen Society Address, 1948.

Furnas, J. C. *How America Lives*. New York: Henry Holt & Co., 1941.

Garrison, Dee. *Mary Heaton Vorse*. Philadelphia: Temple University Press, 1989.

Geller, Max. *Advertising at the Crossroads*. New York: Ronald Press Co., 1952.

Gilbert, Juliet Goldsmith. *Ferber*. Garden City, NY: Doubleday & Co., 1978.

Gilles, Claire Louise. *Materials on Education in Selected Women's Magazines, 1890–99, 1930–39 and 1947–56*. Doctoral Dissertation, University of Pennsylvania, 1962.

Girard, Reverend Cosmas Francis. *American Women's Magazines and the Concept of Marriage, 1901–1951*. Doctoral Dissertation, St. Louis University, 1955.

Glazer, Penina Migdal and Miriam Slater. *Unequal Colleagues*. New Brunswick, NJ: Rutgers University Press, 1987.

Goren, Arthur A. "The Jewish Press." In *The Ethnic Press in the United States*. Sally M. Miller, ed. Westport, CT: Greenwood Press, 1987: 210.

Gould, Bruce and Beatrice Blackmar Gould. *American Story*. New York: Harper and Row, 1968.

Goulden, Joseph. *The Curtis Caper*. New York: Putnam, 1965.

Gundlach, Ernest. *Facts and Fetishes in Advertising*. Chicago: Consolidated Publishers, Inc., 1931.

Hamburger, Estelle. *It's a Woman's Business*. New York: Vanguard, 1939.

Hershey, Lenore. *The Pace and the Pattern*. New York: McCall Corp., 1950.

Hershey, Lenore. *Between Covers*. New York: Coward and McCann, Inc., 1983.

Hinds, Marjorie M. and David L. *Magazine Magic*. Laceyville, PA: The Messenger Book Press, 1972.

Historical Statistics of the U.S., Colonial Times to 1970. Part 1. U.S. Dept. of Commerce, Bureau of the Census, Washington, D.C., 1975.

Hole, Judith and Ellen Levine. *Rebirth of Feminism*. New York: Quadrangle Books, 1971.

Honey, Maureen, ed. *Breaking the Tie that Binds*. Norman: University of Oklahoma Press, 1992.

Honey, Maureen. *Creating Rosie the Riveter*. Amherst: University of Massachusetts Press, 1984.

How Consumers Evaluate Magazines. New York: Parents Institute, Inc., 1938.

Hower, Ralph. *The History of an Advertising Agency*. Cambridge, MA: Harvard University Press, 1949.

Hughes, J.R.T. "Eight Tycoons." In Ralph Andreano, ed., *The New Economic History*. New York, 1970.

Hungerford, Herbert. *How Publishers Win*. Washington, D.C.: Ransdell, Inc., 1931.

Jong, Erica. *Fear of Flying*. New York: Holt, Rinehart and Winston, 1973.

Kallet, Arthur and F. J. Schlink. *100,000,000 Guinea Pigs*. Vanguard Press: New York, 1932.

Kessler-Harris, Alice. *Out to Work*. New York: Oxford University Press, 1982.

Kidwell, Claudia Brush. *Cutting a Fashionable Fit*. Washington, D.C.: Smithsonian Institution Press, 1979.

Kirkland, Edward Chase. *Industry Comes of Age*. New York: Holt, Rinehart and Winston, 1961.

Leading Advertisers, Showing Advertising Investments of Advertisers. Philadelphia: Curtis Co., 1921–37.

Leckie, Janet. *A Talent for Living*. New York: Hawthorn Books, 1970.

Lemons, J. Stanley. *The Woman Citizen*. Urbana: University of Illinois Press, 1973.

Levin, Phyllis Lee. *The Wheels of Fashion*. Garden City, NY: Doubleday & Co., 1965.

Lewis, R.W.B. *Edith Wharton*. New York: Harper & Row, 1975.

Lord & Thomas. *America's Magazines and Their Relation to the Advertiser*. Chicago, 1895.

Macfadden, Mary and Emile Gauvreau. *Dumbbells and Carrot Strips*. New York: Henry Holt, 1953.

Magazine Circulation and Rate Trends, 1937–1952. New York: ANA, Inc., 1953.

Maier, Thomas. *Newhouse*. New York: St. Martin's Press, 1994.

Makosky, Donald Robin. *The Portrayal of Women in Wide-Circulation Magazine Short Stories*. Doctoral Dissertation, University of Pennsylvania, 1966.

Marchand, Roland. *Advertising the American Dream*. Berkeley: University of California Press, 1985.

Martin, Theodora Penny. *The Sound of Our Own Voices*. Boston: Beacon Press, 1987.

Marzolf, Marion. *Up From the Footnote*. New York: Hastings House Publishers, 1977.

Matthews, Glenna. *Just a Housewife*. New York: Oxford University Press.

Mayer, Marvin. *Madison Ave USA*. New York: Harper Brothers, 1958.

Mayes, Herbert. *Magazine Maze*. Garden City, NY: Doubleday and Co., Inc., 1980.

McCall's—Qualitative Study of Magazines. New York: McCall Co., 1946.

McCracken, Ellen. *Decoding Women's Magazines*. St. Martin's Press: New York, 1993.

Mechling, Jay. "The Collecting Self and American Youth Movements." *Consuming Visions*, Simon J. Bronner, ed. New York: W. W. Norton and Co. for the Winterthur Museum, 1989: 260.

The Merchandising of Radio. Philadelphia: Curtis Co., 1925.

Midas Gold. New York: Butterick Co., 1925.

Miller, Alice E. *A Descriptive Analysis of Health Related Articles in the Six Leading Women's Magazines*. Doctoral Dissertation, Southern Illinois University, 1979.

Mott, Frank Luther. *A History of American Magazines, 1741–1850*, I; *1850–1865*, II; *1865–1885*, III; *1885–1905*, IV; *1905–1930*, V. Cambridge, MA: Harvard University Press, 1938, 1957, 1968.

Mrs. John Doe. New York: Butterick Co., 1918.

Naether, Carl. *Advertising to Women*. New York: Prentice Hall, Inc., 1928.

National Advertising. The Modern Selling-Force. Philadelphia: Curtis Co., 1910.

National Advertising Records. New York: Denney Co., 1931–39.

The National Cyclopaedia of American Biography (reprint). Ann Arbor, MI: University Microfilm Incorporated, 1967.

The National Market and Crowell Circulation. New York: Crowell Co., 1933.

Notable American Women, 1607–1950. Cambridge, MA: Belknap Press of Harvard University Press, 1971.

Olney, Martha. *Buy Now Pay Later*. Chapel Hill: University of North Carolina, 1991.

Oppenheimer, Judy. *Private Demons*. New York: Fawcett Columbine, 1988.

Papa Gander. New York: Crowell Co., 1937.

Pease, Otis. *The Responsibilities of American Advertising*. New Haven, CT: Yale University Press, 1958.

Peterson, Theodore. *Magazines in the Twentieth Century*. Urbana, IL: University of Illinois Press, 1964.

Phillips, Mary C. *Skin Deep*. New York: The Vanguard Press, 1934.

Pope, Daniel. *The Making of Modern Advertising*. New York: Basic Books, 1983.

Porter, Michael. *Competitive Strategy*. New York: Free Press, 1980.

Presbrey, Frank. *The History and Development of Advertising*. New York: Doubleday, Doran and Co., Inc., 1929.

A Qualitative Study of Magazines. New York: McCall Co., 1946.

Radway, Janice. *Reading the Romance*. Chapel Hill: University of North Carolina Press, 1984.

Rascoe, Burton. *Bookman's Daybook*. New York: Liveright, 1929.

Regier, C. C. *Era of the Muckrakers*. Chapel Hill: University of North Carolina Press, 1932.

Reid, Margaret. *Consumers and the Market*. New York: F. S. Crofts & Co., 1938.

Richardson, Glenna Crooks. *Portrayal of Birth in an American Medium*. Doctoral Dissertation, University of Indiana, 1978.

Riggio, Thomas, ed. *Dreiser-Mencken Letters*. Vol. 1. Philadelphia: University of Pennsylvania Press, 1986.

Rinehart, Mary Roberts. *My Story*. New York: Rinehart & Co., 1948.

Rorty, James. *Our Master's Voice*. New York: John Day, 1934.

Ross, Ishbel. *Crusades and Crinolines*. New York: Harper & Row, 1963.

Ross, Ishbel. *Ladies of the Press*. New York: Harper and Brothers, 1936.

Rupp, Leila. *Mobilizing Women for War*. Princeton: Princeton University Press, 1978.

Ryan, Mary. *Womanhood in America*. New York: New Viewpoints, 1975.

Ryant, Carl. *Profit's Prophet*. Susquehanna: Susquehanna University Press, 1989.

Sales Opportunities. Philadelphia: Curtis Co., 1948.

Sanders, Marion. *Dorothy Thompson*. Boston: Houghton Mifflin Co., 1973.

Scanlon, Jennifer. *Inarticulate Longings*. Doctoral Dissertation, SUNY Binghamton, 1989.

Schlipp, Madelon Golden and Sharon M. Murphy. *Great Women of the Press*. Carbondale: Southern Illinois University Press, 1983.

Schudson, Michael. *Advertising*. New York: Basic Books, 1984.

Schuler, Marjorie, Ruth Adams Knight and Muriel Fuller. *Lady Editor*. New York: E. P. Dutton and Co., Inc., 1941.

Scott, Walter Dill. *The Psychology of Advertising*. Boston: Small, Maynard, 1908.

Seebohm, Caroline. *The Man Who Was Vogue*. New York: Viking Press, 1982.

Seldin, Joseph. *The Golden Fleece*. New York: The Macmillan Company, 1963.

Shapiro, Laura. *Perfection Salad*. New York: Henry Holt and Company, 1986.

Shi, David E. *The Simple Life*. New York: Oxford University Press, 1985.

Sims, Janet L., comp. *The Progress of Afro-American Women*. Westport, CT: Greenwood Press, 1980.

Sinclair, Upton. *The Brass Check*. Pasadena, CA: published by the author, 1920.

Skocpol, Theda. *Protecting Soldiers and Mothers*. Cambridge, MA: Belknap Press of Harvard University Press, 1992.

Smith, Paul. *Personal File*. New York: Appleton-Century, 1964.

Snow, Carmel, with Mary Louise Aswell. *The World of Carmel Snow*. New York: McGraw-Hill, 1962.

Spalding, John W. "1928: Radio Becomes a Mass Advertising Medium." In John W. Wright, ed., *The Commercial Connection*. New York: Delta Publishing, 1979: 70–79.

Starch, Daniel. *Principles of Advertising*. Chicago: A. W. Shaw Company, 1923.

Statistical Abstract of the United States, 1940. Washington, D.C.: U.S. Government Printing Office, 1941.

Steinberg, Salme. *Reformer in the Marketplace*. Baton Rouge: Louisiana State University Press, 1979.

Stineman, Esther. *What the Ladies Were Reading*. Doctoral Dissertation, Library School, University of Chicago, 1976.

Stineman, Esther Lanigan. *Mary Austin*. New Haven, CT: Yale University Press, 1989.

The Story of a Magazine. Philadelphia: The Press of the Ladies' Home Journal, 1890.

The Story of a Pantry Shelf. New York: Butterick Co., 1925.

Strasser, Susan. *Never Done*. New York: Pantheon Books, 1982.

The Studio Book. New York: Hearst Company, 1930.

A Study of City Markets, 1928–1929. Philadelphia: Curtis Co., 1930.

Swanberg, W. A. *Citizen Hearst*. New York: Charles Scribner's, 1961.

Swanberg, W. A. *Dreiser*. New York: Charles Scribner's Sons, 1965.

Tabachnick, Sharon. "Family Circle." In Alan Nourie and Barbara Nourie, eds., *American Mass-Market Magazines*. Westport, CT: Greenwood Press, 1990: 121.

Taft, William H. *American Magazines for the 1980s*. New York: Hastings House, Publishers, 1982.

Talmadge, John. *Corra Harris*. Athens: University of Georgia Press, 1968.

Tassin, Algernon. *The Magazine in America*. New York: Dodd, Mead & Co., 1916.

Tebbel, John. *The American Magazine*. New York: Hawthorn, 1969.

Tebbel, John and Mary Ellen Zuckerman. *The Magazine in America, 1741–1990*. New York: Oxford University Press, 1991.

Thayer, John Adams. *Astir*. Boston: Small, Maynard and Co., 1910.

Thom, Mary, ed. *Letters to Ms*. New York: Henry Holt and Co., 1987.

Thompson, Dorothy. *The Courage to Be Happy*. Boston: Houghton Mifflin, 1957.

Thompson, J. Walter. *Advertising*, 1895.

Thompson, J. Walter. *Illustrated Catalog of Magazines Compiled for the Use of Advertisers*. J. Walter Thompson Co., 1887.

Tipper, Harry, H. L. Hollingworth, G. B. Hotchkiss and F. A. Parsons. *Advertising*. New York: Ronald Press, 1915.

Towne, Charles Hanson. *Adventures in Editing*. New York: D. Appleton, 1926.

Tucker, Phillip W. *Recollections of My Forty Years with Butterick*. Typescript in Butterick Archives, n.d.

Ulmann, Doris. *A Portrait Gallery of American Editors*. New York: W. E. Rudge, 1925.

Vorse, Mary Heaton. *A Footnote to Folly*. New York: Farrar and Rinehart, 1935.

Waller (Zuckerman), Mary Ellen. *Popular Women's Magazines, 1890–1916*. Doctoral Dissertation, Dept. of History, Columbia University, 1987.

Waller-Zuckerman, Mary Ellen. "The Federal Trade Commision in Historical Perspective." *Marketing and Advertising Regulation*. Patrick Murphy and William Wilkie, eds. Notre Dame: University of Notre Dame Press, 1990: 169–202.

Ware, Susan. *Beyond Suffrage*. Cambridge, MA: Harvard Univeristy Press, 1981.

Weibel, Kathryn. *Mirror, Mirror*. Garden City, NY: Anchor Press, 1977.

Weigley, Emma Seifrit. *Sarah Tyson Rorer*. Philadelphia: The American Philosophical Society, 1977.

Weiland, Barbara, ed. *Needlework Nostalgia*. New York: Butterick Publishing Co., 1975.

Wenner, Sandra. "Ms." In Alan Nourie and Barbara Nourie, eds. *American Mass-Market Magazines*. Westport, CT: Greenwood Press, 1990: 267–69.

Wharton, Edith. *The Age of Innocence*. New York: D. Appleton and Company, 1920.

Who Was Who in America with World Notables. Wilmette, IL: Marquis Who's Who, 1950, 1989.

Who Was Who Among English and European Authors. Detroit: Gale Research Co., 1978.

Wiley, Harvey Washington. *A History of a Crime Against the Food Law*. New York: Arno Press, 1929.

Williams, Tennessee. *The Glass Menagerie*. New York: New Directions, 1966.

Wilson, Christopher P. *The Labor of Words*. Athens: University of Georgia Press, 1985.

Winkler, Allan M. *The Politics of Propaganda*. New Haven, CT: Yale University Press, 1978.

Women in the Influential Homes. New York: Initiated by GH, 1928.

Wood, James Playsted. *The Curtis Magazines*. New York: Ronald Press, 1949.

Wood, James Playsted. *Magazines in the United States*. New York: Ronald Press, 1949.

Wood, James Playsted. *The Story of Advertising*. New York: Ronald Press, 1958.

Woodward, Helen. *It's an Art*. New York: Harcourt, Brace and Co., 1938.

Woodward, Helen. *The Lady Persuaders*. New York: I. Obolensky, 1960.

Woodward, Helen. *Through Many Windows*. New York: Harper and Brothers, 1926.

Wyman, Phillips. *Magazine Circulation*. New York: McCall Co., 1937.

Young, Gerald. *This Is Crowell-Collier*. New York: Crowell-Collier Co., 1947.

Zuckerman, Mary Ellen. "'Family Circle,' and 'Woman's Day.'" In Kathleen L. Endres and Therese L. Lueck, eds., *Women's Periodicals in the United States*, Westport, CT: Greenwood Press, 1995.

Zuckerman, Mary Ellen. *Sources on the History of Women's Magazines, 1792–1960*. Westport, CT: Greenwood Press, 1991.

ARTICLES

"Accent on 'Togetherness'." *The Writer* (October 1955): 322.

Adams, M. "Crusader." *Delineator* (September 1933): 15ff.

Addams, Jane. "The Working Woman and the Ballot." *WHC* (April 1908): 19.

Adler, Felix. "SEX Education." *GH* (January 1912): 22.

"Against All Odds." *LHJ* (December 1995): 66–72.

Alderson, Wroe. "Charles Coolidge Parlin." *Journal of Marketing*, no. 21 (July 1956): 1, 2.

Alexander, Shana. "The Feminine Eye." *McCall's* (December 1969): 7.

Allen, Bonnie. "Essence and Other Thoughts on the Eighties." *Essence* (May 1980): 94, 95.

Allen, Patricia. "Marie Stopes, Crusader." *PR* (April 1934): 26, 27, 77.

Alpert, Hollis. "What Killed Collier's?" *The Saturday Review* (May 11, 1957): 9–11, 42–44.

Anderson, Judith. "Viewpoint. Eating Disorders." *Glamour* (March 1994): 139, 140.

Anonymous. "I Married My Soldier Anyway." *GH* (June 1942): 33, 74.

Antrim, Doron. "New Futures for Girls." *WHC* (April 1943): 72, 73.

Arbanel, Stephanie. "Toxic Nightmare On Main Street." *FC* (1990): 77–80.

Arnot, Bob. "Can Talk Fight Breast Cancer?" *GH* (October 1995): 98.

"Arthur Vance Obituary." *NYT* (September 10, 1930): 25.

Austin, Mary. "Woman Looks at Her World." *PR* (November 1924): 64, 66, 69.

"An Autopsy." *Tide* (January 11, 1957): 23.

Bane, Lita. "New Values in Homemaking." *LHJ* (October 1929): 37, 124.

"Battle Among the Women." *Time* (July 28, 1961): 54.

"Bazaar's Fashion Specialists." HB Promotional Package, 1985.

Bell, Lilian. "Yessum." *WHC* (April 1897).

"Best Man in the Business." *Time* (June 27, 1941): 65, 66.

"The Birth Control Contest." *PR* (February 1916): 31.

Blair, Emily Newell. "Books for the Business Woman." *GH* (July 1929): 104, 214–19.

Blair, Emily Newell. "Where are Women Going?" *LHJ* (March 1919): 37, 58.

Blyth, Myrna. "Women Together." *LHJ* (January 1996): 10.

"Bobby-Sox Forum." *Newsweek* (October 30, 1944): 89–90.

Bogart, Leo. "Magazines Since the Rise of Television." *Journalism Quarterly* (Spring 1956): 153–66.

Bok, Edward. "The Magazine with a Million." *LHJ* (February 1903): 16.

Bok, Edward. "What I Have Seen." *LHJ* (December 1918): 1.

"Boudoir Gossip." *PR* (February 1900): 16.

Boyle, Ruth. "A Business Girl's Investments." *GH* (July 1929): 108.

Boyle, Ruth. "Is this Stock High?" *GH* (August 1929): 112.

Britt, Donna. "Behind the Spirit of Essence." *Washington Post* (May 5, 1990): G1.

Britt, Donna. "Top 300 Magazines by Gross Revenue." *AA* (June 20, 1994): 46.

Brown, Helen Gurley. "Feminism Now." *Cosmopolitan* (May 1994): 195.

Bryant, Gay. "Writing for Family Circle." *The Writer* (August 1985): 22.

Budd, Dorothy. "While Mothers Work." *WHC* (July 1942): 58, 59.

"But I've Never Worked Before!" *McCall's* (March 1944): 88.

Butler, Matilda and William Paisley. "Magazine Coverage of Women's Rights." *Journal of Communication* 28, no. 1 (Winter 1978): 183–86.

"Butterick Magazines to Merge." *NYT* (June 17, 1926): 12.

"By Advice of the Doctor." *WHC* (January 1902): 37, 38.

Cades, Hazel Rawson. "Hands on the Job." *WHC* (March 1943): 118, 119.

Callahan, Jean. "Cosmo's Update on Eating Disorders." *Cosmopolitan* (May 1996): 230–33.

Canby, Henry Seidel. "The Magazine Industry." *The Independent* (December 11, 1926): 666.

Cantor, Muriel and Elizabeth Jones. "Creating Fiction for Women." *Communication Research* 10, no. 1 (January 1983): 111–37.

Carmody, Deirdre. "Helen Gurley Brown Leaving." *NYT* (January 17, 1996): D7.

Carmody, Deirdre. "John Mack Carter to Head New Hearst Magazine Unit." *NYT* (October 14, 1994): D17.

Carmody, Deirdre. "Lear's Magazine Is Expected to Be Closed." *NYT* (March 10, 1994): D20.

Carmody, Deirdre. "New Makeover For Mademoiselle." *NYT* (March 21, 1994): D8.

Carmody, Deirdre. "Why the Plug Was Pulled at Lear's." *NYT* (March 14, 1994): D1.

Casey, Kathryn. "From Beyond the Grave." *LHJ* (May 1996): 104–88, 208.

Casson, Herbert. "The Wonders of Magazine Making." *WHC* (September 1904): 8, 9.

Chalfant, H. Paul. "The Alcoholic in Magazines for Women." *Sociological Focus* 6 (Fall 1973): 19-26.

Chandler, Alfred D., Jr. "The Beginnings of 'Big Business' in American Industry." *BHR* 23 (Spring 1959): 1–31.

Chang, Eva. "A History of the Appeal to Women Readers in American Periodicals." Master's Essay, Columbia University School of Journalism, 1925.

"Chapter XI Filing by WW." *NYT* (December 28, 1977): D8.

"Circulation: 9,496,841." *Fortune* (August 1937): 67, 69, 100–8.

Clark, Kate Upson. "A Chat About Margaret Sangster." *WHC* (September 1904).

Clark, Thomas. "Poisoned Cargo." *FC* (February 1, 1994): 100–3.

Clarke, Ida Clyde. "What the Women Want to Vote For." *PR* (June 1920): 26.

Cohn, Jan. "The Business Ethic for Boys." *BHR* 61 (Summer 1987): 185–215.

Coleman, Willie M. "The Woman's Era, 1884–1897." *Sage* 1, no. 2 (Fall 1984): 36, 37.

Coleman, Kate. "Recipe for Success." *Savvy* (November 1987): 90, 104.

Committee on Public Information. "'They Say': But They Lie." *LHJ* (July 1918): 1, 76.

"Companion Climb." *Time* (July 27, 1936): 43.

A Companion Reader. "A Woman's Club with a Brand–New Idea." *WHC* (September 1920): 66.

"Companion Way." *WHC* (June 1942): 51, 56, 57.

"Conde Nast Dead." *NYT* (September 19, 1942): 39.

Connolly, Vera. "The End of a Long, Long Trail." *GH* (April 1934): 51.

Connolly, Vera. "Every Man For Himself." *GH* (February 1928): 18, 19, 165–81.

Connolly, Vera. "Get the Children Out of the Jails." *WHC* (November 1944): 40.

Connolly, Vera. "Girls Who Run Away." *GH* (July 1927): 40, 41, 194–99.

Connolly, Vera. "Happily Married." *GH* (April 1930): 30, 31, 306–22.

Connolly, Vera. "Is Any Man Worth Fighting For?" *GH* (February 1933): 34, 35, 190–94.

Connolly, Vera. "Is This the End of the Road?" *GH* (May 1929): 15.

Connolly, Vera. "Let's Look At the Home." *GH* (November 1926): 24–29, 264–76.

Connolly, Vera. "Parents Wake Up!" *GH* (July 1923): 67, 166–74.

Connolly, Vera. "Repeat Courses in Matrimony." *GH* (February 1936): 46, 47, 153–60.

Connolly, Vera. "Stampede of Youth." *GH* (August 1926): 36, 37, 170–77.

Converse, Albert. "The Housekeeping of Mr. Smith." *McCall's* (May 1912).

Cook, Elizabeth. "The Kitchen Sink Complex." *LHJ* (September 1931): 12, 148.

Coolsen, Frank. "Pioneers in the Development of Advertising." *Journal of Marketing* (July 1947): 83.

Copperfield, Dora (pseud.). "The Women's Magazines." *Vanity Fair* (January 1934): 22, 23, 53.

Couturier, Lisa. "Protecting Our Fellow Creatures." *New Women* (February 1994): 96-100.

Cowan, Ruth Schwartz. "Two Washes in the Morning and a Bridge Party at Night." *Women's Studies* 3, no. 6 (1976).

Crowther, Samuel. "What YOU Can Do to Help Restore Normal Living and Buying." *LHJ* (March 1932): 3.

Curti, Merle. "The Changing Concept of 'Human Nature' in the Literature of American Advertising." *BHR* 41 (Winter 1967): 335–57.

Dagavarian, Debra. "A Content Analysis of Women's Magazines." Unpublished paper, 1974, copy in possession of MEWZ.

Daggett, Mabel Potter. "An Appreciation of Pictorial Review's Stand for Equal Suffrage." *PR* (November 1918): 7.

Daggett, Mabel Potter. "What the War Really Means to Women." *PR* (November 1917): 13, 14, 36–39.

Daggett, Mabel Potter. "When the Delineator Was Young." *Delineator* (November 1910): 365, 419.

Daggett, Mabel Potter. "Women Who Wear War Jewelry." *PR* (December 1917): 24, 25, 50–52.

Daniels, Jonathan. "What Are Your Veterans' Chances?" *McCall's* (March 1945): 18, 19, 64–68.

D'Antonio, Michael D. "How You (Yes You!) Can Stop Violence in Your Town." *Redbook* (February 1996): 77, 112, 113, 115, 116.

De Kruif, Paul. "Before You Drink a Glass of Milk—." *LHJ* (September 1929): 8, 9, 162.

"The Demographic Woes of the 'Seven Sisters.'" *Magazine Industry Newsletter* (July 12, 1989): 3.

Diamond, Edwin. "Steinem Keeps Moving." *New York* (August 25, 1986): 50, 52.

"Dis-Service." *Delineator* (October 1917): 3.

Donaton, Scott. "'Woman's Day' Now Biggest Sister." *AA* (November 8, 1993): 54.

Donaton, Scott. "'Woman's Day' Cuts Its Rate Base." *AA* (October 16, 1989): 2.

Donor, Kalia. "Women's Magazines." *Social Policy* (Summer 1993): 38, 39, 42.

Dougerty, Philip H. "Advertising: A Magazine for Negro Women." *NYT* (February 11, 1971): 31.

Dreiser, Theodore. "Glory Be McGlathery." *PR* (January 1925): 5–7.

Drewry, John. "Defining the Woman's Home Companion." *Matrix* (December 1936–January 1937): 13.

Drewry, John. "Good Housekeeping—Men Read It Too." *The Writer* (October 1937): 319, 320.

Drewry, John. "The Ladies' Home Journal." *Matrix* (February/March 1937): 11–12.

Drewry, John. "PR-Delineator." *Writer*, no. 50 (December 1937): 56, 383, 384.

Duer, Elizabeth. "Is There a Panic in the Marriage Market?" *WHC* (May 1908): 6.

Dufford, Mabel. "A Business Woman in Politics." *WHC* (February 1912): 17–18.

Dunne, Finley Peter. "Mr. Dooley on the Magazines." *American Magazine*, no. 68 (October 1909).

Dunnigan, Alice E. "Early History of Negro Women in Journalism." *The Negro History Bulletin* (Summer 1965): 178–79, 193, 197.

"Earn Life or Lose It." *McCall's* (March 1912): 85.

Ellenthal, Ira. "Redbook Redux." *Folio* (September 1983): 142, 212.

Elliott, Harriet. "Ten Ways for You to Help National Defense." *GH* (March 1941): 42.

Emmrich, Stuart J. "'Family Circle' Marks 50th." *AA* (September 6, 1982): 10.

Emmrich, Stuart. "The Daughters of Ms." *AA* (September 13, 1982): M2, M3.

"End of an Epoch." *Newsweek* (March 19, 1962): 112.

Engman, Ronda. "The Gould Era—1935-1962." MA, Syracuse University, S. I. Newhouse School of Communications, 1993.

Ernster, Virginia. "Mixed Messages for Women." *New York State Journal of Medicine* (July 1985): 335–40.

"Everything You Wanted to Know about Advertising and Were Not Afraid to Ask." *Ms.* (November 1974): 59.

Fabrikant, Geraldine. "Gruner to Buy Times Women's Magazines." *NYT* (June 17, 1994): D1, D15.

Fabrikant, Geraldine. "As Hard Times Hit Industry, Woman's Day Is Being Sold." *NYT* (May 15, 1990): A1, D17.

"Facts Worth Knowing about the Panama Canal." *WHC* (June 1904): 26–27.

"Famous Women Doctors and Their Pioneer Work." *McCall's* (January 1912): 28, 29.

Fannin, Rebecca. "Image Revision for Magazines." *Marketing and Media Decisions* (January 1984): 121.

Farber, M. A. "Magazine Promoter Wins Over Its Editor." *NYT* (May 22, 1977).

Farley, Jennie. "Women's Magazines and ERA." *Journal of Communication* 28, no. 1. (Winter 1978): 187–92.

Farnham, Marynia and Ferdinand Lundberg. "Men Have Lost Their Women." *LHJ* (November 1944): 23, 132, 133.

Feeney, Sheila Ann. "Man-trap Marks a Milestone." *New York Daily News* (April 24, 1990): 39.

"The Feminine Eye." *Time* (April 25, 1969): 78.

"Feminist Forum." *Newsweek* (November 8, 1972): 104.

Ferguson, Jill Hicks, Peggy J. Kreshel and Spencer F. Tinkham. "In the Pages of Ms." *Journal of Advertising* 19, no. 1 (1990): 40–51.

"A Few Things We Have Done." *LHJ* (November 1908): 3.

Fillmore, Hildegarde. "Little Girl on a Big Plane." *McCall's* (April 1943): 104, 105, 112.

Fisher, Katherine. "Housekeeping Emerges from the Eighties." *GH* (May 1935): 80–83, ff.

Flanner, Janet. "The Generation that Knows Nothing Else." *WHC* (September 1939): 16, 17, 53.

Fleeson, Doris. "100,000 Men and a Girl." *WHC* (February 1944): 4, 116.

Fleeson, Doris. "That Feminine Touch." *WHC* (March 1944): 4, 132.

Fogel, Irene R. "Trends in Advertising in the Fashion Magazine, 1935–1944." Master's Essay, University of Missouri, 1946.

"Food Store Magazines Hit the Big Time." *BW* (February 9, 1952): 108, 110.

Ford, James L. "One Woman in Ten." *Bookman* 63 (March 1926): 37–43.

Fort, Cornelia. "At the Twilight's Last Gleaming." *WHC* (June 1943): 19.

Fraser, C. Gerald. "Ousted Essence Magazine Chief Accuses Playboy." *NYT* (May 6, 1971): 31.

Fried, Lisa I. "Hachette Fallout." *Folio* (November 1990): 41, 42.

Friedman, David. "She Loves Being a Girl." *New York Newsday* (April 26, 1990), Part II, pp. 8, 9.

"From Upstart to Mainstream." *Time* (December 12, 1988): 72.

Gaines, Jan. "War, Women, and Lipstick." *Heresies* 18 (1985): 42–47.

Gale, Harlow. "On the Psychology of Advertising." *Psychological Studies*, no. 1 (1900).

Gale, Zona. "Editors of the Younger Generation." *The Critic* 44 (April 1904): 319, 320.

Gallimore, Rangira Bea. "To Save My Sisters." *LHJ* (February 1995): 66–73.

Gerbner, George. "The Social Role of the Confession Magazine." *Social Forces* (Summer 1958): 29–40.

"Gertrude B. Lane, Noted Editor, Dies." *NYT* (September 26, 1941): 23.

Gibbs, L. D. "Woman's Capture of Congress." *GH* (January 1907): 36–38.

Gilchrist, Ellen. "Blue Satin." *GH* (October 1995): 237–39.

Gilchrist, Ellen. "Brady's Bunch." *AA* (April 6, 1996): 24.

Gilman, Charlotte Perkins. "Housekeeping." *McCall's* (December 1912).

"The Girl who Does Not Marry." *WHC* (January 1914): 5.

"Give Back Their Jobs." *WHC* (October 1943): 6, 7.

Goldman, Debra. "Looks Like a New Woman." *Magazine World* (February 18, 1991): M-26.

"Good Housekeeping Studio Suggests How to Make the Most of a Non-Descript Room." *GH* (August 1929): 68.

"Good Housekeeping and the WAR." *GH* (February 1942): 19.

Goodwin, Jan. "A Brave Widow in Bosnia." *McCall's* (October 1995): 80–84.

Gould, Beatrice. "That Freedom Shall Not Perish." *LHJ* (July 1941): 22, 23.

Gould, Beatrice. "Workshop Housewarming." *LHJ* (May 1949): 189, 214.

"Graduates of Life." *Time* (October 3, 1932): 19.

Graeve, Oscar. "Speaking of Delineator." *The Quill* (January 1937): 10.

Graham, Gordon. "Women Who Fly." *McCall's* (January 1911): 6, 7, 56.

Green, Hetty. "The Benefits of Business Training for Women." *WHC* (February 1900): 8.

Gritz, Ellen. "Warning: Women's Magazines Can Be Dangerous to Your Health." *On the Issues* 7 (1987): 4, 5.

Groeber, Deborah. "Blind, Deaf and Very, Very Successful." *McCall's* (December 1995): 42–48.

Gross, Barbara and Jagdish N. Sheth. "Time-Oriented Advertising." *Journal of Marketing* 63 (October 1989): 76–83.

Guy, Pat. "'Ms.' Takes on Celebrities, Politics." *USA Today* (May 19, 1989): 7B.

Hales, Dianne. "I'm Still Here." *LHJ* (October 1993): 96–100, 192.

Hard, William. "With All My Worldly Goods I Thee Endow, Yes, But Does He?" *Delineator* (October 1911): 217–18.

"Harding and Cox Both Favor the Maternity Bill." *GH* (September 1920): 4.

Harmon, Dudley. "Must I Go to Work?" *LHJ* (January 1919): 22

Harmon, Dudley, ed. "The New Day for Women." *LHJ* (April 1918): 29.

Hartmann, Susan. "Prescriptions for Penelope." *Women's Studies* 5 (1978): 223–39.

Hawes, Elizabeth. "Here Today—Where Tomorrow?" *McCall's* (June 1945): 22, 23, 66–72.

Head of the U.S. Fuel Administration. "Won't You Help to Save Coal?" *LHJ* (February 1918): 31.

Head of U.S. Food Administration. "'I Don't Care What Hoover Says.'" *LHJ* (February 1918): 33.

"Hearst Magazine Earnings." *PI* (March 16, 1939): 16.

"Hearts Divided." *Redbook* (September 1995).

Hellwig, B. and J. Mann. "The Truth About the Salary Gap." *Working Woman* (January 1988): 61.

Henderson, Daniel. "Good Housekeeping's Story." *The Quill* (October 1936): 9.

Herrick, Christine Terhune. "Which Side of the Fence?" *WHC* (November 1912): 16.

Herrick, Christine Terhune. "Do Women Want the Vote?" *WHC* (July 1911): 10.

Hill, Lyn Stiefel. "There Was an American Toy Theater!" *Theater Survey* 16 (November 1975): 165–84.

Hirshfeld, Neal. "Working Woman Caters to the Career Minded." *AA* (April 2, 1984): M-22.

"The History of the Good Housekeeping Seal." *GH* (May 1985): 354.

Hochwald, Lambeth. "Red-letter Days for Redbook." *Folio* (August 15, 1993): 51–53.

Hoover, Herbert. "What Every Woman Can Do to Help." *PR* (October 1917): 3.

Horowitz, Jay. "Arms and the Woman." *HB* (February 1994): 160–66.

"How to Do It Better, Do It Faster, Do It Right." *WD* (November 21, 1995): 23, 24.

"How You Can Help Win the War." *McCall's* (February 1942): 42.

Hughes, Charles Evans. "Women's Interests in the Big Questions of the Day." *WHC* (November 1916): 7, 8.

"The Ideas of a Foreseeing Woman." *LHJ* (March 1919): 43.

"I Didn't Raise My Boy to be a Soldier." *WHC* (November 1915): 23.

"If Baby's Doctor Goes to War." *McCall's* (January 1942): 62–65.

"Infant Mortality." *Delineator* (February 1915): 3.

Inge, Reverend Ralph. "The Question of Birth Control." *PR* (March 1932): 12, 13, 51.

Intrator, Nancy. "What to Do If You Can't Get Pregnant." *Cosmopolitan* (December 1995): 154, 160.

Jambor, Harold. "Theodore Dreiser, the Delineator Magazine, and Dependent Children." *Social Service Review*, 32 (March 1958): 34.

Jancke, Bertha. "The War Comes Home to an American Family." *McCall's* (May 1942): 6, 7, 108.

Johnson, Helen Louise. "The Consumer's Responsibility." *PR* (January 1917): 18, 32.

Johnson, Helen Louise. "The Meaning of the Label." *PR* (August 1914): 10, 54.

Johnson, Helen Louise. "The Right Kind of Food Conservation." *Designer* (December 1917): 22, 47.

Josephs, Ray. "My How You've Changed." *WHC* (February 1946): 4, 140.

"The Journalist's Birthday." *The Journalist* 23 (April 1889): 1, 2.

Kaempffert, Waldemar. "Visit to the Home of Thomas A. Edison." *WHC* (February 1904): 3,4.

"Kate Barnard of Oklahoma." *PR* (November 1912): 7.

Kelly, Keith J. "Gruner & Jahr Thinks Younger." *AA* (June 27, 1994): 4.

Kelly, Keith J. "Innovative 'Lear's' Sinks In a Sea of Red Ink." *AA* (March 14, 1994): 3.

Kennedy, Jane. "Development of Postal Rates 1845–1955." *Land Economics* 33, no. 2 (1957): 93–112.

Kennedy, Shawn. "In Essence, A Celebration of Black Women." *NYT* (May 7, 1990): D8.

Kent, Ruth. "Mental Health Coverage in Six Mass Magazines." *Journalism Quarterly* 39 (1962): 519–52.

Kerr, Sophie. "The First 75 Years." *WHC* (November 1948): 36–38, 118–24.

Kerr, Sophie. "Gertrude B. Lane." Personal memoir, copy sent to MEWZ by SE.

Kessler, Lauren. "Women's Magazines' Coverage of Smoking Related Health Hazards." *Journalism Quarterly* (Summer 1989): 316–22, 445.

Kielbowicz, Richard B. "Postal Subsidies for the Press and the Business of Mass Culture, 1880–1920." *BHR* 64 (Autumn 1990): 451–88.

Kincaid, Jean. "The New England Woman's Press Association." *The Journalist* 19 (January 26, 1889): 7–11.

Kinkaid, Mary Holland. "The Feminine Charms of the Woman Militant." *GH* (February 1912): 146–57.

Kleinfield, N. R. "Grace Mirabella, at 59, Starts Over Again." *NYT* (April 30, 1989): 13.

Knobis, Bertha. "The Only Woman Member of a National Parliament." *Delineator* (January 1912): 7.

Krafft, Susan. "Window on a Woman's Mind." *American Demographics* (December 1991): 44–50.

Kuna, David. "The Concept of Suggestion in the Early History of Advertising Psychology." *Journal of the History of the Behavioral Sciences* 12 (1976): 347–53.

"The Ladies' Home Journal." *The Journalist* (October 22, 1887): 10.

"Ladies' Line-up." *Time* (February 15, 1937): 50.

"Ladies' Man." *Newsweek* (February 17, 1975): 84, 85.

"Lady at the Top." *Newsweek* (April 1969): 88.

Lahman, Marion Sherwood. "Begin at the Beginning." *WHC* (September 1921): 24.

Lang, Susan S. "If You Find a Lump." *GH* (July 1995): 104, 105, 155, 156.

Laurvik, J. Nilsen. "The Modern American Girl." *WHC* (May 1912): 13.

Lazersfeld, Paul and Marjorie Fiske. "The 'Panel' as a New Tool for Measuring Opinion." *Public Opinion Quarterly* 2 (October 1938): 593–612.

Lears, T. J. Jackson. "The Concept of Cultural Hegemony." *American Historical Review* 90 (1985): 567–93.

Lentini, Cecelia. "Balancing Act in Women's Magazines." *AA* (October 19, 1981): S-2, S-64.

Lewis, Edward. "In Celebration of Our Twentieth Anniversary." *Essence* (May 1990): 20, 25.

Lewis, Sinclair and Dorothy Thompson. "Is America a Paradise for Women?" *PR* (June 1929): 14, 15.

"Liberating the Journal." *Newsweek* (August 3, 1970): 44.

"Liberating the Magazines." *Newsweek* (February 8, 1971): 101.

Lippert, Joan. "Women and Heart Disease." *LHJ* (October 1989): 59, 60, 66, 72–80.

Lochridge, Patricia. "I Shopped the Black Market." *WHC* (February 1944): 20.

Lochridge, Patricia. "VD: Menace and Challenge." *WHC* (March 1944): 34, 129–31.

Lockeley, Lawrence. "Notes on the History of Marketing Research." *Journal of Marketing* (April 1950): 733–36.

Logan, Mrs. John A. "Is American Home Life Disappearing?" *McCall's* (January 1912): 12, 73.

Lowry, Beverly. "A Good Killing." *LHJ* (February 1994): 100, 101, 154, 157.

Lynch, Edmund C. "Walter Dill Scott: Pioneer Industrial Psychologist." *BHR* 42, no. 2 (Summer 1968): 151.

Mabie, Janet. "Editor of Good Housekeeping Maintains Common Touch." *CSM* (June 24, 1932): 3.

Mabie, Janet. "Popular Stories Championed." *CSM* (June 1932): 3.

Mabie, Janet. "That an Editor Needs Courage, Wiese of McCall's Well Knows." *CSM* (June 27, 1932): 7.

Mabie, Janet. "Upon Graeve of Delineator." *CSM* (June 23, 1932): 3.

"Magazine Puts Seal of Approval on Its Own Success." *BW* (March 19, 1966): 191, 192.

"Magazines That Mirror Women's Success." *BW* (January 11, 1982): 39.

"The Majesty of the Law." *Delineator* (November 1915): 3.

"Man in a Woman's World." *Time* (January 6, 1947): 68.

"The Man Who Founded the Journal." *LHJ* (June 1950): 11, 12, 103.

Manly, Lorne. "Makeover Contest." *ADWEEK* (February 17, 1992): 30, 31.

Mannering, Mary. "Should an Actress Marry?" *McCall's* (May 1912): 12.

"Marching with Eleanor Roosevelt." *McCall's* (March 1942): 57.

"Martha Van Rensselaer." *DAB* (2) XIX: 208, 209.

Martin, Anne. "Women and 'Their' Magazines." *New Republic* (September 20, 1922): 91–93.

Martin, Jackie. "Here's the American Woman, 1942 Model." *WHC* (June 1942): 52, 53.

Masel-Walters, Lynn. "A Burning Cloud by Day." *JH* 3, no. 4 (1976–77): 103–10.

Masel-Walters, Lynn. "Their Rights and Nothing More." *Journalism Quarterly* 53 (Summer 1976): 242–51.

Masel-Walters, Lynn. "To Hustle with the Rowdies." *Journal of American Culture* (Spring 1980): 167–83.

Masterson, John. "Profit Profile. Family Circle." *Magazine Week* (February 24, 1992): 36.

Maxim, Hudson. "Coming War." *WHC* (March 1904): 7.

Maxim, Hudson. "Wonders of Modern Warfare." *WHC* (May 1904): 13, 54, 289.

Maxwell, Anne. "After the War—Peace?" *WHC* (March 1943): 18.

Maxwell, Anne. "We Asked 1,000 Men." *WHC* (July 1941): 10.

"Maybe 'McCall's' Threatens 'Journal,' but Bruce and Bea Gould Don't Think So." *AA* (May 8, 1961): 154.

Mayers, Robert C. V. "A Deal in Kanuka." *WHC* (January 1900): 7, 8.

"McCall's Century." *McCall's* (April 1976): 10.

"McCall's Store Tie-up." *BW* (September 17, 1938): 28.

McDowell, Margaret. "The Children's Feature." *The Midwest Quarterly* 36, no. 1 (October 1977): 38–44.

McFadden, Maureen. "Sibling Rivalry." *Magazine Age* (January 1982): 51.

McFadden, Maureen. "The Women's Magazines." *Magazine Age* (June 1984): 16, 17.

McKinnie, Adele. "Shall I Let My Child Play with War Toys?" *WHC* (November 1942): 52, 53.

McManus, Marjorie. "The Essence Magazine Success Story." *Folio* (December 1976): 27–29.

"Meet the Up-to-Date Editors of Ladies' Home Journal." *Quill and Scroll* (February/March 1939): 7, 8.

A Mere Masculinity. "This Feminism Business." *WHC* (April 1918): 12, 68, 69.

"Meredith Buys Ladies' Journal." *NYT* (January 4, 1986): 33.

Meyerowitz, Joanne. "Beyond the Feminine Mystique." *Journal of American History* (March 1993): 1455–82.

Milligan, Susan. "Has Ms. Undergone a Sex Change?" *Washington Monthly* (October 1986): 17–21.

Monson, Nancy. "To Your Heart." *WD* (February 22, 1994): 41–47.

Morriss, Tech. Sgt. Mack. "From This Day Forward." *McCall's* (October 1944): 16, 17, 56, 64.

Moskowitz, Milton. "Who Killed Collier's?" *The Nation* (January 5, 1957): 3–5.

Moyne, Ernest. "Baroness Gripenberg Writes an Article for Theodore Dreiser's Delineator." *Scandinavian Studies* 48 (Winter 1976): 85–93.

"Mrs. Louisa Knapp." *The Journalist* (January 26, 1889): 1, 2.

"Ms. A Personal Report." *Ms.* (July 1972): 6.

Mulcahy, Sheila Hogan. "Female Images in Women's and General Interest Magazine Advertising, 1905–1970." Master's Essay, University of Wisconsin-Madison, 1980.

Myers, Francis J. "Don't Take it Out on the Women." *WHC* (January 1946): 13, 76.

Nearing, Scott and Nellie Nearing. "Four Great Things a Woman Does at Home That Makes Her the Greatest Power in America Today." *LHJ* (June 1912): 12.

"Never Underestimate . . ." *Newsweek* (April 17, 1950): 64.

New, Anne L. "Women Wanted." *WHC* (April 1941): 32.

Newkirk, Alice Field. "Has the Woman Past 40 a Chance?" LHJ (January 1919): 23.

Northend, Mary. "Romance of the Fireless Cooker." *McCall's* (November 1912): 66, 67.

"Notes on Some Magazine Editors." *The Bookman* (December 1900): 357.

Ohmann, Richard. "Where Did Mass Culture Come From? The Case of Magazines." *Berkshire Review*, no. 16 (1981): 87–99.

"Origins and Progress of the Publishing House of E. Butterick & Co." *The Metropolitan* (July 1871): 59–61.

Palmer, Greta. "Your Baby or Your Job." *WHC* (October 1943): 4, 137, 138.

Pankhurst, Emmeline. "The Making of a Militant, I." *GH* (January 1914): 4–13.

Pankhurst, Emmeline. "The Making of a Militant, II." *GH* (February 1914): 171–80.

Pankhurst, Emmeline. "Why I am a Militant." *GH* (March 1914): 90.

"Parts for Tank Guns—Made by Women." *McCall's* (August 1943): 71.

Peter, John. "Women's Magazines." *Folio* (April 1977): 75, 76.

"Pictorial Review to Suspend." *NYT* (January 21, 1939): 18.

"A Picture of Tomorrow." *LHJ* (June 1918): 13.

Pollack, Judann. "In Fitful Pursuit of American Women." *AA* (January 8, 1996): S-4, S-38.

Pollay, Richard. "The Distorted Mirror." *Journal of Marketing* 50, no. 2 (April 1986).

Pollay, Richard. "The Subsiding Sizzle." *Journal of Marketing* 49 (Summer 1985): 24–37.

Porter, Jack Nusan. "Rosa Sonnenschien and the American Jewess." *American Jewish History* 68 (September 1978): 57–63.

"Premiums! Premiums!" *PR* (March 1900): 25.

Preston, Alice. "A Girl's Preparation for Marriage." *LHJ* (March 1908): 22.

Pringle, Henry. "High Hat." *Scribner's*, 104 (July 1938): 17, 21.

Pringle, Henry. "What Do the Women of America Think About Advertising?" *LHJ* (May 1939): 22, 60.

Prior-Miller, Marcia. "Vogue, 1929–1942." MA Thesis, University of Missouri-Columbia, 1981.

"Program for Discussion." *Delineator* (May 1912): 437.

"A Quarter Century of Cleavage." *Newsweek* (April 23, 1990): 57.

Quinlan, Roy. "The Story of Magazine Distribution." *Magazine Week* (October 19, 1953): 4, 5.

Raab, Selwyn. "Despite Hint of Mafia Tie, Lottery Let Promoter Take Vending Role." *NYT* (March 1, 1977): 22.

Radziwill and Von Ziekursch. "The Three Women Behind the Demogogue." *PR*: 7, 63–65.

Ray, Cora Corkill. "A Descriptive Comparison of the War-Related Content of Good Housekeeping During Worlld War I and World War II." MA Thesis, Dept. of Journalism, University of Kansas, 1980.

Reilly, Patrick M. "Hard Nosed Allure Wins Readers and Ads." *WSJ* (August 27, 1992): B6.

"Reporters Who Get Results." *Independent Woman* 14 (November 1935): 379.

Reuss, Carol. "The LHJ and Hoover's Food Program." *Journalism Quarterly* (Winter 1972): 740–42.

Rhoads, Geraldine. "How to Sell a Magazine One Issue at a Time." *Saturday Review* (September 11, 1971): 61.

Richardson, Anna Steese. "Good Citizenship." *WHC* (July 1920): 2.

Richardson, Anna Steese. "Is This Woman's War?" *WHC* (August 1918): 2.

Richardson, Anna Steese. "National Defense: What Can WE Do?" *WHC* (June 1941): 42, 43, 84.

Richardson, Anna Steese. "Truth About Equal Suffrage." *WHC* (October 1910): 17–18.

Richardson, Anna Steese. "Women as Municipal Housekeepers." *McCall's* (April 1912): 8, 9.

Richardson, Anna Steese. "Work of the Antis." *WHC* (March 1911): 15.

Ridgway, Erman. "Magazine Makers." *Everybody's Magazine* (January 1912): 56.

Rinehart, Mary Roberts. "The Chaotic Decade." *LHJ* (May 1930): 35, 172, 176ff.

Ripperger, Henrietta. "Are You Going with a Service Man?" *GH* (June 1941): 121.

Ripperger, Henrietta. "Gone with the Draft." *GH* (November 1941): 70.

"Rival Women's Magazines Near Hair-Pulling Stage." *BW* (October 1, 1960): 88.

Roberts, Ina Brevoort. "The Press Committee in the Women's Club." *PR* (November 1916): 28.

Roberts, Willa. "How to Behave in Wartime." *WHC* (March 1942): 2.

Roberts, Willa. "I Am a Woman." *WHC* (February 1943): 4.

Robertson, Alice M. "Woman's Place in Politics." *WHC* (October 1921): 15.

Robinson, Helen Ring. "Women's Work as Wholesale Housekeepers." *PR* (June 1918): 2, 48.

Robinson, Helen Ring. "Ten Million Women in the United States Today Are Getting Ready to Use Their Votes." *PR* (May 1918): 23, 78.

Robinson, Helen Ring. "Where Do We Go from Here?" *PR* (July 1918): 28.

Robinson, R. A. "Use of the Panel in Opinion and Attitude Research." *International Journal of Opinion and Attitude Research*. Vol. 1 (1947): 83–86.

Rock, Andrea. "The Breast Cancer Experiment." *LHJ* (February 1995): 144–51, 220.

Roemer, Michelle S. "That Feminist Ms.tique." *Publishing Economics* (September/October 1991): 46–49.

Rosiere, Gabriele. "How to Give a Suffrage Fair." *PR* (August 1914): 24.

Rothenberg, Randall. "The Cosmo Girl at 25." *NYT* (April 21, 1990): 32.

Rubin, Karen. "McCall's." *MagazineWeek* (May 10, 1993): 13.

Ruggiero, Josephine and Louise C. Weston. "The Popular Approach to Women's Health Issues." *Women and Health* 10, no. 4 (Winter 1985/1986): 47–62.

Sager, Evelyn. "Profile of Success." *WHC* (April 1946): 32, 109.

Salisbury, Philip. "Survey Among 10,000 Housewives Shows Food Advertising Most Liked, Drug Advertising Most Questioned." *Sales Management* (June 1, 1935): 678.

Salisbury, Philip. "10,000 Women Tell Why They Like Certain Advertisements." *Sales Management* (1935): 756–57.

Salisbury, Philip. "What Kinds of Advertisements Do Women Like?" *Sales Management* (July 1, 1935): 10, 11, 31.

Schlesinger, Elizabeth. "They Say Women Are Emancipated." *New Republic* (December 13, 1933): 125–27.

Schlesinger, Elizabeth. "The Women's Magazines." *New Republic* (March 11, 1946): 345–47.

Schmuckler, Eric. "Sob for the Sisters." *Forbes* (April 4, 1988): 112, 113.

"Scoops on Family." *Democrat and Chronicle* (February 24, 1994): 3C.

Schrambling, Regina. "A Sassy Approach." *Profiles, Inc.* (June 1988): 29, 44.

Schuler, Loring. "It's Up to the Women." *LHJ* (January 1932): 3.

Schuler, Loring. "Pocketbook Patriotism. An Editorial." *LHJ* (February 1932): 3.

Schuler, Loring. "Women in Government." *LHJ* (February 1929): 30.

Schuler, Marjorie. "The New Idea in the Woman's Club of Today is Getting Things Done." *WHC* (September 1921): 16.

Searles, Patricia and Janet Mickish. "A Thoroughbred Girl." *Women's Studies* 10 (1984): 261–81.

Seaton, Esta. "Sex and the Nubile Girl in Edward Bok's LHJ (1890–1919)." *University of Michigan Papers in Women's Studies* II, no. 4 (1978): 47, 48.

Shannon, Jacqueline. "Surviving Breast Cancer By Women Who've Been There." *Women's Own* (February 1994): 56, 57.

"Share Your Mail Contest." *WHC* (November 1942): 35, 36.

Shaw, Anna Howard. "If I Were President." *McCall's* (July 1912): 8, 9.

Sherman, James S. "How Laws Are Made." *WHC* (February 1912): 13.

Sloane, Leonard. "Charter To Sell 3 Publishing Interests." *NYT* (July 9, 1982): D4.

Smith, Helena Huntington. "When It's Over, Over Here." *WHC* (November 1944): 4.

Snorgrass, J. William. "Black Women and Journalism, 1800–1950." *Western Journal of Black Studies* 6, no. 3 (1982): 150–58.

"Solving the House-Plan Problem." *PR* (October 1916): 1.

Splint, Sarah Field. "Faith to Remake the World." *WHC* (September 1939): 10.

Splint, Sarah Field. "A Time to Build." *WHC* (October 1939): 10.

Stein, Sally. "The Graphic Ordering of Desire." *Heresies* 18 (1985): 9.

Steinem, Gloria. "A Personal Report." *Ms.* (July 1972): 4–7.

Steinem, Gloria. "Sex, Lies and Advertising." *Ms.* (July/August 1990): 18–28.

Steiner, Linda. "Finding Community in Nineteenth Century Suffrage Periodicals." *American Journalism* 1, no. 1 (Summer 1983): 1–15.

Stevens, Hazel. "An Inquiry into the Present Contents of Women's Magazines as an Index to Women's Interests." Master's Essay, Columbia University Graduate School of Journalism, 1925.

Stoddard, George and Toni Taylor. "Mom's Never Home Anymore." *McCall's* (March 1942): 41, 79.

Stoddard, William. "A Tale of a Broken Oar." *WHC* (April 1897; May 1897; and June 1897).

Stote, Amos. "Crowell." *Magazine World* 1 (August 1945): 9, 10.

"The Strike and the Housewife." *WHC* (November 1904): 15, 37.

"The Subscriber and the Advertisers." *PR* (September 1911): 1.

Sykes, G. A. "Periodicals on the Elevated Railroads." *PI* (December 21, 1892): 830.

Talbott, Mary. "Electricity." *McCall's* (May 1912).

Tarbell, Ida. "The Greatest Story in the World Today." *McCall's* (February 1927): 23, 92–96.

Taylor, Toni. "Women Wanted for War Work." *McCall's* (February 1943): 74, 75.

Teinowitz, Ira. "'First' Shock Wave." *AA* (August 21, 1989): 1, 66.

"Tested and Not Approved." *Time* (June 2, 1941): 51.

"That Freedom Shall Not Perish." *LHJ* (July 1941): 22, 23.

Thompson, Dorothy. "This War and the Common Sense of Women." *LHJ* (April 1942).

Toombs, Elizabeth. "The Golden Praire Biennial." *GH* (September 1920): 23, 172, 175, 176.

Toombs, Elizabeth. "Suffrage Jubilee." *GH* (May 1920): 7, 8.

"Three Things to Remember; Fair Play for Women." *PR* (May 1914): 1.

Ulrich, Carolyn F. "Why Women's Magazines?" *The New Republic* (February 7, 1934): 367.

Upton, Harriet Taylor. "A Woman's View of Practical Politics." *WHC* (September 1921): 4.

U.S. Food Administration's Head of Division of Distribution. "What Your Grocer Has Promised to Do." *LHJ* (February 1918): 32.

Uzzell, Thomas H. "The Love Pulps." *Scribner's* (April 1938): 36–41.

Van Rensselaer, Martha. "The Useless Tragedy of the Farmer's Wife." *Delineator* (April 1909): 778, 813.

Van Rensselaer, Martha. "Big Business, This." *Delineator* (April 1921): 26, 80.

Volek, Thomas W. "Examining the Emergance of Broadcasting in the 1920s Through Magazine Advertising." Paper presented at 1991 AEJMC meeting.

"'Votes for Women'—As Seen by Edward W. Bok." *NYT* (April 18, 1909) part 5, p. 3.

Waller (Zuckerman), Mary Ellen. "The Business Side of Media Development: Women's Magazines in the Gilded Age." In Edwin J. Perkins, ed., *Essays in Economic and Business History*, no. 8 (1989).

Waller (Zuckerman), Mary Ellen. "The Changing Shape of Advertising in Popular Women's Magazines, 1890–1930." Presented at Popular Culture Association of the South, 1987.

Waller (Zuckerman), Mary Ellen. "Delineator and Good Housekeeping." Paper prepared at Columbia University, 1987.

Waller-Zuckerman, Mary Ellen. "Marketing the Women's Journals, 1873–1900." *Business and Economic History*, 2nd Series, vol. 18 (1989): 99–108.

Waller-Zuckerman, Mary Ellen. "Old Homes in a City of Perpetual Change: Women's Magazines, 1890–1916." *BHR* 63 (Winter 1989): 715–56.

Waller-Zuckerman, Mary Ellen. "Vera Connolly, Progressive Journalist." *JH* 15, no. 2–3 (Summer 1988): 80–88.

Waller-Zuckerman, Mary Ellen and Mary Carsky. "Contributions of Women to U.S. Marketing Thought." *Journal of the Academy of Marketing Science* 18, no. 4 (Fall 1990): 313–18.

"Wanted—Letters, Letters, Letters." *WHC* (August 1942): 17.

"The War on Breast Cancer." *LHJ* (October 1989, November 1988).

Ward, Adrienne. "Sibling Rivalry." *AA* (October 6, 1991): 38.

Warner, Fara. "P&G Reads No Family Differences in the Seven Sisters." *WSJ* (March 27, 1995): B5.

"Washington Newsletter." *McCall's* (April 1943): 7, 8.

"Washington Newsletter." *McCall's* (November 1945): 7.

Waterloo, Stanley. "The Hair of the Dog Who Bit Him." *WHC* (February 1897): 5, 6.
Wayne, Leslie. "Australia Concern to Buy Ms." *NYT* (September 24, 1987): D1, D22.
Welles, Chris. "Soaring Success of the Iron Butterfly." *Life* (November 19, 1965): 65–73.
"We Meant It and We Did It." *Delineator* (July 1913): 3.
"We Must Keep Out." *WHC* (December 1939): 2.
"What Your Dollar Will Buy." *Profitable Advertising* (December 1901): 633.
"What Shall We Do About Birth-control?" *PR* (March 1916): 24, 26, 76.
Wheatley, Flo. "Women Who Make a Difference." *FC* (November 21, 1995): 15, 16.
Whelan, Elizabeth M. "Alarm Clocks Can Kill You." *NYT* (September 8, 1992): A19.
White, William Allen. "Simplifying the Business of Politics." *WHC* (November 1924): 21, 22.
"Who Will American's Women Vote?" *WHC* (April 1944): 14.
"Why Your Magazines May Cost More Hereafter." *LHJ* (January 15, 1911): 4.
"Why I Want the Ballot." By a Home Woman, *WHC* (1911): 4.
Wilder, George. "The Delineator's Editor." *Delineator* (March 1921): 1, 72.
Wiley, Harvey W. "The Maternity Bill Explained." *GH* (March 1922): 50, 133, 134.
Williamson, Oscar. "An Inhibition Versus a Market." *Advertising and Selling* (January 26, 1927): 34, 55, 56.
"Will Your Baby Be Born at Home in 1943?" *McCall's* (April 1943): 73.
Wilson, Sally Bolstad. "How Magazines Reflect Social Movements." Masters Essay, University of Missouri, 1972.
Wilson, Woodrow. "The New Meaning of Government." *WHC* (November 1912): 3.
"The Winners!" WHC (September 1942): 60.
Winter, Alice Ames. "The General Federation of Women's Clubs." *LHJ* (June 1926): 26, 202, 205.
Wolberst, Abraham. "The Tragedy of the Marriage Altar." *LHJ* (October 1908): 26.
"Woman Gets High Post." *NY World* (June 20, 1929).
"Woman Toilers." *Delineator* (May 1912): 376, 377.
"Women and Cigarettes." *PI* (February 18, 1932): 25–27.
"Women as Editors." *The Journalist* 23 (April 1889): 1, 2.
"Women in the War." *GH* (September 1942): 62.
"Women of the Campaign." *WHC* (November 1912): 22, 23.
"Women's Magazine's Lose Pep." *BW* (August 30, 1972): 73.
"The Women's Vote." *Delineator* (March 1918): 3.
"Women Want More War News." *WHC* (August 1944): 8.
"Women's War." *BW* (March 7, 1942): 58.
Woodman, Sue. "Life after Breast Cancer." *McCall's* (October 1995): 98–105.
Yang, Mei-ling. "Selling Patriotism." *American Journalism* 12, no. 2 (Summer 1995): 309.
Yoshihara, Nancy. "Women's Magazines Dilemma." *The Los Angeles Times* (December 23, 1979): 5.
Young, Gerald W. "Who's Jim Thayer?" *Timeline* 7, no. 1 (February/March 1990): 50.
Zuckerman, Mary Ellen. "Advertising the New Technology?" Presented at Quality of Life Conference, 1992.
Zuckerman, Mary Ellen Waller. "Aspects of Early Market Research, 1879–1917." *Proceedings of the AMA Winter Educator's Conference* (1988).

Zuckerman, Mary Ellen. "The Career of Mrs. Christine Frederick." Presented at OAH, Spring 1994.

Zuckerman, Mary Ellen. "From Educated Citizen to Educated Consumer." *American Periodicals* 5 (1995): 97, 98.

Zuckerman, Mary Ellen. "Pathway to Success: Gertrude Battles Lane and the Woman's Home Companion." *JH* (Spring 1990): 78–87.

Index

About the Author

MARY ELLEN ZUCKERMAN is Associate Professor of Marketing at the Jones School of Business at SUNY-Geneseo. She is the author of *Sources in the History of Women's Magazines, 1792–1960* (Greenwood, 1991) and coauthor of *The Magazine in America* (1991).